A Study Of The Holy Scriptures From Beginning To The End

A Study Of The Holy Scriptures From Beginning To The End

MYSTERIES AND
PROPHECIES REVEALED

Jerry Hill

Copyright © 2016 Jerry Hill
All rights reserved.

ISBN-13: 9781536853551
ISBN-10: 1536853550
Library of Congress Control Number: 2016915284
CreateSpace Independent Publishing Platform
North Charleston, South Carolina

Sripture taken from The One New Man Bible, copyright ©2011 William J. Morford. Used by permission of True Potential Publishing, Inc.

Scipture taken from the Complete Jewish Bible by David H. Stern. Copyright©1998. All rights reserved. Used by permission of Messianic Jewish Publishers, 6120 Day Long Lane, Clarksville, MD 21029.www.messianicjewish.net.

ISR-The Scriptures 1998 "Scripture taken from The Scriptures ©, Copyright by Institute for Scripture Research. Used by Permission"

Dedication

I dedicate this book on the Scriptures to my wife Brenda Schlosser Hill. With her support and encouragement, I was able to complete this book. She worked and provided for our family in order that I could devote myself full-time to the study and writing of this book. It was a blessing to study the Scriptures, and I hope that the reader will be blessed as I was blessed.

Contents

Acknowledgments ix
Introduction xi
The Use of Holy Names xiii

Chapter 1	The Holy Scriptures	1
Chapter 2	His Hallowed Name.	29
Chapter 3	Written in Hebrew.	40
Chapter 4	Understanding the Book of Matthew	47
Chapter 5	Understanding the Creator's Calendar	61
Chapter 6	YHVH's Instructions to the Israelites	71
Chapter 7	YHVH's Perfect Plan Gone Astray	79
Chapter 8	Babylonian Sun-God Worship	98
Chapter 9	The Birthday of the Messiah	107
Chapter 10	The Seventy-Week Ministry of the Messiah	114
Chapter 11	The Appointed Time of the Passover Lamb of YHVH	123
Chapter 12	The Ark of the Covenant.	133
Chapter 13	The History of the Christian Church.	144
Chapter 14	The Sabbath Day Changed?	166
Chapter 15	The Apostate Church.	180
Chapter 16	The Rise of Islam.	194
Chapter 17	YHVH's Judgment on America.	209
Chapter 18	The Rise of Chrislam.	224
Chapter 19	The Rise of the New World Order	231
Chapter 20	Prophecies in the Scriptures	247

Chapter 21	The Seals	258
Chapter 22	The Trumpets	265
Chapter 23	Holy Roman Empire Reborn	277
Chapter 24	The Antichrist	282
Chapter 25	The False Prophet	296
Chapter 26	The Beginning of the Last Seven Years	307
Chapter 27	Zechariah's War	315
Chapter 28	The Confirmation of the Covenant	322
Chapter 29	The Great Tribulation	326
Chapter 30	The Seventh Trumpet	343
Chapter 31	The Mysteries of YHVH Revealed	352
Chapter 32	Satan's Plan of Deception	373
Chapter 33	The Ten Commandments	382
Chapter 34	Understanding Sin and Repentance	400
Chapter 35	The One New Man	415
Chapter 36	Salvation	422
Chapter 37	The Final Choice	433
Appendix A	The Sinner's Prayer	439
Appendix B	The Lord's Prayer	440
Appendix C	The Power of Blessings	441
Appendix D	A Morning Prayer	444
Appendix E	The Prayer of Transformation	447
References		449
In Memory		467
Jerry's Bio		469

Acknowledgments

I WANT TO ACKNOWLEDGE ALL the followers of the Messiah who are teaching the scriptures all around the world. This book utilizes an overview of their teachings as part of this study of the Holy Scriptures. The following is an abbreviated list; for a full list, see the references section.

Ron Wyatt (deceased) of Wyatt Archaeological Research

Doug Batchelor of Amazing Facts of the Bible

The Nazarite Site

Michael Rood of www.ARoodAwaking.tv

Richard Rives of "Too Long in the Sun"

Ron Johnson of www.666man.net

Dr. Samuel Bacchiocchi (deceased) of "From Sabbath to Sunday"

Hugh Ross of "Journey toward Creation"

Nehemiah Gordon of "The Greek Jesus versus the Hebrew Yeshua."

Keith Johnson of "A Prayer to Our Father" and "His Hallowed Name"

Irvin Baxter of "The End of the Age"

Perry Stone of Manna-Fest

Sid Roth of "It's Supernatural TV"

Walter Shoebat of "God's War on Terror"

Dr. Mark Virkler of "Prayers That Heal the Heart"

Dr. James B. Richards of Heart Physics

Gary Khan of "The Antichrist's Economic, Religious, and Political System Exposed"

Kerry Kirkwood of "The Power of Blessing"

Jonathan Cahn of "The Harbinger"

Rev. William J. Morford of the One New Man Bible

Cassandra Johnson, for her support, guidance and inspiration in helping to complete this mission.

Gregory Denagall for his patience with me on perfecting this beautiful book cover.

To all of our children who loved us through this journey...Robert, Monique, Kelli, Cheryl, Ernie, Michael & Cindy And to all our grandchildren, Gabriella, Mia, Matthew, Riley & Bryce.

To my sisters who always believed in me, Alberta & Thelma. My sister-in-law Mickey for her prayers, and to my big brother James who's in his heavenly place. To all my family members that allowed me to express myself without judgment.

And to all the pastors that let me challenge them!

Introduction

THE APOSTLE PAUL TELLS US that knowing the Scriptures is necessary for wisdom in salvation through faith in Jesus. Paul also tells us that it is faith in Yeshua (Jesus) that provides forgiveness for our sins and how we can receive salvation. He goes on to say that faith comes from hearing the word of God. The Scriptures are the word of God. It is His voice to us. So it is necessary for us to study the word of God in the Scriptures in order to instruct us in righteousness.

This book provides the reader a study guide of the Scriptures that begins in the Garden of Eden and ends at the end of the age when Yeshua returns as prophesied in the book of Revelation. It covers several books that are not in the Scriptures, and scripture verses are quoted for the reader. Several English translations are used in an effort to get away from denominational bias or tradition that could mislead the reader. The goal is for the reader to understand the truth originally penned in the Scriptures.

There are many reasons to read this book. One reason is that God declared the end from the beginning. That means that everything prophesied in the Scriptures by Yeshua will come to pass. In fact, if we understand God's calendar that He gave to us originally and if we understand prophecy, then we can know what time it is on God's calendar. So in this book we have looked at Prophecy in the Scriptures to see how many have already taken place and which ones are future events. There are major prophesies that have recently occurred that indicate that we are approaching the end of the age. If this is true, then the false prophet and the Antichrist are alive today.

There are many mysteries referred to in the Scriptures. A mystery in the Scriptures is something that may not be known to you but is known to God. This book attempts to give the reader a better understanding of some of these mysteries, many of which have recently come to light.

This study also incorporates excerpts from the ministries of many gifted teachers. These teachers have had an encounter with Yeshua, and they are each bringing a message to the followers of Yeshua. For a more in-depth understanding of their ministries, I have referenced briefly their teachings and their websites.

This study will cover the entire Scriptures, and hopefully you will be blessed by reading and pondering what the Scriptures are telling us. This book is not intended to replace, change, add to, or take away from the original penned Scriptures, but it is intended to draw attention to scriptural truths you may not have studied before. It also is not intended to say any particular faith is incorrect. Salvation is between you and Yeshua, the Judge.

Yeshua gave us a grave warning in the Scriptures that He must know you before you can enter into heaven. He also said what you have to do before He will know you. You can know the Scriptures in detail and think you are doing everything you need to do to be saved, but there is something you must specifically do before Yeshua will declare to you: "Enter my faithful servant."

May God bless you in the study of His Word.

The Use of Holy Names

The Name of God

In this book I will refer to name of the Father (God) by using the four-letter Hebrew name that appears in the old Hebrew Scriptures. His name was pronounced Yod-Hey-Vav-Hey (Yehovah) according to the Hebrew letters of His name in the Aleppo Codex and the Leningrad Codex (see chapter 2). The Aleppo Codex and the Leningrad Codex are the oldest Hebrew Scriptures available today. These Hebrew Scriptures contain what we call the Old Testament, and they date back before the early church. Since we are commanded in the Scriptures not to take God's name in vain, I have elected to use the abbreviation YHVH in place of His actual name.

Most English translations of the Scriptures will use the title Lord for the name of God.

The Name of the Messiah

The Messiah was referred to with several different names in Hebrew: Yehoshua or the shortened name of Yeshua. This was the name He was called when He was alive. I have chosen to use the name Yeshua, which means *salvation* in the Hebrew language, in this book. A more in-depth discussion is available in chapter 2.

The English translations will vary regarding the Messiah's name. For example, the Messiah was called "Iesus" in the 1611 King James Bible. Later, in the revised edition, the translators called Him "Jesus."

Most early English translations of the Scriptures used the title *Lord* or *Jesus* for the Messiah.

THE HOLY SCRIPTURES

I have made references to the Holy Scriptures from several English translations in this study in an effort to get the full and correct meaning of a verse. The original Scriptures were penned in Hebrew. Fortunately, we have very old Hebrew scrolls, such as the Aleppo Codex, the Leningrad Codex, and the Dead Sea Scrolls, that can contain the original Hebrew text as best we can find. These scrolls help us to understand the original literal meaning and capture the expressive nature of the original Hebrew language.

The Gospel, record consists primarily of thousands of Greek fragments that were pieced together to form the Greek version of the Gospels. Today we have three versions to choose from for our English translations of the Gospels. In order to use an English translation that is free of denominational biases, I have primarily relied on the One New Man Bible, which uses the fourth edition translation of the United Bible Society Greek text. Also I have referred to verses in The Scriptures translation by the Institute for Scripture Research (ISR), the Hebraic-Roots Version Scriptures (HRV), Complete Jewish Bible (CJB), and the King James Version of the Bible (KJV) in order to convey a good understanding to the reader.

CHAPTER 1

The Holy Scriptures

§

THE TERM *SCRIPTURE* (OR SCRIPTURES) is used once in the book of Daniel and fifty-four times in the New Testament. It refers to the whole book commonly known as "the Bible." The parts of the Scriptures, or individual books, are called "books" or "scrolls," which are *biblos* or *biblion* in Greek. Since these words (*biblos* or *biblion*) do not refer to the complete writings, I prefer to call the whole book the Holy Scriptures.

The word "Bible" was first used for the Scriptures about AD 400. The papyrus on which all the documents were written was imported from Egypt through the Phoenician seaport Gebal, which the Greeks called Byblos or Byblus. This seaport was the home of the Phoenician sun deity. This city was founded by Baal Chronos and was the seat of Adonis and once contained a large temple of Adonis. The sun god was associated with the "Lady of Biblos." Both the city of Byblos in Phoenicia and the city Byblis in Egypt were named after the female deity Byblis (also called Byble or Biblis). This deity was the granddaughter of Apollo, the Greek sun deity. Byblis was also a name for Venus, an astral goddess and a goddess of sensuality among ancient Greeks.[1]

Since it appears that the history of the word "Bible" may have had a pagan background, I prefer to refer to the books as **"The Scriptures,"** just as the apostles referred to them.

What did the Apostles Say about the Scriptures?
Paul says:

> The Holy [set-apart] Scriptures…are able to make thee wise unto salvation through faith which is in [the Messiah]. All scripture is given by inspiration of God [YHVH], and is **profitable** for **doctrine**, for **reproof**, for **correction**, for **instruction** in righteousness. (2 Timothy 3:15–16 KJV, emphasis added)

Paul says:

> And because you have known the sacred writings from childhood, the things that are able to make you wise for salvation through faith in Messiah Y'shua. All Scripture is God-inspired and useful for **teaching**, for **reproof**, **restoration**, for **training** in righteousness. (2 Timothy 3:15–16 OMNB, emphasis added)

What Scripture was Paul Referring to?

> And Paul, as his manner was, went in unto them, and three Sabbath days reasoned out of the **scriptures**. (Acts 17:2 KJV, emphasis added)
> And according to the custom with Paul, he went in to them and on three Sabbaths spoke to them from the **Scriptures**. (Acts 17:2 ONMB, emphasis added)

For three days (Sabbaths), Paul is studying and trying to understand the **Scriptures.** "For he mightily convinced the Jews, and that publicly, shewing by the **scriptures** that [Yeshua] Jesus was Christ [the Messiah]" (Acts 18:28 KJV, emphasis added).

Paul said the Bereans searched the **Scriptures** daily to see if his words were so or not (Acts 17:11).

What **scripture** is Paul referring to? Paul was referring to the **Torah, the Prophets, and the Psalms that were recorded in the Hebrew language on scrolls. That was all that was written at that time.** Yeshua (Jesus) also quoted the Torah, the Prophets, and the Psalms:

And He said to them, "These are the messages I told you while I was still with you, that it is necessary for everything to be fulfilled that has been written about me in the Torah (Teaching) of Moses and in the Prophets and the Psalms." (Luke 24:44 ONMB)

What do the Scriptures Claim about Themselves?

All Scripture is God-inspired and useful for teaching, for reproof, restoration, for training in righteousness. (2 Timothy 3:16 ONMB)

If you understand this first, that no prophecy of Scripture happens by a prophet's own interpretation: for a prophecy was never brought by the will of a person, but people spoke from God, while they were being carried along with the Holy Spirit. (2 Peter 1:21 ONMB)

Y'shua said to the Jews, "If He called those gods to whom the Word of God came, then the Scripture cannot be done away with." (John 12:35 ONMB)

These verses are saying that the Scriptures were written by men who were guided by the Holy Ghost. It cannot be broken or proven untrue.

In Hebrews, Paul says, "For now you ought to be teachers by this time, but you again need someone to teach you the fundamental principles of the words [Oracles] of God from the beginning" (Hebrews 5:12 ONMB).

Peter said, "If any man speak, let him speak as the **oracles of God**; if any man minister, let him do it as of the ability which God giveth" (1 Peter 4:11 KJV, emphasis added).

Stephen said, "This is he [Moses]…who received the **Living Oracles** to give unto us" (Acts 7:38 kjv, emphasis added).

What are these **oracles**? Oracles mean *logion* in Greek. *Logion* means **communication**.

These are **communications from God**. God gave to Moses His communications in the first five books of the Scriptures. These were the **written oracles** from God to be used by the Jews as priests and teachers to the whole world! God gave the Scriptures to the twelve tribes of Israel for safekeeping.

Remember the story when Moses was at Mount Sinai when YHVH asked the Hebrews if they would accept His covenant? They accepted, and this is when they became known as priests to God.

> *Now therefore, if ye will obey my voice indeed, and keep my covenant, then ye shall be a peculiar treasure unto me above all people: for all the earth is mine: And ye shall be unto me a kingdom of priests, and a holy nation. These are the words which thou shalt speak unto the children of Israel. And Moses came and called for the elders of the people, and laid before their faces all these words which the* Lord *commanded him.*
>
> *And all the people answered together, and said, All that the* Lord *hath spoken we will do. And Moses returned the words of the people unto the* Lord. (Exodus 19:5–8 kjv)

These written oracles, which are the first five books of the Scriptures, were called the **Torah** by the Hebrews. The Torah is called the Pentateuch of Moses. The Hebrew word *Torah* means **instructions**. The books are **Genesis, Exodus, Leviticus, Numbers, and Deuteronomy**. Despite popular Christian teaching, the word *Torah* does not mean "Law" as it has been translated in English Bibles.[2]

One of the oldest Hebrew copies in existence today of the Torah is called the Aleppo/Ben-Asher Codex. As best we know, it is exactly word for word just like what was penned originally by Moses 3400 years earlier. It has been maintained by the Masoretes from generation to generation. Today the oldest copy is kept in a vault in Israel.[3]

A Study Of The Holy Scriptures From Beginning To The End

Is there any Proof it came from YHVH?

No one has ever questioned the authenticity of the first five books being from YHVH; however, there is an interesting code in the Torah that only YHVH could have done. Jewish sages conducted a study of the Equidistant Letter Sequences, or ELS, which has been made possible by the modern computer. The study is based on a set pattern of counting letters and selecting a letter within the numbered sequences. The study uses the Hebrew "Aleph-bet" used in the original text. During this study they discovered that every **fiftieth Hebrew letter** of the Hebrew books of Genesis and Exodus from left to right spells **"Torah" over and over again**. They also found every forty-ninth letter from right to left in the book of Deuteronomy spells "Torah" backward, pointing back to the central book. In the book of Numbers, every fiftieth letter from right to left spells "Torah" backward. In Leviticus, **every seventh letter** spells the name of God, **YHVH. Only God (YHVH) could have done this and the books make any sense!**[4]

In the Scriptures there are hundreds of prophecies. In the Old Testament from about 4000 BC to about 430 BC, there are over three hundred Messianic prophecies regarding Yeshua (Jesus). These prophecies were fulfilled by Yeshua in the New Testament and can be categorized as follows:

1. Concerning His Birth: twelve prophecies
2. Concerning His Nature: nine prophecies
3. Concerning His Ministry: eight prophecies
4. Concerning Events after His Burial: three prophecies
5. Prophecies Fulfilled in One Day: twenty-nine prophecies

These prophecies spoke of His betrayal, trial, death, and burial in a twenty-four-hour period.[5]

What are the mathematical odds of prophecies being fulfilled hundreds and thousands of years later?

Peter Stoner said the probability of Yeshua fulfilling eight of the prophecies in the Old Testament to be 1 in 10 to the 17th power. The number would look like this: 1 in 100,000,000,000,000,000.[6]

To fulfill forty-eight of the prophecies would have a probability of 1 in 10 to the 157th power or 1 in 10,00,000,000,000,000,000,000,000,000,000,

000,000,000,000,000,000,000,000,000,000,000,

000,000,000,000,000,000,000,000,000,000,000,

000,000,000,000,000,000,000,000,000,000,000,

000,000,000,000,000,000,000,000,000…Only YHVH could have done this because of the astronomical odds against these prophecies being fulfilled by chance. The Scriptures are absolutely true and give proof that there is a YHVH (God) and Yeshua (Jesus) was the Messiah.

How did Yeshua (Jesus) Demonstrate his Confidence and Belief in the Scriptures?

Yeshua quoted the Scriptures (the Torah, the Prophets, and the Psalms) when meeting the temptations of Satan. Yeshua said, "It is written, Man shall not live by bread alone, but by every word that proceedeth out of the mouth of God [YHVH]" (Matthew 4:4; Deuteronomy 8:3 kjv). Words out of the mouth of God (YHVH) refer to the Torah and the Prophets. Remember, YHVH always told the prophets through His angels to go and prophesy to the Jews that if they don't correct their ways, "consequences" is going to happen to you.

Yeshua often quoted Scripture as the authority for the truth He was preaching. Yeshua was quoting the Torah and the Prophets because **that was all that was written at that time**. The Gospels were not written until long after Yeshua was crucified.

When Yeshua gave the Sermon on the Mount, He said, "Do not think I have come to destroy the Torah (Instructions), or the prophets. I did not come to destroy but to complete. For truly I say to you, till the heaven and the earth pass away, one jot or one tittle shall no means pass from the Torah till all be done" (Matthew 5:17–18 isr). The jot and tittle are extremely small details in the Hebrew language. The quotation means every small detail has received attention and will never change.

How does the Scientific World View the Scriptures?

Dr. Hugh Ross, an astrophysicist, has written many scientific books that show that the physical evidence in the stars and planets of the universe all point to a divine creator of the universe. Dr. Ross and his colleagues present their findings in such a way that both the scientist and the layman can understand. Dr. Ross states that the explanation of the creation of the universe is in complete harmony with the Scriptures. Dr. Ross has a website at www.reasons.org for those who seek scientific proof that God created the universe.[8]

Dr. Jobe Martin has spent the last twenty years studying biblical creation vs. evolution. Dr. Martin has become an expert on the subject and has uncovered countless pieces of evidence that evolution of life on earth is simply not true. In his book *The Evolution of a Creationist* he examines animals whose incredibly complex designs completely defy the ability of evolutionists to come up with any explanation for how the creature could have evolved to its present state. He removes all doubt about the biblical depiction of creation. His website is www.evolutionofacreationist.com.[9]

Are the Historical Statements of the Scriptures Accurate?

Absolutely! The Scriptures say, "The Lord speak righteousness, I declare things that are right" (Isaiah 45:19 KJV). There have always been skeptics of the Scriptures as a historical document. These critics have repeatedly been proven wrong as new discoveries such as the Dead Sea Scrolls were found. One interesting note here is that the Dead Sea Scrolls, which are dated between 150 BCE and 70 CE, proved that the book of Daniel was written before Yeshua was born on this earth. This is important because of the many prophecies regarding Yeshua that are contained in the book of Daniel.[10]

It also is important because the scrolls were almost all written in Hebrew. Even the book of Enoch was among the Dead Sea scrolls.

Archeological Evidence of the Events in the Scriptures

Noah's Ark Found

In September 1960, *Life* magazine published an article about a Turkish army captain who had discovered a boat-shaped form about twenty miles south of Mount Ararat. Ron Wyatt travelled to the area in 1977 to investigate the find and saw a boat-shaped form about five hundred feet long. After investigating the dimensions, it was found to be very close to the dimensions of Noah's ark of three hundred cubits long, a breadth of fifty cubits and the height of thirty cubits (Genesis 6:15 KJV). Also found were anchor stones similar to drogue anchor stones that were common for ancient ships.[11]

In 1978, an earthquake caused the soil surrounding the ship to fall away, exposing about thirty feet of the sides. Finally, in 1985, Ron Wyatt performed subsurface radar scans on the form, and it showed that the object was not a natural object. Finally, in 1987, the site was dedicated as the Noah's Ark Park by the Turkish government. Later, a beam was excavated and tested and found to have once been a living tree. Also, there were no rings in the wood, which would be only be possible before the Flood since it did not rain on the earth until the Flood.[12]

The remains of Noah's ark prove that the Scriptures are true regarding the Flood.

Red Sea Crossing by Moses during the Exodus

Ron Wyatt in 1978 located the Red Sea crossing at the beach at Nuweiba on the Gulf of Aqaba. To get to this area requires driving through the narrow Canyons through the Wadi Watir down to the beach. While diving at the southern end of the beach, Ron found chariot parts. One of these artifacts was a chariot hub with eight spokes. Later, the Egyptian Department of Antiquities dated the hub to be of the eighteenth dynasty.[13]

The underwater site of the crossing is at an underwater bridge, and numerous expeditions have taken place showing the chariot debris on the floor of the area. Solomon marked the site of the crossing on both the Egyptian side and the Saudi Arabian side with giant pillars. The Egyptians removed the one at the Niemba, but the one on the Saudi Arabian side still stands today. It can be viewed on Google Earth.[14]

The remains of the Egyptian chariot wheels under the Red Sea proves that the Scriptures are true regarding the story of Moses leading the Israelites out of Egypt and that YHVH parted the Red Sea to enable their escape from Pharaoh's army.[15]

Mount Sinai Has Been Found

Mount Sinai is where the "burning bush" was located, the location of the rock that split and brought forth water, and the location where YHVH wrote the Ten Commandments in stone. Mount Sinai is located in Saudi Arabia and can be viewed on Google Earth. Archeologist Ron Wyatt was the first to locate Mount Sinai in 1978. Later, Jim Caldwell was an oil field engineer working the area. Jim and his wife Penny took many photographs, which can be seen on their website. They show the top of the mountain at Jabal at Lawz, which is black at the top.[16]

> *And ye came near and stood under the mountain; and the mountain burned with fire unto the midst of heaven, with darkness, clouds, and thick darkness. And the* LORD *Spake unto you out of the midst of the fire: ye heard the voice of the words, but saw no similitude; only ye heard a voice.* (Deuteronomy 4:11–12 KJV)

At the base of Jabal at Lawz, there is evidence of an ancient encampment. Inside the encampment, a large stone altar was found. An image of a calf was found, which was determined to be of Egyptian origin.

The most striking find was the very large rock located on a small mound of rocks that was split and evidence of water that had once poured out of the stone.

> *Behold, I will stand before thee there upon the rock in Horeb; and thou shalt smite the rock, and there shall come water out of it that the*

people may drink. And Moses did so in the sight of the elders of Israel. (Exodus 17:6 KJV)

Also found were the carvings in multiple stones of the feet of the Hebrews who encamped there. There are thousands of these carvings, which were etched with a chisel. It took several hours of hard work to chisel the images of the outlines of feet and sandals in the stones, and they had been there for over three thousand years. A good resource of the archaeological finds are documented in a DVD that can be obtained from the Michael Rood Ministry.

The Ark of the Covenant Has Been Found
Yes, it has been found in Jerusalem by Ron Wyatt, but it cannot be made public at this time. The Israeli Department of Antiquities also knows where it is located. A video was made of the ark by Ron Wyatt, but it will not be shown until the prescribed time by YHVH. I will discuss more about this in a later chapter.[17]

These discoveries give us tangible evidence that the stories and events in the Scriptures actually happened.

One of the Greatest Miracles of the Scriptures is Its Unity
The sixty-six books that are currently in the Bible were originally written in Hebrew by about forty people ranging from kings to shepherds. The books were written over a period of 1500 years by many people, most of whom had never met each other.

These same books maintain harmony with one another, although the same concept may be expressed in a different way. The Old Testament contains more than three hundred passages that prophesy of the coming of Yeshua (Jesus) that are in complete harmony with what the New Testament says about the life of Yeshua.[18] The scientific odds of this happening are more than I can calculate.

So the Scriptures are True And are Inspired By YHVH (God). What does this Mean to me?

It means that you now have a meaning for your life. You are not just a result of one-celled bacteria that mutated in some cosmic soup. You were made in God's image out of clay just below the angels. The Scriptures tell about God's perfect plan for man and how Satan and the other fallen angels interrupted God's plans for this world. The Scriptures tell about how Satan deceived Adam and Eve and brought sin into this world. Now we must all die because of that deception.

The Scriptures not only give us a record of the past and what will happen in the future, but also a plan of **SALVATION**. The Scriptures show how Yeshua gave His life as a sacrifice and how His blood blotted out our sins so that we might not die because the wages of sin are death. In order to save ourselves, we must understand the plan of salvation or instructions given us by YHVH through the words that were penned in the Scriptures.

The Scriptures Foretell our Future

YHVH said,

> *Remember the former things from old! For I AM God, and there is no other God, and there is none like Me, declaring the end from the beginning, and from ancient times the things that are not done saying, My counsel will stand, and I shall do all My pleasure.* (Isaiah 46:9–10 OMNB)

YHVH declared the end from the beginning to Enoch in the prophecy of weeks, and it is recorded in the book of Enoch.

The word of YHVH is written in the Scriptures, detailing events from the beginning till the end. In addition, **YHVH guards every event so that His words are fulfilled as written in the Scriptures.**

> *And the word of YHVH came to me, saying, "What do you see, Jeremiah?" And I said, "I see a branch of an almond tree." And*

YHVH said to me, "You have seen well, for I am watching over my word to do it." (Jeremiah 1:11–12 ISR)

Why is it Important to Study the Scriptures?

Yeshua answered to the trick question asked Him by the Sadducees as follows: **"Yea do err, not knowing the scriptures"** (Matthew 22:29 KJV). I believe Yeshua was warning everyone that if you don't know the originally penned Scriptures, you could be deceived into false worship. Yeshua is referring to the Torah, the Prophets, and the other Old Testament writings since that was all that was written at the time He was preaching.

Yeshua also said, "But seek ye first the kingdom of God, and his righteousness; and all these things shall be added unto you" (Matthew 6:33 KJV). I take this to mean to study the Scriptures, as Paul said above, is to seek instructions in righteousness. Yeshua went on to give us a warning if we don't, saying, "For I say unto you, that except your righteousness shall exceed the righteousness of the scribes and Pharisees, ye shall in no case enter into the kingdom of heaven" (Matthew 5:20 KJV). The scribes and Pharisees followed the Torah religiously. To achieve righteousness will require effort on your part to follow the instruction given by YHVH in the Scriptures.

Yeshua is also saying that we must study the Scriptures to seek YHVH's instructions and learn how to be righteous so that we can someday be found worthy enough to enter into the kingdom of heaven. **We must be very careful to seek the truth from the Scriptures and not follow man-made traditions that may not be the way YHVH wants us to obey and worship Him.** These man-made traditions can lead us astray from our goal of salvation. Yeshua warned us about this when He said, **"But in vain they do worship me, teaching for doctrines the commandments of men"** (Matthew 15:9 KJV).

Early English Translations of the Scriptures

Most Western Gentile Christians are familiar with the King James Version of the Scriptures; however, it was not the first English translation scholars today believe was from the family of the Textus Receptus. The Old Testament was translated from Hebrew text, and the Apocrypha was translated from the Greek and Latin. This was known as the 1611 Authorized King James version of the Scriptures.[24]

Toward the end of the twentieth century, the King James Bible modified the Textus Receptus to bring it in line with the Byzantine manuscripts. Since those texts form the majority of New Testament manuscripts, two Dallas Theological Seminary professors coined the phrase "majority text." None of these texts are older than the tenth century. On the other hand, we have more than thirty Greek texts that date back to the second and third centuries. All of these texts were ignored by people who supported the majority text. Since the majority text is not a critical text, many scholars have done extensive research in the Koine Greek, or common Greek, manuscripts to develop a critical text of the New Testament. As a result, the fourth edition of this Greek text is essentially called the Nestle-Aland text of the early twentieth century and was the product of the United Bible Society (UBS).[25]

Over a period of approximately 1600 years, the English translations of the Scriptures were produced by translators who were influenced by the theology of the early churches. This influence has also affected the final English versions of the Scriptures. Although it is very popular, the revised King James Version of the Scriptures has some translation mistakes that may require you to go back to the original Hebrew or a Greek translation from the UBS to get a better meaning of a verse. For example, to remove anything Jewish from the King James Version, the reference Torah, which means teachings or instructions from God, was changed to *law* in 459 verses. In place of *congregation* in the New Testament, the reference *church* was used seventy-nine times even though the Christian church started up hundreds of years later.

As we said, in order to get to and confirm a verse in Scripture, you must go back to the original language to determine the meaning of a word. This is especially true of the New Testament. The New Testament is entirely based on the fragments of Greek manuscripts. These manuscripts are basically fragments that have been reviewed with of the Scriptures. First there were the original scrolls that were written in Hebrew called the Hebrew Bible.[19] the Hebrew Bible (Old Testament) was translated into Greek from Hebrew and completed by 132 BCE.[20] Jewish scholars in Alexandria, Egypt, made the translation into Greek. The Greek versions of the Hebrew Bible were called the Septuagint or simply LXX. These Greek versions were used to translate the Scripture into other languages.[21]

Eventually, as Christianity spread to Rome, a Latin version of the Scriptures became available. In 382, the Roman Catholic Church commissioned Jerome to update the Latin version of the Scriptures. This "updated" revision became known as *versio vulgate* that is the "commonly used translation" or Vulgate. The Vulgate has been revised several times over the years and is the scripture that was followed by the early Roman Church.[22]

In 1525, William Tyndale undertook the translation of the New Testament, and his work became the first printed scripture in English in 1539. Tyndale's New Testament and his incomplete translation of the Old Testament became the basis for the later Great Bible.

This was the official authorized version of the Scriptures while King Henry VIII was in power. When Mary I succeeded to the throne in 1553, she returned the Church of England back to the Roman Catholic faith. This caused several religious reformers to flee the country, and they established a colony in Geneva. Under the leadership of John Calvin, these reformers produced a translation known as the Geneva Bible. When Elizabeth I took the throne in 1558, it became apparent that the Great Bible and the Geneva Bible did not conform to the ecclesiology and the Episcopal structure of the Church of England and its beliefs of its ordained clergy. In 1558, the Church of England responded with the Bishop's Bible.[23]

In 1601, the new heir to the English throne, King James, proposed a new translation to correct perceived problems by the Puritans, an activist group within the Church of England. The new translation was undertaken by forty-seven clergy, all of whom were members of the Church of England. The New Testament was translated from Greek text that other fragments in order to develop the books of the New Testament. For over a thousand years, clergy in the early church interpreted the Scriptures and translated them. A timeline of the different translations of the Greek Bible are listed on Google.[26] Since there were no Hebrew versions available, these clergy made their own interpretations of the Greek. Now that we have discovered a Hebrew original of the book of Matthew, some differences have come to light. These differences are very significant, and I will explore them in this book!

During this period of revising the Scriptures, the Scriptures and their associated worship doctrine has exploded into many different beliefs. The development of the different Christian theologies over the years has resulted in many different faiths, traditions, and beliefs in the churches. Moreover, the Christian religious system is now so entrenched in their specific theology; no religious leader will accept anything contrary to his beliefs. If you don't study the originally penned Scriptures, most likely you will be deceived in following the true worship of YHVH. So in this book, I will use the King James scripture references where the translation difference is of little consequence. If needed, I will use other translations to get the original meaning of a Scripture verse. Sometimes it is required to go to the Greek or Hebrew word to get the correct original meaning of a verse.

What other Scriptures are Available?

Since there are many different English translations of the Scriptures available today, you should pick one that is the closest to the original penned language. If you read Hebrew, then the best resource for the Tanak (Old Testament) would be the Leningrad Codex written in Hebrew.[27] the Leningrad Codex is highly recommended since it is one of the oldest versions available.[28]

Since most Christians don't read or speak Hebrew, I would recommend The Scriptures published by the Institute of Scripture Research.[29] This translation in English restores the four-letter name YHWH, known as the Tetragrammaton of the name of the Almighty.[30] Also, it restores the Hebraic forms of certain words and titles. It also restores the correct order as follows: the Torah, the words of the prophets, and the writings in the Old Testament (Tanak). The Messianic writings are used in place of the New Testament.

Now that we know that the New Testament was taken from Greek parchment and there are many problems with the translations, you will need to get to the best translation possible to get the original intended meaning of a verse. In many cases this will require you to go back to the meaning of the Greek words to get the original meaning and context of the word or verse. If this is too time-consuming for you, then get a recent translation from the Greek.

Another good English translation is the One New Man Bible, edited by William J. Morford. The Hebrew was translated with help of Rabbi Eliezer Ben-Yehuda, PhD. The New Testament is The Power New Testament, a fresh translation of the fourth edition United Bible Society Greek text. As much as possible this text is free of denominational biases and doctrinal interpretations.[31]

I also recommend the Hebraic-Roots Version of the Scriptures and the Word of Yahweh Bible.

The Pre-Messianic Scriptures

The Tanak is the Hebrew short form of the order of the books of the Old Testament, i.e., **Torah, Nebi'im, and Kethubim.**[32]

The **Torah** is the **instructions from YHVH**. Most of us refer to this as the Law. *Torah* is a Hebrew word referring to the five books of Moses, also known as the *Humash*, meaning law or teaching. They consist of the following books:

The Order of the Books

The following books of the ISR translation are listed with the Hebrew names and are grouped per the original Hebrew order. The order in the King James Version of the Bible is the basic order of most English translations.

ISR(2)	**KJV(1)**
Torah:	
Bereshith	Genesis
Shemoth	Exodus
Wayyiqra	Leviticus
Bemidbar	Numbers
Debarim	Deuteronomy
Nebi'im: Prophets	
Yehoshua	Joshua
Shophetim	Judges
I Shemu'el	1 Samuel
2 Shemu'el	2 Samuel
1 Melakim	1 Kings
2 Melakim	2 Kings
Yeshayahu	Isaiah
Yirmeyahu	Jeremiah
Yehezquel	Ezekiel
Dani'el	Daniel
Hoshea	Hosea
Yo'el	Joel
Amos	Amos
Obadyah	Obadiah
Yonah	Jonah

Mikah	Micah
Nahum	Nahum
Habaqquq	Habakkuk
Tsephanyah	Zephaniah
Haggai	Haggai
Zekaryah	Zechariah
Mal'aki	Malachi

Kethubim: Writings

Tehillim	Psalms
Mishle	Proverbs
Iyob	Job
Shir haShirim	Son of Songs
Ruth	Ruth
Ekah	Lamentations
Qoheleth	Ecclesiastes
Ester	Esther
Ezra	Ezra
Nehemyah	Nehemiah
Dibre haYamim	1 Chronicles
Dibre haYamim	2 Chronicles

The Messianic Writings

Mattithyahu	Matthew
Mark	Mark
Luke	Luke
Yohanan	John

Acts	Acts
Romans	Romans
1 Corinthians	1 Corinthians
2 Corinthians	2 Corinthians
Galatians	Galatians
Ephesians	Ephesians
Philippians	Philippians
Colossians	Colossians
1 Thessalonians	1 Thessalonians
2 Thessalonians	2 Thessalonians
1 Timothy	1 Timothy
2 Timothy	2 Timothy
Titus	Titus
Philemon	Philemon
Ibrim	Hebrews
Ya'aqob	**James**
1 Kepha	1 Peter
2 Kepha	2 Peter
1 Yohanan	1 John
2 Yohanan	2 John
3 Yohanan	3 John
Yehudah	Jude
Revelation	Revelation

Did you notice there never was a book of James in the ISR Scriptures? It was originally named Jacob. The Power New Testament also calls this book Jacob. So how did it get changed? Most biblical scholars agree that the King James translators changed it to honor King James of England for ordering a new translation.

Missing Books in the Scriptures

These are several books that are not in the today's commonly translated Scriptures. One important book you will not find in many translations is the book of Enoch. Enoch was a scribe and the seventh-born child from Adam. The book of Enoch is not in the Scriptures, although it is referred to in Genesis chapter 5 and in Jude. Enoch was said to be so holy that he was translated to heaven without dying. The original book of Enoch was lost for many centuries until three copies were found in Abyssinia in the 1800s and most recently was found with the Dead Sea Scrolls. The book of Enoch has been translated into English and can be found online. The book describes the fall of angels who took an oath to defy YHVH. It also describes how they asked YHVH for forgiveness and they were rejected. In addition, it gives us a picture of why these angels are our adversaries who want to destroy us.[33]

Also not in the Scriptures is the Apocrypha. In the 1611 Bible, the King James Version, the Apocrypha is a section nestled between the Old Testament and the New Testament.[34] the Apocrypha consists of fourteen books such as the Wisdom of Solomon, Additions to Esther, the books of the Maccabees, etc. The books of Maccabees is a must read because it tells of the miracle performed by YHVH to keep the lamp burning in the temple without oil and why the Jews celebrate Hanukkah today.[35]

The Gospels

The Gospels were translated from ancient Greek manuscripts. They tell the story of Yeshua and His teachings to the Jewish nation. They were penned by the disciples in the Hebrew language and later into Greek. They also detail the ministry of Paul as he spread the gospel to the Gentiles.

When studying the Gospels, think of them in this way. Yeshua is **interpreting the Torah or upholding the Torah** to the Jews. Remember He only preached to the Jews. Over a period of time, the

Pharisees had added many traditions to the worship of YHVH that were not found in the Torah. These traditions acted like a "fence" to keep the Jews from breaking the Torah. Yeshua was in constant conflict with the Pharisees over these added rules that were not in the Torah. In the Scriptures He was constantly interpreting the Torah to His followers to overcome the burdensome rules of the Pharisees.[36]

Also, think of the Gospels as layers. In one Gospel, Yeshua has one character trait and in another it is different. For example, in the book of Matthew, Yeshua is the king or ruler of the Kingdom of Heaven:

> *Saying, Where is he that is born **King** of the Jews?* (Matthew 2:2 KJV, emphasis added)

So, in the book of Matthew, Yeshua is the King.

Look for key verses in the Gospels and see if you can tell what character He is within each of them.

In the book of Mark, Yeshua is the Son of Man.

> *But that ye may know that the **Son of man** hath power on earth to forgive sins.* (Mark 2:10 KJV, emphasis added)
>
> *Therefore, the **Son of man** is Lord also of the Sabbath.* (Mark 2:28 KJV, emphasis added)
>
> *Whosoever therefore shall be ashamed of me and of my words in this adulterous and sinful generation; of him also shall the **Son of man** be ashamed.* (Mark 8:38 KJV, emphasis added)

In the book of Luke, Yeshua is the Servant of YHVH

> *The Spirit of the Lord is upon me, because he hath anointed me to preach the gospel to the poor; he hath sent me to heal the brokenhearted, to preach deliverance to the captives, and recovering of sight to the blind, and to set at liberty them that are bruised.* (Luke 4:18 KJV)

In the book of John, Yeshua provides the sinless blood of God.

The next day John seeth [Yeshua] coming unto him, and saith, Behold the Lamb of God, which taketh away the sin of the world. (John 1:29 KJV)

In the book of Revelation, Yeshua is the almighty judge.

And I saw heaven opened, and behold a white horse; and he that sat upon him was called Faithful and true, and in righteousness he doth judge and make war. (Revelation 19:11 KJV)

For a more in-depth teaching, see the teaching by Michael Rood called "The Jonah Code."[69]

Original Scriptures Written by Hebrews

The very first believers in YHVH were called Hebrews. Abraham was Hebrew. When the Exodus took place, they were called Hebrews, and they consisted of twelve tribes. Later, when the twelve tribes settled in the Promised Land, the tribe of Judah settled in the southern part of the land where Jerusalem was built. The tribes eventually separated into two different kingdoms. The kingdom in the southern part of Israel was under the house of David, and it was called the land of Judah. With the demise of the kingdom of Judah, it was later named the land of Judea. The name *Jew* was derived from the Hebrew *Yehudi*, which literally means "Judean" or being of the tribe of Judah. Anyone living in Judea was called a Jew.[38]

The Scriptures were penned by Jews, and they were recorded in Hebrew. They were originally recorded in Palo Hebrew on scrolls. When the Jews took the Scriptures to the rest of the world, the Scriptures were first translated into Greek and Latin by the early church. Unfortunately, the early translators seem to have altered the Scriptures (especially the New Testament) in a way so that the names and many verses would meet the agenda of the early church. The early church made new rules of worship excluding any Jewish feast by changing laws and times of worship. In the King James Version Passover and the Sabbath are not even capitalized so as to lower their importance in the Scriptures. In a later chapter we will review Scripture verses that have been altered, and some verses where words that have been added even change entire meanings.

Paleo-Hebrew was the Very First Hebrew Writing

First, let us look at the history of the Hebrew language. Hebrew was originally written with a pictographic script similar to Egyptian hieroglyphs and is referred to as Paleo- Hebrew script. The ancient Hebrew language is a concrete oriented language, meaning that the Hebrew words are rooted in something that can be grasped by the five senses. Abstract concepts have no foundation in the ancient Hebrew language and are a product of ancient Greek philosophy. The oldest scrolls found to date were written in Paleo-Hebrew script. When the Hebrew were taken into Babylonian captivity, they adopted the Aramaic script of the region.[39]

The ancient Hebrews also wrote the Scriptures within the Eastern culture, whereas most Christians are a product of Western cultures. These two cultures are very different. The authors of the translated biblical texts are writing from within their own culture. So it is easy to see why the original Hebrew texts could be misinterpreted.

Another problem in the translations is that abstract words in ancient Hebrew do not exist; however, we find them throughout the Scriptures. They were added because the Greeks used abstract words in the translations from Hebrew to Greek. Also, Greek thought describes objects in relation to their appearance. Hebrew thought describes objects in relation to their function. For a more detailed discussion of how to understand the correct meaning of a verse as it was written in ancient

Hebrew, get a copy of the *Ancient Hebrew Lexicon of the Bible* by Jeff A. Brenner.[40]

Simply put, you should study the Scriptures with the understanding that it was originally written in ancient Hebrew, copied using Modern Hebrew script, and later translated into the Greek language. With the Greek-to-English translations, it will require you to look at the original language or the Greek language to understand the correct meaning of words in a verse. Translation errors occurred and man interjected some beliefs into the translations that need to be corrected.

Today, we have many old texts that are witnesses to the words of God in the Scriptures. The following is a brief list.

THE FOLLOWING ARE WITNESSES TO THE TEXT OF THE TANAK:

The Hebrew Witnesses
The Masoretic Text
The ancient Hebrew text of the Tanak did not have vowels. The vowels were added by a group of Rabbinic Jewish rationalists between the years 500 and 950 BC. They were known as Masoretes, and the resultant Hebrew text with vowels is known as the Masoretic text. Toward the end of the Masoretic era, the last two Masoretic families (ben Asher and ben Naphtali) finalized two slightly different Masoretic texts. Most printed editions today use the Ben Asher text as their source.[41]

The Masorah
The term *Masorah* refers to the original margin notes by the Masoretes transmitted with the Masoretic text. These notes indicate where the scribes found the words irreverent and changed them to be less offensive.[42]

The Samaritan Pentateuch
The Samaritan Pentateuch is the version of the Hebrew Torah not as preserved by Jewish authorities but as preserved by the Samaritan community.[43]

The Cairo Geniza
The Cairo Geniza discovery is an archive of Jewish manuscripts discovered in the 1890s in the synagogue of Fostat-Cairo, Egypt, which had originally been built in 882 CE. Among the documents discovered were biblical manuscripts from a time when the Masoretic Text was not finalized.[44]

The Dead Sea Scrolls
The Dead Sea Scrolls are a collection of 972 texts of the Old Testament that were found between 1947 and 1956 at Khirbet Quran in caves on the northwest shore of the Dead Sea. These manuscripts generally date between 150 BCE and 70 CE. They were written mostly in Hebrew with a few in Aramaic and Greek. Prior to the Dead Sea discovery, the oldest Hebrew manuscript of the Old Testament was the Masoretic text the Aleppo codex, which dates back to the tenth century. The discovery also has caused scholars to reconsider the development of the Old Testament from only three manuscript families such as the Masoretic text, the Hebrew original of the Septuagint, and the Samaritan Pentateuch.[45]

The Aramaic Witnesses
The Peshitta Aramaic Tanak
The Peshitta Aramaic translation is a literal Aramaic translation made directly from a Hebrew text that closely resembles the current Masoretic text.[46]

The Aramaic Targums
The Aramaic Targums are Aramaic paraphrases of the Tanak. These paraphrases were read in the synagogues along with Hebrew scrolls.[47]

The Greek Witnesses
The Greek Septuagint
The Greek Septuagint is very important because it is the earliest known translation of the Tanak into another language, and it is a translation of a Hebrew text that existed in the third century CE.[48]

These references form the basis for the translators to come close in accurately translating what we call the Old Testament. Remember, you must study the Scriptures based on the Hebrew and the culture of the time in which it was originally written in order to ensure the correct translation into English.

THE FOLLOWING ARE THE WITNESSES FOR THE NEW TESTAMENT:

Hebrew Sources
The Du Tillet Matthew
The Du Tillet version is taken from a Hebrew manuscript of Matthew that was confiscated by Jews in Rome in 1553 by a decree of Pope Julius III. Some scholars say it is close to the Greek text of Matthew.[49]

Munster Matthew
Sebastian Munster (a German cartographer, cosmographer, and a Hebrew scholar) published a Hebrew version of the
Gospel of Matthew in 1537. He had obtained the original copy of Matthew from Spanish Jews.[50]

Shem-Tob Matthew
The Shem-Tob Matthew was transcribed in 1380 by a Spanish Jew called Shem Tob ben-Isaac ben-Shaprut. It first appeared in the polemical treatise *Eben Bohan*, which was writing against Christianity as dictated by the early Roman Church.[51]

Aramaic Sources
The Old Syriac Gospels
There are two ancient Aramaic texts of the four Gospels that date back to the fourth century. They are known as the Codex Syrus Curetonianus and the Codex Syrus Sinaiticus.[52]

The Peshitta New Testament
The Peshitta Bible is an Aramaic version of the Scriptures that is used throughout the Near East.[53]

The Crawford Manuscript of Revelation
The Crawford Aramaic version of Revelation is very rare. The manuscript contains a complete Peshitta text supplemented by the extra Peshitta epistles.[54]

As you can see, there are many sources from which the Scriptures were written. The most common translation for the Tanak or Old Testament is based on the Masoretic Hebrew and Aramaic text of the Scriptures, printed in the 1937 edition of Rudolph Kittel's Biblia Hebraica. This text is based on the ben Asher text of Leningrad. Generally speaking, there are few problems with the Masoretic text.[55]

Unfortunately, this is not true of the Messianic scriptures (New Testament). It was written from the Greek manuscripts, which had over twenty-eight thousand Greek manuscripts or fragments. The alarming fact is that almost all of these handwritten copies differ from every other one. As a result of some of the translations, there are many problems with the New Testament that will require much study and investigation to get to the original meaning of a verse.

Importance of Knowing the Scriptures

Today we have many English translations to choose from. The translations by the early churches seem to have the most translation problems. Sometimes it is difficult to get the correct meaning of a verse consistent with the original Hebrew and Greek scriptures.

This was probably the result of the early church removing everything Jewish from the Gospels and sometimes the Old Testament. Fortunately, we have some new English translations available that have corrected some of these problems without having to go back to the original Hebrew or Greek to get a clear meaning of a verse.

I believe that the translation problems noted have led to much diversity among denominations of Christianity. Wikipedia has reported that there are approximately thirty-eight thousand Christian denominations in the world today. So there are many different theologies in the modern Christian churches, which make it very important to study the originally penned Hebrew Scriptures and Greek manuscripts to get the original meaning intended by the author.

Remember, you do err by not knowing the Scriptures (Matthew 22:29). Now we know this is referring to the originally penned Hebrew Scriptures. So I encourage you not to follow blindly but diligently seek the truth.

CHAPTER 2

His Hallowed Name

In Hebrew, the name of an individual is more than an identifier but is a descriptor of his character. It was thought to reveal the character, reputation, or destiny of the person to whom the name was given.[56] As a result, all Hebrew names have meaning.

The Hebrew Scriptures forbid us from giving false witness against another's name: "Thou shalt not bear false witness against thy neighbour" (Exodus 20:16 KJV).

The Scriptures also say that your name is extremely important: "A good name is rather to be chosen than great riches, and loving favour rather than silver and gold" (Proverbs 22:1 KJV).

So if a name has so much importance, then why do Christians and Jews never speak the actual name of the Creator? In the Lord's Prayer, Yeshua referred to His hallowed name. In all the Scripture translations, His name is replaced with a title or an attribute as though it is forbidden to speak His name. However, the Scriptures say that His name is extremely important. So let's investigate and see what the Scriptures say about His hallowed name.

YHVH Reveals his Name to Moses

When YHVH spoke to Abraham, Isaac, and Jacob, He did not reveal His name to them.

And I appeared to Abraham, to Yitz'chak [Isaac] and to ya`akov (Jacob) as El Shaddai (God Almighty), and by My Name, YHVH, was I not known to them. (Exodus 6:3 ISR)

But when Moses was told by YHVH his mission was to go and free Israel from the Egyptians, He disclosed His name to him.

And Mosheh [Moshe] said to Elohim, "See, when I come to the children of Yisra'el (Israel) and say to them, 'The Elohim of your fathers has sent me to you'; and they shall say to me, 'What is his name?' what shall I say to them?" And Elohim said to Mosheh, "I am that which I am." And He said, "Thus you shall say to the children of Yisra'el (Israel), 'I am has sent me to you.'" And Elohim said further to Mosheh "Thus you are to say children of Yisra'el (Israel), 'YHVH of your fathers, the Elohim of Abraham, the Elohim of Yitshaq (Jacob), has sent me to you.' **This is My Name forever; this is my remembrance to all generations.** (Exodus 3:13–15 ISR, emphasis added)

The *Ancient Hebrew Lexicon of the Bible* defines *remembering* or *remembrances* as follows: "to remember in thought as a memorial or **mention in speech**."[57] This means we are supposed to use His name throughout all our generations. However, almost all the Scriptures do not use His holy name. If you want to be blessed and be saved, call on YHVH by His personal name.[58]

The name will also have a special place in Jerusalem.

And he placed a carved image of Asherah he had made in the house concerning which Adonai had told David and Shlomo his son, "In this house and in Yerushalayim, which I have chosen out of all the tribes of Isra'el, **I will put my name forever.**" (2 Kings 21:7 ISR, emphasis added)

At some point in our future, everyone will know His name.

> *I will make my holy name known among my people Isra'el; I will not allow my holy name to be profaned any longer. Then the Goyim will know that I am* Adonai, *the Holy One in Isra'el.* (Ezekiel 39:7 cjb)

Why is it Important to know the Name of YHVH?

The importance of His name is first expressed in the book of Enoch. Now Enoch was a very holy man. He was a scribe, and he wrote everything down on parchment scrolls. He often had visions and was given many truths about the earth and heaven and what the future held. In the book of Enoch, he writes about the name of YHVH and how the righteous should treat His name.[59]

The lips of the righteous extol (praise) the name of YHVH.

Enoch praised the name of YHVH and received many blessings.

Mighty is His name because He made all the planets, moons and stars.

Sinners who deny His name will be punished by YHVH.

Sinners who deny His name will suffer tribulation.

Sinners will not have any hope because they deny His name.

Finally, those who call on His name will be saved and will be in heaven.

The Scriptures also talk about His name.

> *An altar of earth thou shalt make unto me, and shalt sacrifice thereon thy burnt offerings, and thy peace offerings, thy sheep, and thine oxen: in all places where I record my name **[Yehovah]** I will come unto thee, and I will bless thee.* (Exodus 20:24 kjv, emphasis added)
>
> *"For me you need make only an altar of earth; on it you will sacrifice your burnt offerings, peace offerings, sheep, goats and cattle.* ***In every place where I cause my name [Yehovah] to be mentioned, I will come to you and bless you.***" (Exodus 20:21 (24) cjb, emphasis added)

The Ark of the Covenant was also called by His name.

> *And David arose, and went with all the people that were with him from Baale of Judah, to bring up from thence the ark of God, whose name is called by the name of the LORD of hosts that dwelleth between the cherubims.* (2 Samuel 6:2 KJV)
>
> *And David rose up and went with all the people who were with him from Ba`ale-Yehudah, to bring up from there the ark of Elohim, that is called by the Name YHVH, who dwells between the kerubim.* (2 Samuel 6:2 ISR)

The importance of His name is also expressed in the Old Testament with regard to the forgiveness of sins.

> *Then, if my people, who bear my name, will humble themselves, pray, seek my face and turn from their evil ways, I will hear from heaven, forgive their sin and heal their land.* (2 Chronicles 7:14 CJB)

According to The Scriptures Yeshua answered this when He delivered His last message to the disciples: **"Whosoever shall call upon inthe Name of YHVH (Yehovah) shall be saved."** If you don't know His name, you can't call on his name. Yeshua said, "For I say unto you, from now on you shall by no means see Me, until you say, **Blessed is He who is coming in the Name of YHVH (Yehovah)"** (Matthew 23:39 ISR, emphasis added).

In Exodus 20:24, the Scriptures also say that if we call on His name in blessing others, they will be blessed.

Throughout the book of Enoch, it says over and over that those who praise the name of the Lord of spirits (YHVH) are saved. The ones who do not call on His name are lost. Here is wisdom. You need to know His name in order that you can call His name. In the King James Version, He is called LORD, which is a title. To find His real name requires you to study the oldest Hebrew version that has His four-letter name with three vowel marks. The vowel marks are required so that His name is pronounced correctly.

In the Hebrew scriptures (Tanak or Old Testament), the most often written name of the Hebrew God is the Tetragrammaton, the four-letter name of God, also known as YHWH or YHVH. The Tetragrammaton appears 6,628 times in the Old Testament Hebrew scriptures.[60] Also, the four-letter Hebrew name is most often shown without vowels in an effort to prevent His name being spoken incorrectly.[61]

So what is his Holy Name?

His holy name is the combination of four Hebrew consonant letters: "Yod-Heh-Vav-Heh," which is abbreviated YHVH. His personal name is spoken as **Yehovah**. In order to pronounce His name correctly, three vowels were added to the four letters of His Hebrew name. The vowels were not always shown with the name in some of the earliest Hebrew texts because it was forbidden to speak His name.[62]

In order to demonstrate the sacredness of the name of YHVH, Almighty YHVH chose to reveal His name to the early Jewish scribes through His character and presence by means of His acts and deeds. He also revealed His name in a certain order. Some of these names are as follows:

> *Elohim* is the name for God as the Creator of the universe.
> *In the beginning Elohim created the heaven and the earth.*
> (Genesis 1:1 ISR)

El comes from the root word meaning "might, strength and power," and in Scripture the primary meaning of this root is "god" (pagan or false gods), "God" (the true God of Israel), and sometimes "the mighty" (referring to men and angels). When used of the true God of Israel, El is almost always qualified by additional words that further define the meaning that distinguishes Him from false gods.[63]

El Shaddai is the name of God as the All-Sufficient God.

Adonai is the plural of *Adon* meaning "Lord, master, or owner."

Elah is an Aramaic name for God that means "awesome, fearful one."

After the Babylonian captivity, the rabbis required the four-letter name to be read as "Adonai" (My Lord). To say His name incorrectly was considered blasphemy and the punishment under Jewish law was death. As a result, Adonai was used in Jewish prayers and was referred to as HaShem, "the Name."

Avinu means "our Father." In the book of Matthew, Yeshua tells the disciples not to call anyone father except your Father in heaven.

The Masoretes added vowel-pointing (the inserting of signs used to indicate vowels in certain alphabets) to the four-letter name around the eighth century. Later medieval Christian biblical scholars took the vowel substitution for the actual spelling of the name and interpreted the name as *Jehovah*. I have no explanation how they got the letter *J* to replace the Hebrew letter Yod, although it has been referred to as a substitution word, not translated.

So why is his Personal Name not shown in the Scriptures Today?

Because of church tradition of using titles such as Lord, the personal name of the Holy Father is not even mentioned today. The Jews and the Christians will always justify this by pointing to the third commandment not to take His name in vain as an excuse not to use His personal name. What the verse really says is that you shall not use His name in a lie or make a false vow in His name.

Because of the prohibition of speaking His name, the following are the ways His name is written today in most scriptures:

In the Hebrew and in some English translations, the name of God is expressed by the Hebrew Tetragrammaton YHWH or YHVH. Also, common titles in Hebrew translations are used such as Adonai, El, Eloah, and Elohim.

In Greek, the word *Kyrios* is used for the name of God, which means Lord.

In Latin, the word <u>Dominus</u> is used to replace the Hebrew four-letter Tetragrammaton (YHWH).

In English, the word Lord is used to replace the name of God.

In 2008, Pope Benedict issued a directive to the Roman Catholic Church forbidding the personal Hebrew Name of God to be used or pronounced in songs or prayers. Why? [64]

There is no explanation from the pope regarding the prohibition of sayingYehovah's name. My opinion is that this is part of the Vatican's plan of replacement theology regarding Israel. Replacement theology teaches that the church has replaced the Jewish people and now is the "new Israel."

These traditions and prohibitions directly conflict with the instructions from what Yehovah said to Moses on Mount Sinai.

The Blessing of his Name

Most Christians are familiar with the blessing by Aaron on the people of Israel from Numbers 6:23–27 (**[insert translation]**).

> *And Yehovah spoke to Moses, saying, "Speak to Aaron and his sons, saying, 'this is how you bless the children of Israel, saying unto them,* **"Yehovah** *bless you, and keep you;* **Yehovah** *cause his face shine upon you:* **Yehovah** *lift His face toward you and give you peace." So if they invoke my name on the sons of Israel, I will bless them.'"*

By simply invoking (saying) His name in the blessing, Yehovah's promise is to come and bless them.

Does this apply to the Gentiles? The answer is yes.

> *And the foreigners **[Gentiles]** who join themselves to* **Yehovah** *to serve Him, to love the name* **Yehovah***, and to be his workers, all who keep*

Sabbath and do not profane it, and hold fast to my covenant, even those I will bring them to my holy mountain and make them joyful in my house of prayer; their burnt offerings and sacrifices will be accepted on my altar; for my house will be called a house of prayer for all peoples. (Isaiah 56:6–7, emphasis added)

When Jews or Gentiles bless someone and they invoke His name, Yehovah, then Yehovah will come and bless them.

"'For me you need make only an altar of earth; on it you will sacrifice your burnt offerings, peace offerings, sheep, goats and cattle. **In every place where I cause my name to be mentioned, I will come to you and bless you.'"** (Exodus 20:21 (24) CJB, emphasis added)

What about the Name Jesus?

It is well documented that the Jews always referred to the Messiah as Yeshua. In the Babylonian Talmud, He was referred to as *Yeshu*. They even omitted the letter *a* from His name. "On the eve of Passover Yeshu was hanged" (Babylonian Talmud, Sanhedrin 43a, Soncino Translation).

So when the Hebrew Scriptures were translated from Hebrew to Greek in the Septuagint, the Jewish translators of the Septuagint translated the shortened form (Yeshu) of Yeshua to the Greek *Iesous*. So when the Septuagint was translated to Latin, the Latin Iesus was used. So why the Messiah is called *Jesus* in our English translations today? [65]

How did this happen? It happened because of translation problems from Hebrew to Greek. First there is a *Y* in the Hebrew name, but *Y* did not exist in Greek. So when His name was first written in Greek, they wrote it as *Iesous* in an effort to try to get the Greek name as close as possible to the sound of His Hebrew name and with the correct gender. The Greeks transliterated the short-form Hebrew name Yeshu to Iesous. Then His name Iesous in Greek was transliterated to Latin as *Iesus*. So when you look at the 1611 King James Bible, Yeshua is called Iesus. When Webster invented the letter *J*, the letter *I* in Iesus was changed to

7. Then the Messiah was called Jesus in the King James revised edition of the Scriptures. So you have been tricked into believing the Hebrew Messiah was given a Greek name.[66]

Even today Hebrew scholars disagree over the Hebrew name of the Messiah as recorded in the Scriptures as Yehoshua. Some scholars argue that His name was Yeshua while others argue His name was Yeshuah (Ye-shu-ah) because it is the Hebrew word for *salvation*. Some believe that the name Yeshua is the Aramaic equivalent of Yehoshua.[67]

In addition, the Pharisees of the time when the Messiah was preaching His message would refer to Him by the name Yeshu. Evidence of this is found in the Babylonian Talmud where the Messiah is referred to as Yeshu. Nowhere in the Talmud is He called Jesus.[68]

A very thorough discussion of the importance of knowing the Creator's name is in this book by Keith Johnson. For an in-depth study, get Keith Johnson's book *His Hallowed Name Revealed Again*

How to Speak his Name when Praying

There are hundreds of names and titles of God that reveal His attributes and character. His main name, which is His personal name, is YHVH. Did you realize that Yeshua never referred to His personal name in the Gospels? He always referred to Him as "Father." One good example of this was the Lord's Prayer.

The Lord's Prayer translated from Hebrew from the Hebrew Matthew Version is as follows:

> *Our Father in heaven, May your Name be sanctified. May your kingdom be blessed. Your will shall be done in heaven and on earth. Give us our bread continually. Forgive us the debt of our sins as we forgive the debt of those who sin against us. Do not bring us into the hands of a test, and protect us from all evil. Amen.*[69]

The third commandment is "You shall not lift up the Name of the Lord in vain (*lashav*)," a word that means "in an empty or thoughtless manner." In other words, don't give "lip-service or mechanical expressions of faith or heartless acts of service." The prohibition means that God wants you to engage Him with *kavanah* (concentration). To call upon His name you must first exercise reverence by recognizing His all-consuming glory and power.[70]

When we bless others we are exercising our likeness to God or "lifting up His Name," but when we say negative things about others we are cursing them, and we are doing just the opposite of the likeness of God. Life and death is in the tongue.

> *The tongue has power over life and death; those who indulge it must eat its fruit.* (Proverbs 18:21 CJB)

The Scriptures also tell us not to be weary waiting on a prayer to be answered.

> *So let us not grow weary of doing what is good; for if we don't give up, we will in due time reap the harvest.* (Galatians 6:9)

PRAY IN YESHUA'S NAME

Prior to the crucifixion of Yeshua, the priests offered up prayers to the God of Abraham, Isaac, and Jacob.

> *Go, and gather the elders of Israel together, and say unto them, The Lord God of your fathers, the God of Abraham, of Isaac, and of Jacob, appeared unto me, saying, I have surely visited you, and seen that which is done to you in Egypt.* (Exodus 3:16 KJV)

Yeshua said to pray in His name.

> *And whatsoever ye shall ask in my name, that will I do, that the Father may be glorified in the Son.* (John 14:13 KJV)

Ye have not chosen me, but I have chosen you, and ordained you, that ye should go and bring forth fruit, and that your fruit should remain: that whatsoever ye shall ask of the Father in my name, he may give it you. (John 15:16 KJV)

CHAPTER 3

Written in Hebrew

§

No one would disagree that the Old Testament of the Scriptures was originally penned in Hebrew. But was the New Testament written in Hebrew? First of all, we know that Yeshua (Jesus) and all the apostles were Jewish. As children they had to learn to speak Hebrew and write in Hebrew. So, it is a reasonable assumption to say that the New Testament was originally written in Hebrew. But let's look to the Scriptures and see what it says about the Hebrew language.

First, let's look at the language spoken by Yeshua. There are several examples in the Scriptures that the language spoken by Yeshua was Hebrew.

Paul is on the way to Damascus when he sees a bright light from heaven and he falls to the ground. Then Paul says:

> *I heard a voice speaking unto me, and saying in the Hebrew tongue.* (Acts 26:14 KJV)
>
> "*We all fell to the ground; and then I heard a voice saying to me, in Hebrew, 'Sha'ul! Sha'ul! Why do you keep persecuting me? It's hard on you to be kicking against the ox-goads!*'" (Act 26:14 CJB)

The Aramaic translation of Acts 26:14 in the King James Version uses the word *Hebraidi*, which means Hebrew. Most new Bible translations use the word *Hebrew* in this verse; but not everyone agrees that Yeshua spoke Hebrew. In Mel Gibson's movie *The Passion of the Christ* Yeshua and the disciples spoke Aramaic!

The Aramaic Language
Aramaic is a Semitic language that is based on the name of Aram, which is located in central Syria. It is closely related to both Arabic and Hebrew; however, according to Nehemia Gordon, the relationship of Aramaic to Hebrew is similar to the relationship between German and English. The Aramaic language is about three thousand years old and was spoken throughout the early Middle East. When the Jews were taken into bondage in Babylon for seventy years, they recorded things in the Babylonian Talmud. When Yeshua was preaching, they were still recording in Aramaic in the Talmud.[71]

So did the Jews Speak Aramaic or Hebrew at the Time of Yeshua?
It appears that we must look at some other translations in order to try to resolve this controversy.

In the Greek translation of Matthew 27:46 (KJV), "[Yeshua] cried with a loud voice, saying, Eli, Eli, lama sabachthani? That is to say, My God, my God, why hast thou forsaken me?"

The words spoken by Yeshua—*Eli, Eli, lama sabachthani*—are actually in the Aramaic language.

If I look at the Shem-Tob Hebrew translation of Matthew 27:46, it says "Yeshua cried with a loud voice, saying in the holy language [Hebrew] *Eli, Eli, lama 'azantani*? Why hast thou forsaken me?"

Why is Yeshua speaking in Hebrew (the holy language) in the Shem-Tob version of Matthew and speaking Aramaic in the King James Version?

This was a perplexing question to Nehemia Gordon, a linguistic scholar who had worked on the translation of the Dead Sea Scrolls. He knew that there were more than five thousand manuscripts of the New Testament documented in Greek dating back to the first five centuries after they were penned. He theorized that if the book of Matthew had been written originally in Hebrew, then someone should have known about it. Gordon concluded that if Matthew had been written in Hebrew during the time just after the disciples were teaching to the Gentiles, an early church father would have said something about it. A colleague of Gordon suggested that one of the early church fathers did say the book of Matthew was written in Hebrew and translated into other languages.[72]

At the Mount Scopes Library, Nehemia Gordon reviewed the writings of Papias quoted by Eusebius. Papias had been the Bishop of Hierapolis, a small town in Asia Minor, and he lived about 60–130 CE. Much of the information that Papias had about Yeshua came from people who had studied directly under the disciples. It is recorded that one of the people that Papias knew was the disciple John who wrote the Gospel of John. Papias was well aquatinted with the writings of the disciples, and he wrote the following matter-of-factly: "Matthew collected the oracles (writings) **in the Hebrew language** and each interpreted them the best he could."[73]

The Greek word used here is *hermeneusen*—"interpreted" can also mean "translated" just as in the English language "interpreter" means "translator."

What Papias seems to be saying is that Matthew wrote the Gospel in Hebrew, and speakers of different languages did their best to interpret or translate into their own language.

Apparently, Papias realized that some of the ancient translations of Matthew's Hebrew Gospel were none too accurate, and this is why he says, "Each translated them the best they could."[74]

The evidence is that in ancient times the book of Matthew was originally written in Hebrew, but it was also readily recognized that the Greeks and other non-Hebrews had a difficult time translating the Hebrew Matthew into Greek and other languages.

Now we know the answer to the question of the why Aramaic words were used in the Greek translation in certain versus. Biblical scholars now believe that Yeshua and the disciples spoke in Hebrew and recorded Yeshua's words in Hebrew. As the disciples and others tried to translate the Hebrew writings into Greek, they found this to be very difficult. To solve this problem, they first translated Hebrew into Aramaic.

Then they translated the Aramaic into Greek. As a result, a few Aramaic translations or words appear in the Scriptures.

Did the Early Church change the Scriptures?

There are examples of where the translator interjected the traditions of the early church into the Scriptures. A good example of this is in the book of Acts.

> *And when he had apprehended him, he put him in prison, and delivered him to four quaternion of soldiers to keep him; intending after* **Easter** *to bring him forth to the people.* (Acts 12:4 KJV, emphasis added).

The Greek translation uses the word *pasha* or **Passover, not Easter**. The translator interjected the church's tradition of calling the Jewish Passover Easter. **Easter is not another name for Passover!** Passover is referred to by Yehovah as a feast that occurs on the fifteenth day of the first month of the year. The first month of the year was determined by when the barley was *aviv* I will explain more about this tradition in a later chapter.

Another example is Mark 11:26 in the King James Version. This verse was not in the earliest Greek manuscripts. The translator simply copied Matthew 6:15 and added it as Mark 11:26.

The longest addition of verses to the Scriptures is John 7:53 through 8:11. None of the oldest manuscripts we have which were found in many countries, did not have these verses.

In the King James Version, in the book of Genesis, the words "appointed times" have been changed to "seasons." These changes dramatically change the meaning of the verses Genesis 1:14, Exodus 13:10, Leviticus 23:4, and Daniel 2:21. In the following verses, "seasons" replaced "at all times," changing the meaning of the verse: Exodus 18:22, 26.

Unfortunately, the King James Version has a lot of problems of this type, and many biblical scholars think the changes were a result of the influence of kings on the early church.

Context of the Original Language

In order to truly understand the Scriptures correctly, one must have a sound understanding of the Hebrew language in the context of which it was written. In the book, *The Hebrew Yeshua vs. the Greek Jesus*, Nehemia Gordon explains "Hebraisms" (Hebrew thought patterns written in the original Hebrew text), which the Greek translators did not understand. One must understand the Hebrew style of storytelling to understand the original meaning. A strict mechanical translation from Hebrew to Aramaic to Greek will most likely result in a different meaning from the original. In his book, Gordon explains and gives examples so that the reader of the Scriptures can get a better understanding of the original text.[75]

To study the Scriptures requires you to understand that it was originally written in Hebrew, translated into Aramaic, and then translated into Greek. It was translated into other languages by men, and sometimes the meanings were changed. This requires you to research the truth by going back to the original Hebrew or Greek. Relying on the footnotes in English scriptures for your information is a bad idea. Footnotes are merely interpretations by someone else who may have it wrong.

Also, it may be helpful to read an entire chapter in order to understand the context in which the Scripture was written. Understanding the context a verse was written in may be helpful in understanding the meaning of a verse.

Added Words to the Scriptures

In order to make the English translation make sense, words were added to the King James translation. These words are shown in italics. These are words that are not in the original texts. To have better understanding, you must go back to the best original text available to see the meanings of words in the original text.

Interpretations by Others

Moreover, do not trust interpretations of the Scriptures if they are not consistent with the original context in which the Scriptures were written. They were written for each one of us to read and understand. Remember, at Judgment Day, you are responsible for yourself, not your minister or priest. The Scriptures gives a warning for those who teach us differently by adding to or taking away from the originally penned Hebrew Scriptures:

> ***Whosoever therefore shall break one of these least commandments, and shall teach men so, he shall be called the least in the kingdom of heaven: but whosoever shall do and teach them, the same shall be called great in the kingdom of heaven.*** (Matthew 5:19 KJV)

> "*So whoever disobeys the least of these mitzvot and teaches others to do so will be called the least in the Kingdom of Heaven. But whoever obeys them and so teaches will be called great in the Kingdom of Heaven.*" (Matthew 5:19 CJB)

> *He who shall transgress one word of these commandments (and shall teach) others, shall be called a vain person (in the) kingdom of heaven of heavens; but, whoever upholds and teaches (them) shall be called great in the kingdom of heaven.* (Matthew 5:19 Shem-Tob)

True Understanding of the Scriptures

The bottom line is this: the Scriptures were originally penned in Hebrew. They were written in the context of the Hebrew language and Jewish culture. Events and prophecies were based on a time-keeping system given to the Jews by YHVH that we will review in a later chapter. Although the New Testament was originally written in Hebrew, all we have for the New Testament are three Greek translations. They are the Textus Receptus, the Majority text, and the United Bible Society Text.

CHAPTER 4

Understanding the Book of Matthew

Most scholarly Christians know that there are textural problems in the book of Matthew. Greek scholars are also all familiar with phrases that are considered incomprehensible or "gibberish," and many of these phrases are cautiously noted in the Greek commentaries as "meaning uncertain." These phrases were translated literally from the Greek into English and then "reworked" in an attempt to clarify their uncertain meanings. Some of these textural problems have escalated into doctrinal problems as well.

Most Christians know that the New Testament scriptures were translated from the Greek texts. Most of these Greek texts existed as fragments. When these fragments were organized to form the Greek version of the Scriptures, they did the best they could with what they had to work with. The early Roman Church pieced together the Gospels in Greek and then translated them into Latin to form the Vulgate. These Greek texts are now the basis of the Gospels in English, but, as you might expect, problems began to show up, most notably in the book of Matthew.

One problem that is apparent to most scholarly Christians in the book of Matthew is that there is a problem in the very first chapter. According to the Greek and King James versions, there is no genealogical record that Yeshua is related to King David. Matthew 1:17 states there are **forty-two generations** from Abraham to the Messiah. If you count the generations from Abraham to Yeshua as shown in Matthew 1:1–16, there are only **forty-one generations**. Also, the genealogical records of Yeshua in the book of Luke do not agree with Matthew's account. What's missing from the text that would clear this up? [76]

There are also contradictions as found in Matthew 23:2–3 and Matthew 23:14 (KJV, emphasis added): "The scribes and the Pharisees sit in Moses' seat: **All** therefore whatsoever they bid you **observe, that observe and do**: but do not ye after their works: for they say, and do not." In verse 14, Yeshua says, "Woe unto you, scribes and Pharisees, hypocrites! For ye devour widows' houses, and for a pretence make long prayer: therefore ye shall receive the greater damnation."[77]

The Greek and King James versions clearly teach in verses 2 and 3 that Yeshua is telling His followers to **observe and do all** that the Pharisees teach them to observe. In verse 14, Yeshua is telling His followers that the Pharisees are hypocrites and **not to follow them**. Obviously, this is a major contradiction and needs to be solved.[78]

To solve this problem, Michael Rood (a Messianic teacher) approached Nehemia Gordon (a textural scholar at the Hebrew University in Jerusalem) for assistance. Nehemia Gordon currently works on the Dead Sea Scrolls Publication Project and is fluent in ancient Hebrew, Aramaic, Syriac, and Greek. Although Nehemia was a Karaite (a Jew who only follows the Old Testament), he agreed to help Michael Rood with this and other textural problems in the book of Matthew.[79]

After two years of research, the shocking revelation found by Nehemia Gordon is that he claims that the original book of Matthew, as well as the New Testament, was written in **Hebrew—not Greek or Aramaic.** Furthermore, he discovered that the Greeks had so much difficulty in translating the original Hebrew to Greek that they had to first translate Hebrew to Aramaic and then Aramaic to Greek. Then, later, King James of England had the Greek version translated into English, which we now know as the King James Version. As you might expect, with this many translations there would be mistakes or textual differences from the original text. These differences and mistranslations that changed the original text are very apparent in the book of Matthew. Why is it important to have the correct translation? It is extremely important because of the impact on religious doctrine.[80]

How do we know the book of Matthew was written in Hebrew?

Here are three medieval versions[81] of the book of Matthew, as follows:

1. Shem-Tob's Matthew
2. Du Tillet's Matthew
3. Munster's Matthew

The discovery of Shem-Tob's Hebrew Matthew, which was dated about the year 1380, is one reason that confirms that the Scriptures were first written in Hebrew. Shem-Tob was a Spanish Jew who defended the Jewish religion against the oppression of the Catholics during the Spanish Inquisition. This period was marked with the "Disputations." These Disputations were public debates that were forced on the Jews by their Catholic oppressors. If a rabbi lost a debate in defending the Jewish faith, he and the local Jewish community could be forcibly converted to Catholicism. If he won the debate, he could be charged with insulting the Catholic faith and be forced to flee for his life.[82]

Shem-Tob—a Jewish physician living in Aragon, Spain—in an effort to help his fellow Jews wrote a polemical treatise refuting Catholicism called *Touchstone*. He included in the treatise a Hebrew version of the book of Matthew. Shem-Tob's Hebrew Matthew has been known for centuries, but it was assumed to have been translated into Hebrew from Greek since there are over five thousand manuscripts of the New Testament in Greek. In the 1980s, George Howard at Mercer University in Georgia did a detailed linguistic study of Shem-Tob's Hebrew Matthew that showed that parts of the book could not have been translated from Greek because of the Hebraisms in the text. In 1987, George Howard published *The Gospel of Matthew According to a Primitive Hebrew Text*.[83]

Now that we can read the Shem-Tob's book of Matthew in English, there are some major differences we need to note in the version we now have in the King James.

Shem-Tob's Matthew 12:37:

According to your words you will be judged, and according to your deeds you will be convicted.

The King James Version's Matthew 12:37:

For by thy words thou shalt be justified, and by thy words thou shalt be condemned.

Shem-Tob's Matthew 24:40–41:

Then if there shall be two ploughing in a field, one righteous and the other evil, the one will be taken and the other left. Two women will be grinding at a mill; one will be taken and the other left. This is because the angels at the end of the world will remove the stumbling blocks from the world and will separate the good from the evil.

The King James Version's Matthew 24:40–41:

Then shall two be in the field; the one shall be taken, and the other left. Two women shall be grinding at the mill; the one shall be taken, and the other left.

Shem-Tob's Matthew 28:9:

As they were going Yeshua passed before them saying: **"May the name deliver you."** (Emphasis added)

THIS VERSE IMPLIES THAT THERE IS POWER IN THE NAME!
The King James Version's Matthew 28:9:

And as they went to tell his disciples, behold, Jesus met them, saying, All hail. And they came and held him by the feet, and worshipped him.

Shem-Tob's Matthew 28:19–20:

Go and teach them to carry out all the things which I have commanded you forever.

The King James Version's Matthew 28:19–20:

Go ye therefore, and teach all nations, baptizing them in the name of the Father, and of the Son, and of the Holy Ghost: Teaching them to observe all things whatsoever I have commanded you: and, lo, I am with you always, even unto the end of the world. Amen.

WHAT HAPPENED HERE?

Why is there such a drastic difference between the Hebrew version and the English translations, especially in regard to the Trinity statement? How can we find out the truth? We know that the Jews do not believe in the Trinity. The Protestant churches believe in the Trinity.

Unfortunately, today's church does not seem interested in finding out why this happened. Their response is simply to dismiss the Shem-Tob's biblical Hebrew Matthew version. The idea that YHVH protects the integrity of the Scriptures is true, but this only applies to the original Hebrew-penned version. The English scriptures we have today are transliterated and translated copies that were under the control of the early church that hated and despised the Jews. It is a matter of historical record that almost all the Jewish writings were destroyed. This significant change in Matthew 28:19 alone should prompt us search for the truth of the originally penned Scriptures. You must seek the truth no matter what the obstacles are placed in your path.

WHAT OTHER REASONS LEAD US TO BELIEVE THAT THE BOOK OF MATTHEW WAS ORIGINALLY WRITTEN IN HEBREW?

Hebraisms are an important reason that we know that the book of Matthew was originally written in Hebrew. The Old Testament is full of Hebraisms. The books of Matthew, Mark, Luke, Acts, and Revelation are full of Hebraisms. What are Hebraisms? Hebraisms are thought patterns that only mean something to a Hebrew. If we say "dead as a doornail," we know what it means in America. If we translate that phrase into Chinese, it will be meaningless to the Chinese. The same would be true of Hebrew phrases that would have been meaningless to the Greek translators.

Another example of a Hebraism is a Hebrew word pun. A pun is two similar sounding words that have different meanings. Because there are so many Hebrew puns in the book of Matthew, it is now more accepted theory that the original Matthew was written in Hebrew and translated into Greek. For a more in-depth discussion of Hebraism in the New Testament, see Nehemia Gordon's latest book, *The Hebrew Yeshua vs. the Greek Jesus*.

Additional supporting evidence for a Hebrew Matthew comes from a church father, Papias (60–130 CE). In his writings, he said, "Matthew collected the words in the Hebrew language and translated them the best he could." This seems to say it definitely was written originally in Hebrew and it was difficult to translate it into other languages.

Now that we know most biblical scholars accept that the book of Matthew was written in Hebrew, we now can investigate and try to solve some of the inconsistencies and mistranslations in the Greek and English translations. In the following articles, I will attempt to give you the answers found in the Hebrew Matthew. In addition, there are several clarifications in the Greek and King James Version of the Old and New Testaments.

THE GENEALOGY OF THE MESSIAH

Like most of you, I have tried to count the generations in Matthew 1 to see if they agree with the count of generations shown in verse 17. Since the King James Version was translated from Greek, let's see what the Greek translation says.

Greek Translation:

Matthew 1:17

"So all the generations from Abraham to David are fourteen [14] generations: and from David until the carrying away into Babylon are fourteen [14] generations; and from carrying away into Babylon unto Christ are fourteen [14] generations."

Matthew 1:1–16:

"The book of the generation of Jesus Christ, the son of David, the son of Abraham."

"The generations from Abraham to David are fourteen [14]."

Abraham (1) begat Isaac (2); begat Jacob (3); begat Judas (4); begat Pharez (5); begat Heron (6); begat Ram (7); begat Amminadab (8); begat Nahshon (9); begat Salmon (10); begat Boaz (11); begat Obed (12); begat Jesse (13); begat David (14).

"David until the carrying away into Babylon are fourteen [14] generations."

David begat Solomon (1); begat Rehoboam (2); begat Abijan (3); begat Asa (4); begat Jehoshaphat (5); begat Jehoram (6); begat Uzziah (7); begat Jotham (8); begat Ahaz (9); begat Hezekiah (10); begat Manasseh (11); begat Amon (12); begat Jesiah (13); begat Jechoniah (14).

"From carrying away into Babylon unto Christ are fourteen [14] generations."

Jechoniah begat Salatheel (1); begat Zerubbabel (2); begat Abiud (3); begat Sliakim (4); begat Azor (5); begat Sadoc (6);

begat Achim (7); begat Eliud (8); begat Eleazar (9); begat Matthew (10); begat Jacob (11); begat Joseph (12) the husband of Mary, of whom was born Yeshua (13), who is called Christ.

What happened? Yeshua is supposed to be number 14! What are we missing here?

To solve this problem, we must go to the Aramaic translation of Matthew.

Aramaic Translation:

"And Jacob (11) begat Joseph (12) the Father (not husband) of Mary (13) of whom was born Yeshua (14) who is called Messiah."

When we read the Aramaic translation, verse 17 is absolutely correct! Now we know that the Joseph in the book of Luke was the one that married Mary and Mary was a direct descendant from King David.[84]

Moses's Seat

As we mentioned earlier, there are apparent contradictions in the Greek Matthew 23:15 and Matthew 23:2–3 in the King James Version. In the Greek Matthew 23:2–3, Yeshua is saying to the disciples to obey whatever the Pharisees teach because **they** sit in **Moses's seat** and have his authority.

What is meant by Moses's seat? There are two main opinions on the meaning of the phrase "Moses's seat." Some say that in every synagogue there was an actual seat called "Moses's seat" in which the leaders of the congregation would sit and teach with authority. The other opinion was that "Moses's seat" was a figure of speech indicating someone who teaches with the authority of Moses. Either way, the statement that the Pharisees sit in "Moses's seat" means that the Pharisees have some kind of Mosaic authority. In the book of Matthew, Yeshua seemed to be saying that the words of the Pharisees should be followed, but because they are hypocrites their actions should not be emulated. The implication is that a true follower of Yeshua would need to do whatever the Pharisees taught in order to faithfully obey Yeshua's instructions. In practice, this would mean following all the rules and regulations of the Pharisees that may have been invented without a spiritual basis.[85]

In a later verse, Matthew 23:13, Yeshua definitely warns His disciples not to follow the errors of the Pharisees:

But woe unto you, scribes and Pharisees, hypocrites! For ye shut up the kingdom of heaven against men: for ye neither go in yourselves, neither suffer ye them that are entering to go in.

In Matthew 23:27, Yeshua says:

Woe unto you, scribes and Pharisees, hypocrites! for ye are like unto whited sepulchres, which indeed appear beautiful outward, but are within full of dead men's bones, and of all uncleanness.

Yeshua describes the Pharisees as tombs that contain every type of uncleanness in them. Could Yeshua really be telling His followers to obey the instructions of those He was calling hypocrites and white sepulchres? The answer is no.

In chapter 15, Yeshua seems to be telling His disciples to **stay away from the man-made commandments of the Pharisees.**

In Matthew 15:3, Yeshua says to the Pharisees, "Why do ye also transgress the commandments of God by your tradition?"

In Matthew 15:9, Yeshua says, "But in vain they do worship me, teaching for doctrines the commandments of men."

Yeshua is clearly saying **not to follow the traditions or commandments of the Pharisees.**

In this verse, Yeshua is clearly saying **not to do** what the Pharisees say. So why is there a contradiction? Is there a translation problem? After checking the Greek, the translation is correct. To verify that the original Greek was accurately translated, the only other place to look to see what Yeshua really said was in the Hebrew translation of the book of Matthew. Let's see what the Hebrew says.

Hebrew Translation of verses 2–3:

*Therefore, all that **he (not they)** [Moses] says to you, diligently do, but according to their reforms (takanots) and their precedents (ma'asims) do not do, because they talk but they do not do.*[86]

Explanation:
In the Hebrew Matthew, Yeshua is clearly telling His disciples not to obey the Pharisees. If their claim to authority is that they sit in Moses's seat, **then diligently do as Moses says.**

The contrast is as follows:

In Greek, "…all that **they** (Pharisees) say…"
In Hebrew, "…all that **he** (Moses) says…"

The difference in translation is caused by the addition of one letter to the Hebrew word *yomar*. This mistranslation completely changed the instructions from obeying Moses to obeying the Pharisees!

After Yeshua instructs His disciples to do as Moses says, they **must not do** according to the *takanots* and *ma'aisms* of the Pharisees.

A **takanot** is a reform or enactment by the rabbis that change biblical law.[87]

A **ma'aism** is a precedent or an act or deed set by a rabbi. If a Pharisee does not know what the law is in a particular situation, he looks to a precedent from one of his teachers. Yeshua is warning His disciples not to look to the ma'aism of the Pharisees as a standard of behavior.[88]

In the Greek Matthew 15:8–9, Yeshua then accuses the Pharisees of "teaching for the doctrines the commandments of men." This is supposedly a quote from Isaiah 29:13 (KJV); however, this is not exactly correct.

The Hebrew version of Matthew says "learned commandments of men," which is exactly what the Hebrew version of Isaiah says.

These **doctrines of men** that Yeshua is referring to are the **takanots** and **ma'aisms** of the Pharisees.[89]

The last few words of Yeshua in Matthew 23:3 present a particularly interesting problem:

"[B]ut according to their reforms (takanots) and their precedents (ma'aisms) do not do, **because they talk but they do not do.**"

Yeshua is saying that the Pharisees have their own statues and judgments, which they follow, while at the same time they talk **Torah** but do not do **Torah**.

The Torah is the first five books of the Scriptures. It is the oracles or "communications" of God. *Torah* in Hebrew means *instructions*. The Torah is the written oracles of God to be used by the Jews as priests and teachers to all men, including the Gentiles.

In a letter to the Christian (Gentiles) followers in Rome, Paul explains that a Gentile is a Jew, inwardly when he follows the Messiah (Romans 2:29).

Conclusion: Whenever Yeshua is doing away with the Torah in Greek, the Hebrew Yeshua seems to be upholding the Torah. For Catholics and Christians, this is a major problem because they don't follow the fourth commandment in the Torah, which is to keep the Sabbath. Yeshua says, "If ye love me, keep my commandments." (John 14:15).

The biggest controversy in the King James Version of the Scriptures occurs in the book of Matthew. In Matthew 28:19–20, Yeshua gives the following command: "Go ye therefore, and teach all nations, baptizing them in the name of the Father, and of the Son, and of the Holy Ghost." In the Shem-Tob Hebrew Matthew it says, "Go and teach them to carry out all the things which I have commanded you forever." Ironically, Paul, the most gifted of the apostles, directly contradicts the statement to baptize in the name of the Father, the Son, and the Holy Ghost.[90]

*Then Peter said unto them, Repent, and be baptized every one of you in the **name of Jesus Christ** for the remission of sins, and ye shall receive the gift of the Holy Ghost.* (Acts 2:38 KJV, emphasis added)

And Kepha (Peter) said to them, "Repent, and let each one of you be immersed in the Name of Yeshua Messiah for the forgiveness of sins. And you shall receive the gift of Set-apart Spirit." (Acts 2:38 ISR)

Kefa answered them, "Turn from sin, return to God, and each of you be immersed on the authority of Yeshua the Messiah into forgiveness of your sins, and you will receive the gift of the Ruach HaKodesh!" (Acts 2:38 CJB)

Then they that gladly received his word were baptized: and the same day there were added unto them about three thousand souls. (Acts 2:41 KJV)

So those who accepted what he said were immersed, and there were added to the group that day about three thousand people. (Acts 2:41 CJB)

But when they believed Philip preaching the things concerning the kingdom of God, and the name of Jesus Christ, they were baptized, both men and women. (Acts 8:12 KJV)

But when they came to believe Philip, as he announced the Good News concerning the Kingdom of God and the name of Yeshua the Messiah, they were immersed, both men and women. (Acts 8:12 CJB)

(For as yet he was fallen upon none of them: only they were baptized in the name of the Lord Jesus.) (Acts 8:16 KJV)

For until then he had not come upon any of them; they had only been immersed into the name of the Lord Yeshua. (Acts 8:16 CJB)

When they heard this, they were baptized in the name of the Lord Jesus. (Acts 19:5 KJV)

On hearing this, they were immersed into the name of the Lord Yeshua. (Acts 19:5 CJB)

For as many of you as have been baptized into Christ have put on Christ. (Galatians 3:27 KJV)

Because as many of you as were immersed into the Messiah have clothed yourselves with the Messiah. (Galatians 3:27 CJB)

Know ye not, that so many of us as were baptized into Jesus Christ were baptized into his death? (Romans 6:3 KJV)

Don't you know that those of us who have been immersed into the Messiah Yeshua have been immersed into his death? (Romans 6:3 CJB)

From these verses, Paul is saying **Yeshua commanded the apostles to baptize in Yeshua's name only.** There seems to be a major problem with the text in Matthew 28:19 KJV.[91]

If Yeshua did not issue the command in Matthew 28:19, why would this be a problem?

First, we are not supposed to add or take away from the Scriptures.

Ye shall not add unto the word which I command you, neither shall ye diminish ought from it, that ye may keep the commandments of the LORD your God which I command you. (Deuteronomy 4:2 KJV)

"In order to obey the mitzvot of ADONAI your God which I am giving you, do not add to what I am saying, and do not subtract from it." (Deuteronomy 4:2 CJB)

This commandment is especially true of the book of Revelation:

And if any man shall take away from the words of the book of this prophecy, God shall take away his part out of the book of life, and out of the holy city, and from the things which are written in this book. (Revelation 22:19 KJV)

And if anyone takes anything away from the words in the book of this prophecy, God will take away his share in the Tree of Life and the holy city, as described in this book. (Revelation 22:19 CJB)

Secondly, everyone will know the truth on Judgment Day.

> **For it is written, *as* I live, saith the Lord, every knee shall bow to me, and every tongue shall confess to God.** (Romans 14:11 KJV)
>
> Since it is written in the Tanakh, "As I live, says ADONAI, every knee will bend before me, and every tongue will publicly acknowledge God." (Romans 14:11 CJB)
>
> **That at the name of Jesus every knee should bow, of things in heaven, and things in earth, and things under the earth.** (Philippians 2:10 KJV)
>
> *That in honor of the name given Yeshua, every knee will bow—in heaven, on earth and under the earth.* (Philippians 2:10 CJB)

In this chapter I have gone into a lot of detail to emphasize the importance of studying the Scriptures thoroughly. This may require you going back to the scriptures in the original Greek or Hebrew." I hope you can see how some mistranslations could have crept into the English translations. Our pastors and priests could be preaching something that is not true and you would not even know the difference.

CHAPTER 5

Understanding the Creator's Calendar

YOU CANNOT UNDERSTAND THE SCRIPTURES if you don't understand the Creator's calendar. The events in the Scriptures were based on the Creator's calendar and not on the pagan calendars that we inherited. If you don't know the difference between a weekly Sabbath and a High Sabbath, you are not going to understand the Scriptures, and you will form an incorrect understanding of events, specifically the crucifixion of Yeshua. For example, the Scriptures say that Yeshua was crucified on the eve of Passover, but the Jews wanted Him down from the cross and buried before sunset. Why? Because at sundown was the Passover, a High Sabbath, not a weekly Sabbath (Yohanan 19:31 ISR).

You must understand the **feasts of YHVH** (not the feasts of the Jews) that were given to the Israelites and written in the Torah by Moses. The Israelites were told to **rehearse these feasts forever**. Why? They are rehearsals of things to come and are prophetic shadow-pictures of past and future events. "Let no one therefore judge you in eating or drinking, or in respect of a festival or a new moon or **Sabbaths—which are a shadow of what is to come**—but the Body of the Messiah." (Colossians 2:16–17 ISR). If we understand the feasts as rehearsals for future events that must be fulfilled by Yeshua, then we have a better understanding of the Scriptures and how we are supposed to worship YHVH.

What is the Creator's Calendar?

What do the Scriptures say about His calendar and who followed His calendar?

> *And God said, let there be lights in the firmament of the heaven to divide the day from the night; and let them be for **signs**, and for **seasons**, and for **days**, and **years**.* (Genesis 1:14 KJV, emphasis added)

> *And Elohim said, "Let lights come to be in the expanse of the heavens to separate the day from the night, and let them be for **signs** and **appointed times**, and for **days** and **years**."* (Genesis 1:14 ISR, emphasis added)

Thus the following is the Creator's calendar that was followed by Jews:

Days begin at sundown at any location (Genesis 1:5, 8, 13, 19, 23, 31). Today, if you asked a Jewish person when days start, they will all answer at sundown wherever you are.

Weeks begin at sundown at the end of the weekly Sabbath. Each week has seven days, and the days were numbered 1, 2, 3, 4, 5, 6, and 7. The Sabbath is the seventh day of the week. This means the **Sabbath of YHVH starts at Friday at sundown and ends on Saturday at sundown** on the Gregorian calendar that we follow today (Genesis 2:2–3).

Months start on the first sighting of the first sliver of the new moon and verified by two witnesses. Each month is twenty-nine days due to the lunar cycle. The lunar month is 29.530587 days. **Twelve months make up a year.**

The beginning of the year is determined at the new month when the barley crop in Israel has reached the stage of maturity referred to as *aviv*. Aviv is a Hebrew word, and Abib is the English word that has the same meaning. Why was the month of Aviv the first of the year? "And [Yahweh] spoke unto Moses and Aaron in the land of Egypt saying, This month shall be unto you the beginnings of months: it shall be the **first month** of the year to you" (Exodus 12: 1–2 KJV).

In Exodus 12, the LORD institutes the feast of Passover, for it was in that month that the blood of a lamb was placed over the doors of the Hebrews in Egypt so that the angel of death who killed all the firstborn children in Egypt would pass over their houses. The Hebrew were able to leave Egypt in the month of Abib. "This day came ye out of in the month Abib" (Exodus 13:4 KJV).

This is the calendar given by YHVH for mankind to keep track of *His* calendar. A sample monthly calendar is attached for reference.[92]

WHAT ELSE DO THE SCRIPTURES SAY ABOUT THE CALENDAR?

So, is a day in heaven with YHVH the same as a day on earth? No, because Peter says, "But, beloved, be not ignorant of this one thing, that one day with YHVH is as a thousand years, and a thousand years as one day." This means a thousand years on earth is the same as one day in heaven with YHVH (2 Peter 3:8 and Psalm 90). So the days with the Yahweh are as follows:

First day: 0001–1,000 years
Second day: 1,001–2,000 years
Third day: 2,001–3,000 years
Fourth day: 3,001–4,000 years
Fifth day: 4,001–5,000 years
Sixth day: 5,001–6,000 years
Seventh day: 6,001–7,000 years

A thousand years is commonly known as a millennium.

Now the use of the word *day* in Scripture can be confusing in referring to a weekly day or a day in heaven, which is a thousand years on earth. An easy way to keep it straight is to remember when God says a day He is referring to a day in heaven. So when He says to Adam in Genesis 2:17, "for in the day that thou eatest thereof thou shalt surely die," Adam lived to be 930 years old before dying, so Adam died in the first day.

If each day of creation is a thousand years, then the creation could have gone like this:

> First day: YHVH created light.
> Second day: YHVH created the firmament.
> Third day: YHVH created the seas, land, and vegetation.
> Fourth day: YHVH created the sun, moon, and the heavenly bodies to give light to the earth.
> Fifth day: YHVH created animal life of the sea and air.
> Sixth day: YHVH first created animal life on earth, and then He created man.
> Seventh day: YHVH finished His work and He blessed and sanctified the seventh day.

Christian scientist Dr. Hugh Ross has a study on how to reconcile the fossil record with the biblical creation record. He asks the right questions and provides more insight to answer the doubter's questions.

In remembrance of the creation days, YHVH gave Adam and Eve the weekly calendar of six twenty-four-hour days to work and the seventh day (Sabbath) to rest.

Why is it Important that we understand YHVH's Calendar?

This is the calendar that was followed by the Jews and the authors of the Scriptures. Throughout the Scriptures, the Jewish writers referred to days, times, and events based on YHVH's calendar. **Understanding YHVH's calendar is the key to understanding the Scriptures accurately, as YHVH intended for us. When we don't understand**

YHVH's calendar, we start to misinterpret the Scriptures and are led into false beliefs. Then mistakenly, we start following the traditions of man and not what YHVH intended for us.

Long ago we lost track of time on YHVH's calendar, and now we follow calendars developed by man. These new calendars were developed over a long period of time and were rooted in ancient sun-god worship. The ancient Egyptians started numbering the years when the star Sirius rose at the same time as the Sun. The Egyptian calendar had twelve thirty-day months with five days set as aside as festival days.[93] the ancient Greek (Attic or Hellenic) calendar was based on the moon. Two hundred thirty-five lunar months was equal to nineteen solar years. This calendar was not widely used. The calendar set the days of religious festivals and monthly birthdays of the gods.[94] the ancient Babylonians created a system of zodiacs to describe the position of the planets. In the eighth century, they described the day as starting when the sun was in the highest position point in the sky. Each month started on the first sighting of the crescent moon, and each month had thirty days.[95]

The Roman calendar originally started the year with the vernal equinox and consisted of ten months with a total of 304 days. The 304 days were followed with an unnamed, unnumbered period in winter. The ten months were named after a Roman emperor or a pagan god. The Roman calendar was later replaced by the Julian calendar. In the year 46 BC, Julius Caesar reformed the calendar to a 365-day year with a 366-day leap year. The months were named as follows: [96]

> **January** had thirty-one days and was named after the two-headed god of doorways and gates called Janus, the god of beginnings.
>
> **February** had twenty-eight or twenty-nine days and was called Februarius, the month of expiation or the feast of purification.
>
> **March** had thirty-one days and was named after Mars, the god of war.

April had thirty days and was derived from the Latin verb meaning "to open." The Anglo-Saxons called April *Oster-monath* or *Eostur-monath*, which is the root of the word *Easter*, better known as the Queen of heaven from the Scriptures.

May had thirty-one days and was named after Maia, the goddess of spring and growth.

June had thirty days and was named after Juno, goddess of wisdom and marriage.

July had thirty-one days and was named after Julius Caesar.

August had thirty-one days and was named after Augustus Caesar.

September had thirty days and Septum is the number seven in Latin.

October had thirty-one days and is the number eight in Latin.

November had thirty days and is the number nine in Latin.

December had thirty-one days and is the number ten in Latin.[97]

The days of the week were named after planets and pagan gods as follows:

Sunday is the first day and is named after the sun god.

Monday is the second day of the week and is named after the moon god.

Tuesday is the third day of the week and is named after the pagan god Tew.

Wednesday is the fourth day and is named after the Norse god Odin.

Thursday is the fifth day and is named after Norse god Thor.

Friday is the sixth day and is named after the pagan god Frig.

Saturday is the seventh day and is named after the planet Saturn.[98]

What is wrong with using the Pagan Calendar?

> *I am the* Lord *thy God, which have brought thee out of the land of Egypt, out of the house of bondage.* **Thou shalt have no other gods before me [meaning not even speak their names].** (Exodus 20:2–3 kjv, emphasis added)

The mere mention of other gods was an offense to YHVH. Do you think that Satan put into a place a calendar that in using it we unknowingly continue to speak the names of these gods that YHVH obviously hates?

> *Thus saith the* Lord, *Learn not the way of the heathen, and be not dismayed at the signs of heaven; for the heathen are dismayed at them.* (Jeremiah 10:2 kjv)

YHVH made it clear that we are not to worship the stars or planets.

> *Thou shalt not make unto thee any graven image, or any likeness of any thing that is in heaven above, or that is in the earth beneath, or that is in the water under the earth. Thou shalt not bow down thyself to them, nor serve them: for I the* Lord *thy God am a jealous God, visiting the iniquity of the fathers upon the children unto the third and fourth generation of them that hate me.* (Exodus 20:4–5 kjv)

What else do we know about the Julian Calendar?

The method for keeping time of day or what is known as a twelve-hour clock was adopted from the ancient Egyptians. It is a timekeeping convention in which twenty-four hours of the day are divided into two periods called antemeridian (a.m., Latin for "before noon") and postmeridian (p.m., Latin for "after noon").⁹⁹ Most countries use this convention either verbally or informally except Israel and Ethiopia, which start the day at sunset.

Later, the Julian calendar was modified by the Roman Catholic Church in 46 BC to give a better approximation of the tropical year, which is the actual time it takes for the Earth to complete one orbit around the sun. The Gregorian calendar also changed the way the leap year was calculated. Pope Gregory XII decreed in 1592 that all the Catholic countries would follow the reformed Julian calendar, which is now called the Gregorian calendar. England and the colonies (America) adopted the new calendar in 1752.¹⁰⁰

As you can see, the calendar that we use developed over a period of time and is not the calendar that Yeshua and the apostles followed. **This calendar change has led to a lot of confusion over the Scriptures.** Days always start at sundown. So when we read the Scriptures, the first of a new day is at sundown. The Sabbath is the seventh day and always begins at sundown.

Since we have long ago lost YHVH's original calendar that was given to the Hebrews, do we know what day is the first of the year? The answer is yes. Michael Rood has developed the "Astronomically and Agriculturally Corrected Biblical Hebrew Calendar." The calendar is totally based on the Hebrew Scriptures and correctly determines the years, months, and days based on YHVH's calendar given to the Jews. The calendar can be obtained by going to the website at www.michael-rood.tv. Thousands of people every year watch for the first silver of the new moon. When the new moon is reported by two witnesses, then the barley is tested in Jerusalem to see if it is Aviv. If it is, then the first day of the New Year is declared in Jerusalem.¹⁰¹

Since the year is not exactly 360 days, occasionally there will be an extra day in the year. For example, in 2006, the barley was not Aviv at the first of the thirteenth month, so we had an extra month on the biblical Hebrew calendar or the month of Adar Bet. This meant that the first of the biblical year occurred (for example) on April 1, 2006. This also meant that the Feast of Passover occurred on April 14, 2006.

In 2010, the first day of the month of Aviv occurred on March 18, 2010. Passover was on Aviv 14 or March 31, 2010. The Feast of Unleavened Bread took place from Aviv 15 through Aviv 21, or April 1, 2010, through April 7, 2010. The Day of Trumpets occurred on the first day of the seventh month, which was Tishri 1 or September 11, 2010. The Feast of Tabernacles occurred on Tishri 15 or September 15, 2010. The Last Great Day or Feast of Conclusion occurred on Tishri 22 or October 2, 2010. To understand more about the Creator's Calendar, information can be found on Michael Rood's website.

How does YHVH's Calendar help us in understanding Events in Scripture?

If we know that a day in heaven is one thousand years on earth, then when the Scriptures say 'for in the day that thou eatest thereof thou shalt surely die,' Adam lived for 930 earth years before he died. A day is heaven is one thousand years on earth. So Adam died in the day as the Scriptures stated.

Another reason for using YHVH's calendar when studying the Scriptures is that YHVH's calendar will give you the correct day of when something important happened. I give an important example of this in the chapter called "Appointed Time." This is where I use the calendar and the Scriptures to detail the events of the Passover when Yeshua was crucified and was resurrected after three days and nights in the grave. If you believe in the Scriptures, then there is no way Yeshua was crucified on a Friday and rose on a Sunday. These are man-made traditions of the early Roman Catholic Church. Don't be fooled by the traditions of man because your salvation depends on it.

If you have read the Scriptures then you know salvation depends on you following YHVH's commandments and not man's traditions. Remember, man does not make the rules on worship and forgiveness—YHVH makes these rules. It is not about what something means to you, it is about you following YHVH's commandments.

Which Calendar should we use?

I am not suggesting that we should use the Creator's calendar instead of the secular calendar because of the practicality of the world we live in. However, when studying the Scriptures it will be impossible to understand what happened on what day unless you understand the Creator's calendar that the Jewish writers of the Scriptures followed.

For a calendar for the entire year plus a DVD where Michael Rood explains the calendar, go to the website www.MichaelRood.tv.

CHAPTER 6

YHVH's Instructions to the Israelites

JOHN SAID THAT HE HAD not written all that could or should be written about the Messiah; but these things I have written so that you would know that Yeshua (Jesus) was the Messiah (John 20:30–31).

How did John prove that Yeshua was the Messiah?

He did it by showing that Yeshua fulfilled every detail of the **spring feasts** of YHVH when He was crucified.

For over a thousand years, the Jews had been celebrating the **spring feast (Passover)** as YHVH had commanded them to do in Leviticus 23. It was celebrated in the month of Aviv because it was in that month that YHVH delivered the Jews out of Egypt (Exodus 34:18).

To understand the Feasts of YHVH, we must first understand YHVH's calendar as discussed in chapter 5.

And YHVH said to Moses and Aaron:

*This month [Aviv] shall be unto you the beginnings of months: it shall be the first month of the year to you…And this day shall be unto you for a memorial; and ye shall keep it a **feast to [YHVH]** throughout your generations; ye shall keep it a feast by an ordinance for ever.* (Exodus 12:2, 14 KJV, emphasis added)

And YHVH commanded Moses:

> *Speak unto the children of Israel, and say unto them, concerning the feasts of [YHVH], which ye shall proclaim to be holy convocations, even these are my feasts.* (Leviticus 23:2 KJV)

Three times a year the twelve tribes of Israel were to rehearse the feasts of YHVH. Why were the Jews asked to do this?

To understand this better, a little more background is required.

Yeshua was a Jew, and for the first fifteen years after Yeshua was crucified, there were only Jewish followers of the Messiah. Paul and the apostles preached to the Jews and then they preached to the Gentiles.

In a letter to the Christian followers in Rome, Paul explains that a Gentile is a Jew, inwardly when he follows the Messiah (Romans 2:29). Paul then asks, "What advantage then hath the Jew?" Paul answered this rhetorical question, "Much in every way: chiefly, because that unto them (Jews) were committed the **oracles of [YHVH] God**" (Romans 3:1–2 KJV, emphasis added).

In Hebrews Paul says, "For when for the time ye ought to be teachers, ye have need that one teach you again which be the first principles of the **oracles of [YHVH]**" (Hebrews 5:12 KJV, emphasis added).

Peter said, "If any man speak, let him speak as the **oracles of [YHVH]**; if any man minister, let him do it as of the ability which God giveth" (1 Peter 4:11 KJV, emphasis added).

Stephen said, "This is he [Moses]…who received the **lively oracles** to give unto us" (Acts 7:38 KJV, emphasis added).

What are these **oracles**? Oracles mean *logion* in Greek. *Logion* means **communication.**

These are **communications from God.** God gave to Moses His communications in the first five books of the Scriptures. These were the **written oracles** from God to be used by the Jews as priests and teachers to the whole world! God gave the Scriptures to the twelve tribes of Israel for safekeeping.

The first five books of the Scriptures are called the Torah by the Jews. **Torah means instructions in Hebrew.** The books are **Genesis, Exodus, Leviticus, Numbers, and Deuteronomy.**

The oldest Hebrew text in existence today of the Torah is called the Aleppo/Ben-Asher Codex. It has been claimed that it is exactly word for word just like what was penned originally by Moses 3400 years earlier.

The Written Oracles of YHVH were taught by the Disciples

Paul said the Bereans searched the Scriptures daily (the **Torah**) to see if his words were so or not (Acts 17:11).

Now according to Peter, some of the things Paul preached are hard to understand. But Peter states you must understand the Scriptures (**Torah**) so that you will not be led away **with the error of the wicked and fall from your own stubbornness** (2 Peter 3:16–17).

"Jesus [Yeshua] answered and said unto them, ye do **err**, not knowing the **scriptures**, nor the power of [YHVH]" (Matthew 22:29 KJV, emphasis added). Which scriptures is Jesus referring to? The Torah and the writings of the prophets were all that was written at that time.

Paul states, "I am verily a man which am a Jew, born in Tarsus, a city in Cilicia, yet brought up in this city at the feet of Gamaliel, and taught according to the perfect manner of the law [**Torah**] of the fathers, and was zealous toward [YHVH], as ye all are this day" (Acts 22:3 KJV, emphasis added).

Paul told the Sadducees (second temple believers of the Old Testament only), "I am a Pharisee, the son of a Pharisee" (a Pharisee is a Jewish sect that believed in the oral law allegedly received from Moses). Every word preached by Paul is consistent with the Torah.

What are the Living Oracles of YHVH?

These were the communications or rehearsals that must be lived by each generation in the land of Israel. The living oracles are called the Kadosh Miqrah or holy **convocations**—the **feasts of YHVH** (Leviticus 23:1–44).

> *And [YHVH] spake unto Moses, saying, Speak unto the children of Israel, and say unto them, Concerning the **feasts of [YHVH]**, which ye shall proclaim to be holy **convocations**, even these are my feasts... These are the **feasts of [YHVH]**, even holy **convocations**, which ye shall proclaim in their **seasons**.* (Leviticus 23:1–2, 4 KJV, emphasis added)

Convocation comes from the Greek word *Mikra*. **Mikra means rehearsal.**

God's instructions to the **twelve tribes of Israel** were for them to rehearse the **living oracles** of YHVH at the **appointed time and seasons**. Every seventh day was a **Sabbath** day of rest. No work was to be done on that day. The **spring feast** (Passover) was to be held on the fourteenth day in the first month of the year. This is the month when the barley in Israel is Aviv. The Feast of Unleavened Bread begins on the fifteenth day and lasts for seven days. Then the firstfruits offering of a sheaf of barley is made unto the Lord.

Fifty days after the firstfruits offering, the **Feast of Pentecost** is held. This feast is the conclusion of the Passover celebration seven weeks earlier.

The **fall feast** was to be rehearsed in the **seventh** month after the month of Aviv. The fall feast is a memorial to the blowing of the trumpets when YHVH spoke the Ten Commandments to the twelve tribes of Israel on Mount Sinai (Exodus 19:16). The Day of Trumpets occurs on the first day of the seventh month and it is called Yom Teruah.

On the tenth day of the month is the Day of Atonement. For forty days prior to this day everyone was asked to repent of his sins. On the Day of Atonement, an offering of fire shall be made to YHVH. YHVH then decides to bless you or pass judgment on you. If He blesses you for your offering, there are seven blessings you will receive.

1. A double portion of blessings (Joel 2:23)
2. Financial promises (Joel 2:24)
3. Restoration (Joel 2:25)

4. Special miracles (Joel 2:26)
5. A divine presence (Joel 2:27)
6. Blessings for your sons and daughters (Joel 2:28)
7. Deliverance to whoever calls on His name (Joel 2:32)

The Day of Atonement is a sacred covenant with YHVH that is ageless. The promises are the same for you and me as they were for Moses (Leviticus 16:34).

The fifteenth day of the month and for seven days shall be the Feast of Tabernacles. This is the day Yeshua was born.

YHVH proclaimed that these feasts are to be **rehearsed forever.** Why did YHVH put so much emphasis on the feasts? **Because the feasts are rehearsals for the coming of the Messiah.** Yeshua came as a suffering lamb and was crucified during the spring feast. If you look at the spring feast and the rehearsal that the high priests of the temple did at Passover, you will see that Yeshua fulfilled every ritual that had been rehearsed for over a thousand years before.

Yeshua fulfilled the spring feast the first time He came, and He will come again during the fall feast as detailed in the book of Revelation.

Paul in his letter to the Thessalonians says,

> *But of the **times and seasons**, brethren, ye have no need that I write unto you. [They already understood the feasts.] For yourselves know perfectly that the day of the Lord so cometh as **a thief in the night.** For when they shall say, **Peace and safety;** then sudden destruction cometh upon them, **as travail upon a woman with child**; and they shall not escape. **But ye, brethren, are not in darkness, that that day should overtake you as a thief.** (1 Thessalonians 5:1–4* KJV, emphasis added)

Yeshua said the travail of a woman about to deliver a baby is what it will be like just before He returns. Just as the time gets shorter and shorter between labor pains, travail on the earth will do the same. Natural calamities on the earth will get closer and closer just before He returns.

Feasts are Prophetic Shadow-Pictures of the Return of the Messiah

The feasts are prophetic shadow-pictures of the things that the Messiah must fulfill.

It is not an option. The apostles did not have a good understanding of why the Messiah had to be crucified.

Yeshua did not allow any of His disciples to broadcast to anyone that He was the Son of YHVH.

Remember that He silenced the demons when they recognized Him.

> *And unclean spirits, when they saw him, fell down before him, and cried, saying, Thou art the Son of God. And he straitly charged them that they should not make him known.* (Mark 3:11–12 KJV)
>
> *And devils also came out of many, crying out, and saying, Thou art Christ the Son of God. And he rebuking them suffered them not to speak: for they knew that he was Christ.* (Luke 4:41 KJV)

Yeshua asked the disciples, "Whom do men think I am?" (Matthew 16:13). He also asked whom the disciples thought He was (verse 15). Peter answered, "Thou art the Christ, the Son of the living God." Yeshua answered and said, "Blessed art thou…for flesh and blood hath not revealed it unto thee, but my Father which is in heaven" (Matthew 16:16–17 KJV).

Yeshua told His disciples not to tell anyone that He was the Messiah. And He told them that He "must go unto Jerusalem and suffer many **things** of the elders and chief priests and scribes, and be killed, and be raised again the third day" (Matthew 16:20–21, 20:17–19 KJV, emphasis added).

If Satan had known that Yeshua was to fulfill the spring feast of Passover and be sacrificed as a perfect lamb, he would not have had Yeshua crucified: "Which none of the princes of this world knew: for had they known it, they would not have crucified the Lord of glory" (1 Corinthians 2:8 KJV).

Remember, on the third day after the crucifixion of the Messiah, two disciples walked back to the village of Emmaus in disgust that Yeshua was crucified. Yeshua joined them on their journey, but they did not recognize him. Yeshua asked Cleopas and the other disciple what they were talking about. They described their disappointment in the crucifixion of Yeshua.

Then Yeshua said,

> *O fools, and slow to believe all that the prophets have spoken: Ought not Christ to have suffered these **things**, and to enter into his glory? And beginning at Moses and all the prophets, he expounded unto them in all the scriptures the **things** concerning himself.* (Luke 24:25–27 KJV, emphasis added)

When Yeshua spoke to the disciples, He said, "These are the words which I spake unto you, while I was yet with you, that **all things must be fulfilled, which were written in the [instructions (Torah)] of Moses, and in the prophets, and in the psalms, concerning me**" (Luke 24:44 KJV, emphasis added). And the Scriptures say the disciples understood why Jesus (Yeshua) came as suffering lamb (Luke 24:44–47 KJV).

Since Yeshua has already fulfilled the spring feasts of YHVH, then will He also fulfill the fall feasts of YHVH?

One half of the feasts of the LORD have been fulfilled! The other half will be fulfilled soon. Many scholars believe that we are now living in the seventh millennium and that Yeshua will return to fulfill the fall feasts. No one knows the hour or the day, but we are commanded to be watchful for Him.

To recap, YHVH delivered His oracles (communications) to the twelve tribes of Israel. They were to be priests and teachers to the rest of the world. They were to rehearse the feasts of YHVH as YHVH instructed them. These feasts were to be prophetic shadow-pictures of the things the Messiah had to fulfill. The Messiah fulfilled every detail of the spring feasts of YHVH that the Jews had been rehearsing for over a thousand years. Yeshua will return in the seventh millennium just as the fall feast outlines in the book of Revelation.

You cannot understand the Scriptures without understanding the **feasts of YHVH.** For those who seek a more detailed study of the spring and fall feasts of YHVH that Yeshua must fulfill, see Michael Rood's site for teaching DVDs.[102]

CHAPTER 7

YHVH's Perfect Plan Gone Astray

IN THE BOOK OF GENESIS, we learn the story of Adam. Adam was the first man created by YHVH. The Hebrew word for Adam is *Adamah*, which means "taken out of the earth." Adam was created to live forever. And YHVH created a mate (woman) for him so that he would not be alone. The mate was called a woman because she was created from a rib taken from Adam. YHVH named her Eve. Adam and Eve were created out of the dust of the earth, and they were created just below the angels that YHVH made.

Adam and Eve lived in an earthly paradise with all the earthly creatures and plants created by YHVH. They had all the food to eat that they wanted. The fruit-bearing trees were plentiful. There was no sickness and no disease. They lived with all the creatures that Yahweh had created in paradise. This was YHVH's perfect plan for man.

In the garden YHVH had provided trees with food for Adam and Eve to eat; however, He warned them not to eat of one tree. If they did, YHVH warned that they would surely die in the same day that they ate of the forbidden fruit. The Scriptures tell us that Adam lived 930 years or in the day he ate of the fruit. How? He did because one day with the Lord is one thousand years on earth (2 Peter 3:8).

How did the Serpent Convince Eve to Eat of the Forbidden Fruit?

YHVH told Adam the following:

> *And the* Lord *God commanded the man [Adam], saying, of every tree of the garden thou mayest freely eat: But of the tree of the knowledge of good and evil, thou shalt not eat of it: for in the day that thou eatest thereof thou shalt surely die.* (Genesis 2:16–17 KJV)

When the serpent challenged Eve regarding the tree of the knowledge of good and evil, Eve's response was as follows:

> *And the woman said unto the serpent, we may eat of the fruit of the trees of the garden: But of the fruit of the tree which is in the midst of the garden, God hath said, ye shall not eat of it,* **neither shall ye touch it**, **lest ye die**. (Genesis 3:2–3 KJV, emphasis added)

Eve added to what God had commanded, which exaggerated God's limitation on eating of the fruit. In addition, she says "lest ye die," which tones down the certainty of the penalty of death spoken by God.

Then the serpent said to Eve:

> *And the serpent said unto the woman, ye shall not surely die: For God doth know that in the day ye eat thereof, then your eyes shall be opened, and ye shall be as gods, knowing good and evil.* (Genesis 3:4–5 KJV)

The Scriptures do not give us the exact details of how Eve was convinced to eat the fruit from the tree of the knowledge of good and evil; however, how it was done was revealed to Bill Foss. Bill Foss is a pastor of a church in Keller, Texas. Bill was given a vision of what really happened.

First, Satan used the spirit of **insecurity** by telling Eve that God was lying to her by saying she will die if she eats the fruit. Satan told her that God lied to her. Eve's security up to this point was based on the truthfulness of God. Now Eve does not know what to believe.

In addition, God had already released unto Adam and Eve that they were made in the image of God. Then Satan says to Eve, "You are not really what you think you are" and casts doubt in her of **inferiority**. From these two spirits of **insecurity and inferiority**, Satan then offered her the fruit so that she could regain her sense of value and stature in life.

To learn more about Bill Foss's ministry, get a copy of his teaching *Satan's Dirty Little Secrets*.[103]

The Fallen Angels

The Scriptures tell us some of YHVH's angels were watchers of what YHVH had created on earth. These angels were in awe of what YHVH had created. One of these angels was the one who deceived Eve into eating of the forbidden fruit. Enoch wrote about these fallen angels and even gave us their names. So when the Scriptures refer to Satan, it is referring to the leader of the fallen angels who is YHVH's adversary. He is the one who was created by YHVH who was the most beautiful angel in heaven. He wanted to be like YHVH and he was able to convince other angels to follow him. To learn the story in more detail, one must read the book of Enoch.[104]

We first learn of Enoch in Genesis 5, but it leaves us with a lot of questions. Hebrews 11:5 has a reference to Enoch being translated to heaven because he pleased YHVH. In Jude 1:14, he quotes Enoch's prophecy of the return of the Messiah with ten thousand angels! How did Jude come to know the words of Enoch? They are not in the Scriptures. The answer is Enoch was a scribe and he wrote the book of Enoch, but it was not included in the Scriptures by the Roman Catholic Church as recorded at the Council of Laodicea.

The quote by Jude is as follows:

In the seventh (generation) from Adam Enoch also prophesied these things, saying: Behold, the Lord came with his holy myriads to execute judgment on all, and to convict all the ungodly of all their ungodly deeds which they have committed in such an ungodly way, and all the harsh things which ungodly sinners spoke against him.

This is evidence that the book of Enoch was read by the disciples of Yeshua at the time Yeshua lived. Was it read by the Hebrews for the first four centuries? Most likely it was because it was one of the Dead Sea Scrolls recently found.

What else do we know about Enoch from the Scriptures?

The genealogy of Enoch is as follows: Adam (1) begat Seth (2) who begat Enos (3) who begat Cainan (4) who begat Mahalaleel (5) who begat Jared (6) who begat Enoch (7). Enoch was the seventh generation of man on earth, and Adam lived for several hundred years after Enoch was born. Enoch begat (8) Methuselah, and he begat (9) Lamech. Lamech begat (10) Noah.

So Enoch was the great-grandfather of Noah. The book of Enoch in chapter 68 states, **"And after that my grandfather Enoch gave me all the secrets in the book and in the parables which had been given to him, and he put them together for me in the words of the book of the parables"** (verse 1). This makes it possible for us to believe the book would have survived the flood since Noah would have taken his great-grandfather's writings with him onto the ark.

The book of Enoch gives us the name of the fallen angel who deceived Eve in the Garden of Eden. This is when Eve was deceived by the serpent into eating the fruit of the forbidden tree. She also talked Adam into eating fruit from the forbidden tree. By this act, their eyes were opened and they knew good from evil. Although the Scriptures say it was a serpent that deceived Eve, the book of Enoch says it was the angel Gadreel.

The leader of all the angels who led astray all the angels was named Jeqon. His number-two angel was Asbeel, who gave evil council to the angels who defiled themselves with the daughters of men. The number-three angel was Gadreel who deceived Eve. The other rebellious angels are listed in order of their ranking: (4) Penemue, (5) Kasdeja, (6) Kasbeel.

The book of Enoch and Genesis describe the actions of these angels to take women on the earth as their wives. Here are a few verses from Genesis describing their actions.

> *And it came to pass, when men began to multiply on the face of the earth, and daughters were born unto them, that the sons of God saw the daughters of men that they were fair; and they took them wives of all which they chose. And the* LORD *said, my spirit shall not always strive with man, for that he also is flesh: yet his days shall be an hundred and twenty years. There were giants in the earth in those days; and also after that, when the sons of God came in unto the daughters of men, and they bare children to them, the same became mighty men which were of old, men of renown. And God saw that the wickedness of man was great in the earth, and that* **every imagination of the thoughts of his heart was only evil continually.** *And it repented the* LORD *that he had made man on the earth, and it grieved him at his heart. And the* LORD *said, I will destroy man whom I have created from the face of the earth; both man, and beast, and the creeping thing, and the fowls of the air; for it repenteth me that I have made them.* (Genesis 6:1–7 KJV, emphasis added)

The book of Enoch tells the story in more detail of how two hundred angels swore an oath together to take wives. They swore this oath together on Mount Hermon in Israel. It describes how they taught their wives charms and enchantments. Their wives bore sons who were giants who soon began to exhaust all the food, and they turned to devouring humans and drinking their blood. The fallen angels taught them to make swords and shields and made known to them the metals of the earth. They taught them astrology, the constellations, the use of antimony, the beautifying of the eyelids, and all kinds of costly stones. They taught them about coloring tinctures. Out of this arose godlessness, and they committed fortification. The whole world became corrupt.

YHVH's archangels saw the blood being shed on earth and how lawless the inhabitants had become. YHVH was very displeased with how they taught all unrighteousness on the earth and revealed the eternal secrets that had been preserved in heaven. The children of these angels were giants and soon they exhausted the food supply. They then turned against mankind and became cannibals. They also ate birds, beasts, reptiles, and fish. Then they started drinking the blood.

WHAT WAS THE JUDGMENT OF THE GIANTS?

Then YHVH pronounced judgment against the giants and instructed Gabriel to proceed against the bastards, the reprobates, and against the children of fornication—to destroy (the children of fornication and) the children of the Watchers from among men (and cause them to go forth): send them one against the other that they may destroy each other in battle for length of days they shall not have.

After the giants were destroyed, YHVH said, "And YHVH said the giants that were produced from the spirit and flesh shall be called evil spirits upon the earth and the earth shall be their dwelling." **And these evil spirits (from the giants) shall rise up against the children of men and against the women. These spirits will afflict, oppress, destroy, attack, do battle and work destruction on the earth. And these spirits shall rise up against the children of men and against the women, because they have proceeded from them. They shall destroy without incurring judgment until the Day of Judgment spoken of in the book of Revelation.**

These evil spirits are called demons by the Scriptures and most clergy now are aware that they exist. These demons can come into you and influence your actions. Maybe this is why there is so much brutality against women and children in this world.

WHAT WAS THE JUDGMENT OF THE ANGELS WHO TOOK THE OATH?

YHVH was very unhappy with the actions of His angels and He promised them His judgment. The angels who took the oath to marry women knew their actions were wrong, and they were very concerned about the judgment of YHVH. Because of the impending judgment, they asked Enoch to intervene for them. They wanted to repent. The answer from YHVH was this: "You have been in heaven, but all the mysteries had not yet been revealed to you, and you knew worthless ones, and these in the hardness of your hearts you have made known to women, and by these mysteries women and men work much evil on earth," Say to them "You have no peace."

Semjaza was the leader of these angels who went down to Mount Hermon to make their oath to marry women. Azazel was one of these angels who did the most damage in teaching most of the unrighteousness to the people on earth. YHVH pronounced His judgment and had him bound hand and foot and cast into darkness. **He then was cast into an opening in the desert to stay there until the great Judgment Day when he will be cast into the fire.** The remainder of the angels who married women were imprisoned also.

Semjaza and his associates were to be bound for seventy generations in the valleys of the earth until the great Day of Judgment in which they will be confined in an abyss of fire. The leader of all the angels who disobeyed YHVH and his other close associate angels were not imprisoned, but were left as accusers of men. They are referred to as Satan, which means adversary.

> *And the angels which kept not their first estate, but left their own habitation, he hath reserved in everlasting chains under darkness unto the judgment of the great day.* (Jude 1:6 KJV)

Judgments Pronounced by YHVH

In the book of Enoch, we learn that the fallen angels were condemned to death because of what they had done. Enoch prayed for their forgiveness, but YHVH would not forgive. The fallen angels were condemned to a fiery death that will occur on Judgment Day.

YHVH also pronounced the judgment of the world and shared it with Enoch. Enoch called altogether his children together to show them everything that YHVH had shown him regarding the future. YHVH had established an appointed time for all the future events. YHVH said violence will increase on the earth. He also said that a chastisement will come because of the unrighteousness on the earth. And when sin, unrighteousness, blasphemy and violence in all kinds of deeds increase, including apostasy, transgression, and uncleanness all increase, then a great chastisement will come from heaven upon all the unrighteous of the earth. The holy Lord will come forth with wrath and chastisement to execute judgment on the earth.

Enoch declared to his family what YHVH had written in the books regarding the appointed times for earth and heaven. Each period on earth was described as a week and are listed as best I can understand as:

First Week:
This is a period of judgment and righteousness. **(It is Enoch's time.)**
Second Week:
This is a period of judgment and cleansing. **(It is Noah's time and the great flood.)**
Third Week:
This is a period where righteousness is planted. **(It is Abraham's time.)**
Fourth Week:
During this period, a law was given for all generations to the people on earth. **(It is Moses's time.)**
Fifth Week:
At the end of this period the house of glory and dominion shall be built forever.
(The temple of Solomon was built in Jerusalem and the land given to Abraham belonged to the Jews.)
Sixth Week:
During this period all the people of the earth shall be blinded and their hearts shall godlessly forsake wisdom. **(Yeshua is crucified.)**

And a man shall ascend. **(Yeshua ascends to heaven.)**

And at the end of this period the house of dominion shall be burned with fire. **(Second temple burned by the Romans.)**

And the whole race of the chosen root shall be dispersed. **(The Jews are driven out of Israel by the Romans and scattered around the world.)**

Seventh Week:

During this period an apostate generation shall arise and many shall be its deeds.

And all the deeds are apostate.

Interpretation: *Apostate* **means the abandonment or renunciation of religion. This is referring to the faith once given to the Hebrews by YHVH that is abandoned for the revised beliefs of today's church. We are living in this period of time on earth.**

At the end of this period Yeshua returns to collect the righteous dead and living.

Eighth Week:

During this period the sinners are killed by the sword and the righteous judge the sinners. **(Yeshua returns to kill the Antichrist and his followers. Everyone on earth is killed. The rapture takes place. Judgment by the saints occurs.)**

The righteous are given houses in the new heaven.

Ninth Week:

During this period the righteous judgment is revealed to everyone who had ever lived on the earth. And all the works of the earth are burned up. **(The earth erupts into a fire and all the mountains disappear. Sinners are cast into the burning earth.)**

Tenth Week:

At the end of this period is the great eternal judgment in which YHVH executes vengeance on the fallen angels.

After this, the first heaven shall depart and pass away and a new heaven will appear.

And the power of heaven shall give sevenfold light.
After this and forever there shall be no more sin.

YHVH Declared the End from the Beginning
YHVH declared to Enoch from the beginning to the end what was going to happen on the earth. Remember the following verse in the Scriptures:

> *Declaring the end from the beginning, and from ancient times the things that are not yet done, saying, my counsel shall stand, and I will do all my pleasure.* (Isaiah 46:10 KJV)
>
> *At the beginning I announce the end, proclaim in advance things not yet done; and I say that my plan will hold, I will do everything I please to do.* (Isaiah 46:10 CJB)

Time for Judgment and the Cleansing of the Earth
YHVH was angry with the wickedness of mankind, and He decided to destroy all men, beasts, fowls, and creeping things that He had created. However, YHVH found grace in Noah, the grandson of Enoch. According to the book of Enoch, Methuselah had told Noah about YHVH's judgment of the Flood. So when YHVH told Noah to build an ark, Noah obeyed without hesitation. Noah started the ark in the year 1556BC. It took one hundred years to complete the ark. Then Noah's family and all YHVH's creatures went inside also. Then the doors were shut in the year 1656BC.

For approximately one hundred years Noah and his family knew YHVH's judgment was coming upon the whole earth. The people did not. They probably scoffed about Noah building a boat, especially since it had never rained before. Now they were begging for Noah to let them in the ark so their lives could be saved. What a heart-wrenching day for Noah to hear the cries of the drowning families outside the ark.

YHVH's perfect plan had been interrupted by His own angels. Now a fresh start was made available for mankind on this planet; however, the evil spirits of the giants and the leader of the angels were free to roam the planet and cause men to sin. They want to hurt YHVH for His judgment against them by misleading mankind in any way possible so that they will receive the same judgment.

The Birth of Babylon

Noah begat three sons called Shem, Ham, and Japheth. The sons of Japheth (firstborn) were Gomer, Magog, Madai, Javan, Tubal, Meshech, and Tiras. The sons of Ham (second-born) were Cush, the father of Nimrod, Mizraim, Put, and Canaan. The sons of Shem were Elam, Asshur, Arphaxad, Lud, and Aram. Ham was the son who saw his father's nakedness and got his two brothers to cover him up. Noah placed a curse on Ham for breaking YHVH's law. Ham begat Cush, and Cush begat Nimrod. **Nimrod became a mighty hunter and a powerful leader of the people. His kingdom was Babylon in the land of Shinar.**

> *He was a mighty hunter before the* LORD: *wherefore it is said, Even as Nimrod the mighty hunter before the* LORD. *And the beginning of his kingdom was Babel, and Erech, and Accad, and Calneh, in the land of Shinar.* (Genesis 10:9–10 KJV)
>
> *He was a mighty hunter before YHWH, therefore it is said, "Like Nimrod, a mighty hunter before YHWH." And the beginning of his reign Babel, Erek, Akkad and Kalneh, in the land of Shin`ar.* (Genesis 10:9–10 ISR)

The City of Babel

Nimrod was the father of sun-god worship. He believed that the sun was what gave him and his people life on the earth. He lost the truth about worshipping YHVH and soon began to think he was a god. As the descendants of Noah moved to the east, they eventually settled in the land of Shinar. Soon the population grew larger and they all were of the same language.

With the population increasing, they decided to build a city. And in the city they started building a tower. Most scholars agree that the tower was similar to a Sumerian ziggurat, which is like a temple built on a series of stepped platforms. The Scriptures describe the events as follows: [105]

> *It came about that as they traveled from the east, they found a plain in the land of Shin`ar and lived there. They said to one another, "Come, let's make bricks and bake them in the fire." So they had bricks for building-stone and clay for mortar. Then they said, "Come, let's build ourselves a city with a* **tower (temple)** *that has its top reaching up into heaven, so that* **we can make a name for ourselves** *and not be scattered all over the earth." (Genesis 11:2–4* CJB*, emphasis added)*

Well, this certainly got YHVH's attention!

This is a very significant event because up until this time, Yehovah was the name giver. When Noah's first son was born, he was named Shem. The significance of this name is that it is the Hebrew word for *name*. "Here is the genealogy of Shem" (Genesis 11:10 CJB).

Abraham is of the bloodline of Shem. Yehovah, the name giver, said to Abraham: "And I will make of thee a great nation, and I will bless thee, and make thy **name** great; and thou shalt be a blessing" (Genesis 12:2 KJV, emphasis added).

Yehovah realized that the adversary was seeking a name from his own people and to be worshipped in the highest point of the city of Babel. Then Yehovah steps in to prevent this.

> *A*DONAI *came down to see the city and the tower the people were building. A*DONAI *said, "Look, the people are united, they all have a single language, and see what they're starting to do! At this rate, nothing they set out to accomplish will be impossible for them! Come, let's go down and confuse their language, so that they won't understand each other's*

speech." So from there ADONAI *scattered them all over the earth, and they stopped building the city. For this reason it is called Bavel [confusion]—because there* ADONAI *confused the language of the whole earth, and from there* ADONAI *scattered them all over the earth.* (Genesis 11:5–9 CJB)

According to Strong's Concordance Babel and Babylon are the same. So YHVH caused people to come out of Babylon; in the book of Revelation, YHVH calls for His people to come out of Babylon.

YHVH was able to block another attempt by Satan to establish his own kingdom on the earth. He wants to be like YHWH and be worshipped by the people on earth. We know from the book of Revelation that Babylon exists in the last days of the earth.

Sun-God Worship Spreads all over the World

When YHVH destroyed the tower and renamed it Babel, He also caused their languages to change, creating a problem in communication with one another. As a result, the people who spoke the same language began to move as a group to other parts of the world. When they did that, they took their sun-god worship with them. Now we can see evidence in countries around the world of sun-god worship.[106]

Righteousness is Planted

After this period, there were some who were still close to YHVH and His early instructions of how to worship. This was, of course, Abraham. Because of Abraham and his faith, he was chosen by YHVH to be given the Promised Land, which is in present-day Israel.

And the LORD *[YHVH] had said unto Abram, Get thee out of thy country, and from thy kindred, and from thy father's house, unto a land that I will shew thee. And I will make of thee a great nation, and I will bless thee, and make thy name great; and thou shalt be a blessing:*

And I will bless them that bless thee, *and curse them that curseth thee: and in thee shall all families of the earth be blessed.* (Genesis 12:1–3 KJV, emphasis added)

But before YHVH made Abraham the father of a great nation, He first tested his faith. Abraham went to the land that YHWH told him to go to, which is where present-day Jerusalem is located. YHVH asked Abraham to go up on Mount Moriah and prepare a sacrifice to YHVH for the forgiveness of sins. Remember YHVH first asked Abraham to sacrifice a heifer, a goat, a ram, a turtledove, and a pigeon to Him (Genesis 15:9). **This is extremely important because there is no forgiveness of sins without the shedding of blood. This is repeated throughout the Scriptures.**

YHVH tested Abraham and his faith:

And he said, Take now thy son, thine only son Isaac, whom thou lovest and get thee into the land of Moriah; and offer him there a burnt offering upon one of the mountains which I will tell thee of." (Genesis 22:2 KJV)

And Isaac spake unto Abraham his father, and said, my father: and he said, here am I, my son. And he said, behold the fire and the wood: but where is the lamb for a burnt offering? And Abraham said, my son, [YHVH] will provide himself a lamb for a burnt offering: so they went both of them together. (Genesis 22:7–8 KJV)

And as Abraham was about to kill his son, YHWH stopped him and provided a ram for the sacrifice. **YHVH then reconfirmed His covenant with Abraham to be the father of a great nation.**

YHVH made a covenant with Abraham by having his foreskin circumcised when he was ninety years old. This was a sign of the covenant to indicate that Abraham's offspring were uniquely dedicated to YHVH (Genesis 17:10–11, 14).

YHVH also told Abraham that his offspring would be held as slaves in a strange land and would be afflicted for four hundred years. Israel was taken into bondage in Egypt for four hundred years until Moses led them back to Israel's homeland. Later, King Solomon would build the temple over the spot on Mount Moriah where Abraham was going to offer up Isaac as a sacrifice.

YHVH had set in motion His second plan to save mankind from total destruction by the fallen angels. He had established a nation of people who were to follow His instructions in worshipping YHWH. They are called Jews, which means "Praise YHVH." They are to provide the foundation for the enmity that YHVH will put between the fallen angels and mankind.

As part of this plan of salvation, YHVH sent Yeshua to sacrifice His blood for us so that we might be saved. He also gave us our instructions or commandments on what we must do in order to be saved.

Satan: the Adversary of YHVH

We know that Satan was the leader of the fallen angels who defied YHVH. We also know that he was one of the most perfect angels in heaven. Since he has been condemned to death on Judgment Day, he has great wrath against humans on earth. He is intent on destroying every single person on the planet in order to get even with YHVH.[107]

What was his Name in Heaven?

In the book of Enoch, the leader of the fallen angels was called Jeqon, but in Isaiah, he was called Lucifer.

> *How art thou fallen from heaven, O Lucifer, son of the morning! How art thou cut down to the ground, which didst weaken the nations!* (Isaiah 14:12 KJV)

Lucifer means "in a sense of brightness" or "morning star." So Lucifer must have been a very bright angel in heaven and so he was called Lucifer.

What was Lucifer's Name on Earth?
He is referred to as the King of Babylon.

> *For I will rise up against them, saith the L*ORD *of hosts, and cut off from Babylon the name, and remnant, and son, and nephew, saith the L*ORD*.* (Isaiah 14:22 KJV)

He was referred to as the leader of the Assyrians.

> *That I will break the Assyrian in my land, and upon my mountains tread him under foot: then shall his yoke depart from off them, and his burden depart from off their shoulders.* (Isaiah 14:25 KJV)

He was referred to as the prince and king of Tyrus.

> *Son of man, take up a lamentation upon the king of Tyrus, and say unto him, thus saith the Lord G*OD*; Thou sealest up the sum, full of wisdom, and perfect in beauty.* (Ezekiel 28:12 KJV)

What was the Description of Lucifer in Heaven?

> *Thou hast been in Eden the garden of God; every precious stone was thy covering, the sardius, topaz, and the diamond, the beryl, the onyx, and the jasper, the sapphire, the emerald, and the carbuncle, and gold: the workmanship of thy tabrets and of thy pipes was prepared in thee in the day that thou wast created. Thou art the anointed cherub that covereth; and I have set thee so: thou wast upon the holy mountain of God; thou hast walked up and down in the midst of the stones of fire. Thou wast perfect in thy ways from the day that thou wast created, till iniquity was found in thee.* (Ezekiel 28:13–15 KJV)

Lucifer was a heavenly angel of breathtaking beauty and brightness. He was highly exalted, and he stood next to the YHVH's throne.

> *The LORD reigneth; let the people tremble: he sitteth between the cherubims; let the earth be moved. (Psalm 99:1 KJV)*

SATAN IS VERY POWERFUL
Satan's power is very evident when he tries to claim Moses's body.

> *Yet Michael the archangel, when contending with the devil he disputed about the body of Moses, durst not bring against him a railing accusation, but said, The Lord rebuke thee. (Jude 1:9 KJV)*

SATAN MOVES BETWEEN HEAVEN AND EARTH

> *And the LORD said unto Satan, Whence comest thou? Then Satan answered the LORD, and said, from going to and fro in the earth, and from walking up and down in it. (Job 1:7 KJV)*

SATAN TEMPTS MEN ON EARTH AND THEN ACCUSES THEM IN HEAVEN
The book of Job is a good example of Satan's ability to tempt men to sin and then he accuses them in the throne room of YHVH.

THE EARTH IS UNDER THE CONTROL OF SATAN

> *Again, the devil taketh him up into an exceeding high mountain, and sheweth him all the kingdoms of the world, and the glory of them; And saith unto him, All these things will I give thee, if thou wilt fall down and worship me. (Matthew 4:8–9 KJV)*

Satan has title to the earth and he offers it to Yeshua if He would worship him.

War in Heaven

Yes, there was a war in heaven, and Satan and his followers lost. They were ejected out of heaven. Yeshua was given the title to earth and Satan was banned from heaven.

> *And there was war in heaven: Michael and his angels fought against the dragon; and the dragon fought and his angels, And prevailed not; neither was their place found any more in heaven. And the great dragon was cast out, that old serpent, called the Devil, and Satan, which deceiveth the whole world: he was cast out into the earth, and his angels were cast out with him.* (Revelation 12:7–9 KJV)

Satan Hates You and Me

> *Therefore rejoice, ye heavens, and ye that dwell in them. Woe to the inhabiters of the earth and of the sea! for the devil is come down unto you, having great wrath, because he knoweth that he hath but a short time.* (Revelation 12:12 KJV)

Will Satan use Religion to Deceive and Destroy People?
The answer is yes.

> *For such are false apostles, deceitful workers, transforming themselves into the apostles of Christ. And no marvel; for Satan himself is transformed into an angel of light. Therefore it is no great thing if his ministers also be transformed as the ministers of righteousness; whose end shall be according to their works.* (2 Corinthians 11:13–15 KJV)

What did Yeshua Warn us about?

And Jesus answered and said unto them, Take heed that no man deceive you. For many shall come in my name, saying, I am Christ; and shall deceive many. (Matthew 24:4–5 KJV)

Beware of false prophets [Antichrists], which come to you in sheep's clothing [clergy], but inwardly they are ravening wolves. (Matthew 7:15 KJV)

If you want to avoid being deceived, then you must study the Scriptures as a workmen. Satan has a very complicated attack on the human race. We are no match for his cunning or skill in destroying us. In the following chapters, I will attempt to show just how clever he is.

CHAPTER 8

Babylonian Sun-God Worship

WHY IS IT IMPORTANT THAT we study Babylonian sun-god worship? It is very important because it has been going on since the days of Nimrod in Babylon. This was Satan's first attempt to cause men on earth to worship him. YHVH confused their language, and this caused them to scatter around the world.

However, as they were scattered around the world, they took their sun-god worship practices with them. There are 260 verses about Babylon in the Scriptures. Most of these are in the book of Jeremiah because the Jews were taken into seventy years of captivity in another Babylon.

In the book of Revelation, **YHVH calls for His children to come out of Babylon.**

> *And after these things I saw another angel come down from heaven, having great power; and the earth was lightened with his glory. And he cried mightily with a strong voice, saying, Babylon the great is fallen, is fallen, and is become the habitation of devils, and the hold of every foul spirit, and a cage of every unclean and hateful bird. For all nations have drunk of the wine of the wrath of her fornication, and the kings of the earth have committed fornication with her, and the merchants of the earth are waxed rich through the abundance of her delicacies. And I heard another voice from heaven, saying, Come out of her, my people, that ye be not partakers of her sins, and that ye receive not of her plagues. For her sins have reached unto heaven, and God hath remembered her iniquities.* (Revelation 18:1–5 KJV)

Since the Babylonian empire was destroyed by Alexander the Great, why are the Scriptures telling us to come out of Babylon at a time when Yeshua is about to return to earth? Babylon must have never left, or it comes back to power in the last days for YHVH to call us to come out of Babylon. Will this Mystery Babylon be disguised so we don't recognize it as Babylon?

Could the pagan traditions of old Babylon have become woven into the traditions of the modern church? If so, it could affect the way Christians worship YHVH. It could alter the way we treat YHVH's commandments and how YHVH told us to worship Him. We need to examine the history of Babylonian sun-god worship and determine if we are still following these early traditions but under a different name.

So how did Sun-God Worship Start?

It was a cold, clear night in Chaldea near the Tigris and Euphrates Rivers. The nights revealed the panorama of the moon, plants, and stars. After a long, cold night, the skies would begin to become bright from the rising sun in the east. Finally, the sun would appear over the horizon and begin to warm the inhabitants. This was the experience of the Chaldeans nearly four thousand years ago. The time period was just after the Flood.

The sun gave them life. The earth would turn green in the spring from the warmth of the sun. They knew they were extremely dependent on the sun for life, and soon they began to worship the sun. They even built temples to the sun. These temples were orientated for maximum light to shine on the temple as if to give glory to the sun.

It is easy to see that they might start worshipping the creation instead of the Creator.

Mother-goddess worship was also an important part of the Chaldean culture. Beltis, the wife of Bel-Nimrod and mother of his supposed son Nin, was worshipped as the "Mother of God." The proposed reincarnation of Bel-Nimrod as Nin made Beltis the "mother of god." It has been documented that the worship of Beltis and Nin originated the veneration of the mother and child.[108]

Assyrian Sun-God Worship
The Assyrian monarchy followed the Chaldeans. The worship of the Assyrians seems to be identical with that of the Chaldeans with the exception that Asshur was considered the universal god, "the sun god of the multitude of mankind."

Babylonian Sun-God Worship
The Babylonians followed the Assyrians. They also worshipped the sun. The religious practices of the Babylonians were almost identical to that of the Chaldeans. The same gods were worshipped; the original sun-god worship started under the Chaldeans was still being practiced in 586 BC at the time when Judah was taken captive by King Nebuchadnezzar of Babylon.

Why did this happen to Judah?

> *Only acknowledge thine iniquity, that thou hast transgressed against the* Lord *thy God, and hast scattered thy ways to the strangers under every green tree, and ye have not obeyed my voice, saith the* Lord. (Jeremiah 3:13 kjv)

Is Pagan Worship Mentioned in the Scriptures?
There are many scriptures that detail pagan sun-god worship by the Israelites and the warnings against them by YHVH.

> *And they forsook the* Lord *God of their fathers, which brought them out of the land of Egypt, and followed other gods, of the gods of the people that were round about them, and bowed themselves unto them, and provoked the* Lord *to anger. And they forsook the* Lord, *and served Baal and Ashtaroth.* (Judges 2:12–13 kjv)
> *And the children of Israel did evil again in the sight of the* Lord, *and served Baalim, and Ashtaroth [Easter], and the gods of Syria, and*

> the gods of Zidon, and the gods of Moab, and the gods of the children of Ammon, and the gods of the Philistines, and forsook the LORD, and served not him. (Judges 10:6 KJV)
>
> The children gather wood, and the fathers kindle the fire, and the women knead their dough, to make cakes to the **queen of heaven [Easter]**, and to pour out drink offerings unto other gods, that they may provoke me to anger. (Jeremiah 7:18 KJV, emphasis added)

YHVH BECAME VERY ANGRY WITH THE ISRAELITES OVER THE WORSHIP OF ASHTAROTH.

> Yet ye have forsaken me, and served other gods: wherefore I will deliver you no more. Go and cry unto the gods which ye have chosen; let them deliver you in the time of your tribulation. (Judges 10:13–14 KJV)

SOLOMON WAS NO EXCEPTION TO PAGAN WORSHIP, AS THE SCRIPTURES TELL US.

> And he had seven hundred wives, princesses, and three hundred concubines: and his wives turned away his heart. For it came to pass, when Solomon was old, that his wives turned away his heart after other gods: and his heart was not perfect with the LORD his God, as was the heart of David his father. For Solomon went after Ashtoreth the goddess of the Zidonians, and after Milcom the abomination of the Ammonites. And Solomon did evil in the sight of the LORD, and went not fully after the LORD, as did David his father. Then did Solomon build an high place for Chemosh, the abomination of Moab, in the hill that is before Jerusalem, and for Molech, the abomination of the children of Ammon. (1 Kings 11:3–7 KJV)

Molech was one of the false gods that Israel worshipped in its period of apostasy. One of the practices of the cult that worshipped Molech was to sacrifice their children. The idol was made of metal and had two arms positioned so that it could support an infant. They would build a fire in the idol until it became glowing hot. Then they would place the newborn in the idol's arms and watch the child burst into flames.

ONE PRACTICE OF DECORATING A TREE CAME OUT OF THE WORSHIP OF THE EGYPTIAN SUN GOD RA.

The Egyptians worshipped the sun god Ra. One of their traditions they practiced was to decorate a tree. Does it sound similar to a Christmas tree?

> *Thus saith the LORD, Learn not the way of the heathen, and be not dismayed at the signs of heaven; for the heathen are dismayed at them. For the customs of the people are vain: for one cutteth a tree out of the forest, the work of the hands of the workman, with the axe. They deck it with silver and with gold; they fasten it with nails and with hammers that it move not. They are upright as the palm tree, but speak not: they must needs be borne, because they cannot go. Be not afraid of them; for they cannot do evil, neither also is it in them to do good.* (Jeremiah 10:2–5 KJV)

MEDO-PERSIAN EMPIRE

The Medo-Persian Empire was a kingdom resulting from a combination of the Medes and the Persians. This combination took place under the rulership of Cyrus the Great. The biblical Darius was also one of the famous Medo-Persian kings.

The earliest form of the religion of the Medo-Persians is described in ancient manuscripts known as the Zend-Avesta. Ahura-Mazada was known as the creator of all things: heaven and earth, light and darkness, the originator of all laws and judge of the world. In the earliest periods of Ahura-Mazada worship, the worship of other gods apparently took place also. They included Indra (storm), Aramiti (earth), Agni (fire), Soma (intoxication), Vayu (wind), and most importantly, Mithra (sunlight).

When Cyrus of Medo-Persia conquered Babylon, his policy for conquered people was to restore the worship of their gods. It was because of this policy that Judah was allowed after the seventy years to return to Jerusalem. Unfortunately, when they returned to Jerusalem, they brought with them some traditions that had nothing to do with the worship of God.

The Greco-Roman Sun Gods

The prophet Daniel, relating a vision he had been given, foretold of the fall of the Medo-Persian Empire and the rise of the powerful Grecian empire of Alexander the Great.

As Alexander the Great made conquests, mystery religions came with the territory. The same was true of the Roman Empire that followed the Greek empire of Alexander the Great. The sun gods and goddesses—including Mithra, Phrygian Cybele, and the Egyptian Isis—were brought into the empire as annexations were made. These sun gods were none other than the sun gods worshipped at the time of Nimrod. At the time of Alexander's death, his empire stretched from Greece to India including Egypt and Israel.

After his death, the Roman Empire little by little gained dominance over the Grecian empire. At the time of the death of Caesar Augustus, the Roman Empire stretched from Spain to the Caspian Sea including Egypt, the Sinai Peninsula, and Israel. The Romans worshipped Mithra and they would take a convicted person in these territories and sacrifice them to Mithra. They would nail them to a cross of wood and place the cross upright in the ground. Usually the victim was at eye level so that everyone could see them suffering. He was left on the cross until he finally died. Sometimes it took a week for that to happen. The Romans found that this way of crucifying people was effective in keeping these population under control.

As the Greeks worshipped numerous gods, they instituted several festivals to celebrate their gods. Sun-god worship from the time of Nimrod was extremely important since they were worshipping creation that gave warmth and life to their crops. They determined that the shortest day in winter was the beginning of another cycle of the sun's life. They soon determined that their sun gods are born in winter, and they picked December 25 as that day. So all the sun gods are born on December 25, and they celebrated festivals every year on December 25 to celebrate the birth of their sun gods.

To answer the questions regarding these pagan feasts being adopted by the early church, one needs to look no further than the history of the early Roman Catholic Church. In 1977, Dr. Samuel Bacchiocchi spent five years at the Gregorian University in Rome. He received his doctoral degree for his historical investigation of the rise of Sunday observance in early Christianity. In his thesis, he documents how pagan feasts were just renamed and not done away with by the early Roman church. The pagans in Rome were worshipping *dies natalis Solis invicti*—"the birthday of the invincible sun"—on December 25. In fact, the birthday of all the sun gods that were worshipped was on the date of the winter solstice or December 25.[109]

In order to get the pagans to shift to worshipping Jesus, the leaders in the early church claimed Jesus's birthday was on December 25. The celebration of the birth of the sun gods was accompanied by a profusion of light and torches and the decoration of tree branches and small trees. Sound similar to our celebration with lighted trees? In order to sell this date to the pagans as the birthday of Jesus, the leaders of the early Roman church proclaimed their opinion that both the conception and passion of Christ occurred at the time of the vernal equinox on the twenty-fifth of March. Reckoning from that date the nine months of pregnancy for Mary, the date of the birth of Christ was computed to be the twenty-fifth of December. **Basically, the old Roman church leaders advanced a rational to justify an already existing date and practice.**

So where did Easter Sunday come from? Here again we must look back into history and see what pagan worship was associated with Easter. Easter is derived from the word *Eostre* or *Eastre* or none other than Asthtaroth, the pagan queen of heaven as referred to by the name in the

Scriptures (Judges 10:6; Jeremiah 44:17–19). Easter was observed by the early Romans as the pagan worship of the love goddess Eastre.

History records the words of Hyginus, an Egyptian, who was a librarian at the Palatine Library in Rome during the time of Caesar Augustus. **"An egg of wondrous size is said to have fallen from heaven into the river Euphrates. The fishes rolled it to the bank, where the doves having settled upon it, and hatched it, out came Venus, who afterwards was called the Syrian goddess."** That Syrian goddess, supposedly hatched from the egg, was **Astarte**, from whom came the title **"Easter."** The pagan festival of Easter originated as the worship of the sun goddess, the Babylonian queen of heaven, who was later worshipped under many names including Ishtar. This pagan feast was celebrated in Rome before Christianity arrived.[110]

The early Roman church was very anti-Jewish and rejected the YHVH's celebration of the Passover. This resulted in the pagan tradition of Easter replacing the Passover celebration, which was when Yeshua was crucified. Because the early Christian church in Rome became extremely anti-Jewish and would not celebrate the date of the celebration of Passover, they picked the date of Easter for the celebration of the resurrection of Christ. However, there was much controversy in the Roman Catholic Church over the actual date of when Easter would be observed. After much debate, the Nicaean council of the early Roman church leaders decreed in 325 AD that Easter would be celebrated on the first Sunday after the full moon on or after the vernal equinox. They simply made up some rules to resolve the debate. It was not an apostolic institution; it simply was made up by the early church fathers.[111]

So today we carry on with the old Babylonian celebrations that were based on pagan worship. We just changed the names. Some say that these celebrations break the first commandment of YHVH: **"Thou shalt have no other gods before me"** (Exodus 20:3 KJV).

The Scriptures clearly say in the book of Revelation that you must avoid the sins of Babylon in order to avoid the plagues that will come on the whole earth. These plagues are described in chapter 18, and they occur in the tribulation period.

Are you unknowingly following Christian worship that was rooted in Babylonian sun-god worship that was renamed by the early Roman Catholic Church?

CHAPTER 9

The Birthday of the Messiah

In this book, I discuss how the early Roman Catholic Church decided that Yeshua was born on December 25 of the Gregorian calendar. But, was Yeshua (Jesus) really born on this date? Like me, most Christians have always known there was a problem with the December 25 date that celebrates Yeshua's birth on earth. It has always been confusing, but most Christians don't talk about it. Let's look at the following scriptures from the King James Version and the scriptures published by the Institute of Scripture Research and see if there are any clues to when the Messiah was born.

> *And she bought forth her first born son, and wrapped him in swaddling clothes, and laid him in a manger; because there was no room in the inn.* **And there were in the same country shepherds abiding in the fields, keeping watch over their flocks by night.** (Luke 2:7–8 KJV, emphasis added)
>
> *And she gave birth to her first born Son, and wrapped Him up, and laid Him down in a feeding trough, because there was no room for them in the lodging place.* **And in the same country there were shepherds living out in the fields, keeping watch over their flocks by night.** (Luke 2:7–8 ISR, emphasis added)

It is evident from these passages that the shepherds were still out in the fields, which means that the sheep were still grazing on grass. This means that the event took place no later than early November as this was the time of year that shepherds returned with their flocks from the fields. Winter in the Holy Land is quite cold, and snow occurs often. From this it appears that Yeshua was born before December 25, which is the original date of the winter solstice.

What other clues are there in the Scriptures regarding the birth of the Messiah?

How old was Yeshua when he was baptized by John?

*And [Yeshua] himself began to be **about thirty years of age**." (Luke 3:23 KJV, emphasis added)*

And when Yeshua Himself was about thirty years of age, being as reckoned by law. (Luke 3:23 ISR, emphasis added)

This reading indicates that at the time of his baptism, He was about thirty years old but not quite thirty yet. We know from accounts from the other Gospels that two weeks later Yeshua went to Jerusalem for the Feast of Tabernacles. Could Yeshua actually have been born on the day the Feast of Tabernacles is celebrated?

And the Word was made flesh, and dwelt among us, (and we beheld his glory, the glory as of the only begotten of the Father,) full of grace and truth. (John 1:14 KJV)

The Hebrew translation of word "dwelt" in the King James scripture means "to pitch a tent for the night."[112]

*And the Word became flesh and **pitched a tent** among us, and we saw His esteem, esteem as of the only begotten of the father, complete in favor and truth. (John 1:14 ISR, emphasis added)*

The clue here is "pitched his tent." Part of celebrating the Feast of Tabernacles is to go into the wilderness and live in tents. Yeshua did indeed pitch His tent and tabernacled among us.

If Yeshua (Jesus) was born on the day of the Feast of Tabernacles, what day was that? To answer this question, one must first study the feasts of the Lord that are described in Leviticus 23.

> *And the Lord Spake unto Moses, saying, Speak unto the children of Israel, saying, the **fifteenth day of this seventh month** shall be the feast of tabernacles for seven days unto the Lord.* (Leviticus 23:33–34 kjv, emphasis added)

If indeed Yeshua was born on the day of the Feast of Tabernacles, what month and day would that be? To answer this question, one must first establish the first month of the year as YHVH instructed the Hebrews. Let's look at the Scriptures and see what it says.

> *And the Lord Spake unto Moses and Aaron in the land of Egypt, saying, this month shall be unto you the beginnings of months: it shall be the first month of the year to you. Speak ye unto all the congregation of Israel, saying, In the tenth day of this month they shall take to them a lamb…and ye shall keep it until the fourteenth day of the same month and…the congregation of Israel shall kill it…And they shall eat the flesh in that night…ye shall eat it in haste, it is the Lord's Passover."* (Exodus 12:1–11 kjv)

The Hebrews in Egypt killed a lamb and put the lamb's blood over the doors to protect their firstborn. The angel of death passed over them. When Pharaoh's son was killed, he allowed the Israelites to leave Egypt. The Lord Spake unto Moses, "This day came ye out of in the month of **Abib**" (Exodus 13:4 kjv, emphasis added).

So the first month of the year according to God's calendar is the month of Abib. Abib or Aviv is an agricultural term referring to the maturity of the barley crop in Israel. So the first month of the year on God's calendar is the month in which the barley is Aviv, and it is the month the Passover feast is celebrated. Seven months later on the fifteenth day is the Feast of Tabernacles. If I look at the Creator's calendar and count seven months from the month of Aviv, the first day of the seventh month would be the month of Tishri. For example, in the year 2011, the first day of the seventh of Tishri occurred on September 30, 2011. The fifteenth day of the seventh month will be from sundown on October 14 till sundown on October 15, 2011. So from the Scriptures we know the correct day to celebrate Yeshua's birthday in 2011 was October 14.

Let's look at the Scriptures a different way and see if this date is still the correct date.

Most of you know the story of the birth of John (the Baptist) to Elizabeth, the wife of Zechariah. Zechariah served in the temple service the year that Elizabeth became pregnant with John. In 1 Chronicles 24:10, the order of priestly service in the temple is established. Zechariah's time to serve would be the eighth, which would occur in the third month of the year, or the month of Sivan on YHVH's calendar. At this time is when Zechariah was to burn incense in the temple.[113]

Today we live in a generation that has the computer technology and science of astronomy that enables us to calculate the exact position of the planets and stars. This same technology can take us back in the cycle of the moon and tell us the dates that the first sliver of the new moon was visible over Jerusalem. Thus we can recreate the calendar of the time when Yeshua was born. By taking events described in the Scriptures and historical events from credible sources, we can zero in on the date of Yeshua's birth. The results of this study yield the following:

On Aviv 1, 3997 (4 BCE), the temple course (one week) of services of each of the priests are determined. Zechariah's service has been assigned the eighth course (1 Chronicles 24:10). Herod is king of Judea during this period (Luke 1:5).[114]

Zechariah started his course of service on the ninth day of the month of Sivan (June 3, 4 BCE). The angel Gabriel tells Zechariah that his wife will bear a son. Zechariah returns home after his week of service and his wife conceives and hides herself for five months (Luke 1:24).[115]

After six months from Elizabeth becoming pregnant, the angel Gabriel visited Mary and told her that Elizabeth was with child by six months and that she will bear a child. Mary conceives on the last day of Hanukkah or the second day of the month of Tevet (Luke 1:35–38).[116]

After a 280-day gestation period, John was born on the fifteenth day of Aviv in the year 3998 or April 1, 3 BCE. Yeshua was born on the fifteenth day of Tishri in the year 3998 or September 26, 3 BCE. This day was the Feast of Tabernacles in the year 3998.

In the twenty-fifth year of his reign, Caesar Augustus decreed that an oath of allegiance was to be taken by all his subjects to name him "Father of the Roman Empire." He ordered a census be taken. Everyone in the occupied countries was ordered to return to his or her birthplace to take the census. Since the birthplace of Joseph was Bethlehem, Joseph and Mary made the trip to coincide with Joseph's responsibility to go up to Jerusalem for the Feast of Sukkot. Joseph was required to build a *sukkah* to stay in during the feast. A *sukkah* is a temporary hut constructed for use during the week-long Feast of Sukkot. The *sukkah* is topped with tree branches, palm leaves, bamboo sticks, etc., as long as it is something that grew out of the earth. Mary gave birth to Yeshua in a *sukkah*.

Bethlehem was close to the temple mount and afforded Joseph the ability to participate in all the festivities. Mary was exempt from living in the *sukkah*, but with no other accommodations because of the many people staying in Bethlehem for the census, she stayed in the Sukkot also (Leviticus 23:39–43; Luke 2:7).[117]

Yeshua was born in a sukkah on the fifteenth day of Tishri, the year 3998, or September 26, 3 BCE in Bethlehem, which is the town where all the Passover lambs were raised. Yeshua was the Passover Lamb of YHVH.

The Great Sign in Heaven

YHVH put the moon, stars, and planets in the heavens as signs.

> *And God said, let there be lights in the firmament of the heaven to divide the day from the night; and let them be for **signs, and for seasons**, and for days, and years.* (Genesis 1:14 KJV, emphasis added)

The great sign in the heavens announced His birth, and that for which the Chaldean astronomers had been the watching the heavens for over four hundred years appeared just fifteen days earlier on the first day of the seventh month, which is the memorial to the Feast of Trumpets.

> *And there appeared a great wonder in heaven; a woman [Bethulah] clothed with the sun, and the moon under her feet, and upon her head a crown of twelve stars.* (Revelation 12:1 KJV)

The Hebrew word *Bethulah* means *virgin*. In her left hand is a star called Tzemach, which means *Branch*, a word that is used five times by the Hebrew prophets. Each time it is used, it is referring to the Messiah.[118]

On the first day of Tishri, just as the sun was setting the first sliver of the new moon was just below the feet of Bethulah. At that time the constellation Ariel appeared above the head of Bethulah. Ariel is the lion of the tribe of Judah. There is a star in the Ariel called Ha Melech, which means "The King." At that moment the planet Jupiter (Ha Tzaddig), which means "the Righteous One," came in conjunction with Ha Melech and that was the moment that the birth of Yeshua was announced to the world by YHVH.[119]

This was the sign that the Chaldeans had been looking for over four hundred years. Daniel was the third ruler in Babylon, and he was over the wise men of Babylon.

KING HEROD AND THE LUNAR ECLIPSE

Now the Scriptures say that Yeshua was born during the reign of King Herod. When the Magi arrived in Jerusalem to find the Messiah child, they first went to King Herod. They asked King Herod the following question:

> *Saying, Where is he that is born King of the Jews? For we have seen his star in the east, and are come to worship him.* (Matthew 2:2 KJV)

King Herod in turn asked his priests and scribes, and they quoted the Old Testament.

> *But thou, Bethlehem Ephratah, though thou be little among the thousands of Judah, yet out of thee shall he come forth unto me that is to be ruler in Israel; whose goings forth have been from of old, from everlasting.* (Micah 5:2 KJV)

Then Herod sent the Magi to Bethlehem to find the child.

Now Herod was extremely upset at the thought that the King of the Jews had been born. He had no intention of giving up his throne to the Messiah, so he issued an order to kill all the babies in Judea two years old and younger. Joseph was warned by an angel to flee to Egypt, and so they went to Egypt.

Zechariah hid his son John in the wilderness to protect him from the death order by Herod. When Zechariah refused to tell Herod where his son was, Zechariah was executed while he was in the temple.

It is recorded that King Herod had two rabbis burned alive at the time of a lunar eclipse. We know from astronomy that a total lunar eclipse occurred at midnight on January 10, 1 BC.[120]

Herod became very ill, and he did not expect to live. At the same time, Caesar Augustus had given Herod a choice to exile or to execute one his sons called Antipater. Herod had Antipater killed and named his other son Archelaus as his heir. Five days later, Herod died.

Archelaus was as brutal as his father and, fearing a revolt by the Pharisees of the temple, he had three thousand Pharisees killed. It was so bad that the Passover had to be canceled that year. Later, Archelaus was called to Rome to explain his actions. General Varius was called out of Syria and sent to Judea because of a feared revolt.[121]

Since Herod died just a few weeks after the eclipse, the date of September 26, 2 BCE looks correct. Thanks to historical records, astronomy, and high-tech computer software like Skymap, we now can confirm that Yeshua was born just as the Scriptures said on day of the Feast of Tabernacles on Tishri 15, 3998, or September 26, 2 BCE.

CHAPTER 10

The Seventy-Week Ministry of the Messiah

MOSES TOLD THE HEBREWS IN the desert that YHVH will bring a prophet of His own kind and they were to listen to Him.

> *The LORD thy God will raise up unto thee a Prophet from the midst of thee, of thy brethren, like unto me; unto him ye shall hearken.* (Deuteronomy 18:15 KJV)

THIS WAS PROPHESIED IN THE OLD TESTAMENT AND CONFIRMED IN THE GOSPELS.

> *For Moses truly said unto the fathers, A prophet shall the Lord your God raise up unto you of your brethren, like unto me; him shall ye hear in all things whatsoever he shall say unto you...Yea, and all the prophets from Samuel and those that follow after, as many as have spoken, have likewise foretold of these days.* (Acts 3:22, 24 KJV)

THE MESSIAH WAS FOR EVERYONE.

> *Ye are the children of the prophets, and of the covenant which God made with our fathers, saying unto Abraham, And in thy seed shall **all the kindreds** of the earth be blessed.* (Acts 3:25 KJV, emphasis added)

IN THE BOOK OF JOHN, THE MESSIAH IS DESCRIBED AS THE SON OF YHVH AND WHAT HIS MINISTRY IS ABOUT.

> *In the beginning was the Word, and the Word was with God, and the Word was God. The same was in the beginning with God. All things were made by him; and without him was not any thing made that was made. And the Word was made flesh, and dwelt among us, (and we beheld his glory, the glory as of the only begotten of the Father,) full of grace and truth. For the law [Torah] was given by Moses, but grace and truth came by Jesus Christ [Yeshua].* (John 1:1–3, 14, 17 KJV)

In verse 17, we learn that Yeshua was to teach the truth of the Torah. The Jews over the years since Moses had added many oral instructions and rabbinic traditions to the Torah. They had developed a council or assembly of twenty-three judges called the Sanhedrin. Their purpose was to legislate all aspects of Jewish religious and political life within the parameters laid down by biblical and rabbinic tradition in addition to the written Torah.

There were also two major religious groups in Israel during this period called the Pharisees and the Sadducees. The Sadducees included mostly the priestly and autocratic families who recognized only the written letter of the Torah and the Tanak. The Pharisees held to rabbinic interpretations under Mosaic authority. They believed that by applying Mosaic Law to everyday mundane activities of every Jew, it would prevent the Jews from ever violating the Torah. And so over the years they instituted a corpus of laws in addition to the Torah that created a "fence" so that they would not get close to ever violating the Torah.[122]

During His ministry, Yeshua was in constant debate with the Pharisees over their man-made laws they had instituted. As we pointed out in an earlier chapter, Matthew 23:2–3 tells us that Yeshua is preaching not to follow the teachings of these Pharisees. In the following verses, Yeshua lays out a blistering attack against the Pharisees for making all their man-made laws that take away from the truth of the Torah.

Now the Pharisees were especially overbearing when it came to the Sabbath. The rules were extremely strict, and punishment for violating the Sabbath was death by stoning. Yeshua went to great efforts to show what YHVH really intended for the Sabbath. At sundown on the sixth day (Friday), everyone would come to the synagogues to read from the scrolls of the Old Testament. The Scriptures say days start at sundown. On the following morning and during the daylight hours, no work is to be done. Yeshua preached it was OK to do good for our fellow man on the Sabbath. Yeshua also set many examples of healing on the Sabbath that was forbidden by the Pharisees.

How Long was Yeshua's Ministry?

The Gospels record documents the ministry of Yeshua. It documents Yeshua going up to Jerusalem and attending the feasts. However, there is a discrepancy in the time frame of His ministry. The Roman Catholic Church and most Protestant churches state that His ministry was three and a half years. When you try to harmonize the Gospels with the number of Passovers, there is a problem. It results in about two years of dead space in His ministry.[123]

The problem is in the book of John. It appears that a Passover in chapter 5 and a Passover in chapter 6 are out of place or were mistakenly added. Even if you used these two Passovers in your timeline, it still would not come out to three and a half years. On the other hand, if they are removed, then His ministry is seventy weeks or 490 days. So let's look at other scriptures and get confirmation on the length of Yeshua's ministry.[124]

We know that in order to understand the ministry of Yeshua, it requires that you understand YHVH's calendar that was followed by the Jews as well as an understanding of the Feasts that YHVH said were prophetic shadow-pictures that Yeshua must fulfill. We also know that Daniel was given a prophecy of Yeshua by the angel Gabriel, and it is recorded in chapter 9 of the book of Daniel.

The angel Gabriel spoke to Daniel and foretold of the first and second coming of the Messiah Yeshua. In Daniel 9:24–27, the angel Gabriel gives a time line based on the number **seven or sevens** detailing the ministry of Yeshua and His return in the last days. The angel also told Daniel that the understanding of the prophecy would not be understood until the last days.

Thanks to Michael Rood and his teaching "The Jonah Code," we now have the answer to this mystery. Michael Rood explains that you must understand that there are **three layers of sevens** in the prophecy. Now other biblical scholars are beginning to understand the Jonah Code teaching of Michael Rood regarding the three prophetic layers. Two that I am familiar with are found on the websites www.wwyd.org[125] and www.kayceskorner.blogspot.com.[6]

Let's examine what the Scriptures say and see if we can understand the **three layers of sevens** in the prophecy.

First we must understand that a prophetic day for a year principle in the Scriptures.

> *After the number of the days in which ye searched the land, even forty days, each day for a year, shall ye bear your iniquities, even forty years, and ye shall know my breach of promise.* (Numbers 14:34 KJV)
>
> *And when thou hast accomplished them, lie again on thy right side, and thou shalt bear the iniquity of the house of Judah forty days: I have appointed thee each day for a year.* (Ezekiel 4:6 KJV)

Therefore, a day is equal to a year in these prophecies. This means we must look at the Hebrew words in order to determine what period of time it represents.

So let's look at the prophecy in the book of Daniel concerning Yeshua.

In the book of Daniel, Daniel is praying to YHVH about the seventy years of captivity in Babylon. Daniel wanted to know when it would end and they could go back to Judea. YHVH sent His angel Gabriel to Daniel with the following prophecy. I have added the Hebrew word *shavuim* for a better understanding of the prophecy.

The Seventy Shavuim (490 Years/490 Days) of Daniel[127]

> **Seventy [Shavuim (sevens)]** *are determined upon thy people and upon thy holy city, to finish the transgression, and to make an end of sins, and to make reconciliation for iniquity, and to bring in everlasting righteousness, and to seal up the vision and prophecy, and to anoint the most Holy. Know therefore and understand, that from the going forth of the commandment to restore and to build Jerusalem unto the Messiah the Prince shall be* **seven [shavuim (sevens)]**, *and threescore and two* **[shavuim (sevens)]**: *the street shall be built again, and the wall, even in troublous times. And after threescore and two* **[shavuim (sevens)]** *shall Messiah be cut off, but not for himself: and the people of the prince that shall come shall destroy the city and the sanctuary; and the end thereof shall be with a flood, and unto the end of the war desolations are determined. And He (the Messiah) shall confirm the covenant with many for one* **[shavua]**: *and in the midst of the* **[shavua]** *he shall cause the sacrifice and the oblation to cease, and for the overspreading of abominations he shall make it desolate, even until the consummation, and that determined shall be poured upon the desolate.* (Daniel 9:24–27 KJV, emphasis added)

Yeshua to fulfill his purpose in layers of sevens

The prophecy concerning what Yeshua is to accomplish with my comments are as follows:

To finish the transgression. This means that His death will end the transgression against YHVH's commandments.

To put an end to sins. Since sin is the transgression of YHVH's commandments, then sin is ended with His death.

To make reconciliation for iniquity. Since iniquity means without Torah, then Yeshua's death paid the price for everyone's iniquity.

To bring in everlasting righteousness. The believers and followers of Yeshua will receive everlasting righteousness.

To seal up the vision and prophecy. This means to complete the vision and prophecy given to Daniel by the angel Gabriel—a messenger from YHVH.

To anoint the Most Holy. Yeshua is anointed in heaven and returns to destroy the Antichrist and his armies.

The prophecy spans from the command being given to restore Jerusalem till the return of Yeshua to destroy the Antichrist and set up His millennial reign on earth.

First Layer: Sevens of Years

This layer of 70 sevens is subdivided into 7 sevens plus 62 sevens plus 1 seven, which equals 70 sevens. The sevens in the layer are **sevens of years.**[128]

In Daniel 9:25, the time frame that applies from the time when the command is given to restore and rebuild Jerusalem to the arrival of the Messiah is seven shavuim and sixty-two shavuim. The Scriptures record that the date of the command was 457 BCE until the baptism of Yeshua in 27 CE. The seventh year of the reign of Artaxerxes is 457 BCE and the decree for rebuilding Jerusalem is found in Ezra 7:1–28.

> *Now after these things, in the reign of Artaxerxes King of Persia, Ezra the son of Seraiah, the son of Azariah, the son of Hilkiah, And there went up some of the children of Israel, and of the priests, and the Levites, and the singers, and the porters, and the Nethinims, unto*

> *Jerusalem, in the* **seventh year of Artaxerxes the king.** *And he came to Jerusalem in the fifth month, which was in the seventh year of the king.* **For upon the first day of the first month [Aviv 1]** *began he to go up from Babylon, and on the* **first day of the fifth month came he to Jerusalem,** *according to the good hand of his God upon him. [It took 4 months to walk from Babylon to Jerusalem.]* (Ezra 7:1, 7–9 KJV, emphasis added)

From the Babylonian royal calendar we know that Xerxes, king of Babylon, died in the year 465 BCE, and Artexerxes took the throne but was not sworn in until the following year, 464 BCE. This means that Erza was told by Artexerxes during the seventh year of his reign to go and rebuild Jerusalem, which would have been 457 BCE. The Scriptures also say that Erza left on the first day of the first month of the year. This is Aviv 1, and it took Erza four months to travel to Jerusalem.[129]

So our first benchmark is Aviv 1, 457 BCE, which is when the command was given by Artexerxes to rebuild Jerusalem. This year according to the YHVH's calendar was Aviv 1, 457 BCE, or Aviv 1, 3544.

Remember we said that this layer was 7 sevens of years plus 62 sevens of years plus 1 seven of years.

So if we count 7 sevens or 49 years from Aviv 1, 457 BCE to 408 BCE, that gives us the date when the wall was rebuilt. If we count 62 sevens or 434 years from 408 BCE to Aviv 1, 27 CE, this is the start of Yeshua's ministry when He gathered His disciples to preach. This is the day Yeshua returned from the wilderness and John proclaimed the following:

> *The next day John seeth Jesus coming unto him, and saith,* **Behold the Lamb of God, which taketh away the sin of the world.** (John 1:29 KJV, emphasis added)

Yeshua's was anointed with the Holy Spirit exactly forty-one days earlier when He was baptized. This was on Shevat 19, 27 CE.

So as we said earlier, the first layer is 7 sevens of years plus 62 weeks of years plus 1 seven of years. This totals 70 sevens. However, we are missing the 1 seven of years in the 70 sevens of years. This last 1 seven of years occurs in the third layer and is yet future.

Second Layer: Sevens of Weeks

This layer consists of 70 sevens subdivided into 62 sevens plus 7 sevens plus 1 seven. The sevens in this layer are **sevens of weeks (490 days).**

So the timeframe for this fulfillment is from Yeshua's baptism with water on Shevat 19, 27 CE till Shavuot on Sivan 8, 28 CE, and the day of Pentecost when the Holy Spirit baptized the disciples. During this period, the angel says that He (the Messiah) will be cut off during the middle of the Shevua or seven days. Seven-day weeks start on a Saturday night at sundown and end on sundown on a Saturday night.

Yeshua answered the disciple's questions about His death and resurrection as follows:

> *But he answered and said unto them, An evil and adulterous generation seeketh after a sign; and there shall no sign be given to it, but the sign of the prophet Jonas: For as Jonas was* **three days and three nights** *in the whale's belly; so shall the* **Son of man be three days and three nights** *in the heart of the earth.* (Matthew 12:39–40 KJV, emphasis added)

The angel Gabriel states that the Messiah (Yeshua) would be crucified in the midst of the week. That means He was crucified and died late on Wednesday afternoon on our calendar. Since He was in the grave three days and three nights, then He rose late in the afternoon on Saturday, which is the weekly Sabbath.

This time frame of seventy weeks fits perfectly with the ministry of Yeshua. So why do the Protestant churches all say He was crucified on Friday and spent two days in the grave and rose on Sunday morning? The answer is that this was decided by the early Roman Catholic

Church. It simply is replacement theology of removing the Jewish scriptures and replacing it with scriptures that support papal theology.

Third Layer: Seventy Literal Years

This layer consists of seventy literal years, and it incorporates the **one week** from the first layer that was unfulfilled.

This layer gives the time frame for the rebirth of Israel until the start of the last seven years. So let's look at the date Israel became a nation.

Israel became a nation on May 15, 1948. The next day is May 16, which was Shavuot. Shavuot is the fiftieth day after the firstfruits offering. Since Yeshua left the earth on Shavuot, it is reasonable to assume the starting point for the third layer to start on May 16 or Shavuot. Then we can count seventy years from that date, and we come to the year 2017. This indicates that Yeshua cannot return any earlier than the year 2017.[130]

Since this prophecy incorporates the one seven years, we subtract it and we get the year 2010. This last seven years is understood by most biblical scholars to be the seven-year peace treaty with Israel. Most believe that this peace treaty will be ushered in by Zechariah's Middle East war. Even though this war has not occurred yet and as of this writing, we are in the year 2012, war by the Muslims against Israel seems imminent.

In conclusion, more and more biblical scholars are agreeing with Michael Rood in understanding Daniel's seventy-week prophecy. Daniel could not understand it and the angel said it would be sealed until the time of the end. Sir Isaac Newton spent many years trying to understand it, but he failed. Now that we are beginning to understand the prophecy by the angel Gabriel, we know we are in the last days just before Zechariah's war and the seven-year tribulation. Yeshua will then return to destroy the enemies of YHVH.[131]

CHAPTER 11

The Appointed Time of the Passover Lamb of YHVH

§

MOST OF YOU HAVE SEEN the movie *The Ten Commandments* and understand the story of the Exodus of the Jews from Egypt. The story also is very clear in the Scriptures as to when this occurred. We learned that the Jews were told by YHVH to leave in the month of Aviv. Aviv is an agricultural term that originated in Jerusalem meaning the barley is Aviv or ripe. YHVH also commanded that the month of Aviv would be the first month of the year, and on the tenth day of the month every man was commanded to take a lamb without blemish and keep it until the fourteenth day. On the fourteenth day, the lamb is to be killed and roasted. This is called Preparation Day. Then on the fifteenth day, the Scriptures say, "And they shall eat the flesh **in that night**" **(for days start at sunset and last till the next sunset)**. This is called the Lord's Passover, and it is commanded as a Feast of the LORD forever.

For one to understand the Scriptures and YHVH's **appointed times**, one must understand YHVH's calendar. A review of YHVH's calendar tells us that the first month of the year is the month that the barley is Aviv. We also know that the first of the month occurs when two witnesses see the first silver of the new moon. So when the two witnesses would come up to the temple mount and testify that they saw the first silver of the new moon, then the high priest would declare that it was the first day of the month. Then the priests would determine if the barley was Aviv. If the barley was Aviv or ripe, the high priest would declare that it was the first month of the year. If the barley was not Aviv, then the High Priest would declare the month to be the month of Adar, for that year would have thirteen months instead of the normal twelve.

In the month of Aviv, in addition to the weekly Sabbaths, there are **High** Sabbaths on the following days: the first day of the month of the New Year on the Creator's calendar was a High Sabbath, and the fifteenth day after the first day of the month was the High Sabbath of the Feast of Unleavened Bread. The Scriptures say that the Jews were to eat unleavened bread for seven days as a remembrance of their captivity in Egypt. The seventh day, on the day the Feast on Unleavened Bread concluded, was also a High Sabbath.

So when Yeshua came up the Jerusalem, the Jews had been rehearsing the Passover for over a thousand years. Each year, the temple priests for four days would be inspecting the lambs for the perfect sacrificial lamb. On the fourth day, the perfect lamb was selected by the high priest of the temple. Then the priests of the temple would sacrifice all the lambs that had been provided and the perfect lamb was sacrificed last. Once this was done, the high priest of the temple would announce to all, **"It is finished!"**

Now I would like to establish the exact time of death of Yeshua and with that, we know when Messiah's resurrection took place.

> *And it was the preparation of the Passover, and about the sixth hour: and he saith unto the Jews, behold your king!* (John 19:14 KJV)
>
> *Now it was Preparation Day of the Passover week, and about the sixth hour. And he said the Yehudim, See your Sovereign!* (Yahanan 19:14 ISR)
>
> *"And it was the day of preparation for Pesach and it was about the sixth hour. And he said to the Judeans, Behold your king.* (Yachanan (John) 19:14 HRV).

And again later in another verse we get the exact time again.

> *The Jews therefore, because it was the preparation, that the bodies should not remain on the stake on the sabbath day,* **(for that sabbath**

> *day was an high day) besought Pilate that their legs might be broken, and that they might be taken away.* (John 19:31 KJV, emphasis added)
>
> *Therefore, since it was the Preparation Day, that the bodies should not remain on the stake on the Sabbath—**for that Sabbath was a high** one—the Yehudin asked Pilate to have their legs broken and that they be taken away.* (Yahanan (John) 19:31 ISR, emphasis added)
>
> *And the Judeans, because it was the day of preparation, were saying these bodies should not remain overnight on their gallows because the Sabbath is drawing on, for the day of **that Sabbath was a high day**. And they entreated Pilate that they might break the legs of those crucified and take them down.* (Yochanan [John] 19:14 HRV, emphasis added)

The Sanhedrin also documented the death of Yeshua in the Babylonian Talmud. The Pharisees always called him Yeshu.

> *On the eve of the Passover, Yeshua was hanged. For forty days before the execution took place, a herald went forth and cried, He is going forth to be stoned because he has practiced sorcery and enticed Israel to apostasy. Any one, who can say anything and in his favor, let him come forward and plead on his behalf. But since nothing was brought forward in his favor he was hanged on the eve of the Passover!* (Babylonian Talmud, Sanhedrin 43a9 uncensored version, Soncino Translation)[132]

Now we have an exact time of the execution and death of Yeshua on the Preparation Day, but we see here that it was not on the Preparation Day to the weekly Sabbath but Preparation Day to an annual Sabbath (**High Day**), which was the Passover Feast of Unleavened Bread. We also know that it was about the about the sixth hour that His execution began, which I believe would be close to noon, and that He died about the ninth hour, which is about three o'clock in the afternoon. If He died at about 3:00 p.m., they still had time to carry His body to the tomb and prepare His body for burial before dusk, which is when the High Sabbath began.

This means it was late in the Preparation Day of Passover when they rolled the stone in place and placed the seal on the stone.

Now that we know Yeshua died at approximately three o'clock in the afternoon of the Preparation Day of Passover, which starts at sunset beginning on the fourteenth of the month of Aviv. What do the Scriptures say about this? We know that the high priest must select the Passover lamb for sacrifice on the tenth day of the first month and keep it until the fourteenth day and kill it before evening or dusk (Exodus 12:1–8). Are there any hints in the Scriptures as to what day of the week the triumphal entry by Yeshua may have occurred?

Every year the high priest comes down from the temple mount to go outside the north gate to select the Passover lamb from the many lambs that had been brought to an area near the gate. As he is doing this, thousands of Jews have lined the pathway from the gate to the temple mount waiting for the high priest to walk by with the Passover lamb on the way back up to the temple mount. As they had always done, they would wave branches of trees and cry out, "Hosanna; blessed is he that cometh in the name of the Lord" (Mark 11:9 kjv).

We know that Yeshua went up to Jerusalem for the Passover and the Feast of Unleavened Bread from reading the Gospels. When they reached the Mount of Olives, Yeshua sent His disciples out for a colt that had never been ridden. At the time the high priests was outside the city gate selecting the Passover lamb, Yeshua got on the colt and headed into the city through the north gate. The temple priests could not stop him, and He followed the pathway up to the temple mount. The crowd that was gathered began immediately to cry out "Hosanna in the highest." The high priest and his priests could not stop them from crying out "Hosanna in the highest."

> *And [Yeshua] entered into Jerusalem and into the temple: and when he looked around about upon all things, and now the eventide was come, he went out into Bethany with the twelve. And on the morrow…And they came to Jerusalem: and Jesus went into the temple, and began to cast out them that sold and bought in the temple, and overthrew the*

> *tables of the moneychangers, and the seats of them that sold doves… And he taught, saying unto them, Is it not written, My house shall be called of all nations the house of prayer? But ye have made it a den of thieves.* (Mark 11:11–12, 15, 17 KJV)

Now we know that the temple is a house of prayer on the weekly Sabbath. First at sunset (Friday night) on the start of the weekly Sabbath, the Jews would congregate in their local meeting places (synagogues) to pray and read the Scriptures, which were written on scrolls. After this, they would have supper. When the light part of the day arrived (morning), they would bring their offerings up to the temple This means that His triumphal entry into Jerusalem occurred on the tenth day of the month of Aviv and that it is possible it was a weekly Sabbath (Saturday). Then four days later would be the fourteenth day—it would be a **Wednesday** by our calendar—and it would be the Preparation Day for the Passover.

Then the next day would be the first day (Sunday) of the week; Yeshua again goes up to the temple (Mark 11:27). When He left the temple, He went up to the Mount of Olives. That night he was in Bethany in the house of Simon the leper. After two days was the feast of Passover (Mark 14:1). So it was the first day of the week after the weekly Sabbath and two days to the feast of Passover. Two days would make the feast of **Passover on a Wednesday at sundown**.

So far the Scriptures tell us that Passover was sundown on a Wednesday and that Yeshua died about the third hour and He would spend seventy-two hours in the grave and then be resurrected. That would mean that Yeshua rose from the dead about three o'clock in the afternoon of the weekly Sabbath. Again, are there any clues in the Scriptures?

> *The first day of the week [Sunday] cometh Mary Magdalene early when it was yet dark, unto the sepulchre, and seeth the stone taken away from the sepulchre.* (John 20:1 KJV)
>
> *And on the first day of the week (Sunday) Miryam from Magdala came early to the tomb, while it was still dark and saw that the stone had been removed from the tomb.* (Yahanan 20:1 ISR)

And in the night that was dawning at the first of the week, while it was dark, in the very (early) dawn Miryam from Magdala came to the sepulcher. And she saw the stone that it was taken from the grave. (Yachanan 20:1 HRV)

These passages tell us that late in the day of the weekly Sabbath, just when it gets dark (sunset) starts the next day, which is the first day of the week. So the first day of that week, Miryam went to Yeshua's tomb. When she got there, the tomb was empty.

So we know from this passage of Scripture that on the first day of the week **before the sun had set Yeshua had already departed from the tomb** and was long gone! The first day of the week starts when the sun sets on the weekly Sabbath, and this is probably when she went to the tomb as it was customary to change the burial clothes after three days, and this would have been her first opportunity to do so because it is not customary to touch a corpse on the Sabbath.[133] Also please note that women were not allowed to touch a male corpse, so she isn't going there to change any burial clothes.

WHAT DID YESHUA HAVE TO SAY ABOUT HIS DEATH AND RESURRECTION?

The Messiah told His disciples that He would entombed after His execution. Yeshua also had said that this exact amount of time is the only sign that was to be given to a wicked generation that He was the Messiah.

*But he answered and said unto them, An evil and adulterous generation seeketh after a sign; and there shall no sign given to it, but the sign of the prophet Jonas: For as Jonas was **three days and three nights** in the whale's belly; so shall the Son of Man [Yeshua] be **three days and three nights** in the heart of the earth.* (Matthew 12:39–40 KJV, emphasis added)

But He answering, said to them, "A wicked and adulterous generation seeks after a sign, and no sign shall be given to it except the sign of Yonah the prophet. For as Yonah was **three days and three nights** *in the fish's belly, so will the Son of Man be* **three days and three nights** *in the heart of the earth."* (Mattithyahu 12:39–40 ISR, emphasis added)

But He answered and said to them, "An evil and adulterous generation seeks a sign, but no sign shall be given to it except the sign of Yonah the prophet. For as Yonah was **three days and three nights** *in the fish's belly, so will the Son of Man be* **three days and three nights** *in the heart of the earth."* (Mattitiyahu 12:39–40 HRV, emphasis added)

So we see here that Yeshua said He would be entombed for **three days and three nights,** which is a time frame of seventy-two hours.

Based on the Scriptures, Yeshua was crucified on the eve of Passover before sunset on the fourteenth of the month (Wednesday), and He rose three days and three nights 72 hours) later on the weekly Sabbath (Saturday afternoon). That is the only timing that will work with the Scriptures. This was His appointed time to provide redemption to the sinners on earth.

Yeshua told His disciplines that He would be crucified and would rise on the third day. He also told them **how they were to remember Him.**

And taking bread, giving thanks, He broke it and gave it to them, saying, **"This is my body which is given for you, do this in remembrance of me."** *(Luke 22:19 ISR, emphasis added).*

And having given thanks, He broke it and said, "Take, eat, this is my body which is broken for you; do this in remembrance of Me." In the same way also the cup, after supper, saying, "This cup is the **renewed covenant** *in my Blood. As often as you drink it, do this in remembrance of me."* (1 Corinthians 11:24–25 ISR, emphasis added)[134]

Most scriptures use the word *new* instead of *renewed* in this verse. I have provided an explanation in a later chapter why it is better to use the word *renew.*

This is what the Scriptures tell us to do at Passover in remembrance of Yeshua's crucifixion and His resurrection three days and three nights later.

Every year the Hebrews determined if the barley was Aviv at the first silver of the new moon. If the barley was Aviv, then the Passover would occur on the fourteenth day of the month at sunset. If you don't understand YHVH's calendar, you cannot understand the Scriptures as YHVH intended.

The Current Tradition is incorrect

So how do you get three days and three nights between Friday afternoon and Sunday morning? You can't! Any first grader that can count to three will tell you can't get three days and three nights between Friday afternoon and Sunday morning. The crucifixion on Friday and the resurrection on Sunday morning is a fictional man-made tradition invented by the early church. If you are serious about worshipping Yeshua, then maybe you should read the Scriptures and stop just following along with the crowd.

Today with the science of astronomy and computers, we can tell on what day Yeshua was born and the day He was crucified. The Scriptures were written during a time when YHVH's calendar was practiced, and you must use YHVH's calendar to understand the events in the Scriptures.

Corrected Month of Aviv Calendar

Please refer to the attached calendar for the correct understanding of the crucifixion and resurrection of Yeshua according to the Scriptures.

In order to develop the month of Aviv calendar and show the crucifixion and resurrection events on the correct days, you must meet three criteria:

1. Events are based on the Creator's calendar and the feasts of the LORD rehearsed by the Jews. This is the calendar the Scriptures

referred to when the crucifixion event was penned by the disciples. The calendar we use today was invented in 1752 AD and cannot be used to explain the events of the crucifixion and resurrection.
2. Yeshua was crucified on the eve of Passover (John 19:31).
3. Yeshua said He would be in the grave three days and three nights (Matthew 12:39–40). I will take His word over any attempt by the church to misinterpret the time Yeshua was in the grave.

The following are the events that happened during the month of Aviv or the first month of the year.

1. Two witnesses report seeing the first sliver of the new moon, and the high priest declares this is the first day of the month. If the barley is Aviv, then the high priest declares that this is the first month of the year, which is called Aviv.
2. The anointing at Lazarus's house occurred on the ninth day.
3. The Passover lamb was chosen and the triumphal entry into Jerusalem occurred on the tenth day. This also started the four-day inspection of the lamb.
4. After sunset at the beginning of the fourteenth day, Yeshua and the disciples eat their last meal together. Yeshua is taken into custody and put on trial.

    Then He is scourged and crucified about three o'clock in the afternoon. He is removed from the cross and carried to the tomb before sunset. Nicodemus brought a hundred pounds of myrrh and aloe to the burial site. Then Yeshua was prepared for burial with the spices and wrapped in the burial clothes and prepared with spices by Joseph and Nicodemus (John 19:38–42). Yeshua's crucifixion in the middle (midst) of the week fulfilled the prophecy in the book of Daniel (Daniel 9:26–27).
5. After sunset on the start of the fifteenth day, the Passover meal is eaten. It is called the Seder meal. This starts the High Sabbath of the Feast of Unleavened Bread, which is on the fifteenth

day of the month. From sunset till the next sunset is the High Sabbath, and no one leaves their homes on a Sabbath because it is a day of rest.
6. The sixteenth day is a work day. Mary Magdalene, Mary the mother of Jacob, and Salome bought (purchased) spices for the purpose of anointing Yeshua's body (Mark 16:1). This contradicts the verse in John 19:39–40 where Yeshua was prepared already with spices. And since women in those days were not allowed to touch a male corpse, many believe they only purchased more spices knowing Yeshua had already been prepared for burial.
7. The seventh day is the weekly Sabbath. According to Yeshua Himself, He said He would rise three days and three nights after His death. This means He rose at approximately three o'clock in the afternoon of the weekly Sabbath. Since everyone was at their homes resting on the Sabbath, no one saw the event.
8. On the eighteenth day beginning on the first day of the week, Mary Magdalene came to the tomb. The tomb was empty because Yeshua had already risen in the afternoon on the Sabbath day. The first day of the week is the Hebrew name of Sunday, beginning at sundown Saturday to sundown Sunday.

Yeshua never rose on a Sunday. It was an invention by the early Roman Catholic Church. And you cannot get three days between Friday afternoon and Sunday at sunrise. If you believe and teach others that Yeshua was crucified on a Friday and rose Sunday morning, then the Scriptures are fulfilled when Yeshua quoted Isaiah and said, "to perceive by hearing, you will hear and you will not understand" (Matthew 13:14).

CHAPTER 12

The Ark of the Covenant

MOST PEOPLE KNOW THE STORY of the ark from the Scriptures. The movie *The Ten Commandments* gave us a visual interpretation of how YHVH wrote and gave the Ten Commandments to the Israelites in the desert during the Exodus from Egypt. We know the story about the ark in the tabernacle and in the temple built by Solomon. And we know that it has disappeared, and we see a lot of History Channel stories about its possible location today.

So what is the Real Story?

First, from the time of ancient Israel, the Ark of the Covenant was the focal point of Israel's journey through the wilderness. It was where the throne of YHVH was on the earth, and His Holy Spirit was located over the mercy seat covering the ark.

The ark was a sacred chest made according to YHVH's instructions to house the Ten Commandments written in stone by YHVH. It also was part of the sacrificial system established by YHVH when man fell and was cast out of the Garden of Eden. The sacrificial system was designed to show the awful results of sin and how blood must be shed for forgiveness of sins.

> *And almost all things are by the law purged with blood; and without shedding of blood there is no remission.* (Hebrews 9:22 KJV)

So a sinner would bring a lamb or a dove to the temple, confess his sins, and then take the life of that innocent animal. In this act the sin did not vanish but was transferred to the animal's blood. The temple priest would then put the blood in the golden altar. This act took place every Sabbath all year long. Then once a year on the Day of Atonement, the high priest would sacrifice a young bull for a sin offering and ram for a burnt offering.

> *And he shall take of the blood of the bullock, and sprinkle it with his finger upon the mercy seat **eastward**; and before the mercy seat shall he sprinkle of the blood with his finger seven times. Then shall he kill the goat of the sin offering, that is for the people, and bring his blood within the vail, and do with that blood as he did with the blood of the bullock, and sprinkle it upon the mercy seat, and before the mercy seat: And he shall make an atonement for the holy place, because of the uncleanness of the children of Israel, and because of their transgressions in all their sins: and so shall he do for the tabernacle of the congregation, that remaineth among them in the midst of their uncleanness.* (Leviticus 16:14–16 KJV, emphasis added)

Which Side of the Ark was the Eastward Side?

> *And he brought me into the inner court of the LORD's house, and, behold, at the door of the temple of the LORD, between the porch and the altar, were about five and twenty men, with their backs toward the temple of the LORD, and their faces toward the east; and they worshipped the sun toward the east.* (Ezekiel 8:16 KJV)

So this means the temple faced east. So which way did the ark face? The ark was placed in the Most Holy Place.

> *And the priests brought in the ark of the covenant of the LORD unto his place, into the oracle of the house, to the most holy place, even under the wings of the cherubim.* (1 Kings 8:6 KJV)

The area just outside and east of the Most Holy Place was called the Holy Place.

> *And they drew out the staves, that the ends of the staves were seen out in the holy place before the oracle, and they were not seen without: and there they are unto this day.* (1 Kings 8:8 KJV)

This verse is saying the staves are withdrawn into the Holy Place. That means the ark must be facing either north or south. The verse also says they can't see the staves because of the curtain, but they can see the impression as the staves push against the curtain.

If the ark is facing south, then the right side of the ark would be the eastward side.

Before the time Solomon built the temple for the ark, the ark was housed in a tabernacle per the instructions given to Moses. It was transported through the desert by placing wooden staves through a wooden support structure so that the ark could be moved without touching it. Touching the ark was sure death. Most people believe that there are four angels guarding the ark so man cannot desecrate it. There are many stories in the Scriptures regarding the ark and the destruction that has come upon the enemies of YHVH who tried to violate the ark.

> *And the golden mice, according to the number of all the cities of the Philistines belonging to the five lords, both of fenced cities, and of country villages, even unto the great stone of Abel, whereon they set down the ark of the LORD: which stone remaineth unto this day in the field of Joshua, the Bethshemite. And he smote the men of Bethshemesh, because they had looked into the ark of the LORD, even he smote of the people fifty thousand and threescore and ten men: and the people lamented, because the LORD had smitten many of the people with a great slaughter. And the men of Bethshemesh said, who is able to stand before this holy LORD God? And to whom shall he go up from us?* (1 Samuel 6:18–20 KJV)

What Happened to the Ark?

In the book of Jeremiah, we learn that King Nebuchadnezzar sent an envoy to Jerusalem to check the story out about the ark that was located in Solomon's temple. The envoy was shown the temple, and he returned to Babylon to tell King Nebuchadnezzar about it.

Because of Israel's transgression of the commandments and their wicked acts, YHVH passed judgment on them. The prophets had warned them that judgment would come on the house of Israel if they did not return to the commandments given to them by YHVH. One such commandment that they did not follow was every seven years they were to let the land rest by not planting crops. However, since they had lost their faith in YHVH to provide for them during the Sabbath year, they did not keep the Sabbath year. In addition, every fifth year, they were to free slaves. They also stopped keeping the Jubilee year, which was every fiftieth year.

> *And thou shalt number seven sabbaths of years unto thee, seven times seven years; and the space of the seven sabbaths of years shall be unto thee forty and nine years. Then shalt thou cause the trumpet of the jubile to sound on the tenth day of the seventh month, in the Day of Atonement shall ye make the trumpet sound throughout all your land. And ye shall hallow the fiftieth year, and proclaim liberty throughout all the land unto all the inhabitants thereof: it shall be a jubile unto you; and ye shall return every man unto his possession, and ye shall return every man unto his family. A jubile shall that fiftieth year be unto you: ye shall not sow, neither reap that which groweth of itself in it, nor gather the grapes in it of thy vine undressed. For it is the jubile; it shall be holy unto you: ye shall eat the increase thereof out of the field. In the year of this jubile ye shall return every man unto his possession.* (Leviticus 25:8–13 KJV)

The Ark is Hidden

YHVH was angry with Israel so He issued His judgment on them and they were taken into captivity for seventy years. King Nebuchadnezzar and his army surrounded Jerusalem and breached the walls of Jerusalem. When they then broke into the temple, the golden ark was missing. After ransacking all of Jerusalem, they still could not find the ark.

> *Therefore thus saith the* Lord *of hosts; Because ye have not heard my words, Behold, I will send and take all the families of the north, saith the* Lord, *and Nebuchadrezzar the king of Babylon, my servant, and will bring them against this land, and against the inhabitants thereof, and against all these nations round about, and will utterly destroy them, and make them an astonishment, and an hissing, and perpetual desolations. Moreover I will take from them the voice of mirth, and the voice of gladness, the voice of the bridegroom, and the voice of the bride, the sound of the millstones, and the light of the candle. And this whole land shall be a desolation, and an astonishment; and these nations shall serve the king of Babylon seventy years.* (Jeremiah 25:8–11 kjv)

Jeremiah, being warned by YHVH, hid the ark in one of the caves under Mount Morrow. Jerusalem was under siege, so Jeremiah utilized the secret mechanism that Solomon had put in place at the building of the temple. Solomon had put in place a sand hydraulic system that allowed the stone that the ark rested on to be lowered into the earth. The ark was removed and then the stone was moved back to the surface at the original site. So when King Nebuchadnezzar's army broke into the temple, the ark was already hidden. To learn how this was done, you must get the DVD from Michael Rood named *The Great Secret of Solomon's Temple*.[135]

Clues to how the Ark was hidden

When Solomon built the temple, he had two brass pillars installed in front of the entrance to the temple. The pillar on the left was named Boaz and the pillar on the right was named Jachin.

> *And he set up the pillars in the porch of the temple: and he set up the right pillar, and called the name thereof* **Jachin**: *and he set up the left*

*pillar, and called the name thereof **Boaz**.* (1 Kings 7:21 KJV, emphasis added)

Before the siege, the pillars before the temple were eighteen cubits high. On top of each pillar was a brass chapiter (capital) that was five cubits high.

For he cast two pillars of brass, of eighteen cubits high apiece: and a line of twelve cubits did compass either of them about. And he made two chapiters of molten brass, to set upon the tops of the pillars: the height of the one chapiter was five cubits, and the height of the other chapiter was five cubits. (1 Kings 7:15–16 KJV)

Each pillar was 18 cubits X 20.62 in/cu or 371.16 inches or 30.93 feet tall. The brass chapiter was 5 cubits X 20.62 in/cu or 8.6 feet tall.
After the fall of Jerusalem, the pillars were eighteen cubits high.

The height of the one pillar was eighteen cubits, and the chapiter upon it was brass: and the height of the chapiter three cubits; and the wreathen work, and pomegranates upon the chapiter round about, all of brass: and like unto these had the second pillar with wreathen work. (2 Kings 24:17 KJV)

Now the chapiter is only 3 cubits tall. What happen to the two cubits or 41.25 inches of brass?
What Solomon had built was a sand hydraulic system for the purpose of being able to remove the ark in secret from the temple so it could be hidden. A capstone was placed in the Most Holy Place, which was part of a fulcrum underneath the temple. The other end of the fulcrum was connected to the brass pillars in front of the temple. By unlocking the capstone, the fulcrum would raise the capstone up so the ark could be removed. Once removed, sand from inside the pillars was released, which allowed the capstone to be lowered into place but also caused the chapiter to drop the two cubits.

The ark was transported to a place prepared for by Solomon outside of the walls of Jerusalem in about 605 BC. Jeremiah placed the ark in a stone box that Solomon had placed there earlier.

Solomon gave us a clue in the following:

> *Then spake Solomon, the LORD said that he would dwell in the **thick darkness**. I have surely built thee and **house to dwell in**, a settled place for thee to abide in for ever.* (1 Kings 8:12–13 KJV, emphasis added)

So the ark was hidden outside the walls of Jerusalem.

> *And it shall come to pass, when ye be multiplied and increased in the land, in those days, saith the LORD, they shall say no more, The ark of the covenant of the LORD: neither shall it come to mind: neither shall they remember it; neither shall they visit it; neither shall that be done any more.* (Jeremiah 3:16 KJV)

YHVH had a Plan for the Ark when Yeshua was Crucified

When Yeshua was crucified outside the walls of Jerusalem, the Romans cut holes in the rock to support the wooden cross. At the time, the area was an old road bed and the crosses were low enough that you could look at the victims at almost an eye level. Thanks to Ron Wyatt and his exploration of this area, we now know that the holes cut in the rock to hold the crosses was directly over the place where Jeremiah placed the ark of the covenant over five hundred years earlier.

On the day of the crucifixions, Yeshua says, "It is finished," and He dies. Immediately, there is an earthquake.

> *Jesus, when he had cried again with a loud voice, yielded up the ghost. And, behold, the veil of the temple was rent in twain from the top to the bottom; and the **earth did quake, and the rocks rent;** the*

earthquake caused the rock to rent or split with large cracks. Now when the centurion, and they that were with him, watching Jesus, saw the earthquake, and those things that were done, they feared greatly, saying, truly this was the Son of God. (Matthew 27:50–54 KJV, emphasis added)

The Jews therefore, because it was the preparation, that the bodies should not remain upon the cross on the Sabbath day, **(for that Sabbath day was a high day,)** *besought Pilate that their legs might be broken, and that they might be taken away. Then came the soldiers, and brake the legs of the first, and of the other which was crucified with him. But when they came to Jesus, and saw that he was dead already, they brake not his legs.* (John 19:31–33 KJV, emphasis added)

The Roman soldier, seeing that Yeshua was already dead, did not break His legs. Instead he pierced His side and out came blood and water.

But one of the soldiers with a spear pierced his side, and forthwith came there out blood and water. And he that saw it bare record, and his record is true: and he knoweth that he saith true, that ye might believe. (John 19:35–35 KJV)

THE ARK'S LOCATION DISCOVERED BY RON WYATT

The ark remained hidden until 1988 when Ron Wyatt found the ark in an archeological dig. Ron was privileged to find the ark and live to tell the story of what YHVH showed him. Others from Israel's Department of Antiquities were not as fortunate.[136]

This is what Ron found. The ark was enclosed in a stone case, but the top was broken and set aside. He found the dried blood on the mercy seat where it had fallen through a large crack in the rock above the mercy seat. He had the blood tested in a lab and it was still alive. The lab test revealed that the blood only contained twenty-four chromosomes instead of the normal forty-six. Ron concluded that Yeshua received twenty-three chromosomes from Mary and one Y chromosome from His father YHVH.[137]

This is what happened. The blood and water fell through the cracked rock down through the earth and fell on the left-hand side of the mercy seat of the Ark of the Covenant that was hidden in the cave below the crucifixion area.

WHY BLOOD AND WATER?
The blood and water is necessary to cleanse all unrighteousness. The blood is for forgiveness and the water is the Word, the Torah (see Leviticus 14:51).

By this act, the blood of the perfect Lamb of YHVH was sprinkled on the mercy seat of the ark in atonement for the sins of mankind. Your sins are covered by the blood of Yeshua.[138]

THE SCRIPTURES BEAR WITNESS TO THE BLOOD FALLING ON THE ARK. Remember the first covenant between YHVH and Israel was the regulations for services for the earthly sanctuary. The first covenant required the high priest to enter the Holy of Holies once a year with the blood of animals offered on behalf of both himself and the people for sins committed in ignorance. These are sins committed in error without thinking. When Yeshua's blood fell through the cracks of the rock onto the ark, Paul (Paul is thought to be the author of Hebrews) describes what happened:

> *And not entering by the blood of goats and calves, but through His own blood He entered* **once** *into the Holy of Hollies finding eternal redemption for us...Then because of His death, He is Mediator of a new covenant, by payment of a ransom for transgressions under the first covenant. When His death took place those who have been called could take the promise of eternal inheritance. For where there is a will, death of the testator must be announced. For since a will is valid only*

upon death, then it is not valid while the one made the will is still alive. On this account the first was not inaugurated without blood. for when every commandment was spoken by Moses to all the people according to the Torah (Teaching), then he took the blood of the calves and the goats with water and red wool and hyssop and this he sprinkled on the scroll and all the people. Saying, "This is the blood of the covenant which God commanded for you." And he sprinkled the Tabernacle and all the vessels of the service with the same blood. Then he cleansed every vessel by means of blood according to the Torah (Teaching), and without blood being shed there is no forgiveness. (Hebrews 9:12, 15–22 ONMB, emphasis added)

THE IMPORTANCE OF THE TEN COMMANDMENTS REVEALED TO RON WYATT

Ron also found the original stone with the Ten Commandments written on them by the finger of YHVH. Ron was able to make a video of the mercy seat, the ark, the Ten Commandments, and the other items hidden by Jeremiah. The videotape was placed next to the Ten Commandments.[139]

Ron Wyatt was allowed to see the ark and to tell the story. His story is easy to find on the Internet. No one else has been able to find or see the ark without dying. Even Ron Wyatt died a few years after finding the ark. Ron was able to make a video of the ark and the Ten Commandments, but he was told by the angels guarding the ark to preserve the video until it was time to show the world.[140]

Ron was then told by one of the angels, **"When a worldwide law is passed forcing men to violate the law of God, then they will be shown to mankind."** Then the video and the Ark and the Ten Commandments will be shown to the world. Then the world will see and even test Yeshua's blood. This will cause some to follow God, others will not. It will be your choice. This will be the greatest choice ever made by mankind. If you choose the worship of God, you will be killed. If you choose the Antichrist, then you will be destroyed by Yeshua's return. So if you make the right choice, jump for joy when they kill you because you will be in heaven.[141]

Today, the ark is still hidden in the cave under the crucifixion area outside the walls of Jerusalem, but the Scriptures tell us that we will all see the ark again soon.

CHAPTER 13

The History of the Christian Church

SATAN AND THE FALLEN ANGELS were probably very angry and upset that Yeshua had been crucified and resurrected after three days and three nights. For four thousand years Satan had led the Gentiles into worship of sun gods. Most of the people during this time were lost in sun-god worship except for the Hebrew nation of Israel. This changed when Yeshua's blood covered the mercy seat on the ark, paying the price for everyone's sins who would repent and follow Him. This meant that the Gentiles also could now be saved. Satan and the fallen angels, knowing that they could not be saved, began to pour out their vengeance on all the Jews and Christians. This anger resulted in years of torture and death by the Roman emperors and was continued by the early Roman Church.

JEWISH APOSTLES SPREAD THE GOSPEL TO THE PAGAN GENTILES

After Yeshua's death, the disciples bravely tried to spread the gospel of Yeshua to the Jews in Jerusalem and to rest of the world. This was at a time when the Roman Empire controlled most of Europe and Asia. The emperors of Rome saw this as a threat to their rule of all their conquered countries and sought to kill all of the Jewish disciples who were trying to spread Christianity to the Gentiles and Jews. A gruesome account of the deaths of the disciples of Yeshua is told in *Foxe's Book of Martyrs*.[142]

The first to be killed was Stephen one year after Yeshua was crucified. This occurred at the Passover when Stephen was taken outside the gate and stoned to death.

Ten years later after the death of Stephen, the newly appointed governor of Judea started a sharp persecution of the leaders of the Jews spreading the gospel. He had James, the elder brother of John, beheaded along with his accuser. Also, that year Timothy was also killed in Philippi and Parmenas was killed in Macedonia. The year was about AD 44.

Phillip spread the gospel in Asia until he was scourged, thrown in prison, and afterward crucified in about AD 54.

Matthew wrote his book in Hebrew, which was later translated into Greek by James. Matthew spent most of his time in Parthia and Ethiopia. Matthew was slain with a halberd in the city of Nadabah in AD 60. A halberd is a pole with an axe blade and a spear on the end.

James, the half brother of Yeshua, was elected to the oversight of the churches in Jerusalem. At the age of ninety-four, he was beaten and stoned by the Jews and finally had his brains dashed out by a fuller's club.

Matthias was the replacement disciple for Judas. He was stoned in Jerusalem and then beheaded.

Andrew, the brother of Peter, preached the gospel in Asia. On his arrival to Edessa, he was captured and crucified on a cross, which had two ends fixed transversely to the ground. It is now known as a St. Andrew's cross.

Mark was of the tribe of Levi. He was dragged to death by the people of Alexandria as a sacrifice to the sun god Serapis.

Peter was condemned to death by the Roman emperor Nero. Peter was crucified head down and feet up on a cross in Rome.

Paul was also condemned to death by Nero. Paul was beheaded by a sword.

Jude, the brother of James, was crucified in Edessa in AD 72.

Bartholomew translated the gospel in the language of India only later to be cruelly beaten and crucified.

Thomas preached the gospel in Parthia and India. He was killed by the pagans with a spear.

Luke was supposed to have been hanged on an olive tree in Greece by the idolatrous priests.

Simon, who preached the gospel in Mauritania, Africa, and in Britain, was crucified in AD 74.

John founded the seven churches of Asia known as Ephesus, Smyrna, Pergamos, Sardis, Philadelphia, Laodicea, and Thyatira. The Romans captured John in Ephesus and sent him to Rome. He was sentenced to death by the Roman emperor Domitian and thrown into a cauldron of boiling oil. John was protected by a miracle of YHVH. Domitian was afraid of him after that miracle, so he had John banished to the island of Patmos. This is where John wrote the book of Revelation. John was the only disciple who escaped a violent death.[143]

ROMAN WARS AGAINST THE JEWS

The Romans had occupied Jerusalem even before Yeshua was born. The Jews had suffered greatly under Roman rule. The Romans worshipped the sun god Sol Invictus Mithras for many years, and it was their custom to offer their victims up as a sacrifice to their sun god. They did this by hanging their victims on a cross so that everyone could see them die over a period of days. In the year AD 66 the Jews revolted and took control of Jerusalem. The Roman army led by Titus finally breached the walls in AD 70 and burned Jerusalem and the second temple to the ground. Thousands of Jews were slaughtered. Finally in AD 73, the last Jewish stronghold at Madasa fell, ending the revolt. Titus later became emperor of Rome.[144]

Although there was much hatred for the Jews in Jerusalem, Paul had been successful in bringing Christianity too many Gentiles in Rome. Because these Christians had no previous religious ties to Judaism and their country was in conflict with the Jews, they mostly resisted the Jewish feasts such as the Sabbath, Passover, and the other feasts of YHVH. From the epistles written by Paul, we see that Christians in Rome developed into two groups, one being a Gentile Christian majority and the other a Judeo-Christian minority. The Jewish-Christians, though a minority in the Church of Rome, seems to have provoked "disputes" over the questions regarding the Ten Commandments: "Him that is weak in the faith receive ye, but not to doubtful disputations" (Romans 14:1 KJV).

As a result, much controversy developed over worship. The persecution against the Jews in the Roman Empire began to take its toll.

The Roman Calendar

The Jewish apostles who went to Rome to preach the gospel of Yeshua followed YHVH's calendar. This calendar started on Sunday as day one and ended on the Sabbath or day seven. In trying to teach the Romans YHVH's calendar, the apostles encountered the first-century Roman calendar where each day of the week was named after a planet or the planetary week. The sequence was Saturn (1), Sun (2), Moon (3), Mars (4), Mercury (5), Jupiter (6), and Venus (7). When they converted the pagan Romans to Christianity, they would worship on the Sabbath, which was the day of Venus on the planetary week.[145]

Now the day of the sun or "Sun-day" was the most revered by the pagan Romans. History records that by the end of the first century, the day of the sun replaced the day of Saturn as the first day of the week. The day of the sun emerged as the most important day for the pagan worshippers. The new primitive Christians resented and denied the accusation of being sun-worshippers, and many were martyred because of their denial. Although the Christians tried to avoid sun worship, they continued to celebrate pagan festivals in their communities to avoid hostilities against them.

Influence of Sun Worship on the Early Gentile Christians

Religious scholars tell us that there were three major factors influencing these primitive Christians to become sun-worshippers. The reasons are as follows:

1. Christ—the Sun
2. Eastward orientation
3. The date of Christmas

The sun god, or Mithra, was portrayed as an image of a man with a disk at the back of his head.[146] In the earliest known Christian mosaic (dated ca. AD 240) found in the Vatican necropolis below the altar of St. Peter, Christ is portrayed as the sun (Helios) ascending on the quadriga chariot with a flying cloak and a nimbus behind His head from which radiate seven rays in the form of a T (perhaps alluding to a cross?). This motif of the sun was used by Christian teachers to portray Christ to pagans who were well acquainted with Sun symbology.[147]

The adoption of the east instead of Jerusalem as the orientation of prayer also indicates the significant influence of the sun on the early Christians. The Jews by Daniel's and Solomon's custom were to always pray toward Jerusalem where the temple of YHVH was located. Christian teachers adopted the eastward position of prayer because prayers are offered while looking toward sunrise in the East because the Orient represents the birth of light and the because of the **orientation of the ancient temples for worship of sun gods.** Christians who wanted to disassociate with the Jews automatically accepted the eastward orientation at sunrise and **reinterpreted** the meaning of light with the Christian message.[148]

Adoption of Pagan Feasts into Christian Worship

The adoption of the twenty-fifth of December as the date for the celebration of Christmas is the most explicit example of sun worship's influence on the Christian liturgical calendar. It is a known fact (and not disputed) that the pagan feast of *dies natalis Solis Invicti* is and was the birthday of the Invincible Sun and the birthday celebration was held on the twenty-fifth of December. For Christians today to admit to borrowing a pagan festival and reinterpreting its meaning would be tantamount to an open betrayal of the faith.[149]

Anyone who researches church history in the first and second centuries will agree that the faith originally taught by Paul and other disciples of Yeshua was distorted by the influence of sun worship and the hatred of Jews by the Romans. Christianity was being spread, but it was also changed.

Persecution of Roman Christians

In all, there were ten persecutions of Jews and Christians during the first three hundred years by the Romans.

The First Persecution under Nero, AD 67

Nero reigned from AD 54 through 68. Nero was a sun god worshipper, and he attributed to the sun the merit for the discovery of a plot against him. He erected the famous "Colossus Neronis" at the highest point of the villa, representing the Sun, with the features of Nero and with seven long rays around his head.

In AD 66, a bitter Jewish revolt against the authority of Rome summoned Roman legions, led by Cestius. Nero in AD 67 ordered the city of Rome set on fire and afterward blamed the Christians for the fire. After three and a half years of fighting, a second siege under Titus sealed Jerusalem's fate. The walls were breached and the city and temple were destroyed. Over a million Jews perished.

Nero started persecuting the Christians in Rome with great cruelty. He had some of the Christians sewed up in the skins of wild beasts and then set dogs after them until they finally died. He also ordered Christians to be dressed in wax shirts made stiff and placed in axletrees in his gardens. He then set them on fire to illuminate his gardens.[150]

The Second Persecution under Domitian, AD 81

Domitian carried on with the persecution of Christians. He commanded all the lineage of David be put to death. He had a law passed "that no Christian once brought before the tribunal should be exempted from punishment without renouncing his religion." He also blamed the Christians for all famine, pestilence, and earthquakes suffered by any Roman provinces. When any Christians were brought forth before a magistrate, they were asked to take an oath that they were not Christians. If they refused to take the oath, they were killed, or if they said they confessed they were Christian, they were killed.[151]

The Third Persecution under Trajan, AD 108

Under Trajan's rule, thousands of Christians were put to death daily. Christians who refused to sacrifice to the pagan idols such as Jupiter were beheaded. Many were just burned in the streets. Beneath Rome are excavations called catacombs, which were originally temples and tombs. There are sixty catacombs near Rome in which six hundred miles of galleries of tombs have presently been excavated. When the Christian tombs are opened, they find skeletons where the head has been decapitated and their bones show the awful scars of torture and death.[152]

Persecutions of Jews in Rome

Hadrian become emperor in AD 117 and ruled until AD 138. He is best known for building Hadrian's Wall in Great Britain and rebuilding the Pantheon (a temple with statues of all the sun gods). He was extremely anti-Jewish, and he **outlawed the Jewish religion and the observance of the Sabbath** in the Roman Empire. He also abolished circumcision. He also went to Jerusalem and built a new temple dedicated to the worship of Jupiter at the site of the second temple of Jerusalem that had been earlier destroyed by the Romans. This caused an uprising by the Jews in Palestine and led to Hadrian killing over 580,000 Jews in order to quell the rebellion. With the Jewish religion outlawed, converted Christians were afraid to follow the Sabbath or to celebrate the crucifixion and resurrection of the Messiah at Passover. **Now all Gentile Christians would worship how Rome allowed them to worship.**[153]

A Quiet Period under Antoninus Pius from AD 138–161
Antoninus was adopted by Hadrian after the death of his other adopted son, Aelius Verus. Antoninus also adopted Marcus Aurelius, the son of Aelius Verus.[154]

The Fourth Persecution under Marcus Aurelius Antoninus, AD 162
Marcus Aurelius moved forward with such a fierce and stern persecution of Christians that the spectators shuddered with horror. The Christians suffered the most excruciating tortures that could be devised and then they were destroyed by the most terrible deaths.[155]

The Fifth Persecution Commencing with Severus, AD 192
In spite of the torture and execution of Christians in Rome, Christianity continued to spread. Although Severus was easy on the Christians, the pagans stepped up their persecution of Christians. No one was immune. The bishop of Rome was beheaded along with other notable Romans. Some Christian women had boiling pitch poured on their heads and then set on fire. The rule was to torture first and then to kill the Christian.[156]

The Sixth Persecution under Maximus, AD 235
During this persecution, countless Christians were slain without a trial and were buried in mass graves. Fifty to sixty Christians were thrown into pits like dead animals. Maximus died in AD 249 and the Christians were not persecuted for about ten years.[157]

The Seventh Persecution under Decius, AD 249
Although Christianity had increased in Rome, it had also had become polluted with many errors on how to worship. Decius became emperor and immediately tried to remove the Christian name altogether. Thou-

sands of Christians under his rule were tortured and beheaded, including the bishop of Rome.[158]

The Eight Persecution under Valerian, AD 257
Valerian persecuted Christians for three and half years. Most of the victims were burned to death. Most were scourged first, and then they were pinched with fiery tongs, girded with burning plates, and eventually roasted alive.[159]

The Ninth Persecution under Aurelian, AD 274
Aurelian continued the persecution of Christians and had every Christian beheaded. Later, when Diocletian took over as emperor, his associate Maximiam had a legion of soldiers that happened to be all Christians. Maximian had the entire legion of 6,666 men killed by the sword.[160]

The Tenth Persecution under Diocletian, AD 303
Galerius, the adopted son of Diocletian, persuaded Diocletian to put an end to the Christian churches. They burned churches to the ground, including the homes of Christians. Entire cities were burned to the ground. All Scripture found by Diocletian's soldiers was destroyed by fire. History records that Diocletian's persecution of Christians was the severest in Roman history.[161]

In the year AD 307, Diocletian dedicated a temple to Mithra at Carnuntum. He was a worshipper of the sun god Mithra.

The Influence of Constantine on the Christian Church

Constantine was an emperor of Rome from AD 306 to AD 337. Prior to becoming emperor, he was a soldier in the Roman army and won many battles. While in the Roman army Constantine was not a Christian, but he was tolerant of Christians. The political environment of Rome at the time was that whoever wanted to lead the country would have to defeat his rivals. So eventually Constantine was at war with Maxentius (a rival leader) for control of Rome. Eusebius describes the following while Constantine was marching with his army: "He saw with his own eyes in the heavens a trophy of the cross arising from the light of the sun, carrying the message, In Hoc Signo Vinces or 'In this sign, you will conquer.'" When the battle started, all of Constantine's men had standards painted with the sign Constantine claims he saw. They were victorious. From this victory, Constantine claimed that the sign of the Christ had given him the victory.[162]

In AD 313, Constantine consolidated his authority over his Roman rivals. At a meeting with his rivals, the Edict of Milan was issued, granting full tolerance for Christians and all religions in the empire. Over the next few years, Constantine supported Christians financially and promoted Christians to high office. Constantine established the first Roman political and religious government. In 321, as the supreme ruler of government and religious matters, Constantine instructed that Christians and non-Christians should be united in observing the **venerable day of the sun**, referencing the esoteric Eastern sun-worship that Aurelian had earlier helped to introduce to Rome. Although Constantine was called a Christian, his coinage still carried the symbols of Sol Invictus Mithra until the year 324.[163]

In the year 325, Constantine convened the Council of Nicaea to deal with the problem of Arianism. Arianism is a doctrine attributed to Arius (AD 250–336), a Christian from Egypt, concerning the relationship of Yeshua to YHVH where Yeshua (Jesus) is lesser than God. Arius referred to John 14:28 as the basis for his belief: [164]

Ye have heard how I said unto you, I go away, and come again unto you. If ye loved me, ye would rejoice, because I said, I go unto the Father: for my Father is greater than I. (John 14:28 KJV)

This was in contradiction to the early Roman church belief in the Trinity. The council disagreed and declared Arius a heretic. This was the first time the organized Gentile Christian church had ruled against someone with a different interpretation of the Scriptures, but it would not be the last. The controversy of the Trinity referred to in Matthew 28:19 still rages on.[165]

Also, the council established the construction of the first part of the Nicene Creed, settling the calculation of the date of Easter and establishment of early canon law. Easter would be observed on the first Sunday after the vernal equinox.

A New Gospel is now Official

YHVH gave the Hebrews His communications on how to worship Him. Yeshua came as a suffering lamb and was crucified by the ruling religious body of the Jews. Yeshua's disciples spread the gospel to Rome to convert the pagans to be believers in the Messiah. The Roman pagans were converted over a period of time but, in doing so, brought into the faith sun worship and removed all of the instructions from YHVH regarding the Sabbath, the Passover, and the High Sabbaths. In other words, they made up their own rules and renamed their earlier pagan feasts into new Christian holidays. YHVH knew this would happen, and Paul gave us this warning:

> *But I fear, lest by any means, as the serpent beguiled Eve through his subtilty, so your minds should be corrupted from the simplicity that is in Christ. For if he that cometh preacheth another Jesus, whom we have not preached, or if ye receive another spirit, which ye have not received, or another gospel, which ye have not accepted, ye might well bear with him.* (2 Corinthians 11:3–4 KJV)
>
> *For if indeed who comes is preaching another Yeshua whom we did not preach, or you are taking another spirit which you did not take from us, or a different gospel which you did not take from us, but you put up with it quite easily.* (2 Corinthians 11:4 ONMB)

Changes to the Original Worship Taught by YHVH
Here are a few changes:

1. YHVH's weekly Sabbath changed to Sun-day worship.
2. Passover Feast of YHVH changed to Easter Holiday. Easter was to be the first Sun-day after the spring equinox.
3. Jesus said that He would be in the grave for three days and three nights and this was changed to two days and two nights.
4. Easter Sunday selected as the day the Messiah rose from the grave.
5. Easter was to be celebrated on the same day of the week as opposed to the Passover occurring on the fourteenth day of the first month of the year.
6. High Sabbaths of YHVH totally eliminated.
7. Yeshua's name changed to Iesus. (See the 1611 Bible.) Iesus was later changed to Jesus when Webster invented the letter *J*.
8. The birthday celebration of Tammuz and Mithra celebrated on December 25 was renamed the birthday of Iesus, which became the birthday of Jesus.

What did Jude say about changing the faith once given to the saints?

Beloved, when I gave all diligence to write unto you of the common salvation, it was needful for me to write unto you, and exhort you that ye should earnestly contend for the faith which was once delivered unto the saints. For there are certain men crept in unawares, who were before of old ordained to this condemnation, ungodly men, turning the grace of our God into lasciviousness, and denying the only Lord God, and our Lord Jesus Christ. (Jude 1:3–4 KJV)

The religious hierarchy of the Jewish religious system also began to make up their own rules to suit themselves. They altered the way YHVH had told the Hebrews to worship. Now the new Gentile Christians in Rome were doing the same and altered how we are to worship. They made up new rules.

Before Constantine's edict, the Romans tried to kill all of the Gentile Christians in Rome. They also destroyed Jerusalem and the temple in AD 70. They also destroyed, as much as possible, all the Jewish writings that they could find. After Constantine's edict, Christian and pagan worship in Rome was merged into one new religion. Everything Jewish was removed from the new Christian religion. Now the new era of the Roman Catholic Church was officially launched.

THE ERA OF ROMAN CATHOLIC CONTROL OF THE CHRISTIAN RELIGION

The early Roman church was born out of both the religious rulers and political rulers of Rome. Over time they became one and the same. With their power they dictated the rules of Christian worship. The governance of the early Roman church was divided into four provinces and each province had a bishop over it. Some historians say that in AD 538 (this date is disputed by Catholics), Bishop Justinian declared that the bishop of the Roman province was the rector of the whole church. This put Bishop Justinian in charge of whole church, which included civil power. Also, Bishop Justinian reinforced the doctrine of heresy, which is adherence to a religious opinion contrary to the Roman Catholic Church. Anyone expressing a doctrine different than the opinion of the church could be declared a heretic and could be put to death. This ushered in a period of persecution of heretics by the Christian church that now is referred to as the Dark Ages. The church had the power to torture heretics to make them repent and then kill them. Over a period of about 1260 years, the Roman Catholic Church tortured and killed an estimated fifty to sixty million people they called "heretics" in Europe.[166]

The Holy Roman Empire Born

The rule of the papacy continued until AD 771 when an alliance was formed with a European leader. The leader was Charlemagne, who was the sole ruler of what is now Belgium, France, Luxemburg, the Netherlands, and part of western Germany. He was crowned Emperor of the Romans on December 25, AD 800. This was called the Holy Roman Empire. This empire of European countries and the papacy continued until about AD 1806. The rule of the papacy ended when Napoleon's general, Berthier, took the pope captive and put him in jail in Paris. This ended the rule of the papacy and resulted in the end of the Holy Roman Empire.

Millions of Christians Killed by the Rule of the Papacy

If you disagreed with the early Roman Catholic Church, they would torture you until you would say anything to stop the torture. Then they would kill you anyway. For years the Roman Catholic Church has tried to keep secret this period of time when millions of so-called heretics were tortured and put to death. Different types of torture were used depending on the victim's crimes and social status. Examples of torture used by the church were ripping out teeth, boiling a person alive, bone breaking, branding and burning, castration, cutting, dislocation of bones, roasting, genital mutilation, removing fingers and tongue removal. Examples of executions were tortures and execution by fire, beheading by the sword, quartering, the wheel, the fork dismembering and spiking. Torture was a common practice until finally it was outlawed in England in 1640.[167]

The Inquisition by the Roman Church resulted in the deaths of millions of people. This period of atrocities is best described by John Dowling in *The History of Romanism*:

> *From the birth of the Popery in 600, to the present time, it is estimated by careful and credible historians, that more than fifty millions of the human family, have been slaughtered for the crime of heresy by popish persecutors, and average of more than forty thousand religious murders for every year of the existence of Popery.*[168]

Later, Pope John Paul II partially apologized for the atrocities committed by the early Roman Catholic Church.

Councils by the Church
Also, during this period of time, several councils were held to establish the doctrine of the church so that every church had the same beliefs and doctrines.

Council of Ephesus in 431
This council was held to settle a dispute over the teaching of Nestorius, the patriarch of Constantinople. His doctrine emphasized the disunity between Christ's human and divine natures, which was in conflict with other church leaders, especially Cyril of Alexandria. Nestorius lost and the council condemned his teachings as heresy. Nestorius's followers disagreed, and they left the church to relocate to Persia. There they formed the Church of the East. Today, the Assyrian church of the East still rejects the findings of the council.[169]

Council of Chalcedon in 451
This council was held to overturn an earlier council and to reaffirm that Christ had two natures in one person. They reinforced the doctrine that Christ was the second person of the Trinity. This doctrine resulted in a schism within the church when several members rejected the doctrine and is now known as the Oriental Orthodoxy.

The Apostate Church Exposed
There were certain men who studied the Scriptures and began to see the Roman Catholic Church as an apostate church. Among these people were John Wycliffe, John Huss, and Girolamo Savonarola. John Huss was a Catholic priest, philosopher, and reformer. He was burned

at the stake for heresy against the Roman Catholic Church. Girolamo Savonarola preached against the immoral clergy of the church. The church declared him a heretic, and he was hung from a cross until dead and then a bonfire was set, burning him and the cross into ashes. John Wycliffe is the most well known of the early reformers.

John Wycliffe was an English scholar who taught at Oxford. He was an early dissident and reformer of the Roman Catholic Church during the fourteenth century. His followers were known as Lollards, who preached anticlerical and biblically centered reforms. He translated the Italian Vulgate into vernacular English in 1382, which is now known as the Wycliffe Bible. As Wycliffe's attacks on the supremacy of the pope increased, he identified the pope as the Antichrist of the Scriptures. Finally, the Chancellor of Oxford declared some of Wycliffe's declarations of beliefs to be heretical. Wycliffe was also blamed for the Peasants' Revolt in 1381. Although Wycliffe had a stroke, he was summoned before a synod at Oxford. Since he still commanded the favor of the court, he was not excommunicated.[170]

In December of 1384, he suffered another stroke and died. After his death, the great Hussite movement arose and spread throughout Middle Europe. Although John Wycliffe had escaped being deemed a heretic by the Roman Catholic Church during his lifetime, on May 4, 1415, the Council of Constance declared Wycliffe a stiff-necked heretic and under the ban of the church. In 1428, the Roman Catholic Church decreed all his books to be burned and his remains to be exhumed and burned. His ashes were cast into the River Swift.[171]

Martin Luther Starts the Protestant Movement

Although Martin Luther was not the first to challenge the teaching of the Roman Catholic Church, he was and is well known for his written challenges. As a professor of theology at Wittenberg College in Germany and as a Catholic priest, he wrote "The Ninety Five Theses" or "Disputation on the Power and Efficacy of Indulgences" in 1517. His disputation protested against clerical abuses, especially in regard to indulgences. An indulgence was issued by the Roman Catholic Church to any person for money or a gift to the church. An indulgence is a remission of temporal punishment due to sins that have already been forgiven. You could purchase an indulgence (forgiveness by the church) for a crime you had not committed yet.[172]

In Luther's thesis he strongly disputed the Catholic Church's claim that a person salvation could be purchased by money or good deeds. He rejected the idea of sacerdotalism where the priest acts as the mediator to God. Instead Luther says that Yeshua (Jesus) is the mediator between God and man.[173]

This thesis written by Martin Luther was the catalyst that started the Protestant revolution in the Catholic Church. He checked the thesis for heresy and then forwarded it to the pope in 1517. In 1518, Luther informed the Catholic Church that he did not consider the Catholic Church a part of the biblical Church. Luther was excommunicated from the Catholic Church on January 3, 1521, by Pope Leo X. Just prior to his formal excommunication from the Catholic Church, Martin Luther wrote the "Prelude to the Babylonian Captivity of the Church" and "On the Freedom of a Christian."[174]

In 1526, Martin Luther organized a new church known as the Lutheran Church today. However, he kept the Sunday worship invented by the early Roman Catholic Church. Luther's views were quite blunt. He also called the pope the Antichrist, and he also preached against Islam. He was totally against using violence to compel people to worship as instructed by the church. In his sermons, he often said the following: [175]

> *Do you know what the devil thinks when he sees men use violence to propagate the gospels? He sits with folded arms behind the fire of hell and says with malignant looks and frightful grins: "Ah, how wise these madmen are to play my game! Let them go on; I shall reap the benefit. I delight in it." But when he sees the word running and contending alone on the battle-field, the he shutters and shakes for fear.*[176]

Martin Luther remained defiant of the Roman Catholic Church, and he became the catalyst that started the Protestant movement out of the Roman Catholic Church.

Other Protestant Christian Denominations Formed

Just as Martin Luther protested the Roman Catholic Church and its teachings, so did others as new Protestant churches were formed in the sixteenth century and later. The following is a brief overview of the churches formed.

Anabaptist (Believers in Rebaptism): Direct descendants are the Amish, Brethren, Hutterites, and Mennonites. They rejected normal Christian practices implemented by the Roman Catholic Church, and they were declared heretics by the church. They were also persecuted by the Protestant churches.[177]

Anglicanism (English): They believe that direct descendants of the apostles are the chosen successors or ordained bishops responsible for the teachings of the church. They believe as the Roman Catholic Church but are separate from the Roman Catholic Church. Recently, there has been a move to rejoin the Catholic Church. There are over eighty million Anglicans worldwide. The Puritans and the Methodist Church came out of the Anglican Church.[178]

Calvinism (Reformed Faith): John Calvin (a French reformer) had a strong influence on the reformed views that included predestination and total depravity. Reformed Baptists came out of the reformed churches.[179]

Baptist Church—Protestant: Started as conflict on baptism. They don't believe in infant baptism and they believe in total immersion. The church was started in 1609 in Amsterdam by John Symth.[180]

Presbyterian Church—Protestant: Started in Scotland in 1707 and adheres to the Calvinist theological tradition.[181]

Methodist Church—Protestant: Started as a result of John Wesley's revival movement in the Anglican Church of England. John

Wesley's brother was a professor at Oxford. Because of their methodical preaching, the students at Oxford called them "Methodists." After Wesley's death in 1791, the Methodist church was formed.[182]

Adventist Church—Conservative Protestant: Started in the nineteenth century as the result of the Great Awakening revival the expecting of the "second advent of Christ" or the return of Yeshua (Jesus). The largest segment of the church is the Seventh-Day Adventist Church that formed in the early 1840s.[183]

Present-Day Christian Churches

Today, there are many different Christian churches in the world. Each one has its own creed and basis for worship. The majority follow the old Roman Catholic Church and worship on Sunday. There are others who worship on the Sabbath. Even the Jews have broken into two distinct groups, one being believers in Yeshua as the Messiah and the other that don't believe the Messiah has come yet.

PARTIAL LIST OF GENTILE CHURCHES (See *Wikipedia* for a complete list):

Pentecostal (Assembly of God)
Southern Baptist
Anglican and Episcopal
Roman Catholic
Church of God
Jehovah's Witnesses
Lutheran
Methodist
Nazarene
Presbyterian
Seventh Day Adventists
United Church of Christ

Did the Scriptures say this would happen?
Yes, it did!

Now there seems to be a church for every belief and lifestyle. My experience is that people go to a church because of where their parents went to church. If your parents were Catholic, it is most likely you will attend a Catholic church without questioning anything about church.

Each church has its own doctrine or creed. Each one will say that theirs is the true worship of God. Upon examination of the churches, their doctrines will fall into two distinct categories. Before the cross, there was Judaism, the Torah, and the Sabbath. After the cross, there is Christianity, grace, and Sunday-keeping. This major difference in basic doctrine has created much debate. Biblical scholars on both sides put forth their beliefs regarding which day we should worship on. Recently, with the rise of the Internet, these debates are easily available for review.

Different Church Views of Yeshua

Today, Christians do not agree about the nature of the founder (Yeshua or Jesus) of their religion. First, they cannot agree on the name. Messianic Jews will call Him Yeshua. Catholics and Protestants will call Him Jesus. Christians who profess they are followers of Jesus have very strong disagreements about Jesus Himself. They each seem to interpret His messages in the Scriptures differently and have adopted different theologies. As a result we have thousands of Christian denominations around the world.

Examples of these different views of Yeshua are as follows:

Roman Catholic Church

The Roman Catholic Church is built around a belief that the pope is the intercessor between man and Jesus. It is the oldest Gentile church, and they believe that Jesus bestowed divine power on their church. From this divine power they believe that they speak for Jesus. Priests are called "father" in contradiction to Yeshua's instructions to only call the Father in heaven your Father.

Baptists

The Baptists name themselves after Jesus's practice of baptizing converts, and they traditionally stress conformity to certain behavioral rules: no drinking, no card playing, no dancing. Jesus to them is a moral teacher.

Pentecostals

Pentecostals call themselves after Jesus's promise of the gift of the Holy Spirit, which was fulfilled on the Feast of Pentecost. They are known for their great desire to express the gifts of the Spirit. Their Jesus is a miracle worker.

Seventh-Day Adventists

The Seventh-Day Adventists take their name from the seventh-day Sabbath that Jesus clearly kept. They promote Jesus as the soon-coming rest of God.

Methodists

The Methodists are so-called because John Wesley emphasized a structured, methodical approach to Bible study. They highlight Jesus's many commandments for the individual to be actively involved in his own salvation and Christian growth. They believe that Jesus wants them to exercise their free will to come to Christ.

The Reformed Churches

The Reformed churches are descendants of the teachings of John Calvin, and they underscore the necessity of grace through faith in Jesus. They reject the doctrine of works from the early Roman Catholic Church. They see Jesus as a gracious redeemer.

Messianic Judaism

Messianic Jews believe that Yeshua was the promised Messiah that was prophesied in the Hebrew Bible or Old Testament. They believe He came to teach the Torah, which is the instructions from YHVH.

These different concepts of Yeshua (Jesus) as the central figure determine what one believes and the religion he follows.

The Future of the Church

The Scriptures tell us there will be a one-world religion in our future. That will mean that the Roman Catholic Church and the Protestant churches will be united somehow. It also means Islam and the other religions also will be united with the Christian churches. Since Christianity and Islam are the world's largest religions, some have suggested that this one world-religion will be a confederation between Christianity and Islam. They point to the clay mingled with iron in the statue of Nebuchadnezzar in the book of Daniel.

How these religions unite and what happens to the other religions is not clear; however, it is clear that everyone will be forced by the false prophet to worship the Antichrist. Compliance with this new religion will be mandatory. You will not be able to buy or sell if you don't comply. This will be a life or death choice.

CHAPTER 14

The Sabbath Day Changed?

There is much controversy about the Sabbath in today's Christian churches. The majority of Christian churches worship on Sunday. However, there are millions of Christians who worship on the biblical Sabbath, which is from Friday night until Saturday night. We know that the fourth commandment says to "remember the Sabbath day." So let's look at the Scriptures and church history to see if we can better understand what day we should keep holy.

What did YHVH (God) say about the Sabbath?

> *Remember **the** Sabbath day, to keep it holy. Six days shalt thou labor, and do all thy work: But **the** seventh day is **the** Sabbath of the Lord thy God: in it thou shalt not do any work, thou, nor thy son, nor thy daughter, thy man servant, nor thy maid servant, nor thy cattle, nor thy stranger that is within thy gates. For in six days the Lord made heaven and earth, the sea, and all that In them is, and rested **the** seventh day: wherefore the Lord blessed **the** sabbath day, and hallowed it.* (Exodus 20:8–11 kjv, emphasis added)

What Day is the Sabbath?

1. When did YHVH establish the Sabbath?

> *Thus the heavens and earth were finished, and all the host of them… And God **blessed the seventh day**, and **sanctified it**: because that*

in it he had rested from all his work, which God created and made. (Genesis 2:1–3 KJV, emphasis added)

2. What day of the week is the Sabbath?

*And on **the seventh day** God ended his work which he had made; and he rested on **the seventh day** from all his work which he had made. And God blessed **the seventh day** and sanctified it.* (Genesis 2:2–3 KJV, emphasis added).

Notice YHVH said **the day**. This means a specific day. If I said bring me **a hat**, then any hat would do. If I said bring me **the hat,** you know I am talking about a specific hat. So YHVH has proclaimed a specific day of the week as Sabbath to Him.[184]

3. Has the calendar changed since the time of Adam and Eve?
Yes. In order to keep up with the solar cycle, the Julian calendar was changed to the Gregorian calendar in October 1582, but the weekly seven-day cycle did not change. The whole world still observes a seven-day cycle with the Sabbath on the seventh day. It has not changed from the beginning of time on this earth.

4. Which day of the week is the Sabbath according to the dictionary and encyclopedias?
Look at any dictionary and it will say that the seventh day (Saturday) is the Sabbath.

5. When does the Sabbath day start and end?
According to the Scriptures, each day starts at sundown and ends at sundown (KJV Genesis 1:5, 8, 13, 19, 23, 31). Accordingly, the Sabbath starts at sundown on Friday and ends at sundown on Saturday.

Did the Jews observe the beginnings of days at sunset in Israel? **YES!** Did they observe the Sabbath at sunset? **YES!** Do the Jews observe this today? **YES!** Just ask any Jew and he will tell you that it has never changed since the beginning.

6. Did the Jews ever lose track of the Sabbath?
When Moses was leading the Jews through the wilderness, manna fell from heaven in order to feed them. On the Day of Preparation, twice as much manna fell so that they would have enough for the Sabbath since YHVH did not provide manna on the Sabbath (Exodus 16:25). Since this happened as they were on the way to Mount Sinai, they must have been observing the Sabbath before they received the Ten Commandments from YHVH. Obviously, they had been observing the Sabbath before they were in bondage in Egypt.

6. Did Yeshua (Jesus) and the apostles keep the seventh-day Sabbath?
Absolutely! There are fifty-six verses in the New Testament that say Yeshua and the apostles worshiped on the Sabbath. One of these verses is "And he came to Nazareth, where he had been brought up, and, **as his custom was, he went into the synagogue on the sabbath day, and he stood up for to read**" (Luke 4:16 KJV, emphasis added).

7. Was the Sabbath made just for the Jews?
Mark 2:27 (KJV) says, "And he [Yeshua] said unto them, the Sabbath was made for man, and not man for the Sabbath." **The Sabbath was made for man (all mankind), not only for the Jews**.

Why is it Important to Keep the Sabbath?

1. Why is this important?
In Exodus 20:8–11, God said, "**Remember** the sabbath day, to keep it holy." The Lord blessed the Sabbath day and hallowed it.

YHVH demonstrated the importance of the Sabbath by making it one of the Ten Commandments. It is the only commandment that starts with the word **"Remember."** Did YHVH think we would forget?

2. Is worshipping on the Sabbath a sign between YHVH and man?

> *Wherefore the children of Israel shall keep the Sabbath, to observe the Sabbath throughout their generations, for a perpetual covenant. It is a **sign** between me and the children of Israel forever.* (Exodus 31:16–17 KJV, emphasis added)

Yes! God gave the Sabbath as a **sign** between Him and mankind. Along with it came a stern warning of death if anyone defiles the Sabbath.

In the book of Numbers, it says that a man was gathering sticks on the Sabbath. Moses and Aaron asked the Lord how they should handle the offense against the Sabbath commandment. "And the Lord said unto Moses, The man shall be surely put to death: all the congregation shall stone him with stones without [outside] the camp" (Numbers 15:32–36 KJV).

4. Did YHVH make the Sabbath rest only for the Jews?
"And he said unto them, the Sabbath was made for **man**, and not man for the Sabbath" (Mark 2:27 KJV, emphasis added).

5. Did Yeshua keep the Ten Commandments?
"If ye keep my commandments, ye shall abide in my love, even as I have kept my Father's commandments, and abide in his laws" (John 15:10 KJV).

Also, see 1 Peter 2:21.

6. I have heard that the Ten Commandments are not binding for New Testament Christians. Yeshua (Jesus) said the following about the commandments:

"If thou will enter into life, keep the commandments" (Matthew 19:17 KJV).

"If you love me, keep my commandments" (John 14:15 KJV).

7. Breaking God's laws is a sin. That includes the fourth commandment. Are we saved by keeping the Ten Commandments? No!

> *For by **grace** are ye saved through **faith**; and that not of yourselves; it is the gift of God; **Not of works**, lest any man should boast.* (Ephesians 2: 8—9 KJV, emphasis added)

7. So why do we need to keep the Ten Commandments? **Love.** **"This is the love of God, that we keep his commandments"** (1 John 5:3 KJV).

8. Did Yeshua expect His disciples in the future to be keeping the Sabbath?
Yes. When the disciples asked Him about His future return to the earth, Yeshua said there would be great tribulation on the earth and said to flee to the mountains when it happened. "But pray that your flight not be in the winter or on the **Sabbath day**." Why not on the Sabbath day? The answer is that in modern-day Israel, all the public transportation is shut down on the Sabbath. There is no way you could evacuate the people out of the cities without public transportation.

9. Did the early Gentile Christians keep the Sabbath?
Absolutely! The disciples of Yeshua taught the Gentiles to worship on the Sabbath.

> *And when the Jews were gone out of the synagogue, the Gentiles besought that these words might be preached to them the next Sabbath. Now when the congregation was broken up, many of the Jews and religious proselytes followed Paul and Barnabas: who, speaking to them, persuaded them to continue in the grace of God.* (Acts 13:42–43 KJV)
>
> *But passing through from Perge, they came to Antioch in Pisidia, and went into the congregation on the Sabbath day and sat down.* (Acts 13:14 ISR)

So Why do the Roman Catholic Church and Most Protestant Churches all Worship on Sunday?

As we learned in an earlier chapter, Constantine issued the edict for worship on Sunday in AD 321. In AD 325, Constantine banned any public meetings for Christians wanting the worship on the Sabbath, and Sabbath-keeping Christians were evicted from their homes. The edict made it illegal to worship on the Sabbath in anyone's home and illegal to worship on any day but Sunday. The church backed by the Roman government would only allow Sunday worship, period. That is why most of the Protestant churches that came out of the Roman Catholic Church worship on Sunday. It was by force and the threat of death.[185]

Today in America we have the advantage of knowing church history and freedom of religion guaranteed by the Constitution. However, the majority of Christians still worship on Sunday. So what is the argument made by today's churches for Sunday worship?

Let's examine what the Christians of today say about Sunday worship.

The Lord's Day

Most Protestant Christians claim to worship on Sunday because they say it is the Lord's Day and that is the day of the resurrection of Yeshua (Jesus).

If you read the Westminster Confession of Religious Worship and the Sabbath-day, it says the following:

> *As it is of the law of nature, that, in general, a due proportion of time be set apart for the worship of God; so, in his Word, by a positive, moral, and perpetual commandment, binding all men in all ages, he hath particularly* **appointed one day in seven for a Sabbath**, *to be kept holy unto him: which, from the beginning of the world to the resurrection of Christ, was* **the last day of the week;** *and, from the* **resurrection of Christ, was changed into the first day** *of the*

week, which in Scripture is called the Lord's day, and is to be continued to the end of the world as the Christian Sabbath.[186]

When this was written, the church had long ago removed as much as possible everything Jewish (including the Creator's calendar) from the Scriptures and their worship traditions. Since all the Protestant churches that came out of the Roman Catholic Church claimed the Yeshua's resurrection was on Sunday, it is natural for them to follow suit.

WHAT DO THE SCRIPTURES SAY ABOUT THE LORD'S DAY?
1. What day is the Lord's Day according to the Bible?
"I was in the Spirit on the Lord's day…" (Revelation 1:10 KJV). When John was in prison at Patmos, he refused to work on the Sabbath. It was during the Sabbath that John received his visions from the Lord. John wrote the book of Revelation from his visions.

2. What day did Yeshua say was the Lord's Day?
"For the Son of man is Lord even on the sabbath day" (Matthew 12:8 KJV).

The Jews had always said the Sabbath was the Lord's Day, and they followed His commandment to worship and rest on that day. Jesus said He was Lord even on that day.

To me, this means that the Sabbath is the Lord's Day!

3. What day is blessed and hallowed by YHVH?

> *For in six days the* LORD *made heaven and earth, the sea, and all that in them is, and rested the seventh day: wherefore the* LORD ***blessed the Sabbath day****, and hallowed it.* (Exodus 20:11 KJV, emphasis added)

4. Did YHVH ever say He would change the day? **No.**

> *For I am the LORD, I change not; therefore ye sons of Jacob are not consumed.* (Malachi 3:6 KJV)

5. Did YHVH promise to send a sign on His commandments?
The fourth commandment is to remember the Sabbath day.

> *And the temple of God was opened in heaven, and there was seen in his temple the **ark of his testament**: and there were lightnings, and voices, and thunderings, and an earthquake, and great hail.* (Revelation 11:19 KJV, emphasis added)

Sunday Worship

Now that we have examined the Scriptures about worshipping on the Sabbath, let's look at the basis for Sunday worship. Who started Sunday worship and why?

The Roman Catholic Church takes credit for the change from the biblical Sabbath to Sunday worship!

Since the Roman Catholic Church takes credit for the change to Sunday worship, let's look at what the Catholic Church says about this. We can find this answer in Rev. Peter Geiermann's work *The Catholic Catechism of Catholic Doctrine*.[187]

> Q. *Which day is the Sabbath day?*
> A. Saturday is the Sabbath day.
>
> Q. *Why do we observe Sunday instead of Saturday?*
> A. We observe Sunday instead of Saturday because the **Catholic Church transferred the solemnity of from Saturday to Sunday.**

Q. Why did the Catholic Church substitute Sunday for Saturday?
A. the Church substituted Sunday for Saturday, because Christ rose from the dead on a Sunday, and the Holy Ghost descended upon the Apostles on a Sunday.

Q. By what authority did the Church substitute Sunday for Saturday?
A. The early Church substituted Sunday for Saturday by the plenitude of the **divine power which Jesus Christ bestowed upon her** [the Roman Catholic Church].

In the above, the Roman Catholic Church states that they (the early leaders of the church) changed the day of rest and worship from the Sabbath to Sunday because they claim Yeshua rose on a Sunday. However, the Scriptures say that was not the day He rose.

Also, there is much evidence that the early church in America worshiped on the Sabbath (Saturday). A religious liberty attorney while researching the Notre Dame library discovered a book that recognizes the seventh-day Sabbath. The book is called *The Seventh Day Sabbath Sought Out* (1657) by Thomas Tillman, Minister of the Gospel. It is the oldest book ever found outside the Bible recognizing the seventh-day Sabbath. An excerpt is as follows:

> *The Seventh-day Sabbath Sought out and Celebrated, or, the saints last design upon the man of sin, with their advance of God's first institution to its primitive perfection, being a clear discovery of that black character in the head of the little Horn, Dan. 7:25—the Change of TIMES AND LAWS—with the Christians' glorious Conquest over the mark of the Beast, and the recovery of the long-slighted Seventh day, to its ancient glory.*[188]

The early Catholic Church in America also agreed that correct day of worship was the seventh-day Sabbath. The following was written in the Saint Catherine Catholic Church on May 21, 1995, as follows:

Perhaps the boldest thing, the most revolutionary change the Church ever did, happened in the first century. The holy day, the Sabbath, was changed from Saturday to Sunday. "The Day of the Lord" (dies Dominica) was chosen, not from any directions noted in the Scriptures, but from the Church's sense of its own power. The day of resurrection, the day of Pentecost, fifty days later, came on the first day of the week. So this would be the new Sabbath. People who think that the Scriptures should be the sole authority, should logically become [Seventh] Day Adventists, and keep the Saturday holy.[189]

What else does the Catholic Church say about how it changed?

According to Dr. Samuele Bacchiocchi, the foundation for the change from the Sabbath to Sunday by the bishops of Rome started during the reign of the Roman Emperor Hadrian (AD 117–138) as the result of three major factors:

(1) **Anti-Judaism** by the Roman Christians, which influenced the abandonment of the Sabbath.

(2) **Pagan Sun Worship** by the majority of Romans, which influenced the adoption of the day of the Sun.

(3) **Measures employed by the bishops of Rome,** which promoted the abandonment of the Sabbath and the adoption of Sunday.

How did they do it?

(1) Emperor Hadrian outlawed the Jewish religion and the observance of the Sabbath. In AD 135, he captured Jerusalem and outlawed the Jewish religion.

(2) Pope Innocent I (AD 402–417) prohibited the celebration of the Lord's Supper and assembly on the Sabbath.

(3) Bishop Victor championed the Easter Sunday custom and excommunicated the Asian Christians for not accepting Easter Sunday.
(4) Bishop Sylvester made the Sabbath a day of fasting to kill the joy of the Sabbath.
(5) Pope Sixtest introduced Easter Sunday.

Emperor Constantine has been given credit for formalizing and unifying the Roman Catholic Church in the establishment of Sunday as the official day of worship in the following edicts:

Constantine wrote to Elpidius the following:

All judges, city-folk and craftsmen shall rest on the venerable day of the Sun. But countrymen may without impediment attend to agriculture, because it often happens that this is the most appropriate day for sowing grain or planting vines, so that the opportunity afforded by divine providence may not be lost, for the right season is of short duration. (Justiniauus Codex III, XI, III, March 7, AD 321)

Dr. Samuele Bacchiocchi received his doctorate from the Pontifical Georgian University in Rome. Dr. Bacchiocchi spent five years researching church history to determine how the Sabbath was changed to Sunday by the Roman Catholic Church. **He was awarded a gold medal by Pope Paul VI for attaining the academic distinction of *summa cum laude* for his class work and dissertation "From Sabbath to Sunday."**

To get a PhD from the prestigious Gregorian University in Rome on such a subject and for the pope to give Dr. Bacchiocchi a gold metal illustrates that the Vatican totally agrees with the change of the day of worship instituted by the Roman Catholic Church. However, the debate between John Lewis and Dr. Bacchiocchi indicates that there is strong resistance from worshipping on the Sabbath.[190]

OK, KNOWING THIS, WHY DO CHRISTIANS MAINTAIN THEIR BELIEF IN SUNDAY WORSHIP?

Most Protestant churches have a creed requiring them to hold services on Sunday. If the local pastor tried to change to Sabbath worship, he would be thrown out of the church. To avoid this argument, the pastors now will say that Sunday is now the Sabbath.

If you ask a typical Christian why they worship on Sunday, most will say that is the day Jesus rose from the grave, thereby making it the new Sabbath under the new covenant this is reinforced by the pastors of their church. Over a period of time this becomes the tradition—worshipping on Sunday. If someone asks the pastors why they set apart worship on Sunday, the pastor will usually reply with "Sunday is the day Jesus rose from the grave." However, some pastors have realized that Sunday is not the correct day and have changed to the Sabbath worship only to be thrown out of their church by the leadership of that denomination.

Little do Christians realize that they are just following what Constantine made into law. They also will say you can pray on any day, which no one disagrees with; however, the Sabbath was meant to be a holy (set apart) day. The Sabbath has always been the seventh day of the week starting at sundown Friday and ending at sundown on Saturday. If Jesus and His apostles kept the Sabbath day, then you ought to at least consider doing the same.

Today we have the benefit of church history, computers, and the science of astronomy that allow us to confirm biblical events as witness to the truth. Also, we have the words of Yeshua (Jesus) who prophesied how long He would be in the grave. He said He would be in the **grave three days and three nights, and yet we celebrate His death on Friday and His resurrection on Sunday morning. How can any adult buy into this when any first grader will tell you that you can't get three days and three nights between Friday and Sunday?**

When Christians begin to realize that the Sabbath is not Sunday, the pastors will answer that the Ten Commandments, which include the Sabbath commandment, were nailed to the cross. The Scriptures tell us that when Jesus died, He took on all our iniquities. *Iniquities* means not following the Torah, of which the Ten Commandments is part (Daniel 9:27).

So how do we solve this? Yeshua (Jesus) followed the commandments, and He observed the Sabbath. When He died He took the curse of the Law on Himself for you. He spent three days in the grave, and He was resurrected. By this act, He defeated Satan and death. His sacrifice was to take the curse of the law from you and remove God's wrath for breaking His commandments.

Without His sacrifice, do you think you would be perfect (without sin) and go to heaven? Yeshua suffered for you. Isaiah 53 gives a good portrait of what Yeshua did for you. Do you love Him for that?

If you love Him, then you should want to keep His commandments. Yeshua said, "If you love me keep my commandments." God wrote, "Remember the Sabbath day."

Sunday never appears in the Scriptures. Why? It is a man-made commandment of men.

> *But in vain they do worship me, teaching for doctrines the commandments of men.* (Matthew 15:9 KJV)

The Sabbath is the Seal of YHVH (God)

Have you ever looked at a seal? A seal will have the person's name and title that is sealing the document. It also will have the territory where the power of the seal applies and what is sealed.

> *But the **seventh day is the Sabbath [seal]** of the* Lord ***thy God** [title] in it thou shalt not do any work, thou, nor thy son, nor thy daughter, thy manservant, nor thy maidservant, nor thy cattle, nor thy stranger that is within thy gates: For in six days the* Lord *made **heaven and earth, the sea, and all that in them is [territory]**,*

and rested the seventh day: wherefore the Lord *blessed the Sabbath day, and hallowed it.*

Will We Worship YHVH in Heaven on the Sabbath Day?

For as the **new heavens and the new earth**, *which I will make, shall remain before me, saith the* Lord, *so shall your seed and your name remain. And it shall come to pass, that from one new moon to another, and* **from one Sabbath to another**, *shall all flesh come to worship before me, saith the* Lord. (Isaiah 66:22–23 kjv, emphasis added)

The new heavens and earth occurs after Yeshua's return to the earth, and it states that all shall keep the Sabbath then.

Why would YHVH give the seventh-day Sabbath to mankind at creation (Genesis 2:1–3) then reintroduce it to Israel before Sinai (since they lost it for a while in captivity in Egypt; see Exodus 16:4, 23, 27–29), codify it at Sinai (Exodus 20), then have Yeshua and His disciples and their followers observe it, and then change it to Sunday, and *then* change it back to the Sabbath in Yeshua's kingdom on this earth? This makes no sense.

The answer is Yeshua (Jesus) never changed it. It was changed by the early Roman church to suit her own purposes!

CHAPTER 15

The Apostate Church

IN THE BOOK OF ENOCH, YHVH declared to Enoch the future of man and called it the prophecy of weeks. Enoch wrote what YHVH had shown him and called it the prophecy of weeks. Major events were recorded in each week, which represents a certain period of time. The prophecy has ten weeks or periods of time. The seventh week is called the apostate generation.

> *During this period an apostate generation shall arise and many shall be its deeds. And all the deeds are apostate.*

Interpretation: *Apostate* means the abandonment or renunciation of religion. Not only does this prophecy refer to atheism and worship of other gods, but it is referring to the faith once given to the Hebrews by YHVH that has been abandoned by the people of this generation. It could also mean that the church is itself apostate. Let's look at the different religions that have sprung up recently.

NEW RELIGIONS THAT DO NOT FOLLOW THE TEACHINGS OF YESHUA (JESUS) IN THE SCRIPTURES
SCIENTOLOGY

Scientology is a body of beliefs and related practices created by science fiction and fantasy author Ron Hubbard in 1954. Scientology teaches that people are immortal beings who have forgotten their true nature.

They also teach that you should relive past traumatic experiences so as to free yourself from their limiting effects.

Today there are over eight million followers of scientology in six thousand churches located in 159 countries. Members hold that man is basically good and his spiritual salvation depends on himself, his relationship with his fellows, and his attainment of brotherhood with the universe.

New Age Movement

The New Age Movement started in 1875 with the theosophical teachings of Helena Petrovna Blavatsky. In 1922, Alice Ann Bailey founded the Lucifer Publishing Company, which printed and distributed the New Age teachings. The term *New Age* refers to the coming astrological Age of Aquarius. This is a period of a one-world government and end to all wars, disease, hunger, pollution, poverty, and discrimination by gender, race, or religion. The New Age spirituality also makes references mythological representations of the Earth, moon, and outer space.

Basically, they reject and promote the abolishment of Christianity, Judaism, and Islam. They don't believe that the way to heaven is through Yeshua (Jesus) but claim there are many ways to heaven. One of the biggest supporters is Oprah Winfrey. She has even started her own church called "O." Another prominent member is actress Shirley MacLaine.

Who are they?

There are several publications that list the groups that have the same common beliefs. The *Spiritual Community Guide* and the *New Age Magazine* list many New Age groups. Some of the groups listed and reported as being New Agers are Amnesty International, Greenpeace, The Sierra Club, Zero Population, and many secular and religious organizations.

Apostate Religious Beliefs

The New Age belief is there are many ways to heaven. In Oprah Winfrey's church, they reject any prohibitions against eating certain foods listed in the Scriptures, and premarital sex is acceptable. She has even designated new holidays such as her spring holiday. The tradition of confession has been adopted by her church, and Oprah officiates for the church. To sum it up, the Scriptures' teachings of being born again by accepting Jesus is not followed by the New Agers.

What about the Mainstream Christian Churches?

What do the Scriptures say about being saved?

The Scriptures are very clear on this subject.

> *Jesus answered and said unto him, Verily, verily, I say unto thee, except a man be born again, he cannot see the kingdom of God.* (John 3:3 KJV)
>
> *Marvel not that I said unto thee, ye must be born again.* (John 3:7 KJV)
>
> *Being born again, not of corruptible seed, but of incorruptible, by the word of God, which liveth and abideth for ever.* (1 Peter 1:23 KJV)

The teaching of Yeshua (Jesus) is very clear that you must be born again. However, many churches now don't even mention it. The only way to heaven is by accepting Yeshua as your savior, being born again, and keeping His commandments.

The seven churches of Revelation give us another perspective of the churches today.

In the book of Isaiah, Isaiah sees a vision of seven churches.

> *And in that day seven women [churches] shall take hold of one man, saying, we will eat our own bread, and wear our own apparel: only*

let us be called by thy name, to take away our reproach. (Isaiah 4:1 KJV)

In Isaiah's vision, he is saying that each of these seven churches will claim the right of the correct worship of Yeshua (Jesus). Could these seven churches be the same as the seven churches of the book of Revelation?

The story of the seven churches in John's vision is about seven churches that were located in Asia Minor, or what is Turkey today. The ruins of these churches are tourist attractions today. In the book of Revelation, each one of these churches was given a command to repent or a blessing. Five of these churches are rebuked and two were OK. For the ones who overcome, a blessing is given. However, there is more to this story than what is readily apparent. These churches could also represent different church ages from the first church till today's church. Only YHVH could have done this!

The following is a partial commentary by Perry Stone of Manna Fest Ministries on the seven churches of Revelation.

Ephesus:	Meaning of name: "Desirable." (Revelation 2:1–7)
	Known as the church that left their first love.
	Blessing if they overcome: Eat of the tree of life. (Genesis 2:9 & Revelation 2:7)
Smyrna:	Meaning of name: "Myrrh" (Revelation 2:8–11)
	Known for enduring tribulation and poverty.
	Blessing: Won't be hurt by the second death. (Genesis 3:17–23 & Revelation 2:11)
Pergamos:	Meaning of name: "Height or elevation" (Revelation 2:12–17)
	Known for holding to false doctrines.
	Blessing: Eat from the hidden manna. (Exodus 16:15 & Revelation 2:17)
Thyatira:	Meaning of name: "Continued sacrifice" (Revelation 2:18–29)
	Known for being seduced by a woman.

Sardis:
: Blessing: Given power over the nations. (Joshua 11:17–23 & Revelation 2:26)
: Meaning of name: "Remnant" (Revelation 3:1–6)
Known for some who would die spiritually.
Blessing: Clothed in white raiment. (Matthew 27:35–50 & Revelation 3:5)

Philadelphia: Meaning of name: "Brotherly love" (Revelation 3:7–13)
Known for giving an open door and protection.
Blessing: Will be a pillar in the temple. (1 Corinthians 15:24 & Revelation 3:17)

Laodicea: Meaning of name: "Rights or rule of the people" (Revelation 3:14–22)
Known for being lukewarm and needed to repent.
Blessing: They will sit with Him on the throne. (Revelation 20:6 & Revelation 3:21)

There are the seven church ages as follows:

Ephesus: **The Apostolic Church: AD 30–100**
Smyrna: **The Persecuted Church: AD 100–312**
Christians and Jews persecuted until Constantine legalizes Christianity.
Pergamos: **The Roman Church: AD 313–600**
In this period, there is a lot of doctorial confusion and man's traditions result in changes to the original faith.
Thyatira: **The Dark Ages: AD 600—1517**
Sardis: **The Reformation: AD 1517–1700**
Philadelphia: **The Missionary Church: AD 1648AD–2000**
Laodicea: **The Lukewarm Church: Current Situation**

From this, it appears that these churches represent the seven biblical church ages from the first church age to the present church age. It also appears that we are in the Laodicea church age.

How can we know if we are in the Laodicea church age?
The Philadelphia church was known for its missionary work. Most of the income of these churches during this period was used to sponsor missionaries to countries that had an open door for them. Today, money for missionaries is down about 50 to 60 percent. Only about 2 percent of today's church income is used for sponsoring missionaries. About 85 percent of church income today is used for the local churches to look after their own members. Based on these statistics, most believe that we have shifted from the Philadelphia church age to the Laodicea church age.

What did YHVH say about people in this church age?

> *Because thou sayest, I am rich, and increased with goods, and have need of nothing; and knowest not that thou art wretched, and miserable, and poor, and blind, and naked.* (Revelation 3:17 KJV)

Because we are blessed with lots of stuff, we have lost sight of true worship.

What else did YHVH say about this church?

> *I know thy works, that thou art neither cold nor hot: I would thou wert cold or hot. So then because thou art lukewarm, and neither cold nor hot, I will spue thee out of my mouth.* (Revelation 3:15–16 KJV)

The Scriptures say we should be rich in faith, not material things.

> *Hearken, my beloved brethren, Hath not God chosen the poor of this world* **rich in faith,** *and heirs of the kingdom which he hath promised to them that love him?* (James 2:5 KJV, emphasis added)

Did Yeshua Warn us about the Apostate Church?

Yes. Yeshua warned us about the apostate church.

> *Now the Spirit speaketh expressly, that in the **latter times some shall depart from the faith, giving heed to seducing spirits, and doctrines of devils;** Speaking lies in hypocrisy; having their conscience seared with a hot iron; Forbidding to marry, and commanding to abstain from meats, which God hath created to be received with thanksgiving of them which believe and know the truth. For every creature of God is good, and nothing to be refused, if it be received with thanksgiving: For it is sanctified by the word of God and prayer.* (1 Timothy 4:1–5 KJV, emphasis added)

Yeshua prophesied that the church would depart from the faith once given to the saints. Yeshua also described the people in the last days.

Yeshua also warned us about false prophets in the church who will lead us astray.

> *Beware of false prophets, which come to you in sheep's clothing, but inwardly they are ravening wolves.* (Matthew 7:15 KJV)
>
> *Behold, I send you forth as sheep in the midst of wolves: be ye therefore wise as serpents, and harmless as doves.* (Matthew 10:16 KJV)
>
> *Go your ways: behold, I send you forth as lambs among wolves.* (Luke 10:3 KJV)
>
> *For I know this, that after my departing shall grievous wolves enter in among you, not sparing the flock.* (Acts 20:29 KJV)

These wolves are disguised followers of Satan who have infiltrated the church. Their goal is to lead you astray. So you can see why we have so many different churches and modern beliefs that are not biblical. Yeshua is warning you, so take heed.

Yeshua also said the society would look like this in the last days or end of the age before the tribulation.

*This know also, that in the **last days** perilous times shall come. For men shall be lovers of their own selves, covetous, boasters, proud, blasphemers, disobedient to parents, unthankful, unholy, Without natural affection, trucebreakers, false accusers, incontinent, fierce, despisers of those that are good, Traitors, heady, high-minded, lovers of pleasures more than lovers of God.* (2 Timothy 3:1–4 KJV, emphasis added)

Are there other Warnings in the Scriptures?

Yes, we are warned to turn back to the original faith or face destruction.

Beloved, when I gave all diligence to write unto you of the common salvation, it was needful for me to write unto you, and exhort you that ye should earnestly contend for the faith which was once delivered unto the saints. For there are certain men crept in unawares, who were before of old ordained to this condemnation, ungodly men, turning the grace of our God into lasciviousness, and denying the only Lord God, and our Lord Jesus Christ. I will therefore put you in remembrance, though ye once knew this, how that the Lord, having saved the people out of the land of Egypt, afterward destroyed them that believed not. (Jude 1:3–5 KJV)

What does your Church Teach Compared to the Scriptures?

Is your church following the standards set by the Scriptures? Let's examine in detail the modern church and let's see how they compare. There are many denominations and sects that make up Christianity, a religion that has over two billion adherents whose members exist in diverse countries and cultures. They all claim the teachings of Jesus as their system of beliefs and practices.

So we will use the Scriptures as our standard to see how the churches compare to the standard.

First Comparison—Church Traditions

First let's look at the traditions of the nominal Christian in the modern church. Although the details vary, December 25 is a time when Christmas trees are decorated with bright ornaments and lights. Presents are exchanged, and there is a call to remember the birth of Jesus. Then three to four months later on the first Sunday after the vernal equinox, Easter is celebrated. The homes are decorated with brightly covered eggs and bunny rabbits.

Now it is a well-known fact that pagan influences were brought into the church decades ago. Most Christians and church leaders know that, but it does not matter to them. They will even argue that Jesus freed us to worship as we please. They say these traditions are good and it is a wonderful time and experience. What can be wrong with it?

Now let's compare these traditions to the standard set by the Scriptures.

> *Take heed to yourself that you are not ensnared to follow them, after they are destroyed from before you, and that you do not inquire after their gods, saying, how did these nations serve their gods? I also will do likewise. You shall not worship the LORD your God in that way; for every abomination to the LORD which He hates they have done to their gods; for they burn even their sons and daughters in the fire to their gods.* (Deuteronomy 12:30–31 KJV)

Pagan sun-god worship has been around since the beginning, and children were regularly sacrificed to the sun gods. YHVH is warning us not to have any remnant of pagan worship in the worship of Him.

> *Hear the word which the LORD speaks to you, O house of Israel. Thus says the LORD: Do not learn the way of the Gentiles; do not be dismayed at the signs of heaven, for the Gentiles are dismayed at them. For the **customs of the peoples are futile**; for one cuts a tree from the forest, the work of the hands of the workman, with the ax. They decorate it*

with silver and gold; they fasten it with nails and hammers So that it will not topple. (Jeremiah 10:1–4 KJV, emphasis added)

So what did Yeshua (Jesus) say about all of this?

He answered and said to them, well did Isaiah prophesy of you hypocrites, as it is written: This people honor me with their lips, but their heart is far from me. ***And in vain they worship me teaching as doctrines the commandments of men.*** *He said to them,* ***all too well you reject the commandment of God, that you may keep your tradition.*** (Mark 7:6–9 KJV, emphasis added)

This is a stern warning from Yeshua (Jesus) not to follow the traditions or commandments of men; instead, you should be following the commandments of God.

Second Comparison—Christianity Is Big Business

Christian books and music fill the shelves of bookstores. Musical concerts and television marathon fundraisers are at an all-time high. Television preachers all market their teachings on DVDs, and it has generated a lot of money. So is this OK with the standard set in the Scriptures? Let's look at some verses and see what the standard says about profiting or making financial gain from these activities.

Because people have been ruined by constant irritation of the mind and have destroyed the truth for themselves, thinking that godliness is a means of financial gain. (1 Timothy 6:5 ONMB)

What did Yeshua (Jesus) say about this?

You must continually heal sicknesses, raise the dead, cleanse lepers, cast out demons; you took freely, you must now give freely. (Matthew 10:8 ONMB)

Yeshua is saying you must freely give without any expectation of financial gain. So He expects you to freely give the gospel to others.

The standard in the Scriptures is saying we must not financially gain from giving the word of the Scriptures.

Third Comparison—Prophecy Taught in the Churches
This comparison will look at the approach to prophecy taught in the churches. Actually, most churches will avoid teaching about prophecy in the Scriptures. Most Christians will have to look on the Internet to find what prophecies are in the Scriptures. In fact, the Scriptures have a whole book on prophecy, and it is called Revelation.

> *The Revelation of Jesus Christ, which God gave him to show his servants—things which must shortly come to pass. And he sent and signified it by his angel to his servant John, Blessed is he who reads and those who hear the words of this prophecy, and keep those things which are written in it; for the time is near.* (Revelation 1:1, 3 KJV)

Yeshua is saying we should read and act on the prophecies in the book of Revelation.

> *And so we have the prophetic word confirmed, which you do well to heed as a light that shines in a dark place, until the day dawns and the morning star rises in your hearts.* (2 Peter 1:19 KJV)

Fourth Comparison—Doctrines Taught by the Church
There are many doctrinal differences between churches even within the same denomination. Let's look at a few and see how they compare to the standard in the Scriptures.

1. What happens at death?
Many believe that you either go to heaven or hell directly after death.

What do the Scriptures say?

For the living know that they will die; but the dead know nothing, And they have no more reward, For the memory of them is forgotten. (Ecclesiastes 9:5 KJV)

After the resurrection, Paul is quoting David (a man after God's own heart) who is still dead and not yet been raised to heaven:

"Men, brothers, allow me to say to you with confidence concerning the Patriarch David, that he died and was buried, and his tomb is among us until this day." (Acts 2:29 ONMB)

And we do not want you to be ignorant, brothers, concerning those who have fallen asleep, that you would not grieve as the rest of those who do not have hope. For if we believe that Yeshua (Jesus) died and rose, so God will also bring with Him those who have fallen asleep by means of Yeshua's redemption. (1 Thessalonians 4:13–14 ONMB)

2. What about the commandments?
Most Christians believe that Yeshua kept them but He also took them to the grave. You don't have to keep them because He did away with them at the cross. Yeshua (Jesus) did it all for you.

Let's look at the standard in the Scriptures and compare to see if this doctrine is correct.

What did Yeshua say about the commandments?

Do not think that I came to destroy the Law or the Prophets. I did not come to destroy but to fulfill. (Matthew 5:17)

The Apostle John emphatically said this:

*Now by this we know that **we know Him, if we keep His commandments**. He who says, **I know Him, and does not keep His***

commandments, is a liar, *and the truth is not in him.* (1 John 2:3–4 ONMB) emphasis added)

Yeshua made it clear about keeping His commandments:

> *"Not everyone who says to me, 'Lord, Lord,' shall enter the kingdom of heaven, but he who does the will of My Father in heaven. Many will say to me in that day, 'Lord, Lord, have we not prophesied in your name, cast out demons in your name, and done many wonders in your name?' And then I will declare to them, 'I never knew you; depart from me, you who practice lawlessness!'"* (Matthew 7:21–23)

Yeshua said we are to keep the commandments if we want to make it to heaven!

This subject is covered in more detail in a later chapter.

3. What about the day of worship?
Most of the churches embrace Sunday while others embrace the seventh-day Sabbath. To justify Sunday, some churches actually rename the Sabbath to be on Sunday. Others try to justify Sunday by saying Yeshua rose on a Sunday. In chapter 11, we discussed where the Scriptures say His resurrection was on the seventh-day Sabbath, not on Sunday.

So by comparing the modern church to the standards set in the Scriptures, it appears that the church is not following the original purposes of the church. Moreover, there seems to be much confusion in the churches over the teachings of Yeshua (Jesus) because each seems to have its own interpretation of how to worship.

What does God think about all this confusion in the churches?

> *For God is not the author of confusion but of peace, as in all the churches of the saints.* (1 Corinthians 14:33 KJV)

So what is the purpose of the church?

> *And he said unto them, Go ye into all the world, and preach the gospel to every creature.* (Mark 16:15 KJV)
>
> *And saying, the time is fulfilled, and the kingdom of God is at hand: repent ye, and believe the gospel.* (Mark 1:15 KJV)

Every church and every Christian is called to preach the gospel to their neighbors.

So has the church fulfilled its mission?

These comparisons confirm that the present-day modern church is correctly referred to as the Laodicea church or lukewarm church. The warning in the Scriptures is that the church need to repent and return back to the original faith or risk YHVH's judgment.

> *I know thy works, that thou art neither cold nor hot: I would thou wert cold or hot. So then because thou art lukewarm, and neither cold nor hot, I will spue thee out of my mouth.* (Revelation 3:15–16 KJV)

Finally, Yeshua said this:

> *He that hath an ear, let him hear what the Spirit saith unto the churches.* (Revelation 3:22 KJV)

CHAPTER 16

The Rise of Islam

ISLAM IS THE WORLD'S SECOND-LARGEST religion and it dominates the Middle East. Islam is spreading around the world at a rapid pace, even in America. Muslims are growing at the estimated rate of twenty thousand per year in America. It is estimated there are over three million Muslims in America today. Leaders of Islamic countries are undergoing citzen-led uprisings.In this chapter I will attempt to give the reader a basic understanding of this religion and what the Scriptures say about Islam. For a more in-depth study of Islam, obtain the book *God's War on Terror* by Walter Shoebat.[191]

WHAT DOES ISLAM MEAN?

Islam is the monotheistic religion (belief in the existence of one god), as distinguished from polytheism (the belief in more than one god) that is articulated in the Qur'an. This doctrine is called the Tawhid in Islam. The followers of Islam believe that the Qur'an is the verbatim word of God. The teachings and examples given in the Qur'an were written by Muhammad. The followers of Islam believe that Muhammad was the last prophet of God after Abraham, Moses, and Jesus. The word *Islam* means "submission to God." Followers of Islam are called Muslims. The Qur'an contains the words of Muhammad. The Hadiths are narrations of the words and deeds of Muhammad. More simply put, the Qur'an is the words of Allah and the Hadiths are the words of Muhammad.[192]

When did Islam originate?

Islam was originated by Muhammad. Muhammad was born in the sixth century in the year 570. This is an approximate date because we don't know for sure his actual birth date. In the year 610, Muhammad declared the revelation of the Qur'an in a cave at Hira about two miles from Mecca in Saudi Arabia. This location is where Muhammad claims he received his first revelations from Allah through the angel Jibreel. Muhammad is regarded by Muslims as a messenger and prophet of God. Muslims believe that Muhammad was the restorer of the uncorrupted original monotheistic faith (Islam) of Adam, Noah, Abraham, Moses, and Jesus.[193]

What are the beliefs of Islam?

The Qur'an asserts the existence of one God, and His name in Arabic is Allah. The Qur'an puts forth God whose rule is comprehensive and extends to all aspects of human life, including the domains of state, law, and society. Muslims consider Muhammad as the restorer of an uncorrupted original monotheistic faith (Islam). According to the Qur'an, prayers must be made five times a day with a gathering on Fridays in the mosques.[194]

What is the Difference between Sunni and Shia worshippers?

The Sunni and Shia have different sets of Hadith collections. These collections differ because scholars from the two traditions differ as to the reliability of the narrators and transmitters. Narrators who took the side of Abu Bakr and Umar rather than Ali in the disputes over leadership after Muhammad's death are seen as unreliable by the Shia.

These differences over the Hadiths have contributed to differences in worship practices and Sharia law.[195]

What are the Five Pillars of Islam?

The Pillars of Islam are five basic acts in Islam that are considered an obligation for all believers in Islam. They are

1) the *shahadah* (creed);
2) daily prayers (five times a day);
3) almsgiving;
4) fasting during Ramadan; and
5) The pilgrimage to Mecca at least once in a lifetime.

The *shahadah*, the basic creed of Islam, must be recited under oath with this specific statement: "I testify that there is none worthy of worship except God and I testify that Muhammad is the Messenger of God."[196]

What is the Bismillah?

Muslims have a custom of putting badges on their foreheads and their arms with Arabic words that say "In the Name of Allah." These badges are called Bismillah, which literally means "In the Name of Allah" and is followed by the symbol of crossed swords, which universally throughout the Muslim world signifies Islam.

The Bismillah is worn by Muslims at every Muslim demonstration or gathering. So the Bismillah is the name, mark, or creed of all Muslims. It simply means "In the Name of Islam and Muhammad is his messenger."

What is Sharia law?

Sharia means "the path leading to the watering place." Sharia is Islamic law that has been developed over the years from Islamic scholars, and it constitutes a system of duties that are incumbent upon a Muslim by virtue of religious belief. Different Muslim countries have varying interpretations of Sharia law. Muslims believe that all Sharia is derived from two primary sources: the revelations set forth in the

Qur'an and the sayings of Muhammad. Violations of Islamic law are very severe. An accused person is put in jail for ten days for a trial by an Islamic judges or quadis. There is no trial by a jury of peers. Sharia addresses crimes by secular law such as politics, and economics. It also addresses personal matters such as sexuality, hygiene, diet, prayer, and fasting.

Muslims believe that Sharia law has been revealed to them by God. In Islam, violations of Islamic law are offenses against God. Crime is a sin. Theft is punished by imprisonment or amputation of hands. Adultery requires the party to be stoned to death. If a person is sentenced to death, then he is beheaded with the sword. Homosexual activity is illegal under Sharia law, and the death penalty is required punishment in most Islamic countries.

Conversion of a Muslim to another religion is strictly forbidden, and the punishment is beheading. The eating of pork, blood, meat of dead animals (fish and locusts are excluded), and alcohol is prohibited.[197]

Worship

Muslims believe the purpose of life is to worship God. There are no pastors or clergy. Allah refers to one God, and this is not the God of the Christians. Muslims are required to pray five times a day. Gathering day is on Friday where all Muslims meet in a mosque to worship. As mentioned before, all Muslims must make a trip to Mecca once in their lifetime to touch the Black Stone.[198]

The Black Stone is a Muslim relic that dates back into antiquity. Muslims believe the Black Stone marked the place of worship during pre-Islamic times. Today the Black Stone is the eastern cornerstone of the Kaaba, the ancient stone building toward which all Muslims pray. The Kaaba is in the center of the Grand Mosque in Mecca, Saudi Arabia. The stone is a dark rock, polished smooth by the hands of millions of pilgrims. The stone over the years has been broken into several fragments, but the fragments have been cemented into a silver frame in the side of the Kaaba.[199]

Calendar

The Islamic calendar is very similar to YHVH's calendar given to Moses and practiced by the Jews. It is a lunar calendar. The beginning of the calendar was chosen to be Friday, July 16, 622 CE, which was the year of emigration from Mecca to Medina by the prophet Muhammad, which is called the year of Hijra. The Islamic day began on the preceding day at sunset. Days are from sunset to sunset, and a month is based on a lunar month. Years have twelve months. The ninth month is Ramadan, which means "scorched" in Arabic. This is the month that all Muslims fast between dawn and sunset. The first day of the work week is Saturday.[200]

Symbols

The symbol of Islam is the crescent moon and star. The symbol is featured on the flags of several Muslim countries. The symbol actually predates Islam by several thousand years. Together with the sun, the symbol of the crescent moon appeared on the Akkadian seals as early as 2300 BC. It was the symbol of the Mesopotamian moon gods Nanna in Sumer and Sin in Babylonia.[201]

The city of Byzantium (later known as Constantinople and later Istanbul) adopted the crescent moon as its symbol in honor of the goddess Diana. The symbol was featured on the city's flag. When the Ottoman Empire (Muslims) conquered all this part of Asia Minor in 1453, they adopted the crescent moon symbol. The symbol is also mentioned in the Scriptures in Judges 8:14.[202]

> *Then Zebah and Tsalmunna said, "Rise yourself, and fall on us. For as a man is, so is his might." So Gid'on arose and slew Zebah and Tsalmunna and took the* **crescent ornaments** *which were on their camels' necks.* (Judges 8:14 ISR, emphasis added)

Who is the Mahdi?

The Mahdi is the prophesied redeemer of Islam who will stay on the earth for seven years before the Day of Judgment. The Mahdi, alongside

Jesus, will rid the world of wrongdoing, injustice, and tyranny. The doctrine of the Mahdi is as follows:

1. The Mahdi will be a descendant of Muhammad.
2. He will have the same name as Muhammad.
3. He will be the forerunner to Jesus's Islamic rule.
4. His coming will be accompanied by the raising of the black standard.
5. His coming will be accompanied by the appearance of the Masih ad-Dajjal (Antichrist)
6. There will be a lunar and solar eclipse within the same month of Ramadan.
7. A star with a luminous tail will rise from the east before the coming of the Mahdi.
8. He will establish the caliphate.
9. He will fill the world with justice and fairness at time when the world will be filled with oppression, which is war and calamities.
10. He will have a broad forehead, a prominent nose, and natural mascara will ring his eyes.
11. His face shall shine upon the surface of the moon.
12. The name of the Mahdi's representative will begin with the first letter of a prophet's name and a verse of the Qur'an. (The English letter is *Y*.)[203]
13. The coming Mahdi will be the Mahdi for both Sunni and Shia Muslims.

What is the Caliphate?

The term *caliphate* refers to the first system of government established in Islam. It is a constitutional government headed by a "caliph" or "commander of the believers." It was initially led by Muhammad's disciples as a continuation of the political system the Prophet established as the Rashidun caliphates. Shia followers of Islam believe a caliph must be an imam descended in the line from the Ahl al-Bayt. Sunni followers stipulate that the head of state should be selected by the Shura or elected by Muslims or their representatives.[204]

Caliphates have existed in Islamic countries from the time of Muhammad until the 1920s, or about 1260 years. On March 3, 1924, the first president of the Turkish Republic abolished the caliphate. However, though many Muslims would like to reestablish the caliphate, according to the Hadith the caliphate will be followed by the arrival of the promised Messiah and Imam Mahdi.[205]

One of the stated goals of the group of Al-Qaeda is the reestablishment of a caliphate. They believe that once a caliphate is reestablished, then Egypt would become a rallying point for the rest of the Islamic world to lead a jihad against the West.[206]

What are the Goals of Islam?

The goal of Islam is the same goal of Muhammad; the Khalid (viceregent of Allah), the Mahdi, and all obedient Muslims are to advance Allah's glory as the supreme god by jihad by sending an invitation first, then making war until there are none left who will not say, "There is no God but Allah, and Muhammad is His messenger." Allah's apostle said, "I have been ordered to fight the people till they say: 'None has the right to be worshipped but Allah.'"

To achieve their goals, Muslims are allowed to use tricks, disguises, terrorism, or even war to achieve their goals.

What is Jihad?

A definition of *jihad* by Walter Shoebat is as follows: "Islamic Jihad is religious conditioning, using allusions of misery and glory days of the past in order to convert masses into becoming rage and pride-filled, remorseless killers and seekers of salvation by their own death. The goal is to reestablish a utopian theocratic world order where Allah and Muslims reign supreme and non-Muslims become subservient." You must always remember that Muslims believe that there is no god but Allah and Muhammad is His messenger.[207]

The goal of Islam is to advance Allah as the only god, and this is carried out through jihad. This begins with an invitation to Islam by using political Jihad. If the offer is rejected then, by advancing Allah's glory, comes the jihad war in which the enemy is decapitated.[208]

Jihadism is also a message of salvation to the Muslim. For one to die in the cause of Allah is an assurance of salvation and entry into paradise. Every Muslim has sins. Dying in jihad is the ultimate way to transmit one's soul instantly to heaven. Otherwise, a Muslim must obtain enough merit to outweigh his sins in order to make it to heaven. Muslims reject the idea that Christ died for all humanity. In fact, Islam claims that Jesus is a corruption of the original faith from Abraham. In Islam. Muslims believe it is your own death that gets you to heaven.

A Muslim martyr can be an intercessor for seventy members of his or her family. A suicide martyr is called a *fida'e* from the source word *fidyah* (sacrificial lamb). Salvation occurs upon death and at the first drop of blood. There are six bounties as follows for dying in jihad:

1. He will be forgiven at the first drop of blood.
2. He will see his place in paradise.
3. He will be saved from the great sorrow on the Day of Judgment.
4. He will receive a crown of dignity in heaven.
5. He will have seventy-two virgins in heaven.
6. He will be allowed to intercede for seventy family members.[209]

What is the Role of Women in Islam?

In Islam, women have very few rights. A Muslim woman is treated like property. She can only marry a Muslim. She must be subservient to her husband, or the husband must beat her according to the Qur'an. Rape is also condoned in Islam. Women ages ten to fifty-five have been raped, especially after or during a war. Women who do not wear head scarves are asking to be raped, and if they are, they must prove good conduct or she can be stoned to death.[210]

Islamic view of the Hebrew Prophets
Abraham is recognized in Islam as a prophet and apostle of God and patriarch of many peoples. In Muslim belief, Abraham fulfilled all the commandments and trials with which God tried him over a lifetime. Abraham, in Muslim belief, embodies the type of the perfect Muslim, and the Qur'an mentions Abraham as a model for mankind.[211]

Isaac is recognized in Islam as a prophet and messenger of God. Muslims believe that Isaac and his older half brother Ishmael continued their father's legacy and preached the message of God.[212]

Jacob is recognized in Islam as a prophet, and he preached the oneness of God (Tawhid). The Qur'an frequently mentions Jacob as a man of might and vision and stresses he was of the company of the good and elect.[213]

Jesus is recognized in Islam to be a messenger of the Muslim God Allah, and He was to guide the children of Israel with a new teaching. He is viewed as Muslim just like the other patriarchs (Abraham, Moses, Abraham, Isaac, and Jacob) of the Scriptures. Muslims believe that Jesus was a prophet, but they don't believe He was a savor. In Islam, Jesus comes back as a radical Muslim to lead the armies to abolish Christianity and slaughter the Jews. Remember, the goal of Islam is that everyone on the planet must worship Allah or be killed.[214]

What about the Wars against Christians and Jews?
When did all this start? It started when Muhammad attacked a Jewish settlement in northern Arabia at the oasis of Yathrib, what today is called Medina. In February of 627, Muhammad's forces attacked a Jewish tribe and conquered them after twenty-five days. Muhammad gave the survivors a choice between converting to Islam or death. A few converted, but most did not (approximately nine hundred men), and they were

beheaded. All the women and children were taken as slaves. The women were given to the Muslim warriors as sex slaves. Throughout Islamic history, rape of captured women was justified.[215]

Muhammad first started fighting the idolaters in the Arabian Peninsula. After conquering them, Muhammad turned his attention to the Jews and the Christians. In 638, Muhammad is said to have ascended to heaven from the temple mount in Jerusalem. As a result, a mosque was built on the temple mount at the site of the first temple. After Muhammad's death, Abu Bakr became the leader of the Muslims. Abu Bakr started warring against the Roman cross worshippers. Islam continued to spread and eventually included the Holy Land. The area of Islam included the Middle East, North Africa, and Central Asia. The capital of the Islamic caliphate was initially Bagdad.

As Islam spread over the Middle East, it clashed with the Byzantine or Eastern Roman forces. After years of fighting, Muslim forces expanded deeply into Persian and Byzantine territories. During the Islamic Golden Age (750–1258), the capital of Islam became the city of Babylon, which is located in today's Iraq. By the late ninth century, North Africa, the Middle East, and Central Asia had become Muslim. In the tenth century, Afghanistan and a large part of India had been conquered and became Muslim.[216]

Christians during this period made yearly pilgrimages to Jerusalem. However, the Muslims began to harass them. The Roman Catholic Church was extremely concerned, and eventually Pope Urban II called for a crusade to take back Jerusalem. The first crusade by the church was launched and Jerusalem was captured in 1099. In 1187, the Muslim leader Saladin recaptured Jerusalem and the crusaders were never able to retake Jerusalem.[217]

In 1453, the Roman Empire in Asia Minor fell when the Ottoman Turks took Byzantium (Constantinople). The Greek emperor was killed, and the great church of Saint Sophia was turned into a mosque. The city was then renamed Istanbul. Although the city was claimed for Islam, the Christians were allowed to practice their religion. In the thirteenth and fourteenth centuries, the Ottoman Empire included the Balkans, parts of Greece, and western Anatolia.[218]

During the eighteenth century, the Wahhabi movement took hold in Saudi Arabia. In the nineteenth century, several Muslim states gained independence, and the spread of Islam was halted. Finally, the Ottoman Empire came to a close at the end of World War I, and the caliphate was abolished in 1924.[219]

After World War II, the United Nations gave the Jews a home in Palestine on May 14, 1948. Since the Jews were given a home in Israel there have been seven wars against the Jewish nation, all by Muslim nations. The war in 1967 was significant since Israel defeated the Muslim nations in six days. It is extremely significant since Israel was attacked and significantly outnumbered by overwhelming force, and yet they won the war in only six days. YHVH had to have helped them win. Today, the Muslim neighbors continue to threaten Israel. The Palestinian children are taught to sing songs about killing Jews.

In Africa, Christians are killed by Muslims almost daily. Sometimes whole villages are wiped out. Many huddle in their churches for safety only to find the church was set on fire in an effort to burn them alive. In America we seem not to notice. We don't even pay attention when the Muslim clerics in America vow to kill Christians if they don't convert to Islam. Even the current president seems to side with Muslims over Christians even to the point of violating the first amendment to the Constitution. Wake up, Christians in America, or one day you will see a Muslim flag over the White House.

Are Muslim Countries Mentioned in the Scriptures?

Yes. They are mentioned all through the Old Testament. To understand who they are requires you to identify these countries at the time the prophets wrote about them. You will need old biblical maps in order to locate these countries relative to the present-day nations. Over a period of time, the names of these biblical countries have changed. New nations have arisen, and their borders are different. Walter Shoebat in his book *God's War on Terror* has identified these countries as follows: [220]

Magog:	This area includes Turkey, Syria, northern Iran, and the Turkic regions of central Asia.
Gog:	Gog or Gygez was a real person in Turkey. Also it could refer to Gugu of Lydia in Turkey.
Persia:	Persia is modern-day Iran.
Cush:	Cush of Ezekiel's day was the land immediately south of Egypt, which is the Sudan.
Migdol:	This is northern Egypt.
Aswan:	Today is southern Egypt.
Put or Phut:	This land is west of Egypt or Libya.

In Psalm 82, God rises up to judge the nations.

Arise, O God, judge the earth: for thou shalt inherit all nations. (Psalm 82:8 KJV)

ARE THE NATIONS THAT WILL BE JUDGED BY YESHUA IDENTIFIED IN THE SCRIPTURES?

Yes. They are identified in the Scriptures.

For they have consulted together with one consent: they are confederate against thee: The tabernacles of Edom, and the Ishmaelites; of Moab, and the Hagarenes; Gebal, and Ammon, and Amalek; the Philistines with the inhabitants of Tyre; Assur also is joined with them: they have holpen the children of Lot. Selah. Do unto them as unto the Midianites; as to Sisera, as to Jabin, at the brook of Kison. (Psalm 89:5–9 KJV)

Yeshua (Jesus) returns to fight the Mahdi-Antichrist and the Muslim nations:

I will also gather all nations, and will bring them down into the valley of Jehoshaphat, and will plead with them there for my people and for my heritage Israel, whom they have scattered among the nations, and parted my land. (Joel 3:2 KJV)

The Scriptures say that Yeshua will return to destroy Madhi-Antichrist with his Muslim hordes in the valley of Jehoshaphat.

That I will break the Assyrian in my land, and upon my mountains tread him under foot: then shall his yoke depart from off them, and his burden depart from off their shoulders. This is the purpose that is purposed upon the whole earth: and this is the hand that is stretched out upon all the nations. For the LORD of hosts hath purposed, and who shall disannul it? And his hand is stretched out, and who shall turn it back? (Isaiah 14:25–27 KJV)

WHAT IS THE IMPORTANCE OF THE ARAB SPRING?

The Arab Spring is a revolutionary wave of demonstrations and protests occurring in the Arab world that began on December 18, 2010. As of today, rulers have forced from power in Tunisia, Egypt, Libya, and Yemen. A bloody uprising is now taking place in Syria. Other Arab countries are also experiencing uprisings. So what does this mean? The speculation is that the corrupt and self-serving leaders of these countries are been replaced by a purer Islam and Sharia law.

In a broader context, these regime changes are ushering in Islamic states that will eventually band together. Why? So they can reestablish the caliphate. This means that Mahdi cannot be far behind.

OUR MESSIAH IS THEIR ANTICHRIST AND THEIR ANTICHRIST IS OUR MESSIAH

In Walter Shoebat's book *God's War on Terror*, he shows how Islam's messiah is identical to the biblical Antichrist. He also shows that the man whom Christians believe is the Messiah is the Antichrist of Islam. Yeshua warned us that in the last days there would be false messiahs and false prophets. So when the false prophet commands you to worship the Antichrist, will you know the difference? [221]

He goes on to explain that the Bismillah is the "mark of the beast" spoken about in Revelation 13. The reason is that there are discrepancies in the old Greek manuscripts. Some do not have the number 666 and others have 616 or 665. One explanation for all these variants is that what was thought to be the three Greek letters Chi Xi Stigma were actually three foreign symbols.

> *Here is wisdom. Let him that hath understanding count the number of the beast: for it is the number of a man; and his number is Six hundred threescore and six.* (Revelation 13:18 KJV)

Walter Shoebat believes that if we carefully examine the Greek words of this verse, then it should read as follows:

> *Here is wisdom. Let him that hath understanding reckon (or decide, discern) the multitude of the beast, for it is the number of a man [that is, Muhammad and or the Mahdi-Antichrist] and his multitude [are identified through the following]* "In the Name of Allah and the two swords (or Jihad)."

Bismi means "name of" and *llah* means "Allah." The Bismillah fulfills the biblical requirement that the name and the mark have the same meaning—the name of blasphemy, or the name of Allah. [222]

Is the future Madhi the Antichrist of the Scriptures?

Walter Shoebat makes a strong case that the Mahdi will be the Antichrist of the book of Revelation. [223]

WILL MUSLIMS BE PART OF THE GOVERNMENT OF AMERICA?

Since Revelation 13 says there will be a one-world religion, then I would expect that Muslims and the religion of Islam are going to play a major role in America in the coming days.

CHAPTER 17

YHVH's Judgment on America

Did you know that only two countries on this earth have been dedicated to serving YHVH? Israel was the first, and America was the second. The inauguration of George Washington as the first president of the United States of America occurred on April 30, 1789, at Federal Hall in New York City. On that day, for the first time, America had a constitution, a senate, a house of representatives and a president together. It was the birth of the United States as a fully formed constitutional government.[224]

Buried in the middle of George Washington's address to the newly formed nation on its first official day was a prophetic warning to America.

> *We ought to be no less persuaded that the propitious smiles [ongoing blessings] of heaven can never be expected on a nation that disregards the eternal rules of order and the right which heaven itself has ordained.*[225]

Washington was warning America that YHVH's blessing cannot be expected to continue if the nation ever turns away from the will of YHVH.[226]

The warning that George Washington gave to our nation was the same warning given to the nation of Israel. The warning was that America's future blessing would—as it was with Israel—hang on its relationship to YHVH. If America should begin to depart from YHVH, its blessings, its prosperity, and its protection will disappear.[227]

After the address to the nation, George Washington, the senators, the House of Representatives and the vice president all walked over to a small church that was nearby and went inside. For two hours they all prayed for the new nation and they committed this new nation to YHVH. The entire government was kneeling before YHVH. This small church, known as the St. Paul's Chapel, still stands today, and it is located at the border of Ground Zero in New York City.[228]

According to the Scriptures, judgment came to ancient Israel at the place Israel was dedicated to YHVH. Israel was dedicated to YHVH on the temple mount when Solomon had dedicated the newly constructed temple to YHVH (1 Kings 8:63). When Israel later wavered from following the commandments from YHVH, the prophet Isaiah gave them many warnings to change their ways or punishment from YHVH would be imminent. Isaiah gave this warning in Isaiah 9:9–10:

> *And all the people will know, even Ephraim and the inhabitants of Samaria,* ***they say in the pride and stoutness of heart, the bricks are fallen down, but we will build with hewn stones: the sycamores are cut down, but we will change them into cedars.***

This was a judgment on both houses of Israel. The Scriptures tell us that Israel did not heed the warnings from the prophet Isaiah of impending judgment from YHVH. To get their attention, YHVH sent them several warnings. **First, He removed their hedge of protection.** The Assyrians (they were known as terrorists to the Israelites and their capital city was Nineveh) invaded Israel and destroyed parts of Israel. It was the first warning from YHVH to Israel to turn back to YHVH. The Assyrians then retreated for a period of time.[229]

Although Isaiah had warned them to repent and turn back to YHVH, the Israelites still would not listen to the prophet. Instead they were defiant. They **vowed to rebuild** their homes and walls with stones instead of bricks to make them stronger. At the time, their walls and homes were made of mud bricks, and they were easily broken down by the Assyrians. The prophet Isaiah kept trying to get them to understand that were not doing YHVH's will. To shut Isaiah up, the leaders of Israel killed him by sawing him in two.[230]

The prophets Jeremiah and Ezekiel also warned Israel, to no avail. King Nebuchadnezzar's Babylonian army waged war against Judah, and they took thousands of Jews into bondage in Babylon. Finally, in 586 BC, the temple built by Solomon was destroyed. Later, after the Israelites returned to their homeland, a second temple was built. Then the Romans totally destroyed the second temple. Millions of Jews lost their lives, and the survivors fled to other countries. The final judgment had come to Israel from YHVH because they had turned away from worshipping YHVH as He had instructed them.

Since George Washington dedicated the new nation (America) to YHVH, things have changed. America has moved more and more away from the worship of YHVH. Unfortunately, we have forgotten where our blessing came from. Now we believe that don't need to be dependent on YHVH anymore. We believe that we have superior wisdom and we will always be a wealthy nation. We don't follow YHVH's commandments anymore, and when we try to remind people by publicly displaying them, we are sued to remove them. We removed prayer from the public schools. It is a time of political correctness where conservative Christians are called evil. It is all about our needs and wants. It is a time when we put our personal needs above the will of YHVH. The Scriptures also had something to say about the time we live in now:

Yeshua (Jesus) said:

And the cares of this world, and the deceitfulness of riches, and the lusts of other things entering in, choke the word, and it becometh unfruitful. (Mark 4:19 KJV)

The apostle Paul said:

For the time will come when they will not endure sound doctrine; but after their own lusts shall they heap to themselves teachers, having itching ears. (2 Timothy 4:3 KJV)

> *For we ourselves also were sometimes foolish, disobedient, deceived, serving divers' lusts and pleasures, living in malice and envy, hateful, and hating one another.* (Titus 3:3 KJV)

Peter said:

> *For the time past of our life may suffice us to have wrought the will of the Gentiles, when we walked in lasciviousness, lusts, excess of wine, revellings, banquetings, and abominable idolatries.* (1 Peter 4:3 KJV)
>
> *Knowing this first, that there shall come in the last days scoffers, walking after their own lusts.* (2 Peter 3:3 KJV)

In the book of Jude:

> *These are murmurers, complainers, walking after their own lusts; and their mouth speaketh great swelling words, having men's persons in admiration because of advantage…How that they told you there should be mockers in the last time, who should walk after their own ungodly lusts.* (Jude 1:16, 18 KJV)

On September 11, 2001, a warming was sent to America at the place where the country was dedicated to YHVH. **The hedge of protection was removed.** Isaiah also saw it before it happened and said this about the event:

> *And there shall be upon every high mountain, and upon every high hill, rivers and streams of waters in the* ***day of the great slaughter, when the towers fall.*** (Isaiah 30:25 KJV, emphasis added)

This verse could only apply to the destruction of the twin towers of the World Trade Center in New York City on September 11, 2001. Could this have been the start of many warnings and judgments to the United States from YHVH? Could this warning be similar to the warnings and judgments given to Israel in Isaiah 9:10? Israel was warned by the prophets to repent, and they did not. In the Scriptures, YHVH sent warnings to His people to come back to His true worship, but when they didn't, there came greater judgments.

The leaders of Israel were defiant to YHVH when the warnings came. They were so upset with Isaiah that they had him killed. So let's look at what Isaiah said would happen to Israel and see if it is similar to what happened in New York.

In Isaiah 9:10, the Israelites said the following after they were attacked by the Assyrians:

> ***The bricks are fallen down, but we will build with hewn stones: The sycamores are cut down, but we will change them into cedars.***

Is this verse similar to what happened to America after the September 11, 2001, attack?

1. The Fallen Bricks

In Israel, the Assyrians (terrorists) broke through the walls and homes made out of mud bricks. The bricks fell as rubble and dust.

No one can forget the scene in New York when the terrorists flew planes into the towers and they fell with fire, smoke, dust, and ashes. The bricks of Ground Zero in Manhattan were reduced to ash with only dust and metal remaining.

2. We Will Rebuild with Hewn Stones

The Israelites were defiant and vowed to rebuild with stronger walls to keep the enemy out. They made the vow of Isaiah 9:10.

Just as the Israelites said they would rebuild, so did America. On September 12, 2001, Senator Tom Daschle officially addressed Congress and the world with a defiant speech and said that we would rebuild. He even quoted Isaiah 9:10 in his speech.[231]

The Israelites rebuilt their walls with quarried (hewn) stones to make the walls stronger.

At Ground Zero in New York, the first stone to be used in the construction of the new freedom tower was a twenty-ton Adirondack granite stone block.[232]

3. The Sycamores Are Cut Down
In the Scriptures, the sycamore tree is described as being a sign of judgment.

He destroyed their vines with hail, and their sycamore trees with frost. (Psalm 78:47 KJV)

As part of YHVH's judgment against Israel, the sycamore trees were destroyed by the Assyrians.

On September 11, 2001, when the north tower fell, a steel beam was hurled from the tower, and it struck a sycamore tree. The tree was knocked down and its roots exposed. Just as the sycamores were cut down in Israel, so was the sycamore cut down in New York City at the border of Ground Zero.

Later, a sculptor was commissioned to make a cast of the fallen sycamore tree. He then poured bronze into the cast and made a bronze image of the tree. The bronze image is now displayed on Wall Street. Some say the Sycamore Tree memorial has come to represent the **riches of our nation uprooted, overturned, judged, and displayed in bronze**.

The sycamore tree had been at this location since the time of George Washington. On May 17, 1792, twenty-four stock brokers met underneath a buttonwood (American sycamore) tree outside 68 Wall Street in New York and signed an agreement on trading stocks. The agreement became known as the Buttonwood Agreement, which birthed the New York Stock Exchange.[233]

4. Replant with Cedar Trees
Isaiah said that cedars would replace the sycamores. The Israelites replaced the sycamores with cedars from Lebanon.

As in Israel, two years after September 11, 2001, a cedar tree was planted in the hole left by the sycamore tree that was struck down.

The Church was Protected by YHVH

When the towers came crashing down, many of the surrounding buildings at Ground Zero were heavily damaged except for one—a small church. The protection of the small church that was built in 1766 came from a sycamore tree that was located in the back of the chapel in a graveyard. When the steel beam was flying toward the small church, the sycamore tree blocked the beam from hitting the chapel. This was the same small church where George Washington dedicated America to YHVH.[234]

Inside this small church behind the pulpit is an interesting sight. There is a replica of Mount Sinai with YHVH above it looking down on two stone tablets of the Ten Commandments. On the sculpture of YHVH is written the four letters of the Hebrew Name of YHVH. Could this church have been protected as the following verse implies?[235]

> *For me you need make only an altar of earth; on it you will sacrifice your burnt offerings, peace offerings, sheep, goats and cattle.* **In every place where I cause my name to be mentioned, I will come to you and bless you.** (Exodus 20:24 CJB)

Call to Repent

When the smoke had cleared from Ground Zero and the search was on to find survivors, a strange sight was seen. There in the rubble stood a cross made from fallen steel beams. A cross similar to the one Yeshua (Jesus) was crucified on for our redemption. Perhaps it was a sign from YHVH (God) for **this nation (America) to repent** and turn back toward the Him in true worship.[236]

The Shemittah Connection

One of the commandments from YHVH that the Israelites were not following had to do with the seventh-year rest of the land. Every seven years the land was to rest. The Israelites were not allowed to grow any crops in the seventh year.

> *And six years thou shalt sow thy land, and shalt gather in the fruits thereof: But the seventh year thou shalt let it rest and lie still; that the poor of thy people may eat: and what they leave the beasts of the field shall eat. In like manner thou shalt deal with thy vineyard, and with thy oliveyard.* (Exodus 23:10–11 KJV)

At the end of seven years, **all debts are to be forgiven or canceled**. Slaves are set free, and they are to be given food, supplies, and earnings for the years of service. The Jubilee year (fiftieth year) had an additional feature of returning land back to the original owner. All of this occurred on the last day of Elul, which is a month on YHVH's calendar and was called the **Shemittah.** The Shemittah was always known as the sign of economic and financial blessings, but it also had another meaning. If YHVH's commandments were not followed, then it became a sign of judgment. *Shemittah* means "let fall" or "collapse."[237]

The Israelites had stopped following the Shemittah. It was a test of faith on the national level and personal level that YHVH would provide for them in economic matters. The observance of a whole nation that YHVH is the sole owner and master of their land was difficult for them to follow. Economic blessings or economic disasters were dependent upon their faith in following the commandments of YHVH. So the Shemittah became a sign of judgment on the nation of Israel.[238]

Did the sign of the Shemittah happen in America after September 11, 2001? The following events suggest that that is exactly what happened. On Monday, September 17, 2001, the stock market lost 694 points or 7.1 percent. This happened on the last day of Elul, which was Elul 29 on

YHVH's calendar. Elul 29 was the day of Shemittah. The stock market crash that day had the effect of an economic collapse.[239]

Seven years later, during September 2008, Fannie Mae and Fannie Mac were about to collapse due to the massive foreclosures in the housing markets. On September 7, 2008, they filed for bankruptcy. Lehman Brothers, the fourth-largest global services firm with assets of six hundred billion dollars, filed for bankruptcy on September 15, 2008. On September 29, 2008, the stock market dropped 777.7 points or 6.98 percent. September 29 was Elul 29 on the Hebrew calendar and was exactly **seven years to the day from September 17, 2001**. Amazingly, it looks like the judgment of the Shemittah is on America.[240]

The effect of these financial disasters was to cancel debts, as in home foreclosures. The Lehman Brothers' collapse effectively wiped out many investors. America appeared to be experiencing the sign of the Shemittah just as Israel did. Can we expect the same thing to happen seven years later in the year 2015?

Witnesses for Judgment

As it was in Israel, if America is under judgment from YHVH, the Scriptures say that there must be at least two or three witnesses before judgment can be pronounced. Were there any witnesses that America is under judgment? Yes, there are three witnesses that spoke vows of defiance to rebuild America as Israel vowed in Isaiah 9:10.

First Witness

On September 12, 2001, Tom Daschle spoke the **vow of defiance by quoting Isaiah 9:10**, which linked America to Israel's judgment by YHVH. He then said, "We **will rebuild and we will recover.** The people of America **will** stand strong together because the people of America have always stood together. And those of us privileged to serve this great nation **will stand** with you."[241]

Second Witness
On September 11, 2004, John Edwards spoke at a prayer breakfast and said, "Today on this day of remembrance and mourning, we have the Lord's words." He then **quoted Isaiah 9:10.** Once again a national leader of America had spoken the **vow of defiance by quoting Isaiah 9:10.**[242]

Third Witness
On February 24, 2009, President Obama in his first address to Congress and to the nation said the following: "But while our economy may be weakened and our confidence shaken, though we are living through difficult and uncertain times, tonight I want every American to know this: **we will rebuild, we will recover,** and the United States of America will emerge stronger than before."[243] His statement was eerily out of context in the speech and it was again a **vow to defiance by linking our economic woes to the 9/11 attack to Isaiah 9:10.**

These three witnesses were significant because of their positions in the nation's government. These three witnesses spoke vows of defiance to rebuild.

What is Required to Remove YHVH's Judgment on America?

The Scriptures tell us that YHVH said He would remove judgment against Israel if they would do the following:

> *If my people, which are called by my name, shall humble themselves, and pray, and seek my face, and turn from their wicked ways; then will I hear from heaven, and will forgive their sin, and will heal their land.* (2 Chronicles 7:14 KJV)

Just as Israel suffered under the judgments of YHVH, so it appears America is suffering also. The attack of September 11, 2001, was an attack on the economic and financial foundation of the country. No one can deny that we are in financial decline. The future looks bleak for us and no one seems to want to the truth about our nation's decline. The future looks dark, and Christians can't understand what's happening. One president in our past understood the judgments of YHVH and this is what he said about it.[244]

During the darkest hours of our nation just after the Civil War ended, the future son-in-law of Abraham Lincoln asked the president for a resolution for a national day of prayer to remove YHVH's judgments against America.

On March 30, 1863, Abraham Lincoln proclaimed a national day of prayer.

By the President of the United States of America
A Proclamation
Whereas, the Senate of the United States, devoutly recognizing the Supreme authority and just Government of Almighty God, in all the affairs of men and of nations, has, by a resolution, requested the president to designate and set apart a day for national prayer and humiliation.

And whereas it is the duty of nations as well as of men, to own their dependence upon the overruling power of God, to confess their sins and transgressions, in humble sorrow, yet with assured hope that genuine repentance will lead to mercy and pardon; and to recognize the sublime truth, announced in the Holy Scriptures and proven by all history, that those nations only are blessed whose God is the Lord.

And, insomuch as we know that, by His divine law, nations like individuals are subjected to punishments and chastisements in this world, may we not justify fear that the awful calamity of civil war, which now desolates the land, may be but a punishment, inflicted upon us, for our presumptuous sins, to the needful end of our national reformation as a whole people? We have been the recipients of the choicest bounties of Heaven. We have been preserved, these many years, in peace and prosperity. We have grown in numbers, wealth and power, as no other nation has ever grown. But we have forgotten God. We have forgotten the gracious hand which preserved us in peace, and multiplied and enriched and strengthened us; and we have vainly imagined, in the deceitfulness of our hearts that all these blessings were produced by some superior wisdom and virtue of our own. Intoxicated with unbroken success, we have become too self-sufficient to feel the necessity of redeeming and preserving grace, too proud to pray to the God that made us!

It behooves us then, to humble ourselves before the offended Power, to confess our national sins, and to pray for clemency and forgiveness.

Now therefore, in compliance with the request, and fully concurring in the views of the Senate, I do, by this proclamation, designate and set apart Thursday, the 30th day of April, 1863, as a day of national humiliation, fasting and prayer. And I do hereby request all the People to abstain, on that day, from their ordinary secular pursuits, and to unite, at their several places of public worship and their respective homes, in keeping the day holy to the Lord, and devoted to the humble discharge of the religious duties proper to that solemn occasion.

All this being done, in sincerity and truth, let us then rest humbly in the hope authorized by the Divine teachings, that the united cry of the Nation will be heard on high, and answered with blessings, no less than the pardon of our national sins, and the restoration of our now divided and suffering Country, to its former happy condition of unity and peace.

In witness whereof, I have hereunto set my hand and caused the seal of the United States to be affixed.

Done at the City of Washington, this thirtieth day of March, in the year of our Lord one thousand eight hundred and sixty three, and of the independence of the United States the eighty seventh.

By the President: Abraham Lincoln
William H. Steward, Secretary of State.

This is the kind of leadership we need in Washington to lead our nation back to YHVH.

President Truman initiated a national day of prayer in 1952. It was signed into law and the date was left open for each president to set the day of the prayer. In 1988, President Reagan designated the first Thursday in May of each year as the National Day of Prayer. President George H. Bush had a prayer service in the White House on the National Day of Prayer. However, President Bill Clinton did not have a service in the White House. President George W. Bush held a prayer service in the White House on the National Day of Prayer.[245] But the shocker came on June 28, 2006, when presidential candidate Obama declared the following in a speech:

Whatever we once were, we are no longer a Christian nation—at least, not just; we are also a Jewish nation, a Muslim nation, a Buddhist nation, a Hindu nation, and a nation of nonbelievers.[246]

This has an eerie feeling that we are becoming Babylon.

After President Obama was elected, he distanced himself by not attending any National Day of Prayer services. And then in April 2010, the National Day of Prayer was judged to be unconstitutional by Judge Barbara Crabb. A Wisconsin-based group of atheists and agnostics known as the Freedom from Religion Foundation had filed a lawsuit in 2008 against the National Day of Prayer. In 2010, President Obama changed his mind and did support the National Day of Prayer, but not at the White House. Also in 2010, Franklin Graham was disinvited from the National Day of Prayer service at the Pentagon because he had earlier described Islam as evil and wicked.[247]

So it appears that our government has turned away from its Judeo-Christian roots and President Obama will not be leading the nation to repent.

Warnings in the Year 2011

Similar to 2008, 2011 is also shaping up as a year of economic disasters. If we are under the Shemittah, a sign of judgment, then we can expect to continue to see signs in the financial, labor, employment, commercial, and consumption areas of the economy. Let's look at these areas and see if we are having difficulties.

In the financial area, even though we have extremely low interest rates, banks are not lending money for businesses or churches.

In the labor area, organized labor is a major problem to job growth. One good example is case where the National Labor Relations Board would not let Boeing open a nonunion plant in South Carolina. The unions only want union jobs to be created.

In the employment area, private sector unemployment is at an all-time high. In August 2011, no new jobs were created. Unemployment has skyrocketed in America. No jobs are being created, which has resulted in very difficult economic times. Home foreclosures remain high.

The S&P downgraded the US bond rating and the Dow dropped 1150 points in early August. September was another bad month for the Dow with stocks dropping as several European countries were on the brink of default.

National environmental disasters seem to be getting worse. Low production of food due to weather disasters this year has resulted in the loss of many agricultural crops. The worst drought in Texas's history occurred this summer, resulting in the sale of cattle at very low prices because ranchers could not feed them. Fires and floods destroyed many homes, and the country's infrastructure is deteriorating.

Warnings in the Year 2012

The natural disasters and severe weather seem to be more prevalent. Signs are also being shown on the political side that our government is moving toward becoming either a socialist or communist country. With the Supreme Court upholding the Affordable Care Act, which takes over the entire medical profession, it enables the government to control everyone in this country.

Also, actions by the US Justice Department to promote illegal immigration and to punish states that try to control illegal immigration is another sign of the central control that is coming. I expect after the election that the US Justice Department will enact the already-approved law for everyone to receive a national ID card to be used for identification in voting. This is the forerunner for the economic mark of the beast (kingdom) that will be used to prevent people from buying or selling.

Another pastor has come forward with a vision of the destruction of America. Pastor Shane Warren is warning America that judgment is coming on America. His vision is that the iniquities and sexual sins of America are overflowing and will cause YHVH's judgment to come on America.

Will America Suffer an Economic Collapse?

When the towers came down on 9/11, Federal Hall, where George Washington was sworn in, was damaged. The foundation of the building was cracked by the enormous shock of the collapsing towers. The judgment suffered by America also shook the financial foundation of America. Unless America as a nation repents, then just as the judgments got progressively worse on Israel, so will the judgments on America until our economy collapses. The seven-year Shemittah will again occur on the last day of Elul in 2015. Will this be when America suffers a day of total economic collapse? [248]

Pastor David Wilkerson of the Times Square Church warned people after the attack about the judgments against Israel that seem to be happening to America.[249] Rabbi Jonathan Cahn took up the cause of warning America about our future if we don't repent. For a more in-depth analysis about these judgments coming on America, see Jonathan Cahn's website www.hopeoftheworld.org.[250]

If the Christian and Jewish people of America want to prevent the collapse, again this is what YHVH said to do:

If my people, which are called by my name, shall humble themselves, and pray, and seek my face, and turn from their wicked ways; then will I hear from heaven, and will forgive their sin, and will heal their land. (2 Chronicles 7:14 KJV)

CHAPTER 18

The Rise of Chrislam

MOST OF YOU KNOW THAT the World Council of Churches is a community of churches. It is a worldwide organization dedicated to Christian unity in one faith. They have 349 churches, denominations, and church fellowships in more than 110 countries representing over 560 million Christians. They are leaders in an organized effort to unite Christians, Jews, and Muslims in one faith.[251]

On June 26, 2011, many American churches met to embrace Islam. The organization called Faith Shared organized religious services that included Christians and Muslims. About seventy churches participated, including the National Cathedral in Washington, DC, for the Sunday service. The stated goal of Shared Faith is to strengthen ties between the religious communities of Christians, Jews, and Muslims. The joint services include the clergy reading from one another's sacred texts. Suggested readings would be from the Torah, the Gospels, and the Qur'an. This movement to share worship between Christianity and Islam is known as **Chrislam** by its advocates.[252]

This sounds benign; however, it has prophetic significance. This was the start of the one-world religion talked about in the book of Revelation.

> And **all that dwell upon the earth shall worship him**, *whose names are not written in the book of life of the Lamb slain from the foundation of the world.* (Revelation 13:8 KJV, emphasis added)

Since everyone on the earth will worship the Antichrist, this means at some point in time there will be a one-world religion. This seems hard to imagine since the religions of the world are not in harmony with each another. On the other hand, the Interfaith Alliance movement is a strong movement to bring the religions together. The United Nations even has an interfaith committee dedicated to this purpose. Many see this as a solution to end terrorism and endless wars.

Who is Promoting Chrislam?
Tony Blair

When Tony Blair left office, he set up an interfaith organization. The Tony Blair Foundation is a charity that promotes a greater understanding between religions. The foundation has dedicated a lot of money to promote the foundation's work among the Islamic, Christian, and Jewish faiths. It is composed of individuals from six faiths.

- Dr. Ismail Khudr Al-Shatti (a leader in the Islamic Constitutional Movement of the Muslim Brotherhood)
- Mustafa Cerić (Grand Mufti of Bosnia-Herzegovina)
- Reverend David Coffey (president of the Baptist World Alliance)
- Rabbi David Rosen (chairman of the International Jewish Committee on Interreligious Consultations)
- Chief Rabbi Sir Jonathan Sacks (chief rabbi of the United Hebrew Congregations of the Commonwealth)
- Reverend Rick Warren (founding and senior Pastor of Saddleback Church)[253]

ISNA

The Islamic Society of North America (ISNA), a part of the US Muslim Brotherhood, attended and openly supported the first interfaith presentation by Tony Blair in America on May 30, 2008. The event was opened by **Bill Clinton**.[254]

Rick Warren
Rick Warren has been the leader in promoting Chrislam in America.[255] He is the author of the book *"The Purpose Driven Life*. This book completely contradicts the Scriptures on worship of God, repentance, and salvation by Yeshua (Jesus).

> *But though we, or an angel from heaven, preach any other gospel unto you than that which we have preached unto you, let him be accursed.* (Galatians 1:18 KJV)

Pope Benedict XVI
The pope, on October 27, 2011, presided over the first inter-regional gathering in Assisi, Italy. During the interfaith meeting, he called for peace between all religious parties.[256]

The following appeared in the Common Word, an organization of Muslim scholars and clerics that declares that Islam and Christianity share the same Abrahamic heritage and the two greatest commandments:

> *The more recent A Common Word letter echoed a theme consonant with my first encyclical the unbreakable bond between love of God and love of neighbor, and the fundamental contradiction of resorting to violence or exclusion in the name of God.*[257]

WEA
The World Evangelical Alliance (WEA) responded to the open letters in the Common Word that Christians want peace with Muslims but also expressed their concerns over the repression of Christians throughout the world.[258]

Chrislam: The Coming One-World Religion

The book of Revelation tells us that we will move toward a one-world religion that will worship the Antichrist. The Scriptures also warn us not to be deceived or we will be cursed.

> *I marvel that ye are so soon removed from him that called you into the grace of Christ unto another gospel: Which is not another; but there be some that trouble you, and would pervert the gospel of Christ. But though we, or an angel from heaven, preach any other gospel unto you than that, which we have preached unto you, let him be accursed. As we said before, so say I now again, if any man preach any other gospel unto you than that ye have received, let him be accursed. For do I now persuade men, or God? Or do I seek to please men? For if I yet pleased men, I should not be the servant of Christ.* (Galatians 1:6–10 KJV)

Chrislam appears to be the foundation for this final one-world religion. This blending of Christianity and Islam follows the oath of the interfaith movement that believes that all religions are equal and provide paths to the same destination.[259]

This contradicts the Scriptures, which say there is only one way to salvation and that is by the blood of Yeshua (Jesus). Don't be deceived by this false doctrine.

The Counterfeit Millennium

The late Vince Havner, who was born in "Jugtown," North Carolina, is probably the most quoted preacher in America. He wrote about this period of time in "The Counterfeit Millennium" in which he warned us **"let no man deceive you by any means"** (2 Thessalonians 2:3). He went on to say that "the spirit behind most of the movements now promising a new world is not Christian." Satan is the great imitator. Every time God starts something, the devil comes up with a counterfeit. When our Lord came to earth there was a Roman peace—law and order by imperial force. Before He comes again there will be another Roman peace. That peace will be shattered when the true nature of Antichrist becomes apparent, but he (the Antichrist) will first delude mankind with his program.[260]

COUNTERFEIT AMBASSADOR FOR CHRIST
Vance Havner said, "The devil is not fighting against religion; he is too smart for that. He is producing a counterfeit Christianity so much like the real one that good Christians are afraid to speak out against it." The contemporary churches and the new emerging churches that embrace Islam are worthy examples of counterfeit churches. However, to criticize they can bring on the disdain of the organized church and the government.[261]

WHAT ABOUT COUNTERFEIT CHRISTIANS?
Now we know from the Gospels that there will be counterfeit Christians in the last days of the age. Yeshua made this clear to the disciples when He taught the parable of the tares. He also told us that there would be false apostles in the church to lead us astray.

> *For such are false apostles, deceitful workers, transforming themselves into the apostles of Christ. 14 And no marvel; for Satan himself is transformed into an angel of light. Therefore it is no great thing if his ministers also be transformed as the ministers of righteousness; whose end shall be according to their works.* (2 Corinthians 11:13–15 KJV)

Christians will say their minister is "a man of God" and really he is a minister of the devil.

Do you think you are smart enough to know the difference? If you do not know the Scriptures, there is no way you will know.[262]

WHAT DID YESHUA SAY ABOUT THIS?
The disciples had asked Jesus to explain what would be the signs of His return to earth.

And there was war in heaven: Michael and his angels fought against the dragon; and the dragon fought and his angels, and prevailed not; neither was their place found any more in heaven. And the great dragon was cast out, that old serpent, called the Devil, and Satan, which deceiveth the whole world: he was cast out into the earth, and his angels were cast out with him. (Revelation 12:7–9 KJV)

Could the false Christs and false prophets be fallen angels disguised as church leaders who are manipulating and deceiving Christians? If so, how would we identify them?

Beware of false prophets, which come to you in sheep's clothing, but inwardly they are ravening **wolves**. (Matthew 7:15 KJV, emphasis added)

Sheep refers to the followers of Christ the Shepherd. So there are Antichrists disguised as followers of Christ. Satan will use whatever dirty trick he can to lead you astray.

Paul warned us about these false Christs or ministers as follows:

But I fear, lest by any means, as the serpent beguiled Eve through his subtilty, so your minds should be corrupted from the simplicity that is in Christ. For if he that cometh preacheth another Jesus, whom we have not preached, or if ye receive another spirit, which ye have not received, or another gospel, which ye have not accepted, ye might well bear with him…For such are false apostles, deceitful workers, transforming themselves into the apostles of Christ. And no marvel; for Satan himself is transformed into an angel of light. Therefore it is no great thing if **his ministers also be transformed as the ministers of righteousness;** *whose end shall be according to their works.* (2 Corinthians 11:3–4, 13–15 KJV, emphasis added)

Behold, I send you forth as sheep in the midst of wolves: be ye therefore wise as serpents, and harmless as doves. (Matthew 10:16 KJV)

> *Go your ways: behold, I send you forth as lambs among wolves.* (Luke 10:3 KJV)
>
> *For I know this, that after my departing shall grievous wolves enter in among you, not sparing the flock.* (Acts 20:29 KJV)

So watch out for these Christian ministers who say they are doing YHVH's work by promoting love and peace with Islam. All they are doing is ushering in the new world religion called Chrislam.

CHAPTER 19

The Rise of the New World Order

To understand how close we are to a new world order or one-world government, all you have to do is to look on the back of a one-dollar bill. Underneath the pyramid are the Latin words *Noves Ordo Seculorium* or in English, "New World Order."²⁶³

President Franklin D. Roosevelt had a dream about a future one-world government. As a result of this dream, he had the words "New World Order" put on the one-dollar bill in 1935. Why would he want a one-world government? The answer is simple. He wanted a way to end all wars.²⁶⁴

In World War I, 8.2 million people were killed. People wanted to end the wars of aggression that resulted in all the deaths. President Woodrow Wilson wanted the United States to join the League of Nations, which would have been a centralized government that would result in the end of these wars. However, Congress would not ratify a treaty where the United States was part of the League of Nations.²⁶⁵

In the next war, World War II, 52 million people were killed. When the war was over, Roosevelt, Churchill, and Stalin met at Yalta in 1945 to settle the war and discuss the need for world security. This led to the replacement of the League of Nations and the formation of the United Nations.²⁶⁶

The United Nations is a foundational structure for a future one-world government. Now the Scriptures tell us that at the end of the age, the Antichrist will rule from a one-world government. This should cause some alarm to Christians of today.

> *And I stood upon the sand of the sea, and saw a beast (kingdom) rise up out of the sea, having seven heads and ten horns, and upon his horns ten crowns, and upon his heads the name of blasphemy. And the beast (kingdom) which I saw was like unto a leopard, and his feet were as the feet of a bear, and his mouth as the mouth of a lion: and the **dragon gave him his power, and his seat, and great authority.*** (Revelation 13:1–2 KJV, emphasis added)

Who is the dragon? The Scriptures say that the dragon is Satan.

> *And he laid hold on the dragon, that old serpent, which is the **Devil, and Satan, and bound him a thousand years**.* (Revelation 20:2 KJV, emphasis added)

The Scriptures tell us that Satan will rule the world through the one-world government.

Revelation 13 Tells us the Future of the New World Order

Revelation 13 is broken down as follows:

> Verses 1–8 tell about the coming one-world government.
> Verses 11–14 tell us about the coming one-world religion.
> Verses 16–18 tell us about the coming one-world economic system (this will be managed by the mark of the beast).

This new world order will be made up of countries or kingdoms united together under the rule of a one-world government. These countries are described as beasts in the book of Daniel. In the Scriptures, beasts are kingdoms.

The Beasts (Kingdoms) of the Scriptures

First, let's look at the beasts of Belshazzar's dream in Daniel 7 for an understanding of whom the beasts will represent when the new world order is formed.

> *And four great beasts [kingdoms] came up from the sea, diverse one from another. The first was like a* **lion,** *and* **had eagle's wings***: I beheld till the wings thereof were plucked, and it was lifted up from the earth, and made stand upon the feet as a man, and a man's heart was given to it.* (Daniel 7:3–4 KJV, emphasis added)

What country is represented as a lion today?

The lion represents Great Britain. The lion has been a symbol of Great Britain for a long time.

The eagle wings represent America. Just look at your dollar bill. The wings being plucked represents America being plucked out of Great Britain.

> *And behold another beast, a second, like to a* **bear,** *and it raised up itself on one side, and it had three ribs in the mouth of it between the teeth of it: and they said thus unto it, Arise, devour much flesh.* (Daniel 7:5 KJV, emphasis added)

The bear has always been the symbol of Russia.

> *After this I beheld, and lo another, like a* **leopard,** *which had* **upon the back of it four wings of a fowl; the beast had also four heads***; and dominion was given to it.* (Daniel 7:6 KJV, emphasis added)

The leopard is Germany. The rooster is the official emblem of France.

> *After this I saw in the night visions, and behold a fourth beast, dreadful and terrible, and strong exceedingly; and it had* **great iron teeth***:*

*it devoured and brake in pieces, and stamped the residue with the feet of it: and it was diverse from all the beasts that were before it; and **it had ten horns**. I considered the horns, and, behold, there came up among them another **little horn**, before whom there were three of the first horns plucked up by the roots: and, behold, in this **horn were eyes like the eyes of man, and a mouth speaking great things.*** (Daniel 7:7–8 KJV, emphasis added)

This beast represents the Islamic nations united under the caliphate. One man comes out of one of these nations and takes over two other nations. That means there will be eight nations and one great leader.

To summarize the one-world government in Daniel 7:

The lion is Great Britain.
The eagle wings plucked out of the lion is America.
The bear is Russia.
The leopard is Germany.
The fowl on the back of the leopard is France.
The ten-horned beast is the Islamic nations under the caliphate. The man speaking great things must be the Mahdi Messiah of the Muslims and the Antichrist of the Scriptures.

Here is wisdom. These beasts are grouped by language.

The lion and eagle wings are English-speaking countries.

The bear represents Russian-speaking countries.

The Leopard represents German-speaking countries. There are four countries today that speak German as their official language. Also, we discussed earlier that the Holy Roman Empire consisted of Belgium, France, Luxembourg, the Netherlands, and part of Germany.

The fowl represents French-speaking countries.

The ten-horned beast's countries all speak Arabic.

If this opinion is correct, then the composite beast of Daniel 7 consists of Great Britain, Russia, the Holy Roman Empire reborn, and the Arab alliance of ten countries.

What about the Beast in the Book of Revelation?

And I stood upon the sand of the sea, and saw a beast rise up out of the sea, having seven heads and ten horns, and upon his horns ten crowns, and upon his heads the name of blasphemy. (Revelation 13:1 KJV)

This is the same beast of Daniel that has ten horns. The verse states that the beast (nation) stood on the **sand**. Which countries have lots of sand? They are Arab countries. Sea always refers to multitudes of people. This verse is saying that the beast (nation) came out of the Arab countries.

Notice it also says that the heads have the name of blasphemy. This must be the Bismillah on their heads, which is blasphemous to YHVH. Remember we said that the Bismillah says, "In the Name of Allah, and Muhammad is his messenger."

This is the same beast kingdom of Daniel 7 that represents a federation of Arab countries.

And the beast which I saw was like unto a leopard, and his feet were as the feet of a bear, and his mouth as the mouth of a lion: and the dragon gave him his power, and his seat, and great authority. (Revelation 13:2 KJV)

This is the same composite beast of Daniel except with less detail.

The Scripture say that the **composite beast** has seven heads as follows:

When Daniel interpreted Belshazzar's dream of the four kingdoms, it was about 550 BC. It is estimated that John saw this vision in about AD 96. The vision had the exact same symbols 650 years later.

WHAT ELSE DO THE SCRIPTURES SAY ABOUT THIS COMPOSITE BEAST (KINGDOM)?

> *And I saw* **one of his heads as it were wounded to death;** *and his deadly wound was healed: and* **all the world wondered after the beast**. (Revelation 13:3 KJV, emphasis added)

First, let's look at one possible explanation of the deadly wound that is now healed.

At the end of World War II, Germany was divided between the West and the Soviet Union. In addition, Berlin was also divided between the West and the Soviet Union. This was referred to as the deadly wound against Germany so that they could not start any more wars. However, in 1989, the Berlin Wall came down and East and West Germany were reunited. The deadly wound was healed. This means that the leopard head that had the wound and was healed is Germany.[267]

The second possibility is that this is referring to the Roman Catholic Church. The Roman Catholic Church was dealt a death blow when Napoleon had his general take the pope prisoner. This was a deadly wound to the papacy.

WHAT DOES THE COMPOSITE BEAST REPRESENT?

Next, the word "all" means the **whole world wondered after the beast (kingdom)**.

This means that the composite beast represents a **one-world government**.

*And they **worshipped the dragon** which gave power unto the beast: and they worshipped the beast, saying, who is like unto the beast? Who is able to make war with him? And there was given unto him a mouth speaking great things and blasphemies; and power was given unto him to continue forty and two months.* (Revelation 13:4–5 KJV, emphasis added)

What about the Beast in Revelation 17?

*And there came one of the seven angels which had the seven vials, and talked with me, saying unto me, Come hither; I will shew unto thee the judgment of the **great whore** that sitteth upon many waters: With whom the kings of the earth have committed fornication, and the inhabitants of the earth have been made drunk with the wine of her fornication. So he carried me away in the spirit into the wilderness: and I saw a woman sit upon a **scarlet coloured beast**, full of names of blasphemy, having seven heads and ten horns. And the woman was arrayed in purple and scarlet colour, and decked with gold and precious stones and pearls, having a golden cup in her hand full of abominations and filthiness of her fornication.* (Revelation 17:1–4 KJV, emphasis added)

Notice that this beast has a woman (church) riding on it. The church is referred to as a harlot.

The Scriptures picture a pure woman (church) as the bride of Christ.

For I am jealous over you with godly jealousy: for I have espoused you to one husband that I may present you as a chaste virgin to Christ. (2 Corinthians 11:2 KJV)

A harlot church is also pictured in the Scriptures.

And yet they [Israel] would not hearken unto their judges, but they went a whoring after other gods, and bowed themselves unto them: they turned quickly out of the way which their fathers walked in, obeying the commandments of the LORD; but they did not so. (Judges 2:17 KJV)

The harlot church riding on the composite beast can only be the Roman Catholic Church along with the Protestant churches.

Also please note that this beast is red in color. Red is the color of communism and socialism. This means the one-world government of the false prophet and the Antichrist will be socialist.

Based on Daniel 7 and Revelation 13 and 17, it appears that the composite beast can only be the Roman Catholic Church of the Holy Roman Empire reborn in confederation with the alliance of the ten Islamic nations. The opinion is that the false prophet will be the most important Christian in the world and the Antichrist will be the Mahdi of the ten allied Islamic nations.

ONE-WORLD RELIGION

In Revelation 13:15, the Scriptures tell us there will be a one-world religion.

And he [false prophet] had power to give life unto the image of the beast [antichrist], that the image of the beast should both speak, and cause that as many as would not worship the image of the beast should be killed. (Revelation 13:15 KJV)

This verse is saying that at some point in the future, everyone will be required to worship the Antichrist. Now there are many different religions on earth. The Roman Catholics and Protestants are about two billion. Islam is about 1.5 billion, and Hinduism is about 950 million. These are the three largest groups out of nineteen major world religions.

In order for the prophecy to work in Revelation 13:15, the false prophet will have to get all the world's religions to come under one umbrella of worship. Then through the miracles, they will be coached to worship the Antichrist. If you refuse to worship the Antichrist, you will be killed.

Who is promoting the New One-World Order?

The answer to this was question was surprising to me.

The Vatican

All the popes from Pius XII to Pope Benedict have promoted the formation of a strong one world order or government. This promotion is well documented in position papers issued by the Vatican.[268]

Pope Pius XII

He was the pope during World War II and the formation of the United Nations.

In "Vital Speeches of the Day"—on December 15, 1959, the pope had a lot to say about regarding the United Nations in the following:

Title: "Legacy to World Federalism"

The main points of the speech were as follows:

1. reaffirmation of necessity of a supranational world order
2. support for the United Nations
3. support for agencies that support international cooperation

Pope Pius XII said, "Catholics above all must realize that they are called to overcome every vestige of **"nationalistic narrowness."**

What is "nationalistic narrowness"? This referring to sovereign countries that want to run themselves. He is saying that countries need to overcome this and give up their sovereignty to the United Nations.[269]

Pope John XXIII

In the published encyclical from *Look* magazine on July 2, 1963, the pope issued the "Pacem in Terris," stating that "men's common interests make it imperative that at long last a worldwide community of nations be established." He went on to say this is required because "there is also a growing economic interdependence between States."[270]

Pope Paul VI

In the published encyclical on March 26, 1967, the pope spoke of the need for an effective world authority. He said, "Who can fail to see the need and importance of thus gradually coming to the establishment of a world authority capable of taking necessary effective action on the juridical and political planes." Delegates to international organizations, public officials, gentlemen of the press, teachers and educators…all of you must realize that you have your part to play in the construction of a **NEW WORLD ORDER**.[271]

Pope John Paul I

He was assassinated after 33 days in office.[272]

Pope John Paul II

In the published encyclical on January 2, 2004, the pope called for a new world order. He rang in the New Year with a renewed call for peace in the Middle East and Africa and the creation of a new world order based on respect for the dignity of man and equality among nations.[273]

Pope Benedict XVI

On June 29, 2009, Pope Benedict XVI issued the encyclical letter to the Catholic Church and the whole world. In his message, he calls for a new one-world bank, and all nations would be a subsidiary to a reformed United Nations. In section 67 of the letter, it says the following: [274]

> *In the face of unrelenting growth of global interdependence, there is a strongly felt need, even in the midst of a global recession, for a reform of the* **United Nations Organization**, *and likewise of* **economic institutions and international finance,** *so that the concept of the family of nations can acquire* **real teeth.** *One also senses the urgent need to find innovative ways of implementing the principle of the* **responsibility to protect and of giving poorer nations an effective voice in shared decision making. This seems necessary in order to arrive at a political, juridical and economic order which can increase and give direction to international cooperation for the development of all peoples in solidarity. To manage the global economy; to revive economies hit by crisis; to avoid any deterioration of the greater imbalances that would result; to bring about integral and timely disarmament, food, security and peace; to guarantee the protection of the environment and to regulate migration: for all this there is urgent need of a true world political authority**, as my predecessor Blessed John XXIII indicated several years ago. Such an authority would need to be regulated by law, to observe consistently the principles of subsidiary and solidarity, to seek to establish the common good, and to make a commitment to securing authentic integral human development inspired by the values of charity and truth. Furthermore, such an authority would need to be* **universally recognized** *and to be* **vested with the effective power to ensure security for all**, *regard for justice, and to* **ensure compliance with its decisions from all parties**, *and also with the coordinated measures adopted in various international forums.* (Emphasis added)

This statement from the Vatican is promoting a one-world government (the United Nations) with all countries subordinate.

This would mean we would have to throw out our constitution in America.

The pope wants the United Nations to have "real teeth." He wants teeth for enforcement.

Let's look at his message regarding the United Nations:

1. manage global economy
2. disarmament (only United Nations to have arms)
3. food security (sounds like the mark of the beast)
4. protection of the environment
5. regulation of migration

Pierre Bouillon, Bishop of Verdun, France, said the following:

> Therefore we must emphasize the great moral responsibility to empower an international authority to prevent war. The entire world must become aware that if this institution [UN] is to become effective, every nation must renounce its ultimate sovereignty to this universal authority. This is an obligation. If nations, if rulers of nations, if public opinion will not accept this renunciation, then they are really voting for war, however beautiful may be there speeches on peace.[275]

The Vatican has been promoting a one-world government for a long time. The Scriptures tell us that there will be a one-world government. The Scriptures also tell us that there will be a one-world religion cooperating with the one-world government.

MIKHAIL GORBACHEV'S *PERASTIKA*

In his book *Perastika*, Gorbachev stated that the three main causes of wars on earth as follows:

1. political conflicts

2. religious conflicts
3. economic conflicts

He also said there are three solutions for wars on the earth as follows:

1. a one-world government
2. a global religious system
3. A global economy

Mikhail Gorbachev actually had proposed exactly what the Scriptures say is going to happen in Revelation 13.[276]

Influence on the United Nations

The Roman Catholic Church has exerted much influence on the United Nations since Pope Pius XII was in office. A good example of this is the Genocide Pact by the United Nations.

Catholics have the obligation of insisting on the ratification of the Genocide Pact. The genocide pact was signed on November 11, 1988, by President Ronald Reagan. So what is the Genocide Pact?[277]

The *Encyclopedia Britannica* says the following:

The definition of *genocide* by the encyclopedia is "to cause physical harm or mental harm to a minority."[278]

This treaty makes it a crime to cause mental harm to a minority. There are many examples of how this is being implemented. One example is the hate crime law. Many countries are now passing laws that supposedly prevent mental harm to a minority group.

Mikhail Gorbachev had the following to say about genocide:

In his book *Perastika*, Gorbachev said, "We must **extirpate all genocide, apartheid and religious exclusiveness**."[279]

Extirpate means "to kill off."

Gorbachev is advocating killing everyone that is guilty of genocide, apartheid, and religious exclusiveness as a necessary requirement to usher in the new world order.

So what does he mean by religious exclusiveness? This is when you think your religion is the correct way to worship and all the other religions are wrong. He wants to remove this type of thinking because it prevents your group from becoming part of a one-world religion. It also means that if you refuse, you should be killed.

Trends regarding this have already shown up in the United States government. Military chaplains now are forbidden by the government from using the name of Jesus in their public prayers or sermons. This prohibition is now showing up in veterans' cemeteries around the nation where the name "God," "Jesus," or "God Bless" are banned.

Since Christianity is an exclusive religion, you or your church could be guilty of "exclusiveness," and you could be arrested and put on trial. In some countries now, their governments have passed laws outlawing "exclusiveness." France now has a law that targets religious exclusiveness. The French law proposes that you could get two years in prison for **excessive pressure** in an attempt to **proselytize** people to join your religion.

This could mean that a preacher or a member of the clergy who keeps inviting you to join his or her church could be charged with a crime. So we must be watchful for laws that attempt to stop the church members from trying to encourage people to come to their church. If they can get away with enacting these laws, then it's open season to arrest the clergy under these so-called hate laws.[280]

Are the World Leaders Supporting these Laws?

Absolutely! Bill Clinton and Tony Blair are strong supporters of a one-world government. They obviously believe that would solve all the world's conflicts and provide peace and safety for everyone. Even Russian leaders want this. President Obama has taken it a step closer by bypassing Congress and going to the UN for a war against Libya. Recently the Obama administration has indicated that they are going to other countries to get permission to attack Syria. Our leaders are moving ever closer to a one-world government.[281]

The Roman Catholic Church is also pushing the United States in that direction. They also have a goal to take over the old city of Jerusalem. In 1994, the Vatican signed an agreement with Israel to gain control over the holy sites in Jerusalem. These plans were secret until finally being revealed by Joel Bainerman.[282]

For centuries the Vatican has been pushing its replacement doctrine, which states that the Catholic Church has replaced Israel as "the new Israel." The only way this can happen is for a strong one-world government to be in place that the Vatican can influence to give them control over the old city of Jerusalem.[283]

What is the Vatican's Agenda?

The agenda is first to get a new-world government in place that has teeth to make all the countries subservient. The United Nations will be that one-world government. The second goal is to get control of Jerusalem. Thirdly, they believe there is no place for the restoration of the nation of Israel in its theology. The obstacle to the Vatican claiming to be the New Jerusalem and the rightful heir to the kingdom of God is the occupation of Jerusalem by the Jews. So how is the Vatican going to convince the world that its version of theology is correct?[284]

According to Joel Bainerman, the Vatican is going to have everyone believe this "mysterious individual" who will "unite the faiths" and appear in Jerusalem, which will be under the control of an authority headed by the Vatican. This so-called "messiah" that will be proclaimed will be a false one and it will insist that by having a "world government" that world peace and harmony will be ushered in.[285]

Israel's Leader not caving in to the Vatican

When President Obama put pressure on Prime Minister Benjamin Netanyahu to withdraw to the 1967 borders, the prime minister rejected the plan. The reason given was that Israel could not defend herself with these borders, and he is correct. Also it would mean giving up Jerusalem. The president was pushing the Vatican agenda.[286]

On September 23, 2011, the Quartet—which is made up by the United States, the European Union, Russia, and the United Nations—issued a plan requiring Israel and Palestine to agree on new borders where Palestine shares Jerusalem. The deadline was before the end of 2012.[287]

The New World Order is at our Doorstep

This year a US Navy chaplain was convicted by a military jury of a misdemeanor count for disobeying his commanding officer for wearing his uniform while delivering a prayer "In Jesus's name" at an assembly in front of the White House. In Houston, the veterans' cemetery banned the word "God" from all military funerals. Requests for messages or prayers can be formally submitted for the director's approval, but the mention of God is not allowed. The cemetery chapel was closed to prevent anyone praying there. The present US administration has enacted these requirements in an effort to keep any agency connected to the military from praying to God or using the name Jesus.[288]

Everything is falling into place to institute the new world order. All that is needed is a trigger to initiate it.

CHAPTER 20

Prophecies in the Scriptures

THE SCRIPTURES TELL US EVERYTHING that is going to happen in the future.

> *Remember, the former things of old: for I am [YHVH], and there is none else: I am [YHVH], and there is none like me, **Declaring the end from the beginning**, and from ancient times the things that are not yet done saying, My council shall stand, and I will do all my pleasure.* (Isaiah 46:9–10 KJV, emphasis added)

The Scriptures also state that there is an appointed time for everything:

> *"For every matter there is an **appointed time**, even a time for every pursuit under the heavens."* (Ecclesiastes 3:1 KJV, emphasis added)
>
> *The evil spirits said to Yeshua, and see, they cried out, saying, "What have we to do with You, Yeshua, Son of Elohim? Have you come here to torture us, before the **appointed time?**"* (Matthew 8:29 ISR, emphasis added)

Even the evil spirits on earth know there is an **appointed time** that Satan and his fallen angels will be punished in the lake of fire as described in the book of Revelation and in the book of Enoch.

These prophecies regarding events that will happen at their **appointed times** appear sixty five times throughout the Scriptures in both the Old Testament and the New Testament. So since there is an

appointed time for every event in the future, and if we understand the prophecies in the Scriptures, then we know what is going to happen before it happens.

Why is it Important to understand where we are on YHVH's Calendar?

I believe that the appointed time of Yeshua's return to earth is very close.

> *Therefore be ye also ready: for in such an hour as ye think not the Son of Man cometh.* (Matthew 24:14 KJV)
>
> *And take heed to yourselves, lest at any time your hearts be overcharged with surfeiting, and drunkenness, and cares of this life, and so that the day come upon you unawares.* (Luke 21:34 KJV)
>
> *But as the days of Noah were, so shall also the coming of the son of man be.* (Matthew 24:37 KJV)

We all know the story of Noah: how he was told to build a boat so that he and his family could be saved from the flood that was to come. When Noah shut the door of the ark, the rains had not started. So when YHVH shuts the door in heaven, destruction will again come upon the people of the earth.

There is great danger in becoming so busy with the cares of this life that we don't get our life in order for His return. If we are not ready, we will be surprised, unprepared spiritually and lost. Understanding the prophecies in the Scriptures will help to tell us where we are at on YHVH's calendar and how close we are to Yeshua's return.

Why Cloak Bible Prophecies in Symbols?

The Scriptures are full of references to beasts, water, women, dragons, harlots, etc. One answer may be as follows:

And He said, unto you it has been given to know the mysteries of the kingdom of [YHVH], but to the rest it is given in parables; that seeing they might not see, and in hearing they might not understand. (Luke 8:10 KJV)

We must understand these symbols and their meaning in order to understand prophecy in the Scriptures.

Fortunately, the Scriptures tell us what the symbols represent, and so we can understand the prophecies.

What are some of the Prophetic symbols in Scripture? [289]

Winds: Strife, war, commotion. (Jeremiah 25:31–33; 49:36, 37)

Waters: Peoples, multitudes, and nations. (Revelation 17:15; Isaiah 8:7)

Beasts: Kingdoms, political power. (Daniel 7:17, 23; Rev. 13:2, 3, 7)

Bear: Destructive power/Medo-Persia. (Proverbs 28:15, 2 Kings 2:23–24, Daniel 7:5)

Leopard: Greece. (Daniel 7:6)

Lion: Yeshua/Powerful King. (Revelation 5:4–9, Jeremiah 50:43–44, Daniel 7: 4, 17, 23)

Ram: Medo-Persia. (Daniel 8:20)

Goat: Greece. (Daniel 8:21)

Wolf: Disguised enemies that hunt in a time of darkness. (Matthew 7:15)

Horse: Strength of power in battle (Job 39:19; Psalm 147:10; Proverbs 21:31). Color of horse indicates type of spirit or a belief system. (Zechariah 6:1–8; Revelation 6:1–8)

Harlot: Apostate church or religion. (Isaiah 1:21–27; Jeremiah 3:1–3, 6–9)

Babylon: Apostasy/confusion/ rebellion against how YHVH said to worship Him. (Genesis 10:8–10, 11:6–9; Revelation 2–3; 17:1–5)

Dragon: Satan or his agency. (Isaiah 27:1; 30:6, Psalm 74:13–14; Revelation 12:7–9, Ezekiel 29:3; Jeremiah 51:34)

Serpent: Satan. (Revelation 12:9; 20:2)

Woman: The church/ pure, true church. (Jeremiah 6:2; 2 Corinthians 11:2; Ephesians 5:23–27)

Lamb: Yeshua's sacrifice. (John 1:29; 1 Corinthians 5:7; Genesis 22:7–8)

Time: A year or 360 days. (Daniel 4:16, 23, 25, 32; 7:25)

Times: Two years or 720 days.

Day: (in heaven) A thousand years on earth. (2 Peter 3:8)

Saints: They keep the commandments (first works) of YHVH and have the testimony of Yeshua. They keep the Sabbath day of worship. (Revelation 12:12, 14, 17)

Mark: Sign of approval. (Ezekiel 9:4; Romans 4:11; Revelation 13:17; 14:9–11; 7:2–3)

Seal: Sign of approval. (Romans 4:11; Revelation 7:2–3)

Trumpet: Loud warning of YHVH's approach or judgment. (Exodus 19:16–17; Joshua 6:4–5)

Many of the numbers in the Scriptures have a deeper prophetic meaning or spiritual significance.[290]

Since Yeshua said, "The very hairs of your head are all numbered" (Matthew 10:30 KJV), then let's examine numbers in the Scriptures for any special significance. At least twelve numbers stand out, such as 3, 6, 7, 10, 12, 40, 50, and 70. The following are examples of possible meanings for you to consider:

The **number 3** represents the Godhead. The angels cry "Holy" three times to the triune God (Isaiah 6:3).

The **number 6** represents the worship of man. For example, man was created on the sixth day (Genesis 1:26, 31). In the book of Revelation, 666 identifies the beast, and it is the number of a man (Revelation 13:18).

The **number 7** represents perfection, and it is the sign of YHVH, divine worship, completions, obedience, and rest. It is used 562 times in the Scriptures. It is the most common number in Scripture prophecy. In the book of Revelation, there are seven churches, seven spirits, seven golden candlesticks, seven stars, seven lamps, seven seals, seven horns, seven eyes, seven angels, seven trumpets, seven thunders, seven thousand slain in a great earthquake, seven heads, seven crowns, seven last plagues, seven golden vials, seven mountains, and seven kings.

The **number 10** represents law and restoration. For example, the Ten Commandments.

The **number 12** represents the foundation of YHVH's authority. Yeshua had twelve disciples and there were twelve tribes of Israel. The New Jerusalem had twelve foundations, twelve gates, twelve thousand furlongs, and a tree with twelve kinds of fruits eaten twelve times a year.

The **number 40** represents a generation and a time of fasting. It rained for forty days during the flood. Moses spent forty years in the desert. Yeshua fasted for forty days.

The **number 50** represents power and celebration. The Jubilee came after the forty-ninth year and Pentecost occurred fifty days after Yeshua's resurrection.

The **number 70** represents human leadership and judgment. Moses appointed seventy elders. The Sanhedrin was made up of seventy men. Yeshua chose seventy disciples. YHVH's judgment on Israel was seventy years in Babylon.

Now that we know what these symbols and numbers mean, we can better understand the prophecies in the Old and New Testaments. Since everything has an **appointed time**, understanding the prophecies in the Scriptures can give us a clue to where we are on YHVH's calendar.

Are there Prophecies in the Old Testament for Today's Events?

Yes. Let's look at things prophesied about Israel.

In the book of Genesis, YHVH made a covenant with Abraham.

> *In this same day the L*ORD *made a covenant with Abraham saying, unto thy seed have I given this land, from the river of Egypt unto the great river, the river Euphrates. [YHVH] made a covenant to give Abraham and his children all the land from Egypt to the Euphrates River forever.* (Genesis 15:18 KJV)

YHVH had made a covenant with Abraham and all his children to possess all the land from Egypt to the river Euphrates. They did possess the land until they displeased YHVH. First, they were taken into bondage by the Babylonians. During the Roman occupation, most of Israel was destroyed. The ones who escaped destruction moved to safer parts of the world.

During World War II, the Jews in Russia and Europe were slaughtered by Hitler. After the war, world opinion was to find a safe place for the Jews. So on May 14, 1948, the UN voted them to have their original homeland as their country. So the nation of Israel was born on May 14, 1948, in one day.

This was a prophecy in the book of Isaiah.

> *Who hath heard such a thing? Who hath seen such things? Shall the earth be made to bring forth in one day? Or shall a nation be born at once? For as such Zion travailed, she brought forth her children* (Isaiah 66:8–9 KJV)

THUS THE PROPHECY THE NATION OF ISRAEL WILL BE BORN IN ONE DAY HAS BEEN FULFILLED.

Returning the Jews back to their homeland also created a major problem with the Palestinians. They also claimed this as their homeland, and several wars have broken out between Israel and their surrounding countries. As a result, the world has tried to get Israel to trade some of their land to Palestine for peace. Even certain leaders in Israel agreed with this approach.

Isaiah saw this and he wrote about it.

Because ye [scornful men in Jerusalem] have said, we have made a covenant with death, and with hell are we at agreement…And your covenant with death shall be disannulled, and your agreement with hell shall not stand; when the overflowing scourge shall pass through, then ye shall be trodden down by it. (Isaiah 28:15, 18 KJV)

The Oslo Accords were signed between Israel, and the PLO was signed on **September 13, 1993,** at the White House. It was a framework agreement where Israel would give up land for peace. This agreement directly conflicted with the covenant by YHVH with Abram: "In the same day, the LORD made a covenant with Abram, saying, Unto thy seed have I given this land, from the river of Egypt, unto the great river Euphrates [including the ten tribes that were settled in the land]" (Genesis 15:18–21 KJV).[291]

Also, it has been recently revealed that Cardinal Joseph Ratzinger (now Pope Benedict) signed a secret agreement with Israel's Rabin government on December 30, 1993, to give up control over the old city of Jerusalem to the United Nations. The Vatican would be in charge of the holy sites. Why? The Vatican has been pushing for years its replacement doctrine, which states that the Catholic Church has replaced Israel as "the new Israel." The present government of Israel will not comply with this agreement.[292]

Seven years after signing the Oslo Accords on **September 28, 2000,** Ariel Sharon went up on the temple mount in Jerusalem and read verses in the book of Ezekiel regarding the restoration of Israel (Ezekiel 37:17–19). That same day, violent riots and clashes between the Palestinians and Israelis broke out, ending the truce brought about by the Oslo Accords. Arafat launched a wave of violence against Israel called the Al-Aqsa Intifada. Thus the prophecies in Isaiah were fulfilled. Most of you who saw the event on TV did not realize that Isaiah had prophesied this very event thousands of year's earlier.[293]

THUS THE PROPHECY WITH DEATH HAS BEEN FULFILLED.
What else did Isaiah prophesy about?

> *And there shall be upon every high mountain and upon every high hill, rivers and streams of waters in the **day of the great slaughter**, when the **towers fall**.* (Isaiah 30:25 KJV, emphasis added)

This occurred on **September 11, 2001,** when the **twin towers of the World Trade Center fell** in New York due to the attack by Muslims and thousands were killed (**slaughtered**).

Over three thousand people were slaughtered when the two towers collapsed, fulfilling Isaiah's prophecy.

This prophecy of the fall of the towers was fulfilled on September 11, 2001.

ARE THERE OTHER PROPHECIES IN THE BOOK OF ISAIAH AND OTHER BOOKS THAT ARE NOT YET FULFILLED?
THE BURDEN OF DAMASCUS.

> *Behold, Damascus is taken away from being a city, and it shall be a ruinous heap.* (Isaiah 17:1 KJV)

This prophecy has not occurred yet, so this is a future event.

THE BURDEN OF BABYLON.

> *Howl ye, for the day of the LORD is at hand; it shall come as a destruction from the almighty... [YHVH] himself will return to destroy Babylon. Behold, the day of the LORD cometh, cruel both with wrath and fierce anger, to lay the land desolate: and he shall destroy the sinners therefore out of it.* (Isaiah 13:6, 9 KJV)

This is a future event. This is the battle of Armageddon. It also is described in Revelation 14:8; 16:19; 17:5; 18:2, 10.

Here is wisdom. Just as Satan had orchestrated the first Babylon, so he will again with create the Mystery Babylon, which is the new one-world government.

Thermonuclear War is Prophesied

Yes, it was prophesied in the Old Testament. Read Zechariah 5:1–11:

Then I turned, and lifted up mine eyes, looked, and behold a flying roll…the length of thereof is twenty cubits, and the breadth thereof ten cubits. Then he said to unto me, this the curse that goeth forth over the face of the whole earth. [This means either Israel or literally over the whole earth]: for every one that stealeth shall be cut off [killed] as on this side according to it; and every one that sweareth, shall be cut off [killed] as on that side according to it. I will bring it forth, saith the Lord *of hosts, and it shall enter into the house of the thief, and into the house of him that sweareth falsely by my name: and it shall* **remain in the midst of his house, and shall consume it with the timber thereof and the stones thereof***…And I said, What is it?… And behold there was lifted up a talent of lead: and this is a woman [mistranslation: It should say fire] that sitteth in the midst of the ephah [bucket]…And he cast the weight of lead upon the mouth thereof.* (kjv, emphasis added)

What is a round cylinder of lead with a fire in it that flies through the air? This is a missile with a nuclear warhead. What is this fire that remains in the house? Radiation. This is what Zachariah saw in his vision.

The nuclear war is a future event and many believe that when this happens, the new one-world government will be set up through the United Nations. The United Nations has already started their world dominance by declaring war on Libya.

You must understand the Prophecies in the Scriptures and Historical Events! This in Order to know what Time it is on YHVH's Calendar

By studying historical and current events and prophecies, we can tell where we are at the end of the age spoken about by Yeshua. Yeshua is coming soon, but we don't know the exact day or hour of the day. On the other hand, He has commanded us to be ready and to understand the events so that we will not be deceived by the Antichrist. In Matthew 24, Yeshua describes the events of the end of the age:

> *For there shall arise false Christs, and false prophets, and shall shew great signs and wonders; insomuch that, if it were possible, they shall deceive the very elect. Behold, I have told you before.* (Matthew 24:24–25 KJV)

The book of Revelation contains the final events that lead up to the return of Yeshua. It also describes the terrible events of rule of Satan and his other fallen angels just before Yeshua returns. You and I will be tested to see if we are true followers of Yeshua.

Remember the scene in heaven as John is describing YHVH's throne and the beasts around the throne and the twenty-four elders. The angel has a book in his hand and asks: "Who is worthy to open the book, and to loose the seals thereof?" (Revelation 5:2 KJV).

> *And no man in heaven, nor in the earth, neither under the earth, was able to open the book, neither to look thereon. And I [John] wept much, because no man was found worthy to open and to read the book, neither to look thereon.* (Revelation 5:3–4 KJV)

Why is John weeping? John is weeping because Satan has control of the earth and is determined to cause everyone to worship him. Satan knows his fate, and he wants everyone to be cast into hell with him. We also believe that the book is the book of prophecy because as Yeshua opens each seal, more and more of future history is revealed to John. Once the book is opened, the prophecies written in the book will become an actual event on the earth.

CHAPTER 21

The Seals

IN THE BOOK OF REVELATION, John sees a vision of Yeshua opening the seals. Most believe that these are the seals placed on the book placed there by YHVH. The only person worthy to remove the seals and open the book was the Lamb (Yeshua). When the first seal is opened, John sees a white horse. When the second seal is opened, John sees a red horse. When the third seal is opened, John sees a black horse. When the fourth seal is opened, John sees a pale horse. Let's look at the Scriptures' description.

> *And I saw when the Lamb opened one of the seals, and I heard, as it were the noise of thunder, one of the four beasts saying, come and see. And I saw, and behold a **white horse**: and he that sat on him had a **bow**; and a **crown** was given unto him: and he **went forth conquering, and to conquer**. And when he had opened the **second seal**, I heard the second beast say, Come and see. And there went out another horse that was **red**: and power was given to him that sat thereon to **take peace from the earth**, and that **they should kill one another**: and there was **given unto him a great sword**. And when he had opened the **third seal**, I heard the third beast say, Come and see. And I beheld, and lo a **black horse**; and he that sat on him had a **pair of balances in his hand**. And I heard a voice in the midst of the four beasts say, a **measure of wheat for a penny**, and **three measures of barley for a penny**; and see thou **hurt not the oil and the wine**. And when he*

had opened the **fourth seal**, I heard the voice of the fourth beast say, come and see. And I looked, and behold a **pale horse**: and his name that sat on him was Death, and Hell followed with him. And power was given unto them over **the fourth part of the earth, to kill with sword, and with hunger, and with death, and with the beasts (kingdoms) of the earth.** (Revelation 6:1–8 KJV, emphasis added)

What are these Horses and what do they Mean?

The Scriptures always give us the definitions and meanings of symbols. We have to look in another place in the Scriptures to find the answer, and we found it in the book of Zechariah in chapter 6:

And I turned, and lifted up mine eyes, and looked, and, behold, there came four chariots out from between two mountains; and the mountains were mountains of brass. In the first chariot were **red horses**; *and in the second chariot* **black horses**; *and in the third chariot* **white horses**; *and in the fourth chariot* **grisled and bay** *horses. Then I answered and said unto the angel that talked with me, what are these, my lord? And the angel answered and said unto me, these are the* **four spirits** *of the heavens, which go forth from standing before the* LORD *of all the earth. The black horses which are therein go forth into the North Country; and the white go forth after them; and the grisled go forth toward the south country. And the bay went forth, and sought to go that they might walk to and fro through the earth: and he said, Get you hence, walk to and fro through the earth. So they walked to and fro through the earth. Then cried he upon me, and spake unto me, saying, Behold, these that go toward the North Country have quieted my spirit in the North Country.* (Zechariah 6:1–8 KJV, emphasis added)

The horses represent spirits or major belief systems on earth.

What do the white horse and rider represent?

The first horse (spirit) is white. This is the official color of the **Roman Catholic Church.** The pope's dress is **white**, and his modes of transportation are always **white**. His car, helicopter, and the airplane he uses are all colored white. The rider has a crown, and every pope since Pope Gregory has had a crown. The most famous crown is the one worn by Pope Gregory, and it is kept in the Catholic museum.[294]

The rider also has a bow but no arrows. The Roman Catholic Church became the dominant religion in all of Europe and South America.[295]

What do the red horse and rider represent?

The second horse (spirit) is red. This is the official color of the **communist countries**. The rider has a great sword and power to take peace from the earth. Millions have been killed in the communist revolutions in Russia and China by their own people. In Russia approximately twenty-three million Russians were killed. In China somewhere between forty-nine million and seventy-eight million Chinese were killed. The communist killed their own people, and there was no peace until communism took over the countries.[296]

So when the Scriptures use the word red, it means **socialism** or **communism**.

What do the black horse and rider represent?

The third horse (spirit) is black. This color represents **capitalism.** The rider has a balance, which is used in commerce to buy and sell. Some say the black horse (capitalism) started as early as the fourteenth century. Max Weber wrote his book *The Protestant Ethic and the Spirit of Capitalism* in the nineteenth century. A search on the color black for a symbol of capitalism shows that black is the color accepted worldwide to represent capitalism.[297]

WHAT DO THE PALE HORSE AND RIDER REPRESENT?
To answer this, we must first clear up a translation problem. In verse 8, the Greek word for the color of the horse is *chloros*, which means green. So the color of the horse is really green and not pale. The translator could not visualize a green horse, so he made it pale.[298]

The fourth horse (spirit) is green. The official color of Islam is green. The rider on the green horse is death. In the chapter on Islam, we discussed that a Muslim who martyrs himself goes to heaven, and for centuries Muslim have killed in the name of Allah.[299]

What do the Scriptures say about killing or murdering people?

> *Envyings,* **murders***, drunkenness, revellings, and such like: of which I tell you before, as I have also told you in time past, that* **they which do such things shall not inherit the kingdom of God***.* (Galatians 5:21 KJV, emphasis added)
>
> *But the fearful, and unbelieving, and the abominable, and* **murderers***, and whoremongers, and sorcerers, and idolaters, and all liars, shall have their part in the lake which burneth with fire and brimstone: which is the second death.* (Revelation 21:8 KJV, emphasis added)

So the Scriptures tell us that all murderers will go to hell.

So the rider on the green horse (Islam) kills in the name of Allah and hell follows because the Scriptures say all murders receive the judgment of hell when they die.

The verse also says the rider kills with the sword, which Islam normally kills by beheading by the sword. There cannot be any doubt that this horse is Islam.

FOR WHAT PERIOD OF TIME ARE THESE SPIRITS OR BELIEF SYSTEMS IN POWER?
The white horse (the Roman Catholic Church) started about AD 325.

The red horse (communism and socialism) with the sword started with the Bolshevik Revolution in about 1917 with Stalin's great slaughter beginning in the 1930's. The Cultural Revolution started in 1958.[300]

Some say the black horse (capitalism) started as early as the fourteenth century. Max Weber wrote his book *The Protestant Ethic and the Spirit of Capitalism* in the nineteenth century.[301]

The green horse started when Muhammad wrote the Qur'an in about AD 610.[302]

WHAT TIME IS IT BASED ON THE FIRST FOUR SEALS?
Since we now know what the different colored horses mean, we recognize that the first three seals have occurred, and we now have the fulfillment of the fourth seal. Presently Islam today is about 1.2 to 1.8 million Muslims. This is exactly one-fourth of Earth's population today, just as Revelation 6:8 prophesied.[303]

Conclusion: We are living between the fourth and fifth seals.

THE FIFTH SEAL
The fifth seal is yet future and occurs at the abomination of desolation when the Antichrist stands in the rebuilt temple. This is when the Great Tribulation starts and lasts for three and a half years.

This is a period of time where saints are persecuted and they are all killed. The Scriptures describe them as follows:

> *And when he had opened the fifth seal, I saw under the altar the souls of them that were slain for the word of God, and for the testimony which they held.* (Revelation 6:9 KJV)
> *And one of the elders answered, saying unto me, what are these which are arrayed in white robes? And whence came they? And I said unto him, Sir, thou knowest. And he said to me, these are they which came out of* **great tribulation***, and have washed their robes, and*

made them white in the blood of the Lamb. (Revelation 7:13–14 KJV, emphasis added)

And the dragon was wroth with the woman, and went to make war with the remnant of her seed, which keep the commandments of God, and have the testimony of Jesus Christ. (Revelation 12:17 KJV)

*Here is the patience of the **saints: here are they that keep the commandments of God, and the faith of Jesus.*** (Revelation 14:12 KJV, emphasis added)

The Scriptures say that the saints are identified as the ones who keep the commandments of YHVH. So they are keeping all the commandments including the fourth commandment—the Sabbath.

The Sixth Seal

And I beheld when he had opened the sixth seal, and, lo, there was a great earthquake; and the sun became black as sackcloth of hair, and the moon became as blood; and the stars of heaven fell unto the earth, even as a fig tree casteth her untimely figs, when she is shaken of a mighty wind. And the heaven departed as a scroll when it is rolled together; and every mountain and island were moved out of their places. (Revelation 6:12–14 KJV)

The Seventh Seal

And when he had opened the seventh seal, there was silence in heaven about the space of half an hour. And I saw the seven angels which stood before God; and to them were given seven trumpets. And another angel came and stood at the altar, having a golden censer; and there was given unto him much incense, that he should offer it with the prayers of all saints upon the golden altar which was before the throne. And the smoke of the incense, which came with the prayers of the saints, ascended up before God out of the angel's hand. And the angel took the censer, and filled it with fire of the altar, and cast it into the earth: and there were voices, and thunderings, and lightnings, and an earthquake. And the seven angels which had the seven trumpets prepared themselves to sound. (Revelation 12:1–6 KJV)

The seals give us a dramatic time line of past and future events as we approach the return of Yeshua.

CHAPTER 22

The Trumpets

IN THE SCRIPTURES, THE BLOWING of trumpets represents the loud warning of YHVH's judgment. In the book of Revelation, it speaks about the blowing of seven trumpets and the following judgments by YHVH. Many believe these are future events, but are they? Ron Johnson of 666man.net has made the case that the trumpets began blowing just after Yeshua went to heaven. The following is a discussion of when these seven trumpets were blown and the resulting judgment.[304]

THE SEVEN TRUMPETS

According to the Scriptures, the blowing of the seven trumpets precedes the return of Yeshua. If we compare the scriptural descriptions of events with each trumpet with historical events, then we can date the time of the event. Consider the following comparisons by Ron Johnson that I have taken from 666man.net:[305]

FIRST TRUMPET

> *The first angel sounded* **[judgments]** *and there followed hail* **[Alaric came from the icy north in AD 365]** *and fire mingled with blood, and they were cast upon the earth: and the third* **[The three divisions of the Roman Empire are (1) Constantinople, (2) Britain, Gaul, and Spain, and (3) Africa and Italy]** *part of the*

trees was burnt up and all green grass was burnt up. (Revelation 8:7 KJV, emphasis added)

The first trumpet represents the terrible effects of the Gothic invasion as "hail" from the northern origin of the invaders.

Time line of earthly event: Approximately AD 395 to AD 410.[306]

Second Trumpet

And the second angel sounded, and as it were a great mountain burning with fire was cast into the sea; **[naval conquests under Genseric; also known as Gaiseric, King of the Vandals]** *and the third part of the sea became blood* **[Gaiseric's conquest affected a third of the Roman Empire]**. (Revelation 8:8 KJV, emphasis added)

Time line of earthly event: Approximately AD 428 to AD 468.[307]

Third Trumpet

And the third angel sounded, and there fell a great star **[Attila, king of the Huns]** *from heaven, burning as it were a lamp,* **[Attila wore brilliantly colored clothes. He regarded himself devoted to Mars, the God of war]** *and it fell upon a third part of the rivers* **[running streams]** *and upon the fountains of waters* **[springs, Attila's invasions originated from the streams of the Swiss Alps and rivers flowing down from Italy]**. (Revelation 8:10–11 KJV, emphasis added)

Time line of earthly event: Approximately AD 434 to AD 453.[308]

Fourth Trumpet

And the fourth angel sounded, and the third part of the sun was smitten, and the third part of the moon, and the third part of the stars; so as the third part of them was darkened, and the day shone not for a third part of it, and the night likewise. (Revelation 8:12 KJV)

In AD 476, the Roman emperor's position was dissolved, but the election of the senate and the consul continued.

In AD 538, Belisarius dissolved the Roman Senate and consul. The bishop of Rome was set up as the sole interpreter of the Scriptures and ruler of Europe. The Heruli, Vandals, and the Ostragoths—three of the ten powers in Rome—were destroyed. The bishop of Rome, the pope, became the dominant power in Europe.

Time line of earthly event: Approximately AD 476 to AD 538.[309]

Persecution of Christians

*And he shall speak great words against the most High, and shall wear out the saints of the most High, and think to change times and laws: and they shall be given into his hand until a **time and times and the dividing of time** or 1260 days.* (Daniel 7:25 KJV, emphasis added)

In **AD 533**, Bishop Justinian in Rome issued a decree regarding the power and authority of the church as the sole interpreter of the Scriptures. Anyone not following the church's teachings could be declared a heretic and be killed. This was in the time of war with the Ostragoths, which suddenly ended in **AD 538,** leaving the Roman Church to execute the decree.[310]

Once the Ostragoths had abandoned their siege of Rome, Bishop Justinian issued his decree and punished anyone not following the Roman Catholic Church's instructions on how to worship. For **1260** years, men, women, and children were put to death for defying the Church. This ended in 1798 when Napoleon sent his general Berthier to Rome and had the pope brought to France where he was thrown in prison. This ended the rule of the Roman Catholic Church over the kings of Europe (Daniel 7:25).

Time line of earthly event: Approximately AD 538 till AD 1798.[311] During this same period, there was war in heaven:

And there was war in heaven: Michael and his angels fought against the dragon; and the dragon fought and his angels, and prevailed not; neither was their place found any more in heaven. And the great dragon was cast out, that old serpent, called the Devil, and Satan, which deceiveth the whole world: he was cast out into the earth, and his angels were cast out with him. (Revelation 12:7–9 KJV)

Fifth Trumpet and the First Woe

And the fifth angel sounded and I saw a great star [angel] fall from heaven [many believe this was Satan] unto the earth; and to him was given the **key to the bottomless pit** *[the bottomless pit is the wasted and the desolate places or the unknown wastes of the Arabian Desert]. And he opened the bottomless pit, [reionof wasted Arabian Desert] and there arose a smoke of a great furnace, and the sun [light of the gospel] and the air was darkened by reason of the smoke of the pit. And there came out of the smoke locust [swarms of Saracens like locusts, attacks speedy and vigorous] upon the earth; and unto them was given power as the scorpions of the earth have power. And it was commanded them to not hurt the grass of the earth, neither any given thing, neither any tree; but only those men,* **which have not the seal of God in their foreheads.** *And to them was given that they should not kill them, but that they should be tormented for* **five months.** (Revelation 9:1–5 KJV, emphasis added)

And they had a king over them, which is the angel of the bottomless pit, whose name in the Hebrew tongue is Abaddan, but in the Greek tongue hath his name Apollyon. (Revelation 9:11 KJV)

Another clue to the identity of the great star is in the following verse:

*And when they shall have finished their testimony, the beast that ascendeth out of the **bottomless pit** shall make war against them, and shall overcome them, and kill them.* (Revelation 11:7 KJV, emphasis added)

Muhammad, the father of Islam, was born in AD 570. He is regarded by Muslims as a messenger and prophet of God. (In Arabic, God is called Allah.) Muhammad is the greatest law-bearer in a series of Islamic prophets and is considered by most Muslims to be the last prophet as taught by the Qur'an. Muslims thus consider him the restorer of an uncorrupted original monotheistic faith of Abraham. According to the *Wikipedia*, Muhammad received the revelations from Allah in the year 610 at the age of forty. From these revelations he wrote the Qur'an. Muhammad died in AD 632.

The **first woe** was an attack by Muslims on July 27, AD 1299. Abu Bakr (Muhammad's successor) assembled his armies and commanded his warriors: Destroy no palm tree, nor burn any fields of corn. Cut down no fruitful tree, nor do any mischief to cattle, only kill what you need to eat—but only those men who have not the seal of YHVH in their foreheads.

And to them was given that they should not kill them, but what they should be tormented. Muslim warriors tormented one-third of the Christian world and for five (prophetic) months or 150 years they were at war with the Greek part of the Christian world. Islam was not able to subdue them in 150 years. Remember from Numbers 14:34 and Ezekiel 4:6, a prophetic day is equal to a year. Therefore, five months x thirty days in a month = 150 years.

Time line of earthly event: Approximately AD 1299 till AD 1449.

Sixth Trumpet and the Second Woe

And the sixth angel sounded, and I heard a voice from the four horns of the golden altar which is before [YHVH], saying to the sixth angel which had the trumpet, Loose the four angels which are bound in the great river Euphrates. And the four angels were loosed, which were prepared for an hour, and a day, a month and a year for to **slay a third part of men.** *And the number of the horsemen were two hundred thousand thousand; and I heard the number of them.* (Revelation 9:13–16 KJV, emphasis added)

Please note that there are two prevailing opinions in the Christian world over the blowing of the sixth trumpet. The first is presented in the following paragraphs:

The four principal sultanates of the Muslim empire (Ottoman Empire) were located in country watered by the Euphrates River. These sultanates were at Aleppo, Iconium, Damascus, and Baghdad. YHVH gave the Ottoman Empire the go-ahead to kill or subdue one-third of the Christian world. How long? One prophetic year is 360 years, one prophetic month is thirty years, one prophetic day is one year and one prophetic hour is one-twenty-fourth of a prophetic year or fifteen days. This works out to be 360 years + 30 years + 1 year and 15 days or 391 years and 15 days. Since the sixth angel begins when the fifth angel ends in AD 1449, then the second woe ends on August 11, 1840.[312]

And thus I saw the horses in vision, and them that sat on them, having breastplates of fire, and jacinth, and brimstone; and the heads of the horses were as the heads of lions; and out of their mouths issued fire and brimstone, which issued out of their mouths. For their power was in their tails, for their tails were like serpents, and had heads, and with them they do hurt. (Revelation 9:17–19 KJV)

Muslim warriors discharged their firearms on horseback. They also invented the cannon. The Muslims ended the war on August 11, 1840, and conceded to the Christian world. The Muslims also signed an agreement ending the wars.

Time line of earthly event: Approximately AD **1449 to August 11, AD 1840.**[313]

For a more in-depth study and better understanding of Ron Johnson's analysis of the trumpets, go to his website, www.666man.net.[314]

There is an alternate opinion regarding the sixth trumpet that needs to be covered also. Some biblical scholars believe that the sixth trumpet has not been blown yet. If this is true, then we are looking at World War III where over two billion people could be killed in a nuclear war. They believe that this war would start in the Middle East and involve Russia, China, and the United States. Remember, the Scriptures say that YHVH will bless those who bless Israel, which indicates that the United States should back Israel. If the United States turns her back on Israel, the United States could be cursed because YHVH says He will curse those who curse Israel. This could mean that we will be attacked also. This could be the trigger that ushers in the new world order.

INVESTIGATIVE JUDGEMENTS BEGIN

> *And he said unto me, unto two thousand and three hundred days; then the sanctuary be cleansed.* (Daniel 8:14 KJV)

Most biblical scholars agree that the time line given to Daniel by the angel is based on the decree from the Persian king Artaxerxes authorizing the rebuilding of the temple. The decree as issued in the fall of 457 BC. The account is found in the book of Erza in chapter 7. This means with Satan and his angels cast out of heaven, the sanctuary is cleansed. Thus begins the investigative judgment by Yeshua.

Now we know the investigative judgment must occur before Yeshua returns to earth.

Why? Because the Scriptures say that He has judged you and He is bringing your reward when He returns.

> *And behold I come quickly; and* **my reward is with me, to give every man according as his work** *shall be.* (Revelation 22:12 KJV, emphasis added)

Seventh Trumpet And the Third Woe

And the seventh angel sounded; and there were voices in heaven, saying, the kingdoms of this world are become the kingdoms of our Lord and to his Christ; and he shall reign for ever and ever. (Revelation 11:15 KJV)

*And the **nations were angry** and **thy wrath is come**, and the dead, that they should be judged, and that thou shouldest give reward unto thy servants the prophets, and to the saints, and to them that fear thy name, small and great; and shouldest **destroy them which destroy the earth**.* (Revelation 11:18 KJV, emphasis added)

And the temple of [YHVH] was open in heaven, and then there was seen in the temple the ark of His testament [Ten Commandments] and there were lightnings and voices, and thundering, and an earthquake, and great hail. (Revelation 11:17 KJV, emphasis added)

Has the Seventh Trumpet Blown Yet?

We know that the third woe is an attack by Muslims as they were in the first two woes. On September 11, 2001, when the twin towers were destroyed by Muslims, the third woe began. So is the seventh angel about to blow his trumpet, is he blowing his trumpet, or has he already blown his trumpet?

*But in the days of the voice of the seventh angel, when he shall **begin to sound**, the **mystery of [YHVH] should be finished, as he hath declared to his servants, the prophets.*** (Revelation 10:7 KJV, emphasis added)

What does the mystery of YHVH mean, and why was it declared to the prophets? What is this mystery the prophets knew about? Look no further than the book of Daniel.

> *But you, O Daniel, shut up the words, and seal the book, even to the time of the end: many shall run to and fro, and the **knowledge shall be increased**.* (Daniel 12:4 KJV, emphasis added)
>
> *And he said, Go Daniel! For the words are closed up and sealed until the end time.* (Daniel 12:9)

Most scholars of the Scriptures will say that the knowledge refers to the **knowledge of the Scriptures,** especially the book of Daniel and Revelation.

Some scholars believe that the mystery of YHVH given to the prophets was the gospel of Yeshua that was to come. Also, the prophets were very familiar from the book of Enoch where YHVH declared the end from the beginning in the prophecy of weeks. The prophets were also shown future events by YHVH. Is this the mystery declared to them by YHVH?

So what did YHVH declare to the prophets that is a mystery? First, let's identify the prophets and look at characteristics of their lives.

Joshua:	He was known for a courageous faith centered in the Word of YHVH. His name means "Yahweh is salvation." The book is a record of YHVH's faithfulness to His covenant people. It underscores the need of the believer to be obedient.
Samuel:	He is known for bringing Israel back to worship YHVH. He succeeds in making David the king over Israel.
David:	He is known for YHVH's covenant with him. He was instructed by YHVH to build a house for YHVH, establish a kingdom and a throne for the Messiah to come.
Solomon:	He is known for his wisdom and the building of the first temple to YHVH in Jerusalem. He also devised

	a way to hide the Ark of the Covenant from any enemies that would capture the temple.
Isaiah:	He is known as the greatest of all the prophets. His prophesied the future of Israel, the coming Messiah, His crucifixion, His resurrection, the coming Antichrist, and His return to battle the Antichrist.
Jeremiah:	Jeremiah was a major prophet. He gave timely messages to YHVH's people in the closing days of Judah, prophecies concerning the Messiah and the renewed covenant.
Ezekiel:	He was a prophet who lived in Babylon. He prophesied regarding the judgment of Israel for disobedience to YHVH, the battle against the Antichrist's forces, and how YHVH fights for Israel to defeat them.
Daniel:	The most beloved prophet of YHVH. He was given knowledge of the future by the angel Gabriel.
Hosea:	He was a prophet who called for national repentance from the nation of Israel. He also prophesied about the coming destruction of the northern kingdom of Israel by Assyria.
Joel:	He was a great prophet of repentance on a personal scale and on a national scale. He prophesied about the coming locust plague and the coming of the Messiah.
Amos:	He pronounced judgment on Israel's enemies.

In the book of Amos, the mystery or secret of YHVH is mentioned.

Surely the Lord GOD will do nothing, but he revealeth his secret unto his servants the prophets. (Amos 3:7 KJV)

Obadiah:	His name means "servant of YHVH." He was a prophet who prophesied about the destruction of Edom and the return of the Messiah.
Jonah:	He was a prophet who showed the sovereignty of YHVH at work in his life. He shows that YHVH still wants to save the heathen.

Micah: His name means "who is like Yahweh?" He prophesied about the millennium rule of the Messiah.

Nahum: He was a prophet who delivered a message of judgment against Nineveh and reassured Judea that Nineveh would no longer be able to attack them.

Habakkuk: His name means an "embracer." He embraced faith with YHVH. He prophesied that after the judgment to come the enemies of Israel will be judged.

Zephaniah: His name means "Yahweh hides." He prophesied about the day of the Messiah who will destroy the false remnant of Baal, destroy the YHVH-rejecting nations, and purify the remnant. He painted a dark picture of YHVH's judgment and a brighter picture of Israel's future glory.

Haggai: His name means "feast of YHVH." He was a prophet who told about the need to be obedient to YHVH and to finish building the temple.

Zechariah: His name means "Yahweh remembers."

Malachi: His name means "My messenger." His message was to rebuke the people and call them to repentance.

These scriptures do not clearly unveil the mystery of YHVH.

Does the following verse give you a clue as to the mystery?

*Neither have we obeyed the **voice of the Lord our God, to walk in his laws, which he set before us by his servants the prophets.*** (Daniel 9:10 KJV, emphasis added)

And we have not obeyed the voice of Y'hovah, our Elohim, to walk in His Torah, which He set before us through the servants the prophets. (Daniel 9:10 ISR)

YHVH spoke the commandments to the Hebrews on Mount Sinai, and the Hebrews agreed to follow YHVH's laws. The prophets delivered the voice of YHVH to the Hebrews to return to keeping His commandments.

> *I have sent also unto you all my servants the prophets, rising up early and sending them, saying,* **Return ye now every man from his evil way, and amend your doings, and go not after other gods to serve them,** *and ye shall dwell in the land which I have given to you and to your fathers: but ye have not inclined your ear, nor hearkened unto me.* (Jeremiah 35:15 KJV, emphasis added)

Yeshua spoke about the testimony of the prophets.

> *Do not think that I came to destroy the Torah or the Prophets. I did not come to destroy but to complete.* (Matthew 5:17 ISR)

The Scriptures seem to be saying to follow the Torah and the Ten Commandments. Maybe this is why YHVH opens the heavens and shows us the Ten Commandments in the heaven in the last days.

Are there other clues about the mystery of YHVH?

> *Beloved, when I gave all diligence to write unto you of the common salvation, it was needful for me to write unto to you, and* **exhort** *you that ye should* **earnestly contend for the faith** *which was once delivered unto the saints. For there are certain men crept in* **unawares** *who were before of old* **ordained to this condemnation***, ungodly men, turning the grace of our God into lasciviousness, and denying the only Lord God, and our Lord [Yeshua].* (Jude 1:3–4 KJV, emphasis added)

YHVH told us what His will was in worshipping Him. **Has the faith has been deliberately distorted by YHVH to test you**? Maybe YHVH gave us His commandments and then He subjected us to a test to see if we would keep them. Only by earnestly seeking Him and doing His will can you understand the truth. Is knowledge of the tests by YHVH the mystery?

Once the mystery of YHVH is finished, then the seventh trumpet will be blown. After the seventh angel completes blowing his trumpet, then the end will be near.

CHAPTER 23

Holy Roman Empire Reborn

IT IS IMPORTANT THAT WE understand the rebirth of the Holy Roman Empire because it is out of this empire that the false prophet will come. How do we know this? Remember in Daniel 2, King Nebuchadnezzar sees a vision of a huge statue of a man. Daniel is called before the king, and the king asks why his wise men cannot explain the dream. Daniel answers as follows:

> *Daniel answered in the presence of the king, and said, the secret which the king hath demanded cannot the wise men, the astrologers, the magicians, the soothsayers, shew unto the king; but there is a* **God in heaven that revealeth secrets, and maketh known to the king Nebuchadnezzar what shall be in the latter days.** *Thy dream, and the visions of thy head upon thy bed, are these; Thou, O king, sawest, and behold a great image. This great image, whose brightness was excellent, stood before thee; and the form thereof was terrible.* (Daniel 2:27–31 KJV, emphasis added)

The book of Daniel describes these different metals of the image of a man as different kingdoms that follow one another in time.

> *This image's head was of fine gold, his breast and his arms of silver, his belly and his thighs of brass, His legs of iron, his feet part of iron and part of clay.* (Daniel 2:32–33 KJV)

The head was made out of gold, and it represented the Babylonian kingdom of Nebuchadnezzar. The arms and chest were made of silver, and they represented the kingdom of Medo-Persia. The belly and thighs were made of brass, and they represented the kingdom of Greece under Alexander the Great. The legs were made of iron, and they represented the Roman Empire. The feet (including the ten toes) were made of iron mingled with clay. The two feet represent the kingdoms at the time of the end. They are clearly shown coming out of the two iron legs, which represent the first Roman Empire.

WHAT ELSE DID DANIEL SAY ABOUT THESE DIFFERENT KINGDOMS?

In Daniel 7, Daniel again prophesies about these different kingdoms, and they are described as beasts. Remember that each beast represents a kingdom or nation along with a ruler of that kingdom or nation.

> *And four great beasts came up from the sea, diverse one from another. The first was like a lion, and had eagle's wings: I beheld till the wings thereof were plucked, and it was lifted up from the earth, and made stand upon the feet as a man, and a man's heart was given to it.* (Daniel 7:3–4 KJV)

This beast is Babylon. Approximate time period was 2000 BC to 538 BC.

> *And behold another beast, a second, like to a bear, and it raised up itself on one side, and it had three ribs in the mouth of it between the teeth of it: and they said thus unto it, Arise, devour much flesh.* (Daniel 7:5 KJV)

This beast is Medo-Persia. Approximate time period is 538 BC to 331 BC.

After this I beheld, and lo another, like a leopard, which had upon the back of it four wings of a fowl; the beast had also four heads; and dominion was given to it. (Daniel 7:6 KJV)

This beast is Greece. Approximate time period is 331 BC to 323 BC. His kingdom was then divided into four kingdoms, which lasted until 146 BC.

After this I saw in the night visions, and behold a fourth beast, dreadful and terrible, and strong exceedingly; and it had great iron teeth: it devoured and brake in pieces, and stamped the residue with the feet of it: and it was diverse from all the beasts that were before it; and it had ten horns. (Daniel 7:7 KJV)

This beast is the Roman Empire. Approximate time period is 197 BC to AD 294.

What about the feet and toes?

*And whereas thou sawest the feet and toes, part of potters' clay, and part of iron, the **kingdom shall be divided;** but there shall be in it of the strength of the iron, forasmuch as thou sawest the iron mixed with miry clay.* (Daniel 2:41 KJV)

The kingdom is divided into ten kingdoms. This means the ten toes are also the ten kings. The ten kings are not the kings of the earth. There is a difference. Kings of the earth are political leaders of nations. I believe that the ten kings are religious rulers who rule ten regions of the earth.

And as the toes of the feet were part of iron, and part of clay, so the kingdom shall be partly strong, and partly broken. (Daniel 2:42 KJV)

Most Christians know the story of the potter's clay from the Scriptures. The Potter is God and the clay is man. This could mean that in the last days, men will be molded to one religion and held together with the iron of Rome. This was the case during the period of the Holy Roman Empire.

Birth of the Holy Roman Empire

In AD 771, Charlemagne became the sole ruler of what is now Belgium, France, Luxembourg, the Netherlands, and part of western Germany. He then expanded his kingdom to include northern Italy and southern Germany. He also conquered the Saxons on the main European continent. He forced all these territories to become Christians in the Roman Catholic Church.[315]

Charlemagne followed a policy of friendship and cooperation with the Roman Catholic Church. He protected the church and extended its power. In recognition of Charlemagne's vast power and to strengthen the king's alliance with the church, Pope Leo III crowned Charlemagne Emperor of the Romans on December 25, AD 800. When the pope placed the crown on Charlemagne's head, he said **"I hereby crown you emperor of the Holy Roman Empire."**[316]

The Holy Roman Empire was an alliance in Europe between church and state. This empire lasted until about AD 1806.[317]

Has the Holy Roman Empire been Reborn?

In 1957, several European countries signed the "Treaties of Rome" to form the European Economic Community (EEC). This was the first step in forming a "United States" of Europe.[318]

In 1992, the Treat of Maastricht was signed, and the European Union was born. From this treaty, the euro was born in 1995.[319]

In 2007, twenty-seven member states had ratified the treaties to join the European Union.

On **November 3, 2009**, President Vaclav Klaus of the Czech Republic signed the Lisbon Agreement. This was the last country to sign, completing the European Union. This was the date the Holy Roman Empire was reborn.[320]

Did the Signers know this is the Holy Roman Empire Reborn?

Here are clues that answer that question.

The Euro has picture of **Charlemagne** on it.

The European Union gives a prize to selected world leaders who help the European Union. It is called the **Charlemagne Prize.** President Bill Clinton received the Charlemagne Prize for the United States' efforts in the war in Yugoslavia that removed Yugoslavia's leader who was opposed to joining the European Union.

Applications for membership in the European Union are examined in the **Charlemagne Building.**

A European periodical called the *Economist* has a special page in it devoted to the European Union. It is called the **Charlemagne page.**

The designer of the EU flag was a devout Catholic. He designed a flag with twelve stars on a blue background. The stars came from the reference in the Bible to the pure woman with twelve stars over her head. The Catholics often refer to her as the Virgin Mary. The automobile license plates also have the blue with twelve stars.[321]

Moreover, the signing of the treaty had religious music and took place in a monastery.

The rebirth of the Holy Roman Empire (a union of religion and political forces) took place on November 3, 2009, when the last country signed the European Union constitution. This is the relationship that was prophesied about in Revelation 13. There will be the religious leader who causes everyone to worship the political leader just as was the case in the Holy Roman Empire.

The foundation for the Holy Roman Empire has been reborn. All it needs is for the Antichrist and the false prophet to reveal themselves and take control of the world in the new world government. The Scriptures tell us that the new world government will be a divided government—between a political ruler and a religious ruler.

CHAPTER 24

The Antichrist

THE GREEK WORD *ANTI* ORIGINALLY meant "instead of"—which means that *Antichrist* means anything in the Christian life that replaces the Messiah. There is also a false messiah who is coming who will present himself as the Messiah. So who will this anti-Messiah or Antichrist be?

Yeshua identifies the Antichrist for us in the Scriptures. He is described in Revelation 13 along with the false prophet and the mark of the beast. In Revelation 13, the antichrist and his world government and worldwide religion are described in verses 1–8. The false prophet who enforces the worship is described in verses 11–15. The economic system (mark of the beast) that forces obedience is described in verses 16–18.

Revelation 13 is described by Irvin Baxter as the "Master Plan of the Dragon." The composite beast is the new world government with religious power.

WHO IS THE DRAGON?

> *And the great dragon, the old serpent, the one called Devil, and Satan, the one deceived the entire inhabited world, was cast to the earth, and his angels were cast with him.* (Revelation 12:9 ONMB)

Satan is the Dragon.

According to the Scriptures, Satan's master plan will last for forty-two months and then Yeshua returns. So we need to have a good understanding of the Scriptures to avoid being deceived.

Paul gave us the following warnings:

> *Let no man deceive you in any way. Because when the apostasy would come first, then the man of lawlessness, the son of destruction would be revealed.* (2 Thessalonians 2:3 ONMB)

There is that word Apostasy again. This means the church will be in apostasy or in a state of falling away from the original worship before the Antichrist will be revealed.

> *He is the one who opposes Torah [Teaching] and exalts himself upon every Godly saying or object of worship, and thus seats himself in the Sanctuary of God, proclaiming himself, that he is God.* (2 Thessalonians 2:4 ONMB)

From these verses, he is called the man who opposes God (YHVH) and His Torah and all other religions. He will sit in the rebuilt temple and claim to be God.

> *For the mystery of the one without Torah [Teaching] or lawless one is* **already at work**: *while only He [God] is restraining him at the present time until he would come out from among you.* (2 Thessalonians 2:7 ONMB, emphasis added)

The King James Bible uses "mystery of iniquity." Iniquity comes from the Greek word *anomia*, which means "without Torah."

PAUL IS PREACHING TO THE JEWS AND GENTILES OF THE CITY OF THESSALONICA.

And then the one without Torah [Teaching] will be revealed, whom the Lord Yeshua will destroy by the breath of his mouth, and will abolish by the appearance of His coming. (2 Thessalonians 2:8 ONMB)

Yeshua (Jesus) is going to return and destroy the Antichrist.

Whose coming is through the efficiency of the works of Satan with great power and false signs and wonders. (2 Thessalonians 2:9 ONMB)

These signs and wonders of the Antichrist are going to deceive everyone.

And in every unrighteous deception for those who are being destroyed, because they did not accept the love of the truth for them to be saved. (2 Thessalonians 2:10 ONMB)

Paul is saying good people will be destroyed because they cannot accept the truth that they have been deceived even when the Scriptures say everyone is deceived.

The Scriptures define truth as follows:

Your acts of loving kindness are an everlasting righteousness and Your Torah [Teaching] is the Truth. (Psalm 119:142 ONMB)
  You are near, LORD, and all your commandments are truth. (Psalm 119:151 ONMB)
  And because of this sends them a working of deception so they would believe in a lie, so that all those would be judged who did not believe in the truth, but took pleasure in unrighteousness. (2 Thessalonians 2:11–12 ONMB)

In the above verses, truth is defined as the Torah (Teaching) and the commandments of Yeshua (Jesus).

The Master Plan

Revelation 13:1–8 and 16–18 provides several characteristics of the Antichrist.

> *Then I saw a beast rising from the sea, which had ten horns and seven heads, and upon his horns ten crowns, and slanderous names.* (Revelation 13:1 ONMB)

First, we know that a horn grows out of the head of an animal or beast. So this is saying the composite beast will rise from the sea (refers to multitudes of people or populated areas). Heads means the headquarters of a government of a nation. In this verse, a horn represents a king or ruler.

You must understand that there are two types of kings in the Scriptures. First, there are the kings of the earth. These are political heads of nations.

> *With whom the kings of the earth did fornicate and those who dwell on the earth did become drunk from the wine of her idolatry.* (Revelation 17:2 ONMB)

Then there are the ten kings (religious rulers) that work for the Antichrist.

> *And the ten horns that you saw are ten kings, who did not yet take a kingdom, but they take authority as kings for one hour with the beast.* (Revelation 17:12 ONMB)

It also says the beast will be guilty of slander against God.

And the beast I saw was like a leopard, its feet like a bear, and its mouth like a lion's mouth. And the dragon gave to it its power and its throne, and great authority. (Revelation 13:2 ONMB)

The mouth of a lion (Great Britain) means the composite beast will use English as the official language.

This composite beast (world government) is also described in Daniel 7:4–8:

And one of its heads was as if it had been slain in death, then its fatal wound deadly wound was healed. And the whole world was astonished, and followed the beast. (Revelation 13:3 ONMB)

In the HRV Bible, the correct Greek word is "resurrected" instead of "healed."

Many believe this is referring to the papacy when Napoleon's general, Berthier, entered Rome and took Pope Pius VI captive in February 1798. Napoleon decreed that at the death of the pope, the position of pope would be discontinued. The pope died in France in August 1799.

When was the deadly wound healed or the beast resurrected?

If this is referring to the papacy, then the deadly wound was healed in 1929 when Mussolini signed an agreement with the Vatican, giving them civil power again, which began the healing of the deadly wound. Since then the Roman Catholic Church has gained more and more power. They have gained the support of world leaders and are pushing to bring the Protestant churches back to the Roman Catholic Church. As reported by the Washington Post on November 1, 1999, the Lutheran Church signed an agreement with the Roman Catholic Church to end their disagreements.

What else is said about the Antichrist beast?

*And they paid homage to the **dragon (Satan)** because he gave his authority to the beast and they paid homage to the beast saying, "Who is like the beast and who is able to war against him?"* (Revelation 13:4 ONMB, emphasis added)

The word *homage* means to bend your knees and place your forehead on the ground. This is the way Muslims pray.

> *And the power of speech was given to him, speaking loud and blasphemous sayings, and authority was to him to do miracles during forty-two months.* (Revelation 13:5 ONMB)

The Antichrist will rule for forty-two literal months.

> *And his mouth opened in blasphemies to God to revile His name and His Tabernacle, those who live in His Tabernacle in heaven.* (Revelation 13:6 ONMB)

This verse says he will blaspheme God and His name, Yehovah. In chapter 2, we learned that Pope Benedict issued a directive to all the Catholic churches that the name of God (Yehovah) was not to be mentioned in prayers or songs.

> *Then it was given to him to make war against the saints and to overcome them, and authority was given him over every tribe, and people and language and nation.* (Revelation 13:7 ONMB)

This verse also says that he will make war against Christians who refuse to worship him, and he will be given authority over the entire world at the end of the age.

> *And all those who live on the earth will pay homage to him, whose name is not written in the Lamb's Book of Life, the book of the One Who has been slain from the foundation of the universe.* (Revelation 13:8 ONMB)

WHO IS THE REAL ANTICHRIST?

There is a debate in the Christian world regarding the identity of the Antichrist. Some have made the case that the papacy in the Roman

Catholic Church is the Antichrist. Others have made the case for the coming Muslim Mahdi as the Antichrist. In each case, the beasts are interpreted differently. To investigate this question, let's go and look at the beast prophecies.

First, let's look at the man in Nebuchadnezzar's dream that is interpreted by Daniel.

The image was a great image of like a man. Each part was made of different metals, which represented beasts or kingdoms. See the descriptions of Statue in Daniel 2 below.

STATUE
Head of fine gold, **b.** chest and arms of silver, **c.** belly and thighs of bronze, **d.** Legs of Iron, and **e.** Feet and toes of clay mixed with iron

DANIEL 2
a. Babylon (verse 32), **b.** Medo-Persia (verse 32), **c.** Greece (verse 32), **d.** Rome (Verse 33), **e.** Final kingdom (verses 41, 42)

This prophecy of the succeeding kingdoms is widely accepted, and many believe we are now in the transition to the feet time period. Once we have a new one-world government, this will usher in the Antichrist with ten kings (toes).

After this, when King Belshazzar was the king of Babylon, Daniel had several dreams. In his first dream he saw four great beasts coming up out of the earth.

Beast, Lion with Eagle wings. Daniel 7. Lion like beast (verse4). With eagles'wings plucked, Eagle wings stand on its feet, Eagle has heart like a man. **Revelation 13** Mouth of a lion (verse2).

Bear, Daniel chapter 7. Bear like beast (vs.5)) with 3 ribs in his mouth devours lots of flesh. **Revelation chapter 13** "Feet of a bear" (vs.2).

Leopard, Daniel chapter 7. Leopard like beast (vs.6) with four wings of a fowl and four heads. **Revelation chapter 13**, "Like unto a leopard" (vs2).

Ten Horned Beast, Daniel chapter 7. Dreadful and strong (vs.7), great iron teeth, ten horned beast. **Revelation chapter 14**, "having… ten horns" (vs1) seven heads, crowns on ten horns, slanderous names on horns.

The four beasts of Daniel are the same in Revelation. However, more information is available regarding the ten-horned beast.

Daniel has more detailed description of the final beast, so let's look at the verse in detail.

> *I considered the horns and, behold, there came up among them another little horn, before which three of the first horns were plucked up by the roots and, behold,* ***in this horn were eyes like the eyes of man, and a mouth speaking great things****.* (Daniel 7:8 ONMB, emphasis added).

Sounds like this man is either the Antichrist or the false prophet.

> *I saw and the* ***same horn made war with the holy ones****.* (Daniel 7:21 ONMB, emphasis added).

This verse says he will make war against the holy ones.

> *And he shall speak blasphemous words against the Most High and will wear out the holy ones of the Most High, and* ***think to change times and laws****: and they will be given into his hand until a time and times and half a time.* (Daniel 7:25 ONMB, emphasis added).

Times refer to the seasons of YHVH, which are the feasts of YHVH.

> *And in the latter time of their kingdom, when the transgressors have come to the full, a* ***king will stand up, of fierce countenance, and understanding dark sentences****.* (Daniel 8:23 ONMB, emphasis added).

The Antichrist will have a fierce countenance and an understanding of dark sentences.

> *And his power will be mighty, but not by his own power: and he shall destroy powerfully and will succeed and achieve, and will* ***destroy***

(corrupt) the mighty and the holy people. (Daniel 8:24 ONMB, emphasis added).

These verses say that the Antichrist will make war against the holy people and the mighty people. He will prevail against them.

> *And through his cunning he will succeed by deceit in his hand and he will magnify himself in his heart, and in a period of tranquility he will destroy many; he will also stand up against the prince of princes, but he will be broken without hand.* (Daniel 8:25 ONMB).

The Antichrist will use peace to his advantage so he can cause their destruction.

It has been suggested that this last-day world kingdom or one-world government it will consist of the ten-horned beast. Since the United Nations has already divvyed up the world into ten regional trade and financial centers, many believe that this is the ten-horned beast of the new world order.

Many believe the ten horns are the ten toes of Daniel 2:41–42.

However, there are major disagreements on the beasts of what kingdoms they represent.

Opinion 1:

The lion represents Babylon and the region of the world that is mostly Arab. The wings represent speed in battle.

The bear represents Medo-Persia, which is the beast that follows Babylon. The three ribs represent Lydia, Babylon, and Egypt.

The leopard is represented by a leopard with four heads. The four heads represent the empire of Greece that was divided when Alexander died. The four generals that headed Greece were Cassander, Lysimachus, Ptolemy, and Seleucus. The four wings represent super speed.

The fourth beast is the Roman Empire. Roving barbarian tribes swept into the Roman Empire and carved out land niches for their people. Seven of these ten tribes developed into the countries of modern Western Europe, while three of these uprooted and destroyed. These tribes are as follows:

Visigoths—Spain; Anglo-Saxons—England; Franks—France; Alemani—Germany; Burgundians—Switzerland; Lombards—Italy; Suevi—Portugal; Heruli—Rooted up; Ostrogoths—Rooted up; Vandals—Rooted up.

Who rooted up the three tribes? The pope of Rome rooted up the three tribes because they refused to accept the Roman Church's Christianity.

The "little horn" power appears next. And it is identified by the following:

1. The "little horn" comes out of Western Europe. (Daniel 7:8)
2. It will have a man as its head who speaks for it. (Daniel 7:8)
3. It would pluck up three kingdoms. (Daniel 7:24)
4. It would be diverse from the other from the ten kingdoms. (Daniel 7:28)
5. It would make war with the saints. (Daniel 7:21, 25)
6. It would emerge from the pagan Roman Empire, which is the fourth world kingdom.
7. God's people would be given into his hands for "a time and times and the dividing of time."
8. It would speak great words to slander or blaspheme God.
9. It would think to change times and laws. (Daniel 7:25)

Only the papacy can meet these identifying points.

After the first dream, Daniel has another dream that implies that the beasts have other explanations. Daniel sees a ram with two horns that are high. The second horn was higher than the first. The ram pushed westward, northward, and southward and nothing could stop him.

Then Daniel sees a goat coming from the west, and he had a conspicuous horn between the eyes. The goat overpowers the ram and crushes the ram. During the battle, the great horn on the goat is broken off and four horns replace it.

Gabriel explains to Daniel that the ram with the two horns is Medo-Persia. The goat is the king of Greece or Alexander the Great. The horn between the eyes is the first king. When it is broken, four stood up as four kingdoms for one nation. These are the four generals who replaced Alexander the Great.

Out of one of the horns on the goat came a little horn that grew exceedingly great. This horn is further described as the great dragon.

So in this dream a ram is Medo-Persia and a goat is Greece. Earlier we said Medo-Persia preceded Greece.

So we have two new beasts representing Medo-Persia and Greece.

This leads us to the second opinion, where the beast descriptions are different from Opinion 1.

Opinion 2:

The beasts are characterized by their current symbols of their countries.

The lion is the symbol of Great Britain. There are statues of lions in England that symbolize England as a lion.

The wings plucked represent the United States, which was originally part of Great Britain. The symbol of the United States is eagle wings.

The bear is Russia. The symbol of modern-day Russia is a bear. Every newspaper and magazine always refers to the symbol of Russia as a bear.

The leopard is Germany. The deadly wound of one of its heads is the when East Germany was under Soviet Union control after World War II and West Germany was under control of the Allies. When the Berlin Wall was demolished and the two Germanys reunited, the deadly wound was healed.

The wings of a fowl on the back of the leopard represent France. The unofficial symbol of France has always been the Gallic rooster.

The ten horned beast is the Reborn Holy Roman Empire.

Opinion 3:
There will be an alliance of Muslim countries from which the Mahdi (or Antichrist) will come out. Arab countries that have a leader that is not committed to a caliphate will be overcome by revolutions. We have already seen Libya and Egypt, and now Syria is about to fall. We also know that the United States has pushed for these revolutions to replace their leaders.

This leads us to look at a third option of what the symbols mean in representing the one new world government.

In this opinion, the lion, the bear, and the leopard represent the reborn Holy Roman Empire. The ten-horned beast represents the ten-nation alliance of Muslim countries.

For a more detailed analysis of this opinion, see the book *God's War of Terrorism* by Walter Shoebat.

Clues to his Identity

> *Neither shall he **regard the God of his fathers**, **nor the desire of women**, nor regard any god: for he shall magnify himself above all.* (Daniel 11:37 onmb, emphasis added)

In the Scriptures, the **desire of women is to have children**. This could mean the Antichrist is a woman. This could also mean a man's desire for women. It also could mean a pope because the popes are not allowed to marry.

When will he be Revealed?
The Scriptures say that he will be revealed to the world when he sits in the rebuilt temple in Jerusalem claiming to be God.

> *Therefore when you would see the abomination of devastation placed in a holy place, which was foretold by Daniel the prophet, the one must faithfully consider.* (Matthew 24:15 onmb)

This is when the Antichrist will be revealed to the world.

So How Can we not be Deceived?
Revelation 13 gives us "The Master Plan by Satan" on how he is going to force us to worship him. If you have not studied the Scriptures, especially the writings of Paul and the book of Revelation, then you are susceptible to being deceived. Remember Satan is going to deceive the whole world.

When you see the new world government formed, then you will know what is about to happen. This world government will have authority over the nations and the individuals in the nations. When this happens, there will be a religious figure who will be in charge of all religions.

The only way you can prevent being deceived is to know the Scriptures.

CHAPTER 25

The False Prophet

THE SCRIPTURES ARE CLEAR THAT these two beasts (or two world powers) of Revelation 13 are the Antichrist and the false prophet. We discussed the Antichrist in the previous chapter.

They are the one new world's political leader and the one new world's religious leader. The Scriptures tell us that they will work together to rule the world just as it was during the first Holy Roman Empire.

So what do the Scriptures say about the false prophet?

THE SECOND BEAST OF POWER

Which nation arises about the same time the papacy loses its power?

> *Then I saw another beast rising from the earth, and he had two horns like a lamb, and he was speaking, roaring, like a dragon.* (Revelation 13:11 ONMB)

Earth represents the opposite of waters, so it is coming up out of an unpopulated area before the late 1700s. Satan also speaks through this beast.

The United States declared its independence in 1776, voted the Constitution in 1787, adopted the Bill of Rights in 1791, and was recognized as world power by 1798.

So what are the "two horns like a lamb"?

Horns represent kings or kingdoms. Lamblike horns represent an unoppressive, peace-loving, and spiritual nation. The United States has two governing principles: civil and religious liberty. These two governing principles have long been labeled "republicanism" (a government without a king) and "Protestantism" (a church without a pope). No other nation on earth could match the description in Revelation 13:11.[322]

This suggests that the United States is the second beast of power in Revelation 13.

What does it Mean to Speak as a Dragon?

The dragon is Satan, and his goal is to crush YHVH's church and to force everyone to worship and obey him. The United States will speak as dragon in the end times as follows:

> *And he carried out all the authority of the first beast before him, and he caused the earth and those dwelling in it to bow down and pay homage to the first beast, whose fatal wound was healed.* (Revelation 13:12 ONMB)

This is saying that that the false prophet will be a leader of the United States and will force everyone to worship the Antichrist. Does this mean that a president of the United States could be the false prophet? Also, the United Nations, which has become a world-governing body, is located in the United States. So maybe the false prophet will be the leader of the United Nations.

What Else do the Scriptures Say about the False Prophet?

The false prophet is going to cause miracles to happen that will deceive everyone, and they will accept the mark and worship the first beast (Antichrist).

The false prophet is going to imitate the prophets in the Old Testament. His role is to bring people to worship the first beast. His two horns of a lamb represent an attempt to deceive or give the impression of harmlessness. However, his dragon speech depicts his empowerment by Satan. He will promote the global worship of the Antichrist.

The false prophet will deceive the believers and unbelievers of the world by means and wonders and miracles. This will be spectacular and will be seen on television all around the world.

> *And he [false prophet] performed great miracles, so that he would make fire descend from the sky to the earth before mankind.* (Revelation 13:13 ONMB)

Why does the false prophet bring fire down from heaven? By these miracles of bringing fire down out of heaven, **he is duplicating the prophet Elijah.**

> *Answer me, LORD, Answer me, so this people can know that you are LORD God, and you have turned their heart back again. Then the fire of the LORD fell, and consumed the burnt sacrifice, the wood, the stones, the dust, and licked up the water that was in the trench. And when all the people saw it, they fell on their faces: and they said, The LORD, He is the God. The LORD, He is **the** God.* (1 Kings 18:37–39 ONMB, emphasis added)

The whole world will see this on television or the Internet. By this miracle the false prophet performs a miracle just like Elijah performed, and the whole world will believe that the Antichrist is God.

> *And he deceived those who live on the earth by the miracles which were given to him to do in the sight of the beast saying for those who lived on earth to make an image to the beast that had the wound from the small sword, but still lived.* (Revelation 13:14 ONMB)

> *And Elijah said unto them, Take the prophets of Baal; let not one of them escape. And they took them: and Elijah brought them down to the brook Kishon, and slew them there.* (1 Kings 18:40 KJV)

Yeshua (Jesus) warned the Jews to flee Jerusalem when they see this event. The reason is that the false prophet is going to tell his followers not to let any Jews escape Jerusalem but to capture and kill all of them.

> *Therefore when you see the abomination of devastation, placed in a holy place, which was foretold by Daniel the prophet, the one who reads must carefully consider. At that time those in Judaea must flee to the mountains.* (Matthew 24:15–16 ONMB)
>
> *For then there will be great affliction [tribulation] such as has not happened from the beginning of the world until now and would never happen again.* (Matthew 24:21 ONMB)

Yeshua is saying Jews are going to be killed by the Antichrist because everyone is deceived by these miracles.

> *And it was given to him to give a spirit to the image of the beast, so that the image of the beast could also speak, and could cause as many of those that would not pay homage to the image of the beast, that they would be killed.* (Revelation 13:15 ONMB)

What is the image of the Beast?

We know that the first beast is the Papal Church of Rome. We also know that the Roman Catholic Church is more than a religious body. **It has civil power.** From AD 538 till 1798, Papal Rome exercised religious and civil power. Millions were tortured and killed who would not worship like Papal Rome said to worship. It is a historical fact.

Here is wisdom. Remember the ten kings of the beast. They are not kings of countries, but they are appointed kings for enforcement of worship of the beast.

And the ten horns that you saw are ten kings, who did not yet take a kingdom, but they take authority as kings for one hour with the beast. (Revelation 17:12 ONMB)

The ten horns are churches that will be given civil power just like the mother church (Roman Catholic Church) in order to enforce religious laws.

Could the image of the first beast (Papal Rome) be the Protestant churches of America and Europe?
During this period, false prophets will also arise.

In the book of Matthew, we are warned by Yeshua about false prophets who will arise after this event in Jerusalem.

*And many false prophets **will be raised** and they will lead many astray.* (Matthew 24:11 ONMB, emphasis added)

Yeshua warned that the false prophets and messiahs are going to deceive you into worshipping the Antichrist. They will say by his miracles that the false prophet is the true prophet of God and that we should follow him.

At that time if someone would say to you, "Behold here is the Messiah or here," do not believe it. For false messiahs and false prophets will be raised and they will give great signs and wonders in order to lead astray, if possible, even the elect. Behold, I have told you beforehand. Therefore if they would say to you, Behold, He is in the desert, do not come out: Behold, He is in the inner rooms, do not believe it. (Matthew 24:23–26 ONMB)

So who how does the false prophet cause us to worship the first beast?
He does it by economic power called the mark of the beast.

Mark of the Beast

The false prophet will use economic power to coerce everyone to worship the first beast.

> *And he forces everyone, the small and the great, and the rich and the poor, and the free and the slaves so that he could give them a mark upon their right hand or upon their forehead: and so that no one would be able to buy or sell except the one who had the mark, the name of the beast, or the number of its name.* (Revelation 13:16–17 ONMB)

Today, everyone in the United States uses a number to be able to cash a check or to use a credit card. That number is your driver's license. Soon we may be using a national ID card in order to buy or sell. The law has already been passed in Congress and signed by the president. This ID or number will be managed by a large computer database program. It will be used to identify a person for buying and selling and the ability to have a job.

Today everything is in place to use the economic system to enforce the buying and selling of privileges of individuals if they don't do what the government says.

So we know how the Antichrist will control the world through economic power.

What else does the Scriptures say about the identity of the first beast?

> *Here is the wisdom. The one who has understanding must count the* **number of the beast***, for it is the* **number of mankind***, and its number is* **six hundred sixty-six***.* (Revelation 13:18 ONMB, emphasis added)

Another verse says the following:

> *And I saw like a glassy sea that had been mixed with fire, and those who overcame the beast and his image and the* **number of his name**

were standing upon the glassy sea with harps of God. (Revelation 15:2 ONMB, emphasis added)

Revelation 13 says that 666 is the number of mankind. Revelation 15:2 says that it is the number of the beast's name. This confusion about the number 666 has led to a lot of confusion in identifying the beast.

Some believe the number of his name is referring to the numerical value of a person's name or title. For example, let's look at a typical view of the pope's title.

The title of the Pope of Rome is *Vicarius Filii Dei*. In English, this is "Vicar of the Son of God."

So if we count the number of his name using Roman numerals of his name, it would be the following:

V	=	5
I	=	1
C	=	100
A	=	0
R	=	0
I	=	1
U	=	5
S	=	0

6

F	=	0
I	=	1
L	=	50
I	=	1
I	=	1

6

D	=	500
E	=	0
I	=	1

6

Coincidence? Or does the papacy fit the description of the Antichrist? The problem with this approach of adding up the numerical values of a person's name is that there are many names of actual persons that can be added up to get 666. So I personally do not believe this is what the Scriptures meant.

Some translations use the number of a man, while the latest translations from Greek to English use the word *mankind*. So let's examine the "number of mankind."

The Scriptures say that man is divided into three parts. They are the spirit, soul, and body.

> *And the very God of peace sanctify you wholly; and I pray God your whole* **spirit and soul and body** *be preserved blameless unto the coming of our Lord Jesus Christ.* (1 Thessalonians 5:23 KJV, emphasis added)

Now we know from the Scriptures that man was created on the sixth day.

> *And God said,* **"Earth bring forth the living creature after its kind, cattle and creeping thing and beast of the earth after its kind…"** *And God said,* **"We will make mankind in our image, after our likeness and have dominion over the fish of the sea, over the fowl of the air, over the cattle, over all the earth, and over every creeping thing that creeps upon the earth."** (Genesis 1:24, 26 ONMB, emphasis added)

From the verses, mankind was made in the image of God and His angels. Since there are three parts to man, this could mean the three parts are called 666.

So let's also look at the number 7 or 777, which is a number of perfection.

> *And on the seventh day God ended His work which he had made; and He rested on the seventh day from all His work which he had made. And God blessed the seventh day, and sanctified it: because that in it He had rested from all His work which God created and made.* (Genesis 2:2–3 ONMB)

The Sabbath principle of God is designed to give glory to God as Creator and to encourage man to seek His identity and to be in communion with God and to participate in God's rest.

So the beasts in Revelation 13 could just represent man exercising sovereignty apart from God and conforming to the image of the beast rather than to the image of God.

Therefore, the number 666 simply means worship of the creature instead of the Creator. So, in the context of false worship promoted by the beast (one-world government), the number 666 means the total (spirit, soul, and body) false worship of the image of the beast enforced by the end-time Antichrist.

So the end-time world government will be both political and religious. Only one religion will be allowed, and we will be marked by that religion. So what are the marks of religions that exist now?

What are the current marks that we know about?

We know that YHVH's mark is the Sabbath, which starts at sundown on Friday till sundown on Saturday.

> *Moreover I also gave to them My Sabbaths to be a sign between me and them, so they would know that I am the* Lord *Who sanctifies them.* (Ezekiel 20:12 ONMB)

We know that Sunday is the mark of the Roman Catholic Church.

The Roman Catholic Church responds that "the church substituted Sunday for Saturday by the plenitude of that divine power which Jesus Christ bestowed on her."[323]

We know that Islam also has a mark. The mark of Islam is the Bismillah, which means "in the Name of Allah, and his messenger is Muhammad."

All three religions worship on a different day.

The Coming One-World Government

The one-world government will be established very soon. This is when the national ID numbers will be given to everyone on the planet. This is how the one-world government will control everyone. A time of wars and financial disasters will happen first, and this will usher in the new world order.

Of course, with economic turmoil will also come riots and very dangerous times. Food will be in short supply. This will lead to horrible times resulting in martial law. At some point then, everyone will ordered to worship on the religion of the new world order.

When you see the false prophet and the Antichrist in Jerusalem in the rebuilt temple on TV, then you will know the names of the false prophet and the Antichrist.

The Antichrist is going to sit in the rebuilt temple and claim he is God to everyone. The false prophet (just like Elijah) will bring fire down from heaven and tell everyone to worship the Antichrist as God. When this happens in the temple, it is called the **abomination of desolation. This is the beginning of the great tribulation.**

The Holy Roman Empire

Some Christians believe there will be a confederacy between the Roman Catholic Church and Islam that will result in the establishment of the new one-world religion. Satan is going to use the one-world government and peace to bring about worship of him instead of YHVH. Many believe that this will have the same political and religious structure employed by the Holy Roman Empire, which now has been reborn.

The spiritual leader of the Holy Roman Empire has always been the pope. He anointed a political leader to rule the Holy Roman Empire. Many believe that the pope at the time of the Antichrist will either be the Antichrist or the false prophet. Also, many Catholics believe there is an evil pope coming based on the Prophecy of Saint Malachy. [324]

Saint Malachy was a twelfth-century bishop in Ireland. According to traditional accounts, he was summoned to Rome by Pope Innocent II. While in Rome, he had a vision of future popes, which he recorded. The manuscript was deposited in the Roman archive and forgotten until its rediscovery in 1590.[325]

Malachy listed every pope from his time till the last pope (112th), which will be the successor to the current pope, Benedict XVI. The successor will be known as the "Peter the Roman." He went on to say the following:

> *Peter the Roman, who will nourish the sheep in many tribulations; when they are finished the city of seven hills will be destroyed (this is Rome where the Vatican is located) and the dreadful judge will judge his people.*[326]

At this point we can't say for sure exactly who the false prophet or the Antichrist will be, but we need to be wise by the Scriptures so that we are not deceived.

Remember that Satan deceives the whole world, so if you are doing what the rest of the world is doing, then you must be worshipping the image of Satan.

CHAPTER 26

The Beginning of the Last Seven Years

One of the most popular subjects on the Internet ithat the world will end on December 21, 2012. This is date that the Mayan calendar ends on. It is so popular that books and movies have been made about how the end will come. Predictions of collisions with Planet X and other astronomical events will destroy the Earth. If you go on the Internet, you will find countdown clocks ticking away. On the other hand, the Almighty does not run the universe based on a pagan Mayan calendar. I don't put any confidence in believing the world will end because the Scriptures say it will never end. Now the Scriptures do say that we are close to the end of the age just before Yeshua's return.

In chapter 17, we discussed YHVH's judgment on America. The financial judgment on America continues as of fall 2012. Unemployment continues to climb, and the government continues to waste as much money as possible. Every effort is being made by the present administration to convert this country into a socialist nation. The expectation is that soon the overwhelming debt of the United States is going to collapse the dollar.

Many believe that World War III is about to happen. Some prominent leaders in America have stated that the attack on 9/11 was the start of World War III. The conflict between Israel and the Palestinians has heated up, and a conflict could start at any time. Iran is threatening Israel and the United States as they develop nuclear weapons. Many are convinced that war is imminent in the Middle East.[377]

Although the world's leaders have teamed up to try to get a peace agreement between Israel and the Palestinians before the end of 2012, war appears imminent because Iran is getting very close to having a nuclear bomb. Now the Scriptures tell us that the Muslim countries are going to attack Israel. Israel will come close to losing, except that YHVH will step in and fight for Israel. Israel will win the war.[328]

The present administration of the United States did not want a war between Israel and Iran before the election in November. They have stationed naval battle groups in the gulf near Iran in an effort to keep Israel from attacking Iran. Why? Maybe they are hoping they will get reelected before any war starts.

Of course, any war in the Middle East will shut down the oil supplies, and the cost of fuel will climb at record rates. The economy of America will suffer greatly. In addition, America could also be targeted by terrorists or even be part of a larger war. The result will be extremely hard times for America. Many believe that the America will be in a crisis either caused by the collapse of the dollar or by war.

The election this fall may also determine if the United States will become a subsidiary nation under the United Nations' one-world government. The present administration of the United States has embraced the idea, but it must subvert the US Constitution to move forward with the one-world government. This is evidenced by the Libyan war where the administration bypassed Congress and asked permission from the United Nations to use our military resources to help the rebels overthrow the Libyan government.

Tension between the United States and Israel

The United States has had a long history of supporting Israel. The relationship goes back a long way, and the United States has always been an ally of Israel. Christianity has its roots in Israel, and the Christian churches in the United States have always had a close relationship with Israel. However, this seems to be changing. Some churches have become apostate and embraced Chrislam. The present administration does not get along with Israel, and Israel does not trust the leaders of the United States anymore.

The Scriptures tell us that whosoever blesses Israel will be blessed and that whoever curses Israel will be cursed.

> *"And I shall bless those who bless you (Israel) and curse the one: and in you will all families of the earth be blessed."* (Genesis 12:3 ONMB)

Will YHVH destroy America for her Sins?

According to the Scriptures, YHVH (God) has destroyed mankind before for their iniquities. When the rebellious angels married women and their children were giants, YHVH sent His archangel to destroy the giants and to "lock up" these angels for their later judgment. In addition, in the days of Lot, YHVH destroyed the people of Sodom and Gomorrah for their iniquities by fire and brimstone that rained down from heaven. In both of these cases, destruction came because of sexual sins.

It seems that we are very close to what is called the last seven years before Yeshua will return. We live in a period where knowledge is increased, especially knowledge of the Scriptures (Daniel 12:4). There are rumors of war in the Middle East and even World War III (Matthew 24:6). The weather has resulted in much crop damage and food shortages. There have been earthquakes in places that rarely have earthquakes. The cases of swine flu and other pestilence have arisen (Matthew 24:7). The Scriptures say these events are the beginnings of sorrows (Matthew 24:8).

Christians are now under attack for their beliefs and especially the ones who follow the commandments. Many believe that after the war in the Middle East, the Jews will be blamed for the war and the economic effects on the United States and the rest of the world. This will come after the war in the Middle East, which will usher in the one new world government, which is part of the Dragon's master plan to **get everyone** in the world to worship him.

Many biblical scholars believe the war in the Middle East occurs before the seven-year peace treaty is signed.

Daniel was shown the future by the angel Gabriel as follows:

And after sixty-two weeks the Messiah will be cut off and there be no one to succeed Him, and the people of the people [Romans] of the prince that will come will destroy the city and the Sanctuary; and the end of it will be with a flood and to the end of the war desolations are determined. (Daniel 9:26 ONMB)

Roman legions destroyed Jerusalem in AD 70.

*And **He** will confirm the covenant [peace treaty] with many for one week (seven years) and for half of the week (three and half years after peace treaty signed) He will cause the sacrifice and the oblation to cease, and for the overspreading of abominations He will make it desolate, even until the consummation and that determined will be poured upon the desolate.* (Daniel 9:27 ONMB, emphasis added)

In Daniel 9:27, Daniel speaks of the Messiah (not the Antichrist) that will confirm the covenant for one week or seven years.

So what is the covenant?

On the same day the L<small>ORD</small> cut a covenant with Abram saying, "You're your seed I have given this land, from the river of Egypt to the great river, the river Euphrates." (Genesis 15:18 ONMB)

This is the covenant YHVH made with Abraham and his descendants regarding the land of Israel. Israel's right to the land is not accepted to this day by the Palestinians and most of the Arab neighbors. On the other hand, the verse is saying that there will be a peace agreement for seven years between Israel and the Palestinians. This peace treaty will include an arrangement where the UN has control over the temple mount.

So how long is a week in this verse?
Most translations of the Scriptures translate the word *week* to mean **seven years**.

So the peace agreement will be for seven years. We also know that the Jewish temple will be rebuilt during the first part of this period. How do we know this?

Yeshua said this about the Antichrist: when he stands in the temple, there will be the start of the great affliction or tribulation.

> *Therefore when you would see the* **abomination of the devastation** *stand in the holy place, which was foretold by Daniel the prophet, the one who reads must faithfully consider.* (Matthew 24:15 ONMB, emphasis added)
>
> *For then there will be* **great affliction** *such as has not happened from the beginning of the world until now and would never happen again.* (Matthew 24:21 ONMB, emphasis added)

So how long does the Great Tribulation last?
Daniel 9:27 says that it will start in the midst of the seven-year period and last till for the remainder of the three and half years.

Current Peace Agreement Talks

There have been peace talks going on for the last twenty years with Israel and the Palestinians to reach an agreement for a land for the Palestinians. The talks have two main goals:

1. final Borders between the two nations
2. decide who will control Jerusalem

The United States, United Nations, European Union, and Russia have formed a group called the **Quartet** to negotiate the peace agreement. They have established a schedule for getting the agreement completed.

In addition, the Vatican continues to push for an agreement where the Vatican controls the holy sites in Jerusalem.

These is a list some of the events that occurred in 2011 and planned events for 2012.

May 20, 2011: President Obama meets with Prime Minister Netanyahu in the White House. President Obama proposed that the borders be changed to the 1967 borders. That would put Jerusalem in the Palestinian territory. No one can forget the stare by President Obama toward Netanyahu when the proposal was rejected by Prime Minister Netanyahu.

September 23, 2011: Palestinian president Abbas formally asks the UN for recognize Palestine as a state. To prevent this proposal from going to the Security Council, President Obama threatened to veto any resolution giving the Palestinians statehood. The goal is for the Quartet to resolve the agreement that both countries will live by. After Abbas finished his address to the UN, Secretary of State Hillary Clinton announced that the Quartet had an alternative proposal as follows:

1. Within a month of both parties agreeing to implement the Quartet's proposal, Israel and the Palestine will attend a "preparatory meeting" to determine procedures and agendas.
2. Within three months, both parties would submit proposals on borders and security.
3. Within six months, the quartet would convene an international meeting in Russia to review the final agreement.
4. Israel and Palestine must agree to and have a **peace agreement in place before December 31, 2012. The Quartet insists that this date cannot change.**[329]

The following are actual events that occurred up to December 31, 2011:

October 23, 2011: Quartet travels to Israel for peace talks. Palestinians will not negotiate because of Jewish settlements in east Jerusalem. Israel refuses to halt settlements.

November 10, 2011: The pope meets with Jewish religious leaders to commit to peace and free access to Israel's holy sites for all religions.

November 14, 2011: The Quartet resumes trying to start peace talks but without success.

December 2, 2011: Vatican calls for special "Internationally Guaranteed Status."

December 15, 2011: Vatican demands control of temple mount and holy sites and tells Israel there will not be a peace agreement until they give them up.

December 17, 2011: President Obama gives a speech to Jewish conference affirming that US support for Israel is unshakeable.

The scheduled meeting on January 23, 2012, did not happen since the Palestinians refused to attend.

Was there be an agreement before the end of 2012?

If the peace agreement does happen in 2012, then it will usher in the last seven years of tribulation and rule of the Antichrist before Yeshua returns. It appears that Prime Minister Netanyahu will not agree to give up Jerusalem and go back to the 1967 borders or give up the settlements in east Jerusalem. This frustration by the Palestinians will again lead to a war against Israel.

War is Coming

The Scriptures tell us there will be a war with Israel. This war is described in the books of Zechariah, Ezekiel, and Joel. This war will be nuclear, and Israel will come close to annihilation, but YHVH again will deliver them. Will it turn into a world war? Many scholars say yes, but we can't be sure. Some biblical scholars believe this war will be the catalyst that causes the peace agreement to be implemented.

The peace agreement initiates the last seven years before Yeshua returns.

My prediction is that after the war, the peace agreement will be signed. The world is not going to allow any more wars over Jerusalem. Everyone will say, "Finally, we have peace." This agreement, called the "confirmation of the covenant," will start the clock on the last seven years of the earth.

CHAPTER 27

Zechariah's War

WE BELIEVE THAT THE THIRD woe started on September 11, 2001. If true, then we are living in the end of the age, and the events just before the Messiah returns are about to happen. We know from the Scriptures that we are going to see a war in the Middle East where the Muslims attempt to destroy Israel, the confirmation of the covenant with the seed of Abraham, a one-world government, the revealing of the Antichrist, tribulation, and the return of the Messiah. Since most Christians have not understood YHVH's calendar and the book of Revelation, they may not realize how close we are to these events taking place. The angel Gabriel explained to Daniel what was to come, and he fainted. Also, Gabriel told Daniel to seal up the book until the time of the end. The book of Daniel is now being understood, and so the mystery can now be better understood.

The Scriptures tell us that there is a war between YHVH and Satan. Satan won the earth when Adam and Eve sinned. Yeshua, the sinless Lamb of YHVH, was sacrificed on the cross. Because He was worthy, Yeshua was able to remove the seals from the scroll, giving Him the title to the earth. The scroll has the appointed times of the return of the Messiah to the earth where He will rule with a rod of iron. Many Christian scholars believe that the writings on the front and back of the scroll are recorded as part of the book of Revelation in the Scriptures.

After this event, there was a war in heaven between YHVH and Satan. Satan and his angels lost, and they were kicked out of heaven and fell to the earth. Satan is angry and his goal is to have **us worship**

his image (the Antichrist) on earth before he is destroyed by YHVH. To get even with YHVH, he is going to destroy anyone who worships YHVH, especially the Jewish nation.

We all know about Iran. Iran has publicly stated that they are going to destroy Israel. They are busy developing a nuclear bomb, and this has given rise to much tension in Israel. The present US administration doesn't support Israel, and this has emboldened Israel's enemies. Most people now believe that a war is imminent between Israel and its Muslim neighbors.

Tensions are very high between Israel and Iran's strategic alliance of Syria, Hezbollah, and Hamas. Syria has threatened to launch missiles into Israel if NATO tries to intervene in Syria's on-going revolution. Hezbollah has accumulated forty thousand rockets in Lebanon for use against Israel. Hamas in the Gaza area has shoulder-fired rockets. Israel is preparing its citizens for a missile war.

Although it has not happened yet, it appears that a war against Israel is imminent.

Are Israel's Enemies in the Scriptures?

In Psalm 83, it describes clearly Israel's neighbors as enemies.

> *They have said, Come, and let us cut them off from being a nation; that the name of Israel may be no more in remembrance. For they have consulted together with one consent: they are confederate against thee: The tabernacles of Edom, and the Ishmaelites; of Moab, and the Hagarenes; Gebal, and Ammon, and Amalek; the Philistines with the inhabitants of Tyre; Assur also is joined with them: they have helped the children of Lot. Selah.* (Psalm 83:4–8 KJV)
>
> *Son of man, set thy face against Gog, the land of Magog, the chief prince of Meshech and Tubal, and prophesy against him, And say, Thus saith the Lord God; Behold, I am against thee, O Gog, the chief prince of Meshech and Tubal: Persia, Ethiopia, and Libya with them; all of them with shield and helmet: Gomer, and all his bands; the house of*

> *Togarmah of the north quarters, and all his bands: and many people with thee. Sheba, and Dedan, and the merchants of Tarshish, with all the young lions thereof, shall say unto thee, Art thou come to take a spoil? Hast thou gathered thy company to take a prey? To carry away silver and gold, to take away cattle and goods, to take a great spoil?* (Ezekiel 38:2–3, 5–6, 13 KJV)

This Psalm 83 coalition referenced in the Scriptures includes Palestinian, Jordanian, Hezbollah, Lebanese, and Syrian forces. Most of these groups have already had several battles with the Israel's army and lost. Scholars believe that Israel can win this war on its own.

Ezekiel says that a Russian-Iranian coalition will attempt to invade Israel after Israel defeats the Psalm 83 coalition. This war is called the Gog-Magog War, and it will occur shortly after the Psalm 83 invasion. This coalition includes Russia, Iran, Sudan, Ethiopia, Libya, Algeria, Tunisia, Turkey, Armenia, and the Turkish-speaking people of Asia Minor and Central Asia. This is the war in which YHVH alone destroys the enemy. They come to take a spoil.

The Palestinians have for years fought against Israel in order to get Israel to give up land for peace. By giving up land, they have violated YHVH's covenant with Abraham and his seed. This obviously has angered YHVH, and it is apparent what will happen to them in the book of Isaiah.

Israel is to be overrun by her enemies.

> *And your covenant with death shall be disannulled, and your agreement with hell shall not stand; when the **overflowing scourge shall pass through, then ye shall be trodden down by it.** From the time that it goeth forth it shall take you: for morning by morning shall it pass over, by day and by night: and it shall be a **vexation only to understand the report**.* (Isaiah 28:18 19 KJV, emphasis added)

Israel will be stunned and confused by YHVH, allowing the country of Israel to be overrun by the Muslim armies.

Zechariah's Vision

Zechariah was a prophet who was born when Israel was in captivity in Babylon, and his name means "YHVH remembers." In the book of Zechariah, he often is receiving messages from an angel sent by YHVH. He also had several visions as follows:

> *Then I turned, and lifted up mine eyes, and looked, and behold a flying scroll. And he said unto me, what seest thou? And I answered, I see a flying scroll; the length thereof is twenty cubits, and the breadth thereof ten cubits.* (Zechariah 5:2 KJV) [330]

These are very close dimensions of a Scud missile.

> *Then said he unto me, This is the curse that goeth forth over the face of the whole earth: for every one that stealeth shall be cut off as on this side according to it; and every one that sweareth shall be cut off as on that side according to it.* (Zechariah 5:3 KJV)

The curse referred to are missiles capable of delivering nuclear bombs on every nation of the earth.

> *I will bring it forth, saith the LORD of hosts, and it shall enter into the house of the thief, and into the house of him that sweareth falsely by my name: and it shall remain in the midst of his house, and shall consume it with the timber thereof and the stones thereof.* (Zechariah 5:4 KJV)

Nuclear explosions will consume timber and stones as well as leaving radiation for a long period of time.

Then the angel that talked with me went forth, and said unto me, Lift up now thine eyes, and see what this that goeth forth is. And I said, what is it? And he said, this is an ephah that goeth forth. He said moreover, this is their resemblance through all the earth. (Zechariah 5:5–6 KJV)

An ephah is a container.[331]

And, behold, there was lifted up a talent of lead: and this is a woman (fire) that sitteth in the midst of the ephah. (Zechariah 5:7 KJV)

Woman is a mistranslation. The Hebrew word means fire. Lead is used to protect people from the radiation.[332]

And he said, this is wickedness. And he cast it into the midst of the ephah; and he cast the weight of lead upon the mouth thereof. Then lifted I up mine eyes, and looked, and, behold, there came out two women, and the wind was in their wings; for they had wings like the wings of a stork: and they lifted up the ephah between the earth and the heaven. (Zechariah 5:8–9 KJV)

Two missiles are launched against Israel.

Then said I to the angel that talked with me, whither do these bear the ephah? (Zechariah 5:10 KJV)

Zechariah asks the angel who sent the missiles.

And he said unto me, to build it and house in the land of Shinar: and it shall be established, and set there upon her own base. (Zechariah 5:11 KJV)

The angel answers that they came from the land of Shinar.

The land of Shinar is Iraq. Many believe that this prophecy is saying that the two missiles were built in Iraq. Others believe that these missiles were built in Iran. I assume that the Scriptures are correct, so maybe these are the missiles that the United States did not find in Iraq during the second Gulf war.

We do know that Syria has a lot of these scud missiles. There are four versions of Scud missiles, each having different sizes and range. The dimensions of the missile in Zechariah's vision appear to be the same as a Scud–C or a Scud-D, which have a range of 550 km or 300 km. We also know that Syria has given Hezbollah Scud missiles. This would put most of Israel in range for an attack by Hezbollah, and they have already threatened to hit the Ben Gurion Airport.[333]

A war could break out at any time. This war is also described in the book of Ezekiel.

Gog-Magog War

In Ezekiel 38:7–39, it describes the Gog-Magog war where Israel is overrun by her enemies and YHVH has to defend Israel. This war will be an attack by Muslims against Israel. This war is also described by three prophets in the Old Testament. Ezekiel 38 and 39 describe the war and how **YHVH defends Israel**. In Joel 2:20, Joel describes how **YHVH defends Israel**. In Isaiah 17:1–3, it describes the total destruction of Damascus.

If the Muslims can launch a surprise attack and knock out the air bases where Israel has its air force located, then it will be difficult to stop them from being overrun. Hezbollah itself has over forty thousand rockets it could launch against Israel. The armies of Gog and Magog will overrun most of Israel, and Israel as a last resort will have to use their nuclear armed submarines to counter the attack.[334]

The Scriptures say that YHVH will utterly destroy the enemy and the world will know that He fought and destroyed the enemy.

*And I will call for a sword against him throughout all **my mountains**, saith the Lord GOD: every man's sword shall be against his brother.* (Ezekiel 38:21 KJV, emphasis added)

YHVH is making it clear that this is **His land**.

And I will plead against him with pestilence and with blood; and I will rain upon him, and upon his bands, and upon the many people that are with him, an overflowing rain, and great hailstones, fire, and brimstone. (Ezekiel 38:22 KJV)

Supernatural forces will come against the enemy that only YHVH could do.

Thus will I magnify myself, and sanctify myself; and I will be known in the eyes of many nations, and they shall know that I am the LORD. (Ezekiel 38:23 KJV)

WHEN WILL THE MUSLIMS ATTACK AND START THE WAR?

No one knows the answer to this question. On the other hand, the recent war against Libya gives rise for concern that it may be a precursor to the big war. Also, large deposits of oil and gas have been found in Israel, which would make them a prosperous country. This could tempt the nations to attack before their military gets even more powerful.[335]

When the war starts, it is extremely significant because most biblical scholars agree that when this war ends, the world will usher in the seven-year peace agreement brokered by the Antichrist where Israel is recognized as a country by the Muslim world. So Ezekiel's war is a critical milestone to the start of the last seven years before Yeshua returns.

CHAPTER 28

The Confirmation of the Covenant

AFTER ZECHARIAH'S WAR IS OVER, it takes seven months to bury the dead in Israel. The world also has been devastated due to war. No one can say for sure what countries outside of Israel will be affected, but most believe that America will also be hit. If America is hit by nuclear weapons, then there will much destruction, and our economy will be destroyed also. There could be rioting and much lawlessness in America. Many will have been killed by the nuclear blast. The war could be the trigger that ushers in new world order run by the United Nations.

The end of the war will usher in a cry for peace. The world is not going to tolerate any more wars, especially over Jerusalem. The UN will become the new world government, and it will place Jerusalem under the control of the Roman Catholic Church. In order to get the Israel to agree, the Antichrist will broker a deal where the Muslims recognize Israel as a nation. This agreement is known as the confirmation of the covenant, which refers to the covenant made by YHVH with Abraham.

Daniel said the following would happen:

> ***And he shall confirm the covenant with many for one week** [seven years] and in the midst of the week he shall cause the sacrifice and the oblation to cease, and for the overspreading of abominations he shall make it desolate, even until the consummation, and that determined shall be poured upon the desolate.* (Daniel 9:27 KJV, emphasis added)

This event marks the beginning of the first half of the seven-year period. During this period, the Jews will start rebuilding the replica of Solomon's temple on the temple mount in Jerusalem. The location will be near the existing Muslim mosque. After the temple is completed, it will be furnished with replicas of the major furniture pieces that were in the original temple.

Speculation is the Ark of the Covenant will be placed in the temple. The hidden location of the ark has been known for many years. Ron Wyatt had discovered the ark with the Ten Commandments and Moses's staff many years before. At that time, Ron Wyatt said it could not be removed because it was protected by angels.

The Fulfillment of the Fall Feasts

In order to understand the events that are to follow Zechariah's war, we must understand that Yeshua's return will fulfill the fall feasts of YHVH. Remember in chapter 6 we said that the feasts were prophetic shadow-pictures of the return of the Messiah. The Scriptures said Yeshua after two days would revive us and in the third day He would raise us up.

> *After two days will he revive us: in the third day he will raise us up, and we shall live in his sight.* (Hosea 6:2 KJV)

Remember Peter said that a day in heaven is a thousand years on earth. So Yeshua was crucified about two thousand years ago or two days, and now we are in the third day. Aviv 1, 6001, or March 26, 2001, was the first day of the seventh millennium and commenced the day of the Lord. This day is also known as the "Time of Jacob's Trouble." This date has been declared unanimously by the rabbinic council in Jerusalem.[336]

The following is a description cy Michael Rood of the confirmation of the covenant—how things are expected to happen if the covenant is confirmed on Yom Kippur, the Day of Atonement.[337]

Tishri 1: The Overflowing Scourge—Ten days of Awe during Zechariah's War. This is the first day of the seventh month on YHVH's calendar. It is the day of the blowing of trumpets.

Tishri 10: The Day of Atonement. This is the day that Judea is reborn. This is when the global peacemaker shows up on the scene to confirm a covenant with **many** for seven years. **Many** in the church and in **many** in Israel abandon the faith and sign the covenant agreement.

Tishri 15: Sukkot (Feast of Tabernacles).

Tishri 22: The Last Great Day. The Feast of Tabernacles is observed for seven days, and on the last day (The Last Great Day) is celebrated with prayer and thanksgiving.

This when the **Latter Day rains (outpouring of the Holy Spirit) begins.** When YHVH's people realize no rapture is evident, they will be on their knees praying and repenting. They will receive the outpouring of the Holy Spirit to prepare them for the tribulation against the saints.[338]

> *And it shall come to pass afterward, that I will pour out my spirit upon all flesh; and your sons and your daughters shall prophesy, your old men shall dream dreams, your young men shall see visions: And also upon the servants and upon the handmaids in those days will I pour out my spirit. And I will shew wonders in the heavens and in the earth, blood, and fire, and pillars of smoke. The sun shall be turned into darkness, and the moon into blood, before the great and the terrible day of the LORD come. And it shall come to pass, that whosoever shall call on the name of the LORD shall be delivered: for in mount Zion and in Jerusalem shall be deliverance, as the LORD hath said, and in the remnant whom the LORD shall call.* (Joel 2:28–32 KJV)

Kislew 25: Feast of Hanukkah initiates the eight-day altar dedication.

Tevet 3: Oblation sacrifice begins. This initiates the 2300 evening and morning oblations (1150 days).

The construction of the replica of Solomon's temple begins. It will be constructed on the temple mount adjacent to the existing Dome of the Rock mosque. The UN will provide security, and the Vatican will rule over all the holy sites. This will be part of the agreement where the Muslims and Jews share the temple mount.[339]

The Falling Away

At the same time there will be a **great falling away**. The Antichrist will lead many of YHVH's people into a deeper apostasy and to an abandonment of worship of YHVH and Yeshua.

> *Let no man deceive you by any means: for that day shall not come, except there come **a falling away first,** and that man of sin be revealed, the son of perdition.* (2 Thessalonians 2:3 KJV)

From this Bible verse we know the falling away begins before the Antichrist is revealed at the midpoint of the seven-year peace agreement. So this must happen in the first three-and-a-half-year period.

The Antichrist will be revealed in Jerusalem at the midpoint of the seven years, and it is called the abomination of desolation (or devastation).

During this period, I expect to see the foundation of a new world government, a one-world religion and a one-world economic system put in place. A one-world religion also will have to be in place.

CHAPTER 29

The Great Tribulation

YESHUA (JESUS) SAID THE FOLLOWING to the disciples:

*When ye therefore shall see the **abomination of desolation**, spoken of by Daniel the prophet, stand in the holy place, (whoso readeth, let him understand).* (Matthew 24:15 KJV, emphasis added)

Who opposeth and exalteth himself above all that is called God, or that is worshipped; so that he as God sitteth in the temple of God, shewing himself that he is God. (2 Thessalonians 2:4 KJV)

The false prophet will bring fire down from heaven in sight of the world, and this will convince most of the world to worship or pledge allegiance to the Antichrist who sits in the temple.

And he [the second beast] doeth great wonders, so that he maketh fire come down from heaven on the earth in the sight of men. (Revelation 13:13 KJV)

The false prophet is imitating Elijah, who proved to the worshippers of Baal that YHVH is the true God.

And it came to pass at the time of the offering of the evening sacrifice, that Elijah the prophet came near, and said, LORD God of Abraham, Isaac, and of Israel, let it be known this day that thou art God in Israel, and that I am thy servant, and that I have done all these things at thy

> *word. Hear me, O LORD, hear me, that this people may know that thou art the LORD God, and that thou hast turned their heart back again. Then the fire of the LORD fell, and consumed the burnt sacrifice, and the wood, and the stones, and the dust, and licked up the water that was in the trench.* (1 Kings 18:38 KJV)

By bringing fire down from heaven at the temple he is trying to convince the whole world that the Antichrist is the true god of the world. When the world sees this on worldwide television, almost the whole world will be convinced to worship him.

He will sit in the rebuilt temple of Jerusalem and make a great proclamation to the world claiming to be god of all religions including Islam, Christianity, Buddhism, etc. So when you see this happen, you will have no doubt that he is the Antichrist.

Immediately he puts an end to the sacrifices and daily oblations by the Jewish priests in the temple.

> *And he shall confirm the covenant with many for one week: and in the midst of the week he shall* **cause the sacrifice and the oblation to cease**, *and for the overspreading of abominations he shall make it desolate, even until the consummation, and that determined shall be poured upon the desolate.* (Daniel 9:27 KJV, emphasis added)

From the following, the Antichrist most likely will issue a death sentence to the Jews in Jerusalem. His speech will motivate the Palestinians living in Jerusalem to go after all the Jewish families to kill them. Maybe that's why Yeshua gives them this warning.

Yeshua tells the Jews in Jerusalem that when they see this event to flee for their lives: "Then let them which be in Judaea flee into the mountains" (Matthew 24:16 KJV).

The Jews are told to run for their lives. This will be difficult, and many will not make it. A remnant will flee into the mountains of Jordan to a place called Petra. During the journey and in Petra for three and half years, they will be protected by YHVH.

As they are walking out of Israel to the mountains, the Antichrist will send an army after them to destroy them:

And the serpent [Satan] cast out of his mouth water as a flood [overwhelming number of soldier] after the woman, that he might cause her to be carried away of the flood. (Revelation 12:15 KJV)

But YHVH protects them just as He had done during the exodus from Egypt.

And the earth helped the woman, and the earth opened her mouth, and swallowed up the flood which the dragon cast out of his mouth. (Revelation 12:16 KJV)

An earthquake opened up the earth and swallowed up the army. This protection allows time for the remnant of Israel to get to Petra in Jordan. There the remnant of Israel is protected from the Antichrist for three and half years.

*And to the woman were given **two wings of a great eagle** that she might fly into the wilderness, into her place, where she is nourished for a time, and times, and half a time from the face of the serpent.* (Revelation 12:14 KJV, emphasis added)

This will be the second time that YHVH will protect Israel during their flight.

*Ye have seen what I did unto the Egyptians, and how I bare you on **eagles' wings**, and brought you unto myself.* (Exodus 19:4 KJV, emphasis added)

Why Jordan?

> *He [Antichrist] shall enter also into the glorious land, and many countries shall be overthrown: but **these shall escape out of his hand**, even Edom, and Moab, and the chief of the children of Ammon.* (Daniel 11:41 KJV, emphasis added)

Edom, Moab, and Ammon are in modern-day Jordan. Obviously Jordan will escape control by the Antichrist. Apparently from the Scriptures, the Antichrist will not control the entire world.

> *But tidings out of the east and out of the north shall trouble him: therefore he shall go forth with great fury to destroy, and utterly to make away many.* (Daniel 11:44 KJV)

War against the Saints

Now that the remnant of the Jews is protected from the Antichrist in Jordan, the Antichrist starts his persecution of the Gentiles. They are ordered to worship the Antichrist. Everyone will be given a choice to worship either the Antichrist and live or to worship Yeshua by keeping His commandments and face death.

> *And the dragon was wroth with the woman, and went to make war with the remnant of her seed, which keep the commandments of God, and have the testimony of Jesus Christ.* (Revelation 12:17 KJV)
> *For then shall be great tribulation, such as was not since the beginning of the world to this time, no, nor ever shall be.* (Matthew 24:21 KJV)

The world has seen tribulation before. The Flood during the time of Noah was certainly tribulation. During the Spanish Inquisition, countless millions were tortured and murdered. Hitler had six million Jews exterminated. Joseph Stalin had twenty million Russians killed, and Mao Zedong had sixty million killed over a fifty-year period.

Yeshua says the Great Tribulation is worse than any of these prior tribulation periods.

The Mark of the Beast

> *And he causeth all, both small and great, rich and poor, free and bond, to receive a mark in their right hand, or in their foreheads: And that no man might buy or sell, save he that had the mark, or the name of the beast, or the number of his name.* (Revelation 13:16–17 KJV)

Everyone is given this choice of either receiving his mark and worshipping the Antichrist or rejecting the mark. The law that will be passed will carry a death penalty.

> *And he had power to give life unto the image of the beast that the image of the beast should both speak, and* **cause that as many as would not worship the image of the beast should be killed.** (Revelation 13:15 KJV, emphasis added)

Warning from YHVH if you accept the Mark

> *And the third angel followed them, saying with a loud voice, If any man worship the beast and his image, and receive his mark in his forehead, or in his hand,* **The same shall drink of the wine of the wrath of God, which is poured out without mixture into the cup of his indignation; and he shall be tormented with fire and brimstone in the presence of the holy angels, and in the presence of the Lamb:** *And the smoke of their torment ascendeth up for ever and ever: and they have no rest day nor night, who worship the*

beast and his image, and whosoever receiveth the mark of his name. (Revelation 14:9–11 KJV, emphasis added)

So if you are alive when this happens, you will be given a choice of accepting the mark or be killed. The easy road is to accept the mark. If it is Sunday worship, then it will seem OK to you. Remember the Scriptures say everyone is deceived.

If you accept the mark, then you will not be forgiven by YHVH, and you will spend eternity in hell. If you refuse the mark, then you will be thrown in jail and killed after ten days. But, you will be in heaven for all of eternity.

Millions of Christians will refuse the mark and will be killed. John saw them in his vision:

And one of the elders answered, saying unto me, what are these which are arrayed in white robes? And whence came they? And I said unto him, Sir, thou knowest. And he said to me, these are they which came out of **great tribulation**, *and have washed their robes, and made them white in the blood of the Lamb. Therefore are they before the throne of God, and serve him day and night in his temple: and he that sitteth on the throne shall dwell among them.* (Revelation 7:13–15 KJV, emphasis added)

This will be a tough choice for every Christian.

When the saints refuse, they will be killed. Who are the saints?

Here is the patience of the saints: here are **they that keep the commandments of God, and the faith of Jesus.** (Revelation 14:12 KJV, emphasis added)

The saints are all killed. All the saints who keep the commandments of YHVH and believe in Yeshua are eliminated. The whole world now will worship the Antichrist.

After the millions of the followers of Yeshua are killed, then the wrath of YHVH comes on the ones who accepted the mark of the beast.

Everyone will be made to make a choice to either follow YHVH or be killed or to accept the mark to worship the Antichrist and be sentenced to hell forever.

How will the Mark be Implemented Worldwide?

Technology makes everything easy. During the Bush administration, Congress passed the National ID Act, but it has not been implemented yet. This law allows the federal government to issue every citizen an ID card with a number on it. The number will locate you in the database. This ID card will be used by everyone to obtain employment, buy goods, and sell goods. It also could be used against you if you don't comply with the government. Technology makes it easy to implement, and the European Union is trying to implement this also.

So if you don't comply with the directives from the government, then it will be easy to identify you. Then you will be arrested and thrown in jail for ten days before execution.

The two witnesses

At the time the abomination of desolation occurs in the temple in Jerusalem, the Gentiles will overrun Jerusalem and the temple mount.

> *But the court which is without the temple leave out, and measure it not; for it is given unto the Gentiles: and the holy city shall they tread under foot forty and two months.* (Revelation 11:2 KJV)

YHVH sends two witnesses to testify in Jerusalem. Although the Scriptures do not say who they are, many suggest it will be Elijah and Moses.

And I will give power unto my two witnesses, and they shall prophesy a thousand two hundred and threescore days, clothed in sackcloth. (Revelation 11:3 KJV)

They will be prophesying in Jerusalem for three and a half years. *Prophesying* means to speak for YHVH or that they utter the words of YHVH.

Why are two witnesses required? The Scriptures give us the answer to this question.

> *At the mouth of two witnesses, or three witnesses, shall he that is worthy of death be put to death; but at the mouth of one witness he shall not be put to death.* (Deuteronomy 17:6 KJV)
>
> *One witness shall not rise up against a man for any iniquity, or for any sin, in any sin that he sinneth: at the mouth of two witnesses, or at the mouth of three witnesses, shall the matter be established.* (Deuteronomy 19:15 KJV)
>
> *And all the people that were in the gate, and the elders, said, we are witnesses. The* LORD *make the woman that is come into thine house like Rachel and like Leah, which two did build the house of Israel: and do thou worthily in Ephratah, and be famous in Bethlehem.* (Ruth 4:11 KJV)
>
> *But if he will not hear thee, then take with thee one or two more, that in the mouth of two or three witnesses every word may be established.* (Matthew 18:16 KJV)
>
> *But found none: yea, though many false witnesses came, yet found them none. At the last came two false witnesses.* (Matthew 26:60 KJV)
>
> *This is the third time I am coming to you. In the mouth of two or three witnesses shall every word be established.* (2 Corinthians 13:1 KJV)
>
> *Against an elder receive not an accusation, but before two or three witnesses.* (1 Timothy 5:19 KJV)
>
> *He that despised Moses' law died without mercy under two or three witnesses.* (Hebrews 10:28 KJV)

Satan has gained complete control of the earth, but the **two witnesses testify daily a message of judgment and the need for turning away from the worship of the Antichrist.** They are compared to olive trees.

> *These are the two olive trees, and the two candlesticks standing before the God of the earth.* (Revelation 11:4 KJV)

In the Scriptures, Zerubbabel and Joshua are pictured as the two olive trees furnishing oil for a lampstand or Israel. They provided help and power to Israel in a time of need. Just as Zerubbabel and Joshua provided these things to Israel in the past, they will provide the same to Israel in the 1260 days or three and a half years before judgment.

Their testimony will not be well received, and many will try to stop them without success.

> *And if any man will hurt them, fire proceedeth out of their mouth, and devoureth their enemies: and if any man will hurt them, he must in this manner be killed.* (Revelation 11:5 KJV)

The testimony of the two witnesses occurs in the same period of time that the last seven plagues take place.

Mystery Babylon

Then an angel descends from heaven with a call for people to come out of Mystery Babylon. You see, Babylon has never gone away. It started at the tower of Babel and will exist to the end when Yeshua returns. This is the one-world religion that worships the Antichrist.

Let's examine the Scriptures and look at what the angel told John in the book of Revelation.

> *And after these things [Revelation 17] I saw another angel come down from heaven, having great power; and the earth was lightened with his glory. And he cried mightily with a strong voice, saying,* **Babylon the**

great is fallen, is fallen, and is become the habitation of devils, and the hold of every foul spirit, and a cage of every unclean and hateful bird. (Revelation 18:1–2 KJV, emphasis added)

This is a religion that has fallen from God. God is about to pour out His plagues on them:

And there came one of the seven angels which had the seven vials, and talked with me, saying unto me, come hither; I will shew unto thee the judgment of the great **whore** *that sitteth upon many waters.* (Revelation 17:1 KJV, emphasis added)

In the Scriptures, a woman is the church. In Revelation 12, the woman is shown as a pure woman. In these verses, the woman is called a **whore**.

With whom the kings of the earth have committed fornication, and the inhabitants of the earth have been made drunk with the wine of her fornication. So he carried me away in the spirit into the wilderness: and I saw a woman [church] sit upon a scarlet colored beast, full of names of blasphemy, having seven heads and ten horns. And the **woman [church] was arrayed in purple and scarlet colour**, *and decked with gold and precious stones and pearls, having a golden cup in her hand full of abominations and filthiness of her fornication.* (Revelation 17:2–4 KJV, emphasis added)

I have likened the daughter of Zion to a comely and delicate **woman**. (Jeremiah 6:2 KJV, emphasis added)

For thy Maker is thine husband; the L*ord* *of hosts is his name; and thy Redeemer the Holy One of Israel; The God of the whole earth shall he be called. For the* L*ord* *hath called thee as a woman forsaken and grieved in spirit, and a wife of youth, when thou wast refused, saith thy God.* (Isaiah 54:5–6 KJV, emphasis added)

For I am jealous over you with godly jealousy: for I have espoused you to one husband that I may present you as a chaste virgin to Christ. (2 Corinthians 11:2 KJV)

> *And upon her forehead was a name written, MYSTERY, BABYLON THE GREAT, AND AND AND THE MOTHER OF HARLOTS AND ABOMINATIONS OF THE EARTH.* (Revelation 17:5 KJV)

So who are the harlots (prostitutes) referred to in this passage? In the Old Testament, YHVH often referred to the Jews as **harlots** for they were in **rebellion to His laws**. This is one of forty verses in the Scriptures that describes a harlot:

> *The LORD said also unto me in the days of Josiah the king, hast thou seen that which backsliding Israel hath done? She is gone up upon every high mountain and under every green tree, and there hath played the **harlot**.* (Jeremiah 3:6 KJV, emphasis added)

Historically, only one church system fits this description, and it is the Roman Catholic Church. The old Roman Catholic Church became the church for the Gentiles throughout Europe. There was no other church in Europe, and as a result, the Roman Catholic Church expanded and gained much power and influence over the nations of Europe. The Roman Catholic Church became the sole interpreter of the Scriptures and exercised great authority over the Europeans in how to worship. To go against the church was to invite torture or death, and so the church was in total control of the nations of Europe.

However, Revelation 17:5 could be referring to the church system during the great tribulation.

> *And I saw the woman [church] drunken with the blood of the saints, and with the blood of the martyrs of Jesus: and when I saw her, I wondered with great admiration.* (Revelation 17:6 KJV)

This verse fits also the church of the dark ages. During the dark ages (AD 538 to AD 1798), the Roman Catholic Church tortured and killed millions of Christians as heretics against the church. For 1260 years, millions were brutally tortured and burned at the stake. Thirty-one thousand people were burned alive in Spain alone. Read *Foxe's Book of Martyrs* for a better understanding of what happened during this period of church history.

On the other hand, John is seeing these terrible events in the latter days. When John saw this vision, he could not understand how the church in the name of Jesus could do such a thing.

> *And the angel said unto me, wherefore didst thou marvel? I will tell thee the mystery of the woman [Church], and of the beast [Kingdoms, political power] that carried her, which hath the seven heads and ten horns. The* **beast** *that thou sawest was, and is not; and shall ascend out of the* **bottomless pit**, *and go into perdition: and they that dwell on the earth shall wonder, whose names were not written in the book of life from the foundation of the world, when they behold the beast that was, and is not, and yet is.* (Revelation 17:7–8 KJV)

John is seeing this prophecy of 1798 when the papacy has lost its power. Napoleon (an atheist) decreed on February 10, 1798, that the papacy's power over the European nations was over. He dispatched his general to Rome and put the pope in prison. The word **"was"** is referring to the period of time from 538 to 1798 that the church had power over the nations of Europe. The **"is not"** is referring to the period after 1798 when the Roman Catholic Church has no power. The bottomless pit is the period of time that the church is restrained or has no control.

PERDITION MEANS TO DESTROY.

> *Let no man deceive you by any means: for that day shall not come, except there come a falling away first, and that man of sin be revealed, the son of perdition; Who opposeth and exalteth himself above all that is called God, or that is worshipped; so that he as God sitteth in the temple of God, shewing himself that he is God. Remember ye not, that, when I was yet with you, I told you these things? And now ye know what*

withholdeth that he might be revealed in his time. For the mystery of iniquity doth already work: only he who now letteth will let, until he be taken out of the way. And then shall that Wicked be revealed, whom the Lord shall consume with the spirit of his mouth, and shall destroy with the brightness of his coming. (2 Thessalonians 2:3–8 KJV)

The son of perdition is a man and will be destroyed.

The phrase **"yet is"** is the church/state that will return to power and will be destroyed by the return of Yeshua.

And here is the mind which hath wisdom. The seven heads are seven mountains, on which the woman sitteth. (Revelation 17:9 KJV)

The final state and church system seems to be the following:

1. The United Nations will be the political organization that will rule the world. All nations will be subservient to the United Nations. The false prophet will be the leader of the United Nations, and the seat will be in New York City.
2. The religious system will be the Roman Catholic Church with the Protestant churches under her control in a confederacy with Islam. This is the clay mixed with iron in Daniel's prophecy. The seat of the religious system will be in Rome.

This one of many scenarios that are plastered across the Internet. The Scriptures say that the Antichrist will not be revealed until the midpoint of the peace treaty. Only then will we know for sure.

BACK TO THE TWO WITNESSES
After three and a half years, the two witnesses have finished their testimony, and they are killed by Satan.

And when they shall have finished their testimony, the beast that ascendeth out of the bottomless pit shall make war against them, and shall overcome them, and kill them. And their dead bodies shall lie in the street of the great city, which spiritually is called Sodom and Egypt, where also our Lord was crucified. And they of the people and kindreds and tongues and nations shall see their dead bodies three days and an half, and shall not suffer their dead bodies to be put in graves. And they that dwell upon the earth shall rejoice over them, and make merry, and shall send gifts one to another; because these two prophets tormented them that dwelt on the earth. And after three days and an half the Spirit of life from God entered into them, and they stood upon their feet; and great fear fell upon them which saw them. And they heard a great voice from heaven saying unto them, Come up hither. And they ascended up to heaven in a cloud; and their enemies beheld them. (Revelation 11:7–12 KJV)

The two witnesses are called before Yeshua to report on the completion of their testimony.

*And the same hour was there a great earthquake, and the tenth part of the city fell, and in the earthquake were slain of men seven thousand: and the **remnant were affrighted, and gave glory to the God of heaven.*** (Revelation 11:13 KJV)

THE PLAGUES COME

The saints have been killed. The ones left are in the Christian church and other religions that are followers of the Antichrist. Maybe they think they did the right thing. Many had asked their pastors, who told them they would be right; however, the Scriptures tell us very vividly what happens to everyone who accepts the mark, whether you are Christian or another religion.

First probation in heaven closes when it fills with smoke. No prayers of forgiveness can be heard until all the plagues come on the earth.

> *And one of the four beasts gave unto the seven angels seven golden vials full of the wrath of God, who liveth for ever and ever. And the temple was filled with smoke from the glory of God, and from his power; and no man was able to enter into the temple, till the seven plagues of the seven angels were fulfilled.* (Revelation 15:7–8 KJV)

Then a voice is heard from the sanctuary of YHVH for the seven angels to pour out their vials of YHVH's wrath on the earth. As we discussed in the prior chapter, a call had been given to come out of Babylon. After a period of time, YHVH sends the plagues to the ones who worship the Antichrist. They are described as vials of the wrath of YHVH.

First are the seven vials.

First Vial

> *And the first went, and poured out his vial upon the earth; and there fell a **noisome and grievous sore upon the men which had the mark of the beast**, and upon them which worshipped his image.* (Revelation 16:2 KJV, emphasis added)

So if you get this sore, that's a real bad sign. You have made a bad choice.

Second Vial

> *And the second angel poured out his vial upon the **sea; and it became as the blood of a dead man:** and every living soul died in the sea.* (Revelation 16:3 KJV, emphasis added)

Third Vial

*And the third angel poured out his vial upon the **rivers and fountains of waters; and they became blood.*** (Revelation 16:4 KJV, emphasis added)

Fourth Vial

*And the fourth angel poured out his **vial upon the sun;** and power was given unto him to scorch men with fire.* (Revelation 16:8 KJV, emphasis added)

Fifth Vial

*And the fifth angel poured out his **vial upon the seat of the beast**; and his kingdom was full of darkness; and they gnawed their tongues for pain.* (Revelation 16:10 KJV, emphasis added)

Sixth Vial

*And the sixth angel poured out his **vial upon the great river Euphrates;** and the water thereof was dried up, that the way of the **kings of the east** might be prepared. And I saw three unclean spirits like frogs come out of the mouth of the dragon, and out of the mouth of the beast, and out of the mouth of the false prophet. For they are the **spirits of devils, working miracles**, which go forth unto the **kings of the earth** and of the whole world, to gather them to the battle of that great day of God Almighty.* (Revelation 16:12–14 KJV, emphasis added)

These are not kings of nations but are the ten kings of ten regions appointed by the one-world government to rule the world.

These spirits cause the kings of the earth to send their troops to Israel to do battle with Yeshua (Jesus). They know that Yeshua will return to Jerusalem on the Mount of Olives. They gathered their armies on the plain of Har-Megiddo or Armageddon.

Then Yeshua is seen by everyone returning to earth.

And I saw heaven opened, and behold a white horse; and he that sat upon him was called Faithful and true, and in righteousness he doth judge and make war. His eyes were as a flame of fire, and on his head were many crowns; and he had a name written, that no man knew, but him himself. And he was clothed with a vesture dipped in blood: and his name is called The Word of God. And the armies which were in heaven followed him upon white horses, clothed in fine linen, white and clean. (Revelation 19:11–14 KJV)

Then the battle of Armageddon is about to begin.

CHAPTER 30

The Seventh Trumpet

When the seventh angel blows his trumpet, the world becomes the kingdom of Yeshua as He returns to earth.

> *And the seventh angel sounded; and there were great voices in heaven, saying, the kingdoms of this world are become the kingdoms of our Lord, and of his Christ; and he shall reign for ever and ever. And the four and twenty elders, which sat before God on their seats, fell upon their faces, and worshipped God, Saying, We give thee thanks, O Lord God Almighty, which art, and wast, and art to come; because thou hast taken to thee thy great power, and hast reigned.* (Revelation 11:15–17 KJV)

The nations on earth are not happy about this event.

> *And the nations were angry, and thy wrath is come, and the time of the dead, that they should be judged, and that thou shouldest give reward unto thy servants the prophets, and to the saints, and them that fear thy name, small and great; and shouldest destroy them which destroy the earth.* (Revelation 11:18 KJV)

As the inhabitants of earth are looking at the supernatural events in the heavens, an unbelievable supernatural event happens.

*And the temple of God was opened in heaven, and there was seen in his temple the **ark of his testament**: and there were lightnings, and voices, and thunderings, and an earthquake, and great hail.* (Revelation 11:19 KJV, emphasis added)

What is the ark of His testament? **The Ten Commandments. The whole world is shown this by Yeshua before they are destroyed. These are His commandments and He wants the whole world to know it.**

The Rapture

*Immediately **after** the tribulation of those days shall the sun be darkened, and the moon shall not give her light, and the stars shall fall from heaven, and the powers of the heavens shall be shaken: And then shall appear the sign of the Son of man in heaven: and then shall all the tribes of the earth mourn, and they shall see the Son of man coming in the clouds of heaven with power and great glory. And he shall send his angels with a great sound of a trumpet, and they shall gather together his **elect** [the church] from the four winds, from one end of heaven to the other.* (Matthew 24:29–31 KJV, emphasis added)

In other translations, *the elect* are called *the chosen*.

Therefore, there is no pretribulation rapture according to Yeshua.

Rapture after the Great Tribulation

Then there is a strange sight as the dead saints with new bodies come up out of the grave and ascend into the heavens to Yeshua in the air.

After this, the remnant of the saints on the earth who are alive will also ascend into the heavens and will receive new heavenly bodies.

In a moment, in the twinkling of an eye, at the last trump: for the trumpet shall sound, and the dead shall be raised incorruptible, and we shall be changed. (1 Corinthians 15:52 KJV)

For many generations the church has preached that the **rapture of the saints would occur before the Great Tribulation. However, the Scriptures say the saints are killed during the Great Tribulation. So there must not have been a rapture of saints before the tribulation or during the tribulation. The pretribulation rapture theology is a false doctrine according to the Scriptures.**

The following are seven points by Doug Batchelor of the Amazing Facts Ministry, outlining the events of the rapture.[340]

First, Yeshua will return just as He left.

Which also said, ye men of Galilee, why stand ye gazing up into heaven? This same Jesus, which is taken up from you into heaven, shall so come in like manner as ye have seen him go into heaven. (Acts 1:11 KJV)

Seven Points of His Return

1. There will be audible evidence.

*And he shall send his angels with a great **sound of a trumpet**, and they shall gather together his elect from the four winds, from one end of heaven to the other.* (Matthew 24:31 KJV, emphasis added)

*In a moment, in the twinkling of an eye, at the last trump: for the trumpet shall **sound**, and the dead shall be raised incorruptible, and we shall be changed.* (1 Corinthians 15:52 KJV, emphasis added)

*For the Lord he shall descend from heaven with a **shout**, with the voice of the archangel, and with the **trump** of God: and the dead in Christ shall rise first.* (1 Thessalonians 4:16 KJV, emphasis added)

> *Our God shall come, and shall **not keep silence:** a fire shall devour before him, and it shall be very tempestuous round about him.* (Psalm 50:3 KJV, emphasis added)

> *Therefore prophesy thou against them all these words, and say unto them, The LORD shall **roar** from on high, and utter his voice from his holy habitation; he shall mightily roar upon his habitation; he shall give a shout, as they that tread the grapes, against all the inhabitants of the earth.* (Jeremiah 25:30 KJV, emphasis added)

> *And there were **voices, and thunders**, and lightning's; and there was a great earthquake, such as was not since men were upon the earth, so mighty an earthquake, and so great.* (Revelation 16:18 KJV, emphasis added)

2. There will be visible evidence.

> *Behold, he cometh with clouds; and **every eye shall see him**, and they also which pierced him: and all kindred's of the earth shall wail because of him. Even so, Amen.* (Revelation 1:7 KJV, emphasis added)

> *And then shall appear the sign of the Son of man in heaven: and then shall all the tribes of the earth mourn, and they shall **see** the Son of man coming in the clouds of heaven with power and great glory.* (Matthew 24:30 KJV, emphasis added)

> *Jesus saith unto him, Thou hast said: nevertheless I say unto you, hereafter shall ye **see** the Son of man sitting on the right hand of power, and coming in the clouds of heaven.* (Matthew 26:64 KJV, emphasis added)

> *For as the lightning cometh out of the east, and **shined** even unto the west; so shall also the coming of the Son of man be.* (Matthew 24:27 KJV, emphasis added)

3. There will be physical evidence.

> *The earth is utterly **broken down**, the earth is clean dissolved, and the earth is **moved** exceedingly.* (Isaiah 24:19 KJV, emphasis added)

*And there were voices, and thunders, and lightnings; and there was a great **earthquake**, such as was not since men were upon the earth, so mighty an earthquake, and so great.* (Revelation 16:18 KJV, emphasis added)

*And the **heaven departed as a scroll** when it is rolled together; and every mountain and island were moved out of their places.* (Revelation 6:14 KJV, emphasis added)

4. There will be supernatural evidence.

And this is the will of him that sent me, that every one which seeth the Son, and believeth on him, may have everlasting life: and I will raise him up at the last day. (John 6:40 KJV)

For as in Adam all die, even so in Christ shall all be made alive. But every man in his own order: Christ the firstfruits; afterward they that are Christ's at his coming. (1 Corinthians 15:22–23 KJV)

For the Lord himself shall descend from heaven with a shout, with the voice of the archangel, and with the trump of God: and the dead in Christ shall rise first. (1 Thessalonians 4:16 KJV)

5. There will be recompense evidence.

And, behold, I come quickly; and my reward is with me, to give every man according as his work shall be. (Revelation 22:12 KJV)

For the Son of man shall come in the glory of his Father with his angels; and then he shall reward every man according to his works. (Matthew 16:27 KJV)

6. There will be astronomical evidence.

Then the moon shall be confounded, and the sun ashamed, when the LORD of hosts shall reign in mount Zion, and in Jerusalem, and before his ancients gloriously. (Isaiah 24:23 KJV)

> *The earth shall quake before them; the heavens shall tremble: the sun and the moon shall be dark, and the stars shall withdraw their shining.* (Joel 2:10 KJV)
>
> *And it shall come to pass in that day, saith the Lord GOD, that I will cause the sun to go down at noon, and I will darken the earth in the clear day.* (Amos 8:9 KJV)
>
> *Immediately after the tribulation of those days shall the sun be darkened, and the moon shall not give her light, and the stars shall fall from heaven, and the powers of the heavens shall be shaken.* (Matthew 24:29 KJV)
>
> *And I beheld when he had opened the sixth seal, and, lo, there was a great earthquake; and the sun became black as sackcloth of hair, and the moon became as blood; and the stars of heaven fell unto the earth, even as a fig tree casteth her untimely figs, when she is shaken of a mighty wind. And the heaven departed as a scroll when it is rolled together; and every mountain and island were moved out of their places.* (Revelation 6:12–14 KJV)

7. There will be emotional evidence.

> *Men's hearts failing them for fear, and for looking after those things which are coming on the earth: for the powers of heaven shall be shaken. And then shall they see the Son of man coming in a cloud with power and great glory.* (Luke 21:26–27 KJV)
>
> *And it shall be said in that day, lo, this is our God; we have waited for him, and he will save us: this is the LORD; we have waited for him, we will be glad and rejoice in his salvation.* (Isaiah 25:9 KJV)

As the angel with the seventh vial pours out the wrath of YHVH, a loud voice is heard saying, **"It is finished."** Then there are such great earthquakes that the islands disappear into the ocean and the mountains disappear.

> I beheld the earth, and, lo, *it was* without form, and void; and the heavens, and they *had* no light. *I beheld the mountains, and, lo, they trembled, and all the hills moved lightly. I beheld, and, lo, there was no man, and all the birds of the heavens were fled. I beheld, and, lo, the fruitful place was a wilderness, and all the cities thereof were broken down at the presence of the* Lord, *and by his fierce anger. For thus hath the* Lord *said, the whole land shall be desolate; yet will I not make a full end.* (Jeremiah 4:23–27 KJV)

Everyone on earth is now destroyed. The planet is void of life for the first time since YHVH created earth.

> *And the slain of the* Lord *shall be at that day from one end of the earth even unto the other end of the earth: they shall not be lamented, neither gathered, nor buried; they shall be dung upon the ground.* (Jeremiah 25:33 KJV)

Then an angel descends from heaven and binds Satan for a thousand years. Satan is cast into the Abyss for a thousand years so that he cannot deceive anyone. The Holy City comes to a rest on the plains of Israel for its final eternal location.

The Millennial Reign

The righteous who were raised from the grave and the remnant who were alive when Yeshua returned are with Him in the Holy City. There is where and when the judgments are determined for the ones in the grave. This is the millennial reign of Yeshua that will last for a thousand years.

During this period the saved live in heaven on earth with Yeshua. There they learn all the mysteries of YHVH and the deceptions of Satan. They also participate in the judgment of the dead.

After a thousand years, the rest of the dead come alive and surround the Holy City. Satan was loosed to deceive them to go to war against heaven, which is now on earth. The dead surround the Holy City, spurred on by Satan. The ones located behind the wall in heaven see the enormous multitude that surrounds the city. Suddenly, they see Yeshua rise above the Holy City, and they now can see all their sins. They understand the truth and how they were misled. They bow down and confess their sins as spoken of in the Scriptures. This is when every knee will bow to Yeshua.[341]

> *For it is written, as I live, saith the Lord, every knee shall bow to me, and every tongue shall confess to God.* (Romans 14:11 KJV)

Yeshua then casts Satan into the lake of fire. The rest of the dead were also cast into the lake of fire. YHVH had fulfilled to the day the prophecies in the book of Enoch.

The saved inside the safety of heaven watch as the earth erupts with fire and the dead are destroyed. They are weeping because many of the lost were relatives or friends from their days on earth. There will be much sorrow and crying in heaven on this great Day of Judgment.

> *And God shall wipe away all tears from their eyes; and there shall be no more death, neither sorrow, nor crying, neither shall there be any more pain: for the former things are passed away.* (Revelation 21:4 KJV)

Then there was a new sky and a new earth. There will no longer be a sea on earth.

> *And he shewed me a pure river of water of life, clear as crystal, proceeding out of the throne of God and of the Lamb. In the midst of the street of it, and on either side of the river, was there the tree of life, which bare twelve manner of fruits, and yielded her fruit every month: and the leaves of the tree were for the healing of the nations. And there shall be no more curse: but the throne of God and of the Lamb shall be in it; and*

his servants shall serve him: And they shall see his face; and his name shall be in their foreheads. And there shall be no night there; and they need no candle, neither light of the sun; for the Lord God giveth them light: and they shall reign for ever and ever. (Revelation 22:1–5 KJV)

CHAPTER 31

The Mysteries of YHVH Revealed

IN OUR JOURNEY THROUGH THE Scriptures, we have learned that the Scriptures are infallible. Almost everything that YHVH prophesied in the Scriptures has happened, and we can see those events in history. With this information, we can now determine what time it is on YHVH's calendar. Everything points to the fact we are living in the last days of the age. We now know that the war against Israel will be the event that ushers in the last seven years before Yeshua returns. Knowledge of the Scriptures has increased and is spreading. There is an overwhelming number of evangelists who all agree we are in the last days.

In the previous chapter, we discussed what happens when the seventh trumpet is blown. There is also another verse that talks about the mystery of YHVH.

> *But in the days of the voice of the seventh angel, when he shall begin to sound, the mystery of God should be finished, as he hath declared to his servants the prophets.* (Revelation 10:7 KJV)

In the book of Amos, the mystery or secret of YHVH is mentioned.

> *Surely the Lord GOD will do nothing, but he revealeth his secret unto his servants the prophets.* (Amos 3:7 KJV)

What was the mission of the prophets whom the mystery was declared to?

Remember, the prophet was a messenger to Israel from YHVH exhorting them to return to the Torah, the instructions from YHVH (God).

The prophets also prophesied about the coming Messiah. Isaiah spoke of the coming Messiah as follows:

He was despised and rejected by men; a Man of pains, and having known about sickness, disease, and as one from whom men hide their face: He was despised, and we esteemed him not. Surely He has borne our sicknesses, our pains. He carried them, yet we esteemed him stricken, smitten of God, and afflicted. (Isaiah 53:3–4 ONMB)

Who took away our sins Himself by means of His body on the tree; so that by dying to our sins we could live in righteousness: by whose wound you were healed. (1 Peter 2:24 ONMB)

But He was wounded because of our transgressions, bruised because of our iniquities: the chastisement of our peace was upon him; and we have been healed by His wounds. *All we like sheep have gone astray. We have turned, each one to his own way; and the* LORD **has caused the iniquity of us all to fall upon Him**…*He will see of the travail of His soul, and be satisfied. By His knowledge My Servant will justify the righteous before many, and He will bear their iniquities.* (Isaiah 53:5–6, 11 ONMB, emphasis added)

These Old Testament prophets were clearly telling the Jewish nation to follow the Torah, and they prophesied of the coming of another prophet, Yeshua.

Yeshua spoke about the testimony of the prophets:

Do not think that I came to destroy the Torah or the Prophets. I did not come to destroy but to complete. (Matthew 5:17 ISR)

Yeshua did not come to do away with Torah and the Ten Commandments, but instead He paid the price for our iniquities against the Torah. As a man He took on the curse of the Torah (law) and our iniquities and took them to the grave.

After three days and three nights in the grave, YHVH raised Him from the dead in His glorified body.

By the power of His resurrection, Yeshua conquered all of our iniquities, sins, and sicknesses. Yeshua (Jesus) did everything as a man so He could defeat Satan who had power over death.

Supernatural Mysteries

In the last days, many have been gifted with the supernatural power of YHVH. In fact, Sid Roth has a television program dedicated solely to the supernatural power of YHVH. His guests tell the story of the supernatural power of YHVH on their lives. Many of these guests tell their stories of being able to pray and bring healing to people. Many have the ability to actually see angels and the evil spirits.[342]

Do you remember Yeshua's charge to His disciples?

> *And while you are going you must preach, saying that The Kingdom of the Heavens has come near. You must continually heal sickness, raise the dead, and cleanse lepers, cast out demons: you took freely, you must now give freely.* (Matthew 10:7–8 ONMB)

Yeshua is saying that we can also have the power to heal sickness and cast out demons. Today we have many teachers who have the ability through prayer to heal. These same ministers have teaching materials on the supernatural that can help you to understand the power of the Spirit. This new awareness brings greater meaning to the teaching in the Scriptures. The following are some good examples:

1. We are both spirit and flesh.

The Scriptures tell us that we are divided into three parts. These three parts are the **spirit**, the **soul**, and the **body**.

> *And the very God of peace sanctify you wholly; and I pray God your whole **spirit and soul and body** be preserved blameless unto the coming of our Lord Jesus Christ.* (1 Thessalonians 5:23 KJV, emphasis added)

Throughout the Scriptures, they tell us about the spirit. There are 456 verses in the Scriptures that talk about the spirit. As our brains think and reason and we communicate with words, our spirit communicates in a different way. The language of the spirit—or as we often refer to it as "our heart"—communicates with flow, imagination, dreams, visions, emotions and pondering.[343]

The language of the heart is flow.

> *And on the final Sabbath day of the feast [this is the eight day of the feasts of booths, Sukkot], Yeshua (Jesus) stood and cried out saying, "If anyone would thirst, **he must continually come to me and he must continually drink**. The one who believes in me, just as the Scripture said, **rivers of living waters will flow** out of His inner being.* (John 7:37–38 ONMB, emphasis added)
>
> *The words of a man's mouth are like deep waters: the **fountain of wisdom like a flowing brook**.* (Proverbs 18:4 ONMB, emphasis added)
>
> *And the LORD will guide you continually and satisfy your very being in drought, and relieve your bones. Then you will be like a watered garden and like a spring of water, whose waters do not fail.* (Isaiah 58:11 ONMB)
>
> *And He said this about the Spirit, which those who believed Him were about to take: for the Spirit was not yet given, because Yeshua was not yet glorified.* (John 7:39 ONMB)

The language of the heart is imagination.

> *And the LORD smelled a sweet savor and the LORD said in His heart, "I shall not again curse the ground any more for man's sake; for **the***

imagination of man's heart is bad from his youth. Neither will I again strike any more everything living, as I have done." (Genesis 8:21 ONMB, emphasis added)

The language of the heart is dreams and visions.

*And it will be in the last days, says God, I shall pour out my Spirit upon all flesh, and your sons and your daughters will prophesy, and your youths will see **visions** and your elders will dream **dreams**.* (Acts 2:17 ONMB, emphasis added)

The language of the heart is emotions.

*And the LORD was sorry that he had made man on the earth, and it **grieved Him in His heart**.* (Genesis 6:6 KJV, emphasis added)

The language of the heart is pondering.

*I call to remembrance my song in the night: I **meditate [ponder]** with my own heart and my Spirit makes diligent search.* (Psalm 77:7 ONMB, emphasis added)

So the language of the heart is flow, imagination, dreams, visions, emotions, and pondering.

So when you pray, stay tuned to flowing thoughts, flowing pictures/ visions, and emotions.[344]

2. Are there are evil spirits and demons in the world?
Yes, as we discussed in chapter 7. YHVH allowed the spirits of the giants in the world to lead us astray. Also, there are fallen angels who also are trying to control us. These spirits can prevent the Holy Spirit from coming into your heart. We know they are real because Yeshua spent about 25 percent of His ministry casting these evil spirits out of the people in Israel. These demons and evil spirits are very prevalent

today and may explain all the evil atrocities we see around us on the six o'clock news.[345]

In Matthew 12, Yeshua is talking about casting out demons; He speaks about the **strong man.**

> *Or else how can one enter into a **strong man's** house, and spoil his goods, except he first bind the strong man? And then he will spoil his house.* (Matthew 12:29 KJV)

Yeshua says that the assignment of a demon to you is a test common to everyone and is called a strong man.

> *A trial has not taken you except what is common to mankind: but God is faithful, who will not permit you to be tested beyond what you are able, and therefore He will then in the test make you able to patiently bear the way out.* (1 Corinthians 10:13 ONMB)

Then Yeshua goes on to say that if you don't bind the **strong man**, he will let other demons in that are far worse than the **strong man**.

Mel Bond in his teachings calls him the **door opener.**

Mel Bond goes on to say that is the reason most Christians have all sorts of problems, especially health problems.[346]

During Yeshua's teaching on casting out demons and the strong man demon, He immediately starts teaching about idle words:

> *But I say unto you, that every **idle word** that men shall speak, they shall give account thereof in the Day of Judgment. For by thy words thou shalt be justified, and by thy words thou shalt be condemned.* (Matthew 12:36–37 KJV, emphasis added)

Yeshua says that every word spoken by you will be brought into account, and you will be declared righteous or condemned because of your words.

Mel Bond believes that the **strong man** demon is **your idle words**.

An example of this is a statement like how "I was scared to death" is actually a lie. To you it may only be a figure of speech, but you have opened the door for the spirit of death to come into you—an idle word because it is a lie is a dangerous thing for your soul.

Remember Yeshua said, "Let your words be yea or nay." (Matthew 5:37 KJV) The power of the spoken word is very misunderstood by Christians and will affect their lives and their salvation. More on this in item 5.

3. Why did YHVH allow these evil spirits to test us?

One-third of the angels in heaven tried to overthrow YHVH and establish their own kingdom. YHVH is going to make sure that evil never again comes into heaven. So we are going to be tested or put in a trial. How do we know this? Let's look at the Lord's Prayer where it uses the word *temptation*. The Greek word here can also be translated as the word *trial*. So let's read the prayer as shown in the Hebrew Matthew version.

> *Our Father in heaven, May your name be sanctified. May your kingdom be blessed. Your will shall be done in heaven and on earth. Give us our bread continually. Forgive us the debt of our sins as we forgive the debt of those who sin against us.* **Do not bring us into the hands of a test**, *and protect us from all evil.*[347]

The Scriptures are full of stories of how the saints were tested. Abraham and Job were tested, and they passed the test. The Israelites were also tested at Mount Sinai, and they failed. As a result, they wandered in the desert for forty years. Moses also failed the test when he became angry at the complaining Israelites and struck the rock in anger for water. As a result, he did not get to go into the Promised Land. A great teaching on this subject is available from Pastor John Hagee's teaching The Promise, the Problem, and the Provision."

Once you become a follower of Yeshua, most likely you will also be tested. You may not even know you are in the middle of a test. These tests may come in the form of poverty, prosperity, sickness, or suffering, but you must remain faithful to the Word of YHVH. Remember, these tests are designed to test your attitude and faithfulness.

4. The blessing and the curse.
The Scriptures tell us that we have a choice of a blessing or a curse. There are 397 verses in the Scriptures regarding the meaning of the words you speak. You either speak a blessing to someone or you speak a curse. Every negative word you use is a curse against something or someone. This curse will come back against you. We reap what we sow.[348]

This is especially true with Israel.

> *And I will make of thee a great nation, and I will bless thee, and make thy name great; and thou shalt be a blessing: And I will bless them that bless thee, and curse him that curseth thee: and in thee shall all families of the earth be blessed.* (Genesis 12:2–3 KJV)

The Scriptures give us a good example of this. We learn in Genesis that the pharaoh of Egypt was very concerned that the Israelites were multiplying and growing in great numbers. He was afraid that at some point their large number could overthrow Egypt. So he gave an order to drown all the newborn male children of the Israelites. Moses was spared, and we all know the story of Moses.

When the Egyptians chased after the Israelites into the Red Sea, suddenly the seas crashed in on them and they were drowned. The curse of drowning the newborn Israelites was returned by drowning Pharaoh and his army.

5. The blessing and curses of your words.
We are created in the image of YHVH. **The Scriptures tell us that YHVH spoke the universe into existence** (Genesis 1:3, 6, 9, 11, 14, 20, 24, 25, and 26). Then He said "Let's make man in our image, after our likeness" (Genesis 1:25).

The One New Man Bible says it this way: the first image is the physical resemblance to God; the second is love, the feelings and emotions of God.[349]

So the power of YHVH's words created us. He actually spoke us into existence. So do our words have the same kind of authority? Yes.

In the Scriptures, it clearly shows that blessings were spoken out loud over many people. It is mentioned in sixty-four verses in the Scriptures. It also speaks of curses spoken over people.

However, most of us are guilty of speaking negatively about someone or something. This is against the word of YHVH.

Every Christian would agree that YHVH loves everyone, even the evil ones.

For God so loved the world, that he gave his only begotten Son, that whosoever believeth in him should not perish, but have everlasting life. (John 3:16 KJV)

So when we speak against someone in a negative way, this is in opposition to the Word of YHVH. As a result, if what we speak is against someone, it becomes a word curse and God turns it back against us. If we forgive and bless everyone, even our enemies, then the Scriptures tell us that YHVH will bless us.

Yeshua (Jesus) said it is our words that defile us.

Not that which goeth into the mouth defileth a man; but that which cometh out of the mouth, this defileth a man. (Matthew 15:11 KJV)

If you bless your enemies, you will be blessed by YHVH. If you curse anyone by saying anything negative about them, then the curse comes back at you.[350]

The Scriptures tell us the tongue has power of life and death.

Death and life are in the power of the tongue: and they that love it shall eat the fruit thereof. (Proverbs 18:21 KJV)

The Scriptures have a lot to say on tongues that speak iniquity, crafty words, wickedness, viper's words; tongues that are full of deceit, flattery, cursing, fraud, guile, devised mischiefs, or devouring; tongues that are against heaven; tongues that lie, give false words, backbite, are perverse, or boast; tongues of blasphemers, false accusers, grumblers, complainers, and gossipers.

The Scriptures tell us to hold our tongue and guard our words.

> *He that hath knowledge spareth his words: and a man of understanding is of an excellent spirit. Even a fool, when he holdeth his peace, is counted wise: and he that shutteth his lips is esteemed a man of understanding.* (Proverbs 17:27–28 KJV)

6. The power of healing.

Christians know that Yeshua spent a lot of time healing people. Before He could heal some of them, He first had to cast out demons. Yeshua also told His disciples that they also could cast out demons and heal people. To do this requires that you have great belief that you can pray for healing and it will actually happen.

> *And these signs shall follow them that believe; in my name shall they cast out devils; they shall speak with new tongues.* (Mark 16:17 KJV)

The Scriptures also say that we are protected if we believe.

> *They shall take up serpents; and if they drink any deadly thing, it shall not hurt them; they shall lay hands on the sick, and they shall recover.* (Mark 16:18 KJV)

Today, many people are being healed by prayer. Sometimes the sickness is associated with demons or evil spirits. When these spirits are cast out, healing comes to these individuals. Stress and trauma is another factor in illness. By prayer, trauma can be removed and healing will take place in the body.[351]

7. The mystery of prayer.
The secret to answered prayer is a great mystery. I have often heard Christians say, "I have been praying, but my prayers just don't seem to be answered." Sometimes weeks or months go by and there is no spiritual breakthrough. Most Christians just don't know what the Scriptures say about prayer, and this can result in unanswered prayers.

To get a good understanding of how to pray and receive answers to your prayers, you must be familiar with the spiritual laws of prayer given to us in the Scriptures. There are certain things we must do in order to get our prayers answered. The following is taken from the book *Opening the Gates of Heaven* by Perry Stone.[352]

One of the rituals of the Levite priests was to go into the Holy Place—where the golden altar was positioned before the veil in the tabernacle and the temple—to offer up his prayers. First he would mix the incense and coals from the brass altar outside the Holy Place and place the coals and incense in a golden bowl. He would then take the bowl into the Holy Place and place it in the golden altar before the veil. The smoke as it rose represented the prayers of the high priest and the Israelites.

The incense was made up of four types of incense and seven spices. These were thoroughly mixed together to make the holy incense. When burned by the coals of the altar, it created a smoke containing the prayers of the priests going up before YHVH.

> *Let my prayer be set forth before thee as incense; and the lifting up of my hands as the evening sacrifice.* (Psalm 141:2 KJV)

The smoke from the burning incense is holy and bans any demons or evil spirits from the prayers.

From Tobit 6:7, the angel is replying to the young man's question regarding what to do with the heart, liver, and gall of the great fish. He replied, "As for the heart and liver, if a demon or evil spirit gives trouble to any one, you make a smoke from these before the man or woman, and that person will never be troubled again."

So the same process that once took place on earth in the temple now takes place in heaven where Yeshua is the high priest.

And when he had taken the book, the four beasts and four and twenty elders fell down before the Lamb, having every one of them harps, and golden vials full of odours, which are the prayers of saints. (Revelation 5:8 KJV)

When you pray, your prayers go to heaven and they are placed in a golden bowl. So if your prayer contains faith, hope, and belief in Yeshua, then your prayer will be placed before YHVH in heaven by the high priest, Yeshua. The prayer will be answered immediately.

*And this is the confidence that we have in him, that, if we ask any thing **according to his will**, he heareth us.* (1 John 5:14 KJV, emphasis added)

*Likewise the Spirit also helpeth our infirmities: for we know not what we should pray for as we ought: but the Spirit itself maketh intercession for us with groanings which cannot be uttered. And he that searcheth the hearts knoweth what is the mind of the Spirit, because he maketh intercession for the saints according to **the will of God.*** (Romans 8:26–27 KJV, emphasis added)

Now there are two types of prayer.
1. Prayer with fasting:

Howbeit this kind goeth not out but by prayer and fasting. (Matthew 17:21 KJV)

2. Prayer with anointing:

And it shall come to pass in that day, that his burden shall be taken away from off thy shoulder, and his yoke from off thy neck, and the yoke shall be destroyed because of the anointing. (Isaiah 10:27 KJV)

Prayer is very serious. First, you are going to say something to the Creator of the universe, and He is going to answer. It is imperative that your prayers be based on faith, hope, belief, and obedience to YHVH's commandments if you want a positive response.

Seven Spiritual Laws for Answered Prayer

Believing and confessing are spiritual laws that create a supernatural result for the believer and the confessor.[353]

The mysteries above mentioned that are coming to light are not necessarily a complete list. They are many others that we are discovering every day. May YHVH bless you in your search for the mysteries of the Scriptures.

1. You must ask.
2. You must ask in faith.
3. You must ask in faith, nothing wavering.
4. You must be in full agreement with another.
5. You must ask the Father in Jesus's (Yeshua's) name.
6. You must hold fast to your confession.
7. You must ask in line with the will of God (YHVH).

8. The mystery of iniquity.

*For the **mystery of iniquity** doth already work: only he who now letteth will let, until he be taken out of the way.* (2 Thessalonians 2:7 KJV)

Yes, the mystery of iniquity has been at work since Satan took his stand against YHVH. Satan is working behind the scenes to deceive us from true worship.

In whom the god [Satan] of this world [age] **hath blinded the minds of them which believe not,** *lest the light of the glorious gospel of Christ, who is the image of God, should shine unto them.* (2 Corinthians 4:4 KJV)

Satan has blinded Christians to the obvious truth of life and the worship of YHVH. Yes, even the most elect have been deceived.

Iniquity is defined as "the deviation from that which is just or upright. A deed of injustice, or maleficent act." The Greek word for iniquity is *anomia*.

The letter *A* in Greek means "without."

Nomia in Greek means "Torah."

Then anomia simply means "without Torah."

The King James Bible translates *anomia* as lawlessness or "in the state of being without or in opposition to the law (Torah)." Therefore, lawlessness means you are in opposition to the originator, or author, of the Torah (YHVH).

So every time you see the word *iniquity* **in the Scriptures, it means "without Torah."**[354]

THE INIQUITY OF YOUR ANCESTORS IS PASSED ON TO YOU.

Most people do not realize that the iniquity of their fathers could have passed on to them to the third and fourth generations.

> *The* LORD *is longsuffering, and of great mercy, forgiving iniquity and transgression, and by no means clearing the guilty, visiting the iniquity of the fathers upon the children unto the* **third and fourth generation.** (Numbers 14:18 KJV, emphasis added)

Sexual sins can be passed on to the **tenth generation**.

> *No one of illegitimate birth does enter the assembly of YHVH, even a tenth generation of his does not enter the assembly of YHVH.* (Deuteronomy 23:2 ISR)

These iniquities that are passed on to future generations are commonly known as generational sins and curses. How can you break these sins and curses? The answer is special prayers of repentance of your ancestor's sins and obedience to His commandments.[355]

> *Know therefore that the L*ORD *thy God, he is God, the faithful God, which keepeth covenant and mercy with them that love him and keep his commandments to a* **thousand generations**. (Deuteronomy 7:9 KJV, emphasis added)

The good news is that if you are obedient to His commandments, then your iniquities are forgiven for a thousand generations.

For a wealth of understanding on this subject, read *The Mystery of Iniquity* by Michael Rood.

9. How to activate YHVH's promises in your life.

Dr. James B. Richards has spent many years investigating the heart and the influence on our ability to pray and be heard by YHVH. In his teaching, Dr. Richards explains the principles of the relationship of the heart to rest of our body and how to heal sickness. By applying these principles, **we are able to persuade our heart to believe the truth in Yeshua.**

Many Christians who follow Yeshua and are trying their best to serve Him still get sick. Their prayers don't seem to be answered. Why is this?

You must believe in your heart before you can receive the promises of YHVH. But when you are still sick or you still have more bills than you can pay, **this is evidence that you don't believe in your heart**. This says that the promises of YHVH (God) are not yours.

The Scriptures say the following about this:

Now faith is the substance of things hoped for, the evidence of things not seen. (Hebrews 11:1 KJV)

Dr. Richards goes on to say that there are emotions and feelings trapped in the body both from our own experiences and even from past generations. Even the scientific world is catching up to understand this phenomenon.

The Scriptures say that these experiences can even originate in the womb and the cells in our body remember them. It is called **cellular memory**, and the phenomenon has been recognized by medical scientists.

These memories are passed down to the third and fourth generations. In the fourth generation, these memories can become "hardwired" as normal behavior.

For example, your grandfather and your father lived in poverty. When the fourth generation comes along, mostly likely you have been "hardwired" to expect to live in poverty.

The LORD is longsuffering, and of great mercy, forgiving iniquity and transgression, and by no means clearing the guilty, visiting the iniquity of the fathers upon the children unto the third and fourth generation. (Numbers 14:18 KJV)

Painful experiences and emotions are literally taken into our bodies and they stay there in our cellular memory.

The words of the wicked are to lie in wait for blood: but the mouth of the upright shall deliver them. (Proverbs 12:6 KJV)
The heart is deceitful above all things, and desperately wicked: who can know it? (Jeremiah 17:9 KJV)

Paul even became aware of these experiences in his body.

But I see another law in my members, warring against the law of my mind, and bringing me into captivity to the law of sin which is in my members. (Romans 7:23 KJV)

Paul is saying that his body parts are in opposition to the law of YHVH.

Now we know that YHVH spoke everything into existence, including our bodies. Every word He spoke had a different frequency and so every organ or body part has a different frequency. So when we retain these memories in our cells that are opposed to law of YHVH, our body parts are warring against our mind and spirit in following YHVH.

So what can we do to prevent this?

When someone does an offense against you and you are hurt, you must forgive them and send the pain away. If you hold on to it, then the hurt literally becomes a vibration in one of your body parts. This disrupts that perfect frequency of YHVH's words for that body part. So when you pray for healing, you are literally holding on to that memory that is making you sick!

Yeshua said that when someone sins against you, you have two choices. First, you can send it away by forgiving them, or second, you can retain it.

How do we know all of this true?

There are many cases that show this when organs are transplanted. One example is the heart of a murdered young girl that was transplanted into another young girl. After transplant she began to have dreams of someone hurting her. She could describe the person in the dreams, and the police were able to make an arrest of the person who murdered the donor. There are many documented cases like this of transplanted organs that retained the memories of what happened to them.

How does a person correct this problem?

Dr. Richards states that you **put off** or send away any feeling, emotion, or anything that is **inconsistent** with the promises of YHVH (God) in Yeshua (Jesus).[356]

If you hold on to a feeling about yourself, or a belief about yourself, that is not consistent with your belief that you are righteous, saved, healed, prospered, blessed, and protected, then the cells in your body will not function consistently with the promises of God.

He further states that you must **put on** who you are in Yeshua (Jesus).

Dr. Richards explains that a prayer of transformation works to do this. A prayer to YHVH would be to search you for the source of the problem. Once you can identify the emotion or feeling, then you command that emotion or feeling to leave your body. When it leaves, then you can be healed by prayer.

Dr. Richards further states that science has found that each time the heart beats it sends an encoded message to every cell in your body regarding what you believe about yourself. We also now know that when you have certain emotions it affects certain body parts. For example, fear affects the kidneys, abiding anger affects the liver, abiding sorrow and grief affect the respiratory system, and fright and panic attacks affect the heart.[357]

10. Healing the soul.

Katie Souza began her ministry while in prison. Today she is a gifted teacher of how to heal your soul wounds. When we accepted the Messiah, we understand that our spirit man became instantly perfect when the Messiah came into our hearts, but we don't understand that our soul man was not instantly made perfect. Throughout our lifetime we have had traumas that have wounded our soul, and we have sinned, resulting in wounds to our soul.

The Scriptures talk about the wounds of our souls:

Moreover, the light of the moon will be like the light of the sun, and the light of the sun seven fold, like the light of seven days, in the Day that the LORD *binds up the* **hurt** *of His people and heals the bruise of their wound.* (Isaiah 30:26 ONMB)

So our sins actually wound our souls. When this happens, it starts affecting our relationships, such as marriages resulting in divorces, businesses starting to have problems, finances starting to deteriorate, and our physical health being affected. Even Christians have missed this teaching, and we even see Christians who have been affected by these soul wounds as a result of sin accumulated throughout their life.[358]

We start getting sick when our soul is wounded.

Beloved, I pray that concerning everything, for you to do well and to be in good health, just as your inner being [soul] is well. (3 John 1:2 ONMB)

The inner being is referred to as your soul in the King James Version.

Katie Souza goes on to explain that even Christians get offended. We know that being offended is an offense that wounds your soul. This wound to your soul actually short-circuits the presence of God.

In John 5, Yeshua heals a man who had an infirmity for thirty-eight years.

And a certain man was there, which had an infirmity thirty and eight years. When Jesus saw him lie, and knew that he had been now a long time in that case, he saith unto him, Wilt thou be made whole? (John 5:5–6 KJV)

From the Strong's Concordance

The word *infirmity* means "weakness or infirmity of the body and the soul." When Yeshua healed the infirmities of the people, He also healed their souls. So Yeshua healed both the man's body and soul.

Remember we are body, soul, and spirit.

God does not want Christians to be **hurt**. He wants us to be freed from sickness, abuse, addiction, depression, mindsets, or any oppression of any sort.

The Scriptures are drawing a connection of our souls to sickness. Now we also know that many believers also have health issues. So what are believers doing or not doing that would cause health issues in them? We know that there is a direct connection between sin and sickness.

The answer is very simple. When you are offended by someone or something, it literally wounds your soul. If you are offended, the offense you have is a sin wound to your soul!

In James 5, when he is speaking to the twelve tribes of the Diaspora, he talks about bridling the tongue and how to be patience and prayerful. He instructs them as follows:

Do not murmur, brothers, against one another so that you will not be judged. (James 5:9 ONMB)

Murmur means to grumble or complain about someone or something. This means something that is an offense to you.

Now that we know more about when you are offended and that it is a sin to your soul, what can we do about it?

There are two things that affect repentance.

First, there is the cross where Yeshua's blood was shed for us. Second, there is the power of the resurrection, which in the Greek is called *Dunamis*. There are two basic uses of the word *Dunamis* from the Greek lexicon in the Scriptures:

1. It means power to perform miracles such as the resurrection.
2. It means moral power and excellence of the soul.

*As God anointed this Yeshua, the one from Nazareth, in the Holy Spirit and **power**, Who came through doing good and healing all those who were oppressed by the devil, because God was with Him.* (Acts 10:38 ONMB, emphasis added)

Yeshua healed the sinners both in their bodies and their souls.

The words of your mouth and anything that offends you is a wound to your soul and is a sin you must answer for on Judgment Day. Chapter 26 of Proverbs explains the things you should do as follows: You should ignore foolish talk and not try to correct it (verse 4); correct other speakers only when they are in error (verse 5); don't say things and call them just kidding around (verse 18–19); and don't gossip and slander anyone because it is harmful for your belly (verses 22). If you listen to gossip or slander, then you are an accomplice and equally guilty. The proper response is to excuse yourself.

For example, your reaction to cars that cut you off or when someone cuts in line is what you must manage. You are to be patient, and your response should always be yea or nay or nothing at all. Always be in control. One way to stop the habit of offending is just to bless them to come into the full knowledge of Yeshua.

The Scriptures are very clear on how believers are to manage themselves and their tongues. It takes practice to manage your words, but it reduces the number of times you have to repent for your words.

Katie Souza's ministry is very similar to the ministry of Dr. James Richards and is another sign that knowledge will increase in the last days.

Today these mysteries that are in the Scriptures are being revealed. For a greater in-depth understanding, please obtain the teachings of these authors.

CHAPTER 32

Satan's Plan of Deception

SATAN WANTS YOU TO WORSHIP him, not God. Only two groups of people worship God, and they are Jews and Christians. All the other religions worship other gods. So Satan only has to deceive Christians and Jews in order to deceive the whole world.

> *And the great dragon was cast out, that old serpent, called the Devil, and Satan, which **deceiveth the whole world**: he was cast out into the earth, and his angels were cast out with him.* (Revelation 12:9 KJV, emphasis added)

So what is Satan's plan of deception for Jews and Christians?

The Scriptures very clearly state that the proof of love for God is following His instructions and commandments. Yeshua said doing His commandments is the only way He will know you on Judgment Day.

> *And then will I profess unto them, I never knew you: depart from me, ye that work iniquity [without Torah].* (Matthew 7:23 KJV)

Yeshua also said that unless you do the will of God you will not enter into heaven.

> *Not every one that saith unto me, Lord, Lord, shall enter into the kingdom of heaven; but he that doeth the will of my Father which is in heaven.* (Matthew 7:21 KJV)

Yeshua has been given the authority to judge each of us, and it will be based on you showing your love for Him, which He says is doing His commandments. Yeshua has given each of us this standard by which will be judged.

Satan's Nullifies God's Commandments

So Satan's plan of deception is centered on the first five books of the Scriptures. These Scriptures are YHVH's words given to Moses as instructions to His chosen people to be priests to the Gentiles. Of course, the Ten Commandments are the most recognized of YHVH's teachings. So let's look and see how His plan was carried out.

First, Satan had to stop the Jewish apostles from converting the Gentiles to following the Torah. He accomplished this by corrupting the faith that God and Yeshua had given to the Jewish apostles, which resulted in a new faith based on something different. Jude gave us this warning before it happened:

> *Beloved, when I gave all diligence to write unto you of the common salvation, it was needful for me to write unto you, and exhort you that ye should earnestly contend for the faith which was once delivered unto the saints. For there are certain men crept in unawares, who were before of old ordained to this condemnation, ungodly men, turning the grace of our God into lasciviousness, and denying the only Lord God, and our Lord Jesus Christ.* (Jude 1:3–4 KJV)

Rome invents a new Religion

With the destruction by the Romans of Jerusalem and Jewish evangelism, Rome was free to reinvent the worship of YHVH for its benefit. First, they destroyed or altered all the Jewish instructions in the Scriptures, which gave the early Roman church a freehand in the translations into Latin. They basically changed Jewish Scriptures to reflect the new Gentile religion. Since no one could own a Bible except the church, the church became to sole interpreter of the Scriptures. Although there were many that were not deceived by the early church, they were all singled out, tortured, and killed.

This ushered in the doctrine of Romanism, which declared the pope as the visible head of the universal church of Christ who is invested with supreme authority over bishops and pastors in all parts of the world. The very titles of deity were claimed for the pope. He styled himself "Lord God the Pope," assumed infallibility, and demanded that that all men pay him homage.[359]

The pope was set up as the earthly mediator for the forgiveness of sins, and no one could approach God except through him. The people were instructed to look to the pope or the bishops or priests to whom he had delegated authority for confession of sins. Priests were to be addressed as "Father" in direct contradiction to the Scriptures. In the Gospels, Yeshua refers to YHVH in heaven as the "Father" 369 times, and He gives this warning:

> *And call no man your father upon the earth: for one is your Father, which is in heaven.* (Matthew 23:9 KJV)

Once Satan had control of the church, the next step was to anger God by deceiving Christians into corrupting the first four commandments that show love for God. Satan knows the rules of salvation, so he wants you to anger God by corrupting the first four commandments of the Ten Commandments.[360]

SATAN'S DECEPTION THAT ATTACKS THE LOVE OF GOD IN THE COMMANDMENTS

Let's look at the first four commandments.

1. YOU WILL HAVE NO OTHER GODS BEFORE ME

The early Roman church renamed the feast of the pagan god Eastre to what we call Easter for the resurrection of Yeshua. Secondly, the birthday of Yeshua was ordered to be the December 25 to coincide with the birthday of all the other pagan gods. It seems to be like it was deliberately done to make sure we keep pagan remembrances in God's face each time Christians celebrate these holidays.

To make matters worse, every time we speak the day of the week and the month of the year—all of which were named after fallen angels, pagan gods, or evil Roman emperors—we are unintentionally bringing the names of these gods before the God in heaven in violation of the first commandment.

2. YOU WILL NOT MAKE ANY GRAVEN IMAGE FOR YOURSELF, OR ANY LIKENESS OF ANYTHING THAT IS IN HEAVEN ABOVE, OR THAT IS IN THE EARTH BENEATH, OR THAT IS IN THE WATER UNDER THE EARTH. YOU WILL NOT BOW DOWN YOURSELF TO THEM, OR SERVE THEM.

The early Roman Church erased the second commandment, which prohibits the worship of idols or graven images. This resulted in nine commandments instead of the original ten. So to keep number the same as ten, they split the original tenth commandment into two commandments.[361]

3. THOU SHALL NOT TAKE THE NAME OF THE LORD IN VAIN.

The early Roman Church changed the Jewish name Yeshua of the Messiah to, eventually, Jesus. And the name of God, which is Yehovah, to just plain God or Lord. Well, you can't take His name in vain if it's not His name.

4. REMEMBER THE SABBATH, TO KEEP IT HOLY. YOU WILL LABOR SIX DAYS AND DO ALL YOUR WORK, BUT THE SEVENTH DAY IS THE SABBATH OF THE LORD YOUR GOD, YOU WILL NOT DO ANY WORK.

The early Roman church ordered that the day of worship to be changed from the Sabbath to Sunday, which was the day that the worship of the sun god took place.

So the first deception was to corrupt the first four commandments that show our love for God in the early church skimpily by inserting Babylonian Sun God into the worship of God. The new religion sets the foundation for the last days when everyone is deceived.

A new Religion is born based on the commandments of men

As a result of these changes by the early Roman Church, all the commandments that are based on the love and worship of God were nullified. Satan was successful in influencing the early church in corrupting the true worship in order to set the foundation of traditions followed by most Christians today.

> *This people honors me with their lips, and but their hearts are far from me and they are worshipping me in vain* **teaching, teachings that are the commandments of men.** (Matthew 15:8–9 OMNB, emphasis added)

The message from this is "Do not add to God's Torah or instructions, period." If you do, then you are following the commandments of men.

After two thousand years of being misled in worship, it is a difficult task for a Christian to grasp the truth. Traditions in worship have been passed down from generation to generation and have taken on a totally different meaning to Christians. And since Christians have developed the attitude that worship is about what they think, you cannot change their minds. For example, if you seek to follow the fourth commandment, you will be scorned by Christians. Why is this? It is because Christians are taught by the church that Yeshua rose on a Sunday, and this fits the new covenant of salvation by grace.

So what is this new covenant?

*In that he saith, a **new covenant**, he hath made the **first old**. Now that which decayeth and waxeth old is ready to **vanish away**.* (Hebrews 8:13 KJV, emphasis added)

To get a better understanding of the meaning of the covenant requires first that we understand what covenant means. *Covenant* means a bond between the parties of the covenant, each saying "Everything I have is yours." In making covenant with Him, we are to give everything we have to Him, and then He gives all His love and prayer and eternal life. **All the covenants are between YHVH and Israel.**[362]

There are three types of covenants in the Scriptures. There are conditional, unconditional, and reinforcing covenants. Conditional requires each individual in the covenant to do something. The unconditional is given by YHVH and is an eternal promise. The third type simply reinforces the previous covenants. Since Christians are grafted into Israel, all the conditional covenants apply to Christians. There are twenty-two covenants in the Scriptures.[363]

So when the church reads this verse (Hebrews 8:13), their interpretation is that the Ten Commandments are no longer required to be followed since Yeshua took them on at the cross. A common term by Christians today is that they were nailed to the cross with Yeshua and that they are no longer required to be kept under the new covenant. This was contradicted by Paul.

Who are Israelites; to whom pertaineth the adoption, and the glory, and the covenants, and the giving of the law, and the service of God, and the promises. (Romans 9:4 KJV)

The root of the Hebrew word usually translated *new* has the meaning of ***renew***, so this is really a renewal of the previous covenants with a new blessing, made possible with a deeper relationship through His blood.[364]

So this is a renewed covenant with the Jews. All the covenants are between God and the Jews. There are no covenants between God and the Gentiles except where the Christian is grafted into the olive tree of the Jews. And since all the Jews worship on the Sabbath…**are the commandments of men woven into our church worship traditions?**

Yes.

In addition, everything Jewish was removed from the Scriptures, such as the feasts of YHVH and the Sabbath day of worship. In addition, many of the verses in the Scriptures were tampered with so as to perpetuate the non-Jewish scriptures. Why? It is because the mission of the mother church now is to replace Israel with Roman Catholicism. This has become known as replacement theology.

As a result, tradition has won out over truth. Tradition in the *Merriam-Webster Dictionary* is defined as "the handing down of information, beliefs, and customs by word of mouth or by example from one generation to another without written instruction." Truth is defined as "the body of real things, events, and facts."

It appears that these changes were made in order to make it easy to deceive Christians in the last days when the new world order is put in place. For example, if the new one-world religion incorporates Sunday worship, then Christians who already worship on Sundays are more likely to be accept it. Of course, there will be Christians in all faiths who will understand what's happening and refuse to worship the Antichrist.

Yeshua gave us a warning about this:

And Jesus answered and said unto them, Take heed that no man deceive you…And many false prophets shall rise, and shall deceive many. (Matthew 24:4, 11 KJV)

Beware of false prophets, which come to you in sheep's clothing [this means clergy], but inwardly they are ravening wolves. (Matthew 7:15 KJV)

Yeshua is warning us about clergy in the church who are compromising Scripture truths in order to gain popularity or power. Yes, you could be deceived in church if you don't know the Scriptures. How else could Satan deceive the whole world?

> *For there shall arise false Christs, and false prophets, and shall shew great signs and wonders; insomuch that, if it were possible, they shall deceive the very elect.* (Matthew 24:24 KJV)

This chapter is not written to judge a person, a faith, or a church, but we cannot ignore the warnings of Yeshua about the church. With free will comes the risk of judgment.

It is extremely important for all Christians to understand the difference between following the commandments of YHVH and following the commandments of men in our churches. It is important because each person will have to make a choice in the future that will determine how he or she worships.

Remember, you don't make the rules of worship of God—God makes the rules of how you are to worship Him. The rules are in the Scriptures, and even Yeshua came to interpret them for us.

The book of Revelation describes the events of the last days during which Satan will have complete control of the planet. You will be given a choice to either worship the image of the beast (the Antichrist) and his commandments or to worship according to the commandments of YHVH. If you accept the mark, you will damned to hell. If you refuse the mark of the beast (kingdom), then you may be killed. Then Yeshua returns to defeat the defeat the Antichrist and the false prophet.

The master plan to create the new one-world government is laid out in Revelation 13. We also know that the whole world will be deceived.

> *And **all that dwell upon the earth shall worship him**, whose names are not written in the book of life of the Lamb slain from the foundation of the world.* (Revelation 13:8 KJV, emphasis added)

The Scriptures tell us that the one whom we will all worship when he is revealed will be called the lawlessness one or "without Torah."

> *He is the one who opposes Torah [Teaching] and exalts himself above every Godly saying or object of worship, and thus seats himself in the Sanctuary of God, proclaiming himself, that he is God. (2 Thessalonians 2:4 ONMB)*

CHAPTER 33

The Ten Commandments

IN THE PREVIOUS CHAPTER, WE learned that Yeshua was crucified for our iniquities and sins. We also have learned that legalism and faith are different. In fact, the Scriptures say that if you are under legalism, then you are cursed. Paul said the following:

> *For as many as are from works of legalism, they are under a curse: for it has been written that "Cursed is everyone who does not abide in all of the things which have been written in the scroll of the Torah (Teaching)" [Deuteronomy 27:26]. And no one will be made righteous in God by legalism is clear, because "The righteous will live by faith" [Hebrews 2:4]. Messiah redeemed us from the curse of the legalism when He became a curse instead of us, because it is written, "Cursed is everyone who is hung from a tree [Deut. 21:23].* (Galatians 3:10–11, 13 ONMB)

SO WHY DID YESHUA CONTINUE TO TEACH THE TORAH?

The Scriptures tell us that Yeshua and the disciples continued to teach and observe the Torah, which included the original Ten Commandments that were given to Moses. In fact, Yeshua declared to the people of Israel the following:

> *Think not that I am come to destroy the law, or the prophets: I am not come to destroy, but to fulfill.* (Matthew 5:17 KJV)

> *"Do not think I have come to destroy the Torah or the Prophets. I did not come to destroy but to complete."* (Matthew 5:17 ISR)

"The Law and the Prophets" is a term used in the pre-Messianic Scriptures. Yes, the Law and the Prophets without Messiah are incomplete.

The One New Man Bible says it like this:

> *Do not think that I came to do away with, or to bring an incorrect interpretation to, the Torah or the Prophets: I did not come to do away with but to bring spiritual abundance, for the Torah (Teaching) to be obeyed as it should be and God's promises to receive fulfillment.* (Matthew 5:17 ONMB)

From the previous chapter, we learned that Yeshua gave us the renewed covenant of blessings for those who love Him and keep His commandments. So if we look at the Gospels, we should see that the commandments spoken by Yeshua and the disciples are the same as the commandments in the Old Testament.

First Commandment: No One and Nothing between You and YHVH.

Old Testament:

> *I am the* LORD ***thy God,*** *which have brought thee out of the land of Egypt, out of the house of bondage. Thou shalt have no other gods before me.* (Exodus 20:2–3 KJV, emphasis added)

New Testament:

> *Then saith Jesus unto him, get thee hence, Satan: for it is written,* ***Thou shalt worship the Lord thy God, and him only shalt thou serve.*** (Matthew 4:10 KJV, emphasis added)

> *No man can serve two masters: for either he will hate the one, and love the other; or else he will hold to the one, and despise the other. Ye cannot serve God and mammon [wealth].* (Matthew 6:24 KJV)

Second Commandment: Idolatry
Old Testament:

> *Thou shalt not make unto thee any graven image, or any likeness of any thing that is in heaven above, or that is in the earth beneath, or that is in the water under the earth: Thou shalt not bow down thyself to them, nor serve them: for I the* LORD ***thy God*** *am a jealous God, visiting the iniquity of the fathers upon the children unto the third and fourth generation of them that hate me; And shewing mercy unto thousands of them that love me, and keep my commandments.* (Exodus 20:4–6 KJV, emphasis added)

There are many verses regarding idolatry in the New Testament as follows:

> *But that we write unto them, that they **abstain from pollutions of idols**, and from fornication, and from things strangled, and from blood.* (Acts 15:20 KJV, emphasis added)
>
> *Forasmuch then as we are the offspring of God,* **we ought not to think that the Godhead is like unto gold, or silver, or stone, graven by art and man's device.** *And the times of this ignorance God winked at; but now commandeth all men every where to repent.* (Acts 17:29–30 KJV, emphasis added)
>
> *But now I have written unto you not to keep company, if any man that is called a brother be a fornicator, or covetous, or an **idolater**, or a railer, or a drunkard, or an extortioner; with such a one no not to eat.* (1 Corinthians 5:11 KJV, emphasis added)
>
> *Know ye not that the unrighteous shall not inherit the kingdom of God? Be not deceived: neither fornicators, nor **idolaters**, nor*

adulterers, nor effeminate, nor abusers of themselves with mankind, nor thieves, nor covetous, nor drunkards, nor revilers, nor extortioners, shall inherit the kingdom of God. (1 Corinthians 6:9–11 KJV, emphasis added)

*Neither be ye **idolaters**, as were some of them; as it is written, the people sat down to eat and drink, and rose up to play.* (1 Corinthians 10:7 KJV, emphasis added)

*Wherefore, my dearly beloved, flee from **idolatry**.* (1 Corinthians 10:14 KJV, emphasis added)

*Ye know that ye were Gentiles, carried away unto these dumb **idols**, even as ye were led.* (1 Corinthians 12:2 KJV, emphasis added)

And what agreement hath the temple of God with idols? For ye are the temple of the living God; as God hath said, I will dwell in them, and walk in them; and I will be their God, and they shall be my people. (2 Corinthians 6:16 KJV)

*Now the works of the flesh are manifest, which are these; Adultery, fornication, uncleanness, lasciviousness, **Idolatry**, witchcraft, hatred, variance, emulations, wrath, strife, seditions, heresies, envyings, murders, drunkenness, revellings, and such like: of the which I tell you before, as I have also told you in time past, that they which do such things shall not inherit the kingdom of God.* (Galatians 5:19–21 KJV, emphasis added)

*For this ye know, that no whoremonger, nor unclean person, nor covetous man, who is an **idolater**, hath any inheritance in the kingdom of Christ and of God.* (Ephesians 5:5 KJV, emphasis added)

*Mortify **therefore your members which are upon the earth; fornication, uncleanness, inordinate affection, evil concupiscence, and covetousness, which is idolatry**.* (Colossians 3:5 KJV, emphasis added)

*For they themselves shew of us what manner of entering in we had unto you, and how ye turned to God from **idols** to serve the living and true God.* (1 Thessalonians 1:9 KJV, emphasis added)

*Little children, keep yourselves from **idols**. Amen.* (1 John 5.21 KJV, emphasis added)

*And the rest of the men which were not killed by these plagues yet repented not of the works of their hands, that they should not worship devils, and **idols** of gold, and silver, and brass, and stone, and of wood: which neither can see, nor hear, nor walk.* (Revelation 9:20 KJV, emphasis added)

*But the fearful, and unbelieving, and the abominable, and murderers, and whoremongers, and sorcerers, and **idolaters**, and all liars, shall have their part in the lake which burneth with fire and brimstone: which is the second death.* (Revelation 21:8 KJV, emphasis added)

*For without are dogs, and sorcerers, and whoremongers, and murderers, and **idolaters**, and whosoever loveth and maketh a lie.* (Revelation 22:15 KJV, emphasis added)

The Third Commandment: Vain Use of YHVH's Name
Old Testament:

*Thou shalt not take the name of the Lord thy God in vain; for **the Lord** will not hold him guiltless that taketh his name in vain.* (Exodus 20:7 KJV, emphasis added)

New Testament commandments on vain use of YHVH's name:

*After this manner therefore pray ye: Our Father which art in heaven, **Hallowed be** thy name.* (Matthew 6:9 KJV, emphasis added)

*But I say unto you, that **every idle word** that men shall speak, they shall give account thereof in the Day of Judgment.* (Matthew 12:36 KJV, emphasis added)

*This people **draweth nigh unto me with their mouth**, and **honoureth me with their lips**; but their heart is far from me. But in vain they do worship me, teaching for doctrines the commandments of men.* (Matthew 15:8–9 KJV, emphasis added)

*And **call no man your father** upon the earth: **for one is your Father, which is in heaven**.* (Matthew 23:9 KJV, emphasis added)

> *Let as many servants as are under the yoke count their own masters worthy of all honour, that the **name of God** and his doctrine be not blasphemed.* (1 Timothy 6:1 KJV, emphasis added)

The Fourth Commandment: Seventh-Day Sabbath
Old Testament:

> *Remember the Sabbath day, to keep it holy. Six days shalt thou labour, and do all thy work: But the seventh day is the sabbath of the* LORD ***thy God**: in it thou shalt not do any work, thou, nor thy son, nor thy daughter, thy manservant, nor thy maidservant, nor thy cattle, nor thy stranger that is within thy gates: For in six days the* LORD *made heaven and earth, the sea, and all that in them is, and rested the seventh day: wherefore the* LORD *blessed the sabbath day, and hallowed it.* (Exodus 20:8–11 KJV, emphasis added)

New Testament verses on the seventh-day Sabbath:

> *For the **Son of man is Lord even of the Sabbath day**.* (Matthew 12:8 KJV, emphasis added)
>
> *How much then is a man better than a sheep? Wherefore it is lawful to do well on the **Sabbath** days.* (Matthew 12:12 KJV, emphasis added)
>
> *And they went into Capernaum; and straightway on the **Sabbath** day he entered into the synagogue, and taught.* (Mark 1:21 KJV, emphasis added)
>
> *And he said unto them, the **Sabbath** was made for man, and not man for the Sabbath: Therefore the Son of man is Lord also of the **Sabbath**.* (Mark 2:27–28 KJV, emphasis added)
>
> *And when the **Sabbath** day was come, he began to teach in the synagogue: and many hearing him were astonished, saying, from whence hath this man these things? And what wisdom is this which is given unto him, that even such mighty works are wrought by his hands?* (Mark 6:2 KJV, emphasis added)

And he came to Nazareth, where he had been brought up: and, as his custom was, he went into the synagogue on the **Sabbath** *day, and stood up for to read.* (Luke 4:16 KJV, emphasis added)

And came down to Capernaum, a city of Galilee, and taught them on the **Sabbath** *days.* (Luke 4:31 KJV, emphasis added)

And the women also, which came with him from Galilee, followed after, and beheld the sepulchre, and how his body was laid. And they returned, and prepared spices and ointments; and **rested the Sabbath day according to the commandment**. (Luke 23:55 KJV, emphasis added)

But when they departed from Perga, they came to Antioch in Pisidia, and went into the synagogue on the **Sabbath** *day, and sat down.* (Acts 13:14 KJV, emphasis added)

And when the Jews were gone out of the synagogue, the Gentiles besought that these words might be preached to them the next **Sabbath**. (Acts 13:42 KJV, emphasis added)

And the next **Sabbath** *day came almost the whole city together to hear the word of God.* (Acts 13:44 KJV, emphasis added)

And Paul, as his manner was, went in unto them, and three **Sabbath** *days reasoned with them out of the scriptures.* (Acts 17:2 KJV, emphasis added)

And he reasoned in the synagogue every **Sabbath**, *and persuaded the Jews and the Greeks.* (Acts 18:4 KJV, emphasis added)

For he spake in a certain place of the seventh day on this wise, And God did rest the seventh day from all his works. (Hebrews 4:4 KJV)

There remaineth therefore a rest to the people of God. (Hebrews 4:9 KJV, emphasis added)

The Fifth Commandment: Honor Your Parents
Old Testament:

Honour thy father and thy mother: that thy days may be long upon the land which the LORD **thy God** *giveth thee.* (Exodus 20:12 KJV, emphasis added)

New Testament verses on honoring your parents:

> But he answered and said unto them, why do ye also transgress the commandment of God by your tradition? For God commanded, saying, **Honour thy father and mother**: and, He that curseth father or mother, let him die the death. (Matthew 15:3 KJV, emphasis added)
>
> Obey your parents in the Lord: for this is right. **Honour thy father and mother**; (which is the first commandment with promise ;) That it may be well with thee, and thou mayest live long on the earth. (Ephesians 6:1 KJV, emphasis added)
>
> Children, **obey your parents in all things**: for this is well pleasing unto the Lord. (Colossians 3:20 KJV, emphasis added)
>
> But if any widow have children or nephews, let them learn first to shew piety at home, and to requite their parents: for that is good and acceptable before God. (1 Timothy 5:4 KJV, emphasis added)

The Sixth Commandment: Do Not Murder
Old Testament:

> Thou shalt not kill. (Exodus 20:13 KJV)

New Testament verses on "do not murder":

> (Ye have heard that it was said by them of old time, **Thou shalt not kill**; and whosoever shall kill shall be in danger of the judgment. (Matthew 5:21 KJV, emphasis added)
>
> For he that said, do not commit adultery, said also, **do not kill**. Now if thou commit no adultery, yet if thou kill, thou art become a transgressor of the law. (James 2:11 KJV, emphasis added)
>
> But let none of you suffer as a **murderer**, or as a thief, or as an evildoer, or as a busybody in other men's matters. (1 Peter 4.15 KJV, emphasis added)

*We know that we have passed from death unto life, because we love the brethren. He that loveth not his brother abideth in death. Whosoever hateth his brother is a murderer: and ye know that **no murderer hath eternal life** abiding in him.* (1 John 3:14–15 KJV, emphasis added)

The Seventh Commandment: Do Not Commit Adultery
Old Testament:

Thou shalt not commit adultery. (Exodus 20:14 KJV)

New Testament on "Do not commit adultery":

*Ye have heard that it was said by them of old time, **Thou shalt not commit adultery:** But I say unto you, that whosoever looketh on a woman to lust after her hath committed adultery with her already in his heart.* (Matthew 15:27–28 KJV, emphasis added)

*But I say unto you, that whosoever shall put away his wife, saving for the cause of fornication, causeth her to commit adultery: and whosoever shall marry her that is divorced **committeth adultery**.* (Matthew 5:32 KJV, emphasis added)

*He saith unto him, which? Jesus said, Thou shalt do no murder, **Thou shalt not commit adultery**, Thou shalt not steal, and Thou shalt not bear false witness.* (Matthew 19:18 KJV, emphasis added)

*And he saith unto them, whosoever shall put away his wife, and marry another, committeth adultery against her. And if a woman shall put away her husband, and be married to another, **she committeth adultery**.* (Mark 10:11 KJV, emphasis added)

*(Whosoever putteth away his wife, and marrieth another, committeth adultery: and whosoever marrieth her that is put away from **her husband committeth adultery**.* (Luke 16:18 KJV, emphasis added)

The Eight Commandment: Do Not Steal
Old Testament:

Thou shalt not steal. (Exodus 20:15 KJV)

New Testament verses on "do not steal":

He saith unto him, which? Jesus said, Thou shalt do no murder, Thou shalt not commit adultery, **Thou shalt not steal,** *and Thou shalt not bear false witness.* (Matthew 19:18 KJV, emphasis added)

Nor thieves, nor covetous, nor drunkards, nor revilers, nor extortioners, shall inherit the kingdom of God. (1 Corinthians 6:10 KJV)

Let him that stole **steal no more**: *but rather let him labour, working with his hands the thing which is good, that he may have to give to him that needeth.* (Ephesians 4:28 KJV, emphasis added)

But let none of you suffer as a murderer, or as a **thief**, *or as an evildoer, or as a busybody in other men's matters.* (1 Peter 4:15 KJV)

The Ninth Commandment: Do Not Lie
Old Testament:

Thou shalt not bear false witness against thy neighbour. (Exodus 20:16 KJV)

New Testament verses on "do not lie":

But I say unto you, that every idle word that men shall speak, they shall give account thereof in the Day of Judgment. For by thy words thou shalt be justified, and by thy words thou shalt be condemned. (Matthew 12:36–37 KJV)

For out of the heart proceed evil thoughts, murders, adulteries, fornications, thefts, false witness, and blasphemies: These are the things which defile a man: but to eat with unwashen hands defileth not a man. (Matthew 15:19–20 KJV)

He saith unto him, which? Jesus said, Thou shalt do no murder, Thou shalt not commit adultery, Thou shalt not steal, **and Thou shalt not bear false witness**. (Matthew 19:18 KJV, emphasis added)

Ye are of your father the devil, and the lusts of your father ye will do. He was a murderer from the beginning, and abode not in the truth, because there is no truth in him. **When he speaketh a lie, he speaketh of his own: for he is a liar, and the father of it.** (John 8:44 KJV, emphasis added)

Lie not one to another, *seeing that ye have put off the old man with his deeds.* (Colossians 3:9 KJV, emphasis added)

The Tenth Commandment: Do Not Covet or Lust
Old Testament:

Thou shalt not covet thy neighbour's house, thou shalt not covet thy neighbour's wife, nor his manservant, nor his maidservant, nor his ox, nor his ass, nor any thing that is thy neighbour's. (Exodus 20:17 KJV)

New Testament verses on "do not covet":

And he said unto them, Take heed, and beware of covetousness: for a man's life consisteth not in the abundance of the things which he possesseth. (Luke 12:15 KJV)

What shall we say then? Is the law sin? God forbid. Nay, I had not known sin, but by the law: for I had not known lust, except the law had said, Thou shalt not covet. (Romans 7:7 KJV)

For the love of money is the root of all evil: which while some coveted after, they have erred from the faith, and pierced themselves through with many sorrows. (1 Timothy 6:10 KJV)

> *Let your conversation be without covetousness; and be content with such things as ye have: for he hath said, I will never leave thee, nor forsake thee.* (Hebrews 13:5 KJV)

From the teaching of Yeshua and His disciples it is a fact that they taught the Ten Commandments. So they were still relevant during Yeshua's ministry, and the disciples also preached to keep them after Yeshua's crucifixion.

Yeshua explained the greatest commandment to the Pharisees in the following:

> *But when the Pharisees heard that He silenced the Sadducees they gathered together against Him, and one of them a teacher of the Torah (Teaching), testing Him asked, "Teacher, which is the greatest commandment in the Torah (Teaching)?" And He said to him, "You will love the Lord your God with all your whole heart and with your whole being and with your whole mind: this is the greatest commandment and first commandment. And the second is like it, 'you will love your neighbor as yourself.' The whole Torah (Teaching) and the Prophets are hanging on these two commandments."* (Matthew 22:34–40 ONMB)

Please picture two stone tablets hanging from a rod. On one tablet it says "Love to God," and underneath it contains the first five commandments. On the second hanging stone tablet it has the words "Love to Man," and underneath it has the last five commandments. Yeshua's reply to the Pharisees makes good and logical scriptural sense. However, false teachers spin this to say Yeshua did away with the Ten Commandments. Please read it carefully because these two great commandments are the source of the more detailed Ten Commandments. Yeshua also said that the Torah (teaching in the first five books) and the Prophets also hang on these two great commandments.

Confusion exists over following the Commandments of God

Some church pastors teach that Yeshua paid the price for our sins against the commandments of YHVH when He was crucified. This is true according to Isaiah 53 and many other verses in the Scriptures. He took our transgressions and sins so that we would not be under the curse of the law. This has led to the doctrine of legalism where the church teaches that following the commandments is legalism. They say that Yeshua was crucified for us and we are no longer under the Torah (Teachings) or God's law. So let's examine what the Scriptures actually say and see if we can clear up the confusion.

First what did Yeshua say about the commandments?

During the Sermon on the Mount, Yeshua preached to the multitudes.

The scene is Judgment Day, and everyone (including some Christians) is standing before Yeshua. Yeshua is speaking to the Christians and says the following:

> *Not everyone that saith unto me, Lord, Lord, shall enter into the kingdom of heaven; but, he that* **doeth the will [commandment]) of my Father** *which is in heaven...And then will I profess unto them,* **I never knew you: depart from me, ye that work iniquity***.* (Matthew 7:21, 23 KJV, emphasis added)

Earlier we discussed that *iniquity* comes from the Greek word *anomia*, which means "without Torah."

So Yeshua is talking about Christians on Judgment Day who did not follow the commandments of YHVH while they were on this earth.

These are the most terrifying words of Yeshua in the Scriptures because Christians realize they did not follow the commandments of YHVH and they are being sentenced to eternity in hell.

Many Christians are very concerned about this and really don't have a good understanding of what is required in following the commandments.

Paul offers an explanation:

> *For you are saved by* **grace** *through* **faith**. *And this is not from your selves, it is a gift from God.* (Ephesians 2:8 ONMB, emphasis added)
>
> *For as many as are from legalism, they are under a curse: for it has been written in the scroll of the Torah [Teaching] to do them. And that no one is made righteous in God by legalism is clear, because "The righteous shall live by faith."* (Galatians 3:10–11 ONMB)

From these verses it is clear that keeping the commandments does not justify us to be saved. **We still need grace to be saved.** Let's look further at the Scriptures to see what is missing to be saved.

> *Messiah redeemed us from the curse of legalism when He became a curse instead of us, because it is written, "Cursed is everyone who is hung on a tree."* (Galatians 3:13 ONMB)

From this, Yeshua **took our place** on the cross as penalty for sins against YHVH's commandments.

Yeshua took the punishment for our iniquities.

So what did Yeshua say we should do?
"For the righteous shall live by faith."

Does this mean we don't need to be concerned about keeping Torah?

> *Therefore do we cancel Torah [Teaching] through faith? God forbid! But we cause Torah to stand.* (Romans 3:31 ONMB)

What is Paul trying to tell us?

Paul is telling us to keep faith and the gospel.

If indeed you remain in the faith, since you have laid the foundation for yourselves and are steadfast and not moving away from the hope of the gospel that you heard, the one that has been preached in all creation to everyone under heaven, of which I, Paul, have become a servant. (Colossians 1:23 ONMB)

What did Yeshua say about the Torah and the commandments?

Whosoever therefore shall break one of these least commandments, and shall teach men so, he shall be called the least in the kingdom of heaven: but whosoever shall do and teach them, the same shall be called great in the kingdom of heaven. (Matthew 5:19 KJV)

If ye love me, keep my commandments. (John 14:15 KJV)

He that hath my commandments, and keepeth them, he it is that loveth me: and he that loveth me shall be loved of my Father, and I will love him, and will manifest myself to him. (John 14:21 KJV)

If ye keep my commandments, ye shall abide in my love; even as I have kept my Father's commandments, and abide in his love. (John 15:10 KJV)

And hereby we do know that we know him, if we keep his commandments. (1 John 2:3 KJV)

And whatsoever we ask, we receive of him, because we keep his commandments, and do those things that are pleasing in his sight… And he that keepeth his commandments dwelleth in him, and he in him. And hereby we know that he abideth in us, by the Spirit which he hath given us. (1 John 3:22–24 KJV)

> *By this we know that we love the children of God, when we love God, and keep his commandments. For this is the **love of God, that we keep his commandments:** and his commandments are not grievous.* (1 John 5:2–3 KJV, emphasis added)
>
> *And this is love that we walk after his commandments. This is the commandment, that, as ye have heard from the beginning, ye should walk in it.* (2 John 1:6 KJV)
>
> *And **love is this that we should walk according to His commandments**: the commandment is this, just as you have heard from the beginning, that you should walk in this love.* (2 John 1:16 KJV, emphasis added)
>
> *Here is the patience of the saints: here are they that **keep the commandments of God, and the faith of Jesus**.* (Revelation 14:12 KJV)
>
> *Blessed are they that **do his commandments** that they may have right to the tree of life, and may enter in through the gates into the city.* (Revelation 22:14 KJV)

There is no confusion here. Yeshua repeats it many times that we are to keep the commandments.

The Promise

There was a curse on everyone who did not abide in all things that were written in the Torah (Teachings) and did not do them (Deuteronomy 26:26). Yeshua redeemed us from the curse of legalism when He became a curse instead of us. Remember it was written that cursed is everyone who is hung on a tree (Deuteronomy 21:23). No one is made righteous in God by legalism because the righteous shall live by faith (Habakkuk 2:4).

Abraham believed in God and his acts of lovingkindness were from faith. God made a promise to Abraham that the Gentiles would be blessed because of his faith. The Torah was given to the Hebrews four hundred years after the promise. However, the Torah did not invalidate the promise. It was added on account of transgressions, until the Seed (Yeshua) would come for whom it has been promised.

The Torah was the guide to righteousness until the Messiah came. The Torah was the teaching or instructions from God on how He wants us to live. Now we are made righteous by faith in the Messiah. We are all made children of God through faith in Yeshua. Therefore, by faith in Yeshua you are the seed of Abraham and made heirs of the promise.

Yeshua took on all our iniquities (*iniquity* means not following the Torah, which includes the Ten Commandments) when He was crucified. He rose three days and three nights later and defeated death for us. He has defeated Satan for us.

So when we read Matthew 7:21–23 where Yeshua says He doesn't know you because you didn't keep the commandments, we now can understand why He said that He did not know you. The Scriptures are telling us that we express our love for Yeshua by keeping His commandments. Then this means He did not do away with the Torah and the Ten Commandments, but instead He expects you to keep them. It is proof of your love to Him if you do.

What about the ones who reject the Torah and the Ten Commandments?

The Scriptures explains that the ones who are deceived and reject truth will be destroyed.

> *And in every unrighteous deception for those who are being destroyed, because they did not accept the love of the truth for them to be saved.* (2 Thessalonians 2:10 ONMB)

They rejected the truth in the Scriptures.

> *And because of this God sends them a working of deception [delusion] so they would believe in a lie.* (2 Thessalonians 2:11 ONMB)

Sadly, most Christians will reject the truth about following the Torah and the commandments. They reject the Sabbath and just go along with the crowd. So YHVH gives them a delusion so they cannot understand the truth.

> *So that all those would be judged who did not believe in the truth, but took pleasure in unrighteousness.* (2 Thessalonians 2:12 ONMB)

CHAPTER 34

Understanding Sin and Repentance

IN ORDER TO UNDERSTAND YHVH's requirements of salvation from each of us, we first must understand sin and the different levels of sin. Paul gave us a sermon in the book of Romans that reveals to us the truth regarding sin. This sermon was preached after Yeshua (Jesus) had risen from the grave and gone back to heaven. Recently Perry Stone of Manifest presented a teaching on sin, and I have included excerpts from his presentation.[365]

WHAT ARE THE DIFFERENT LEVELS OF SIN?

The Scriptures refer to sin as having four levels. These are sin, trespass, transgression, and iniquity. What are the definitions of each of these in the Greek language?

1. Sin
   Sin means "to miss the mark." An example is an archer who misses the target with his arrow.
2. Trespass
   Trespass means "to pass over and go beyond your rights." Literally it means to cross a line.
3. Transgression
   Transgression means "to choose to cross the line." It also means to intentionally or willfully disobey.
4. Iniquity

Iniquity means "to be willfully lawless (without Torah) and without fear of punishment." It is the highest level of the four categories of sin.

YHVH JUDGES THE NATIONS BY THE INIQUITIES OF THE FATHERS

YHVH spoke to Israel and said the following:

> *You shall not bow down to them nor serve them. For I, the LORD your God, am a jealous God, visiting the **iniquity of the fathers upon the children to the third and fourth generations** of those who hate Me, but showing mercy to thousands, to those who love me and keep my commandments.* (Deuteronomy 5:9–10 KJV, emphasis added)

So when YHVH judges the iniquities of the fathers, it comes on the fourth generation. This is sometimes delayed because He is also long-suffering and wants us to give us time to repent.

> *And I gave her time to repent of her **sexual immorality,** and she did not repent.* (Revelation 2:21 KJV, emphasis added)

The Scriptures tell us that YHVH has destroyed nations and groups of people for the iniquity of the fathers.

> *But in the fourth generation they shall come hither again: for the iniquity of the Amorites is not yet full.* (Genesis 15:16 KJV)
>
> *Keeping mercy for thousands, forgiving iniquity and transgression and sin, and that will by no means clear the guilty; visiting the iniquity of the fathers upon the children, and upon the children's children, unto the third and to the fourth generation.* (Exodus 34:7 KJV)
>
> *For I have told him that I will judge his house for ever for the iniquity which he knoweth; because his sons made themselves vile, and he restrained them not.* (1 Samuel 3:13 KJV)

> *I acknowledged my sin unto thee, and mine iniquity have I not hid. I said, I will confess my transgressions unto the* Lord; *and thou forgavest the iniquity of my sin. Selah [pause or silence].* (Psalm 32:5 kjv)

Iniquity of a nation or a group that does not repent can be described as a vessel that continues to fill up with iniquities. In Revelation, it describes **iniquities as filling up the golden cup** carried by the mother of harlots.

> *And the woman was arrayed in purple and scarlet colour, and decked with gold and precious stones and pearls, having a golden **cup** in her hand **full** of abominations and filthiness of her fornication.* (Revelation 17:4 kjv, emphasis added)

Think of iniquities like this. When iniquity is practiced continually and without repenting by the person then the **iniquity reaches a level of unnatural affection**. Then the mind of the individual is turned over to a **reprobate mind**.[366]

Paul described this phenomenon as follows:

> *And even as they did not like to retain God in their knowledge, God gave them over to a **reprobate mind**, to do those things which are not fitting.* (Romans 1:28 kjv, emphasis added)

In the New King James Version, the word used is *debased* mind. In the One New Man Bible it is called the *unrighteous* mind.

This verse is saying that when men continually reject the true worship of God, God gives them a reprobate or debased mind. This is a worthless person—morally and spiritually.

Webster's definition of *reprobate* is as follows: "To condemn strongly as worthless; unacceptable or evil; to foreordain to damnation; rejected as worthless or not standing the test; refusal to accept."

This was first described in Isaiah 5:18–24 how the continued practice of iniquity led to the reprobate mindset of the people of Israel.

Today there are groups of people in the United States and the world who mock God and Jesus.

When a person walks in iniquity without repentance and when the cup of iniquity becomes full, **God gives him over to a reprobate mind.** When this happens, you cannot reason with a person who has reprobate mind. When people reach the highest level of disobedience where they worship the creature instead of the Creator, then God turns them over to a worthless, reprobate mind.

Progressions of Sins

Just as there are progressions in walking in a life with God, there are progressions in walking in a life of sin.

1. Sin is natural.

One man allowed sin into the world and death is the reward of sin.

2. Falling into sin after knowing God.

This is what Peter did when he denied the Lord.

3. Presumptuous sin.

This is where Sampson continued to sin thinking it was all right with God.

4. Premeditated sin.

This is where David committed adultery and set up a situation where the husband would be killed.

5. Willful sin.

This is when you choose to disobey God on a daily and consistent basis with no fear of God's judgment.

The Scriptures tells us what happens if we sin willfully:

> *For if we sin willfully after that we have received the knowledge of the truth, there remaineth no more sacrifice for sins.* (Hebrew 10:26 KJV)

If a person willfully sins **without repentance**, it leads to a life of iniquity.

Let's look at King David's prayer of repentance.

> *To the chief Musician, A Psalm of David, when Nathan the prophet came unto him, after he had gone in to Bathsheba.*
>
> *Have mercy upon me, O God, according to thy lovingkindness: according unto the multitude of thy tender mercies blot out my* **transgressions***. Wash me thoroughly from mine* **iniquity***, and cleanse me from my* **sin***. For I acknowledge my transgressions: and my sin is ever before me. Against thee, thee only, have I sinned, and done this evil in thy sight: that thou mightest be justified when thou speakest, and be clear when thou judgest.* (Psalm 51:1–4 KJV, emphasis added)

He used the words "sin," "iniquity," and "transgression" in his prayer. Iniquity represented the perverseness of what he did, sin means he missed the mark and should not have done it, and transgression is the sum of his sins. He crossed the line in his actions. His prayers say that he sinned against God by breaking His commandments on adultery, murder and covetousness. He broke at least three commandments of God.

Again, when the sin is continually practiced without repentance and the person isn't trying to stop the sin, eventually it becomes a level or state of unnatural affection or state of perversion; then if the person is at the iniquity level when the sins continue, she is turned over to a reprobate mind. These are people who are rapists, pedophiles, child molesters, people who are involved in all types of perverted-type sins, abusers of themselves, men with men going against the natural law of God.

Sins of the body, without the body and of the spirit

There are sins with the body, there are sins without the body, and there are sins of the human spirit. In addition, if you hold iniquity in your heart, then YHVH (God) will not hear your prayers.

> *If I regard iniquity in my heart, the Lord will not hear me.* (Psalm 66:18 KJV)

You must repent and turn away from your iniquities in order for YHVH to forgive you.

Examples of the three types of sin:

Sins of the Body
Examples are adultery, fornication, same-sex relations, and drunkenness.

Sins without the Body
Examples are conspiring, evil, and occult practices.

Sins of the Human Spirit
Examples are unforgiveness, hate, jealousy, bitterness, and strife.

Why is it important that we recognize sin, repent, and turn away from the sin?

> *For all have sinned, and come short of the glory of God* (Romans 3:23 KJV)

Paul also addressed this when he preached about the moral decay of the Gentiles.

Moral decay of the gentiles

1. All men at one time knew God, and they kept His commandments, but there came a point in the Gentile society when the true God was rejected and they stopped following the commandments of God.

For the wrath of God is revealed from heaven against everything godless and unrighteous of men, of those who hold back the truth by their wickedness. For what is known of God is evident among them: for God revealed Himself to them. For the unseen things, both His eternal power and divine authority, from His creation of the world, are seen clearly, being understood by His works things that are made, even his eternal power and Godhead; so they are without excuse: Because although they knew God, they did not glorify Him as God or give thanks, but their thoughts became directed to worthless things and their foolish hearts and minds became covered in darkness. (Romans 1:18–21 ONMB)

2. God was replaced with gods of man's imagination, copied after things found in creation.

Although they claim to be wise they were made foolish, and they transformed the glory of the incorruptible God into a likeness of an image of a corruptible man and of birds, and four-footed beasts and reptiles. (Romans 1:22–23 ONMB)

3. Once truth is exchanged for a lie, man's impulse is to indulge his physical appetite, especially in the realm of sex.

For this reason God gave them over in the lusts of their hearts into uncleanness, their bodies to suffer disgrace among themselves: Who exchanged the truth of God for the false and worshipped and served the created thing contrary to the creator, who is blessed for ever, amen. (Romans 1:24–25 ONMB)

4. Then disgusting and unnatural forms of sex are sought.

Because of this God gave them over into vile passion of disgrace, and indeed their females exchanged the natural function for that contrary to nature: And likewise also the males who neglected the natural function with the females. They were inflamed in their lustful passion with one another, males performing the unseemly deed with males and receiving the reward which was necessary for their deceit in repayment for their sin. (Romans 1:26–27 onmb)

5. The results of the decay of society are described by Paul as follows:

And since they did not see fit to have true knowledge of God, God gave them over into an unrighteous [reprobate] mind, to do the shameful things. (Romans 1:28 onmb)

Being filled with all unrighteousness, fornication, wickedness, covetousness, maliciousness; full of envy, murder, debate, deceit, malignity; whisperers, Backbiters, haters of God, despiteful, proud, boasters, inventors of evil things, disobedient to parents, Without understanding, covenant breakers, without natural affection, implacable, unmerciful: Who knowing the judgment of God, that they which commit such things are worthy of death, not only do the same, but have pleasure in them that do them. (Romans 1:29–32 kjv)

Let's examine each of these sins in more detail from the Greek words:

Unrighteousness (*adika*): The Greek word means "iniquity or wickedness." Since he is focused on himself, he disregards the commandments of God.

Fornication (*pomeia*): The Greek word means "sexual immorality or unchastity." It refers to sexual acts (whoring) outside the bounds of marriage as defined by God.

Wickedness (*poneria*): The Greek word means "wickedness." This refers to the desire to harm others, such as to deliberately corrupt or inflict injury.

Covetousness (*pleonexia*): The Greek word means "greed or to have more." It is the lust to get and possess. It sometimes is connected to sexual sins.

Maliciousness or malice (*kekia*): The Greek word means "evil or wickedness." It is the opposite of goodness.

Full of envy (*mestous phthonos*): These Greek words mean "full of jealousy." It means to wish ill will stemming from the good fortune of others.

Murder (*phonos*): The Greek word means "to slay." It can mean both the physical act and in the intent in the heart.

Debate (*eridos*): The Greek word means "quarreling, fighting, wrangling, contention or strife."

Deceit (*dolos*): The Greek word means "to decoy or trick." It refers to the bait used for fishing and means "trickery, deception, craftiness, and treachery."

Malignity (*kakoetheias*): The Greek word means "bad character or ill natured." It also refers to mischievousness or evil habits.

Whisperers (*psithuristas*): The Greek word means "a secret calumniator." This is a gossiper who defames another behind her back.

Backbiters (*katalalos*): The Greek word means "talkative against or slander."

Haters of God (*theostugeis*): The Greek word means "hateful to God." God places restrictions on behavior, and the hater of God wants to do as he pleases. These are lovers of pleasure rather than the lovers of God.

Despiteful (*hubristas*): The Greek word means "insulter or a maltreater." It refers to someone who is insolent. It describes a man who is so proud that he will defy God. It describes a person who is wantonly cruel and insulting. He is a violent person who delights in hurting others.

Proud (*huperephanous*): The Greek word means "appearing above others or haughty." This is a person who trumpets himself above others.

Boasters (*alazonas*): This Greek word means "a braggart." This is an attitude of pretending to have what you do not have in order to gain advantage.

Inventors of evil things (*epheuretas kaklon*): This is when a person actually seeks out new sins. Old sins are no longer thrilling, so he seeks out new thrills in new sins.

Disobedient to parents (*goneusin apeitheis*): This is a person who rebels against his parents' rules. This person wants to do what he wants to do.

Without understanding (*asunetous*): This literally means "unintelligent, stupid, or foolish." These are people with a sense of foolishness in their sins.

Without understanding (*asunthetous*): These are covenant breakers. They are treacherous, without faith, and cannot be relied upon or trusted.

Without natural affection (*astrogous*): "Being without the natural love between parents and children."

Implacable or irreconcilable (*aspondous*): This word is not in the later Greek translations. It means "not willing to make peace or come to an understanding."

Unmerciful (*aneleemonas*): This means "without pity or compassion."

PAUL SAYS THAT THESE SINNERS APPLAUD OTHER SINNERS.

> *Who, although they know the ordinances of God thoroughly, because they are practicing such things as these that are worthy of death, not only are they doing them but they are also applauding others who do them.* (Romans 1:32 ONMB)

THE RIGHTEOUS JUDGMENT OF GOD

In Romans 2, Paul describes the righteous judgment of God. God makes it very clear that He has no partiality. There are only two kinds of people at judgment, and they are the ones without Torah teaching and the ones that sin in Torah teaching.

> *For however many sin without Torah [Teaching] or God's commandments, will also perish without Torah (Teaching), however many who sin in Torah [Teaching] will be judged through Torah [Teaching]. As many as have sinned without law shall also perish without law: and as many as have sinned in the law shall be judged by the law.* (Romans 2:12 ONMB)

So who are the ones who will be saved?

> *For it is not the hearers of Torah [Teaching] who are righteous before God, but* **those who do the commandments of Torah (Teaching) will be declared righteous.** (Romans 2:13 ONMB, emphasis added)

So how do we break the cycle of sin?

First, you must recognize that any logical presentation will not cause someone to seek the truth in worship of God. Paul said in the Scriptures that if you have a belief and you continue with this belief in your actions, God will give you over to a reprobate mind. You will have a delusion from God, and no one will ever convince you that you are not following the true worship of God.

Fortunately, because God and Yeshua love us with *agape* love, we can repent, change our ways, and live in faith that we will be saved. No matter what our situation is, we can repent for our sins and transgressions just as King David did. Repenting is the starting point. Since sin is the transgression of the commandments of God, then I encourage everyone to **repent for breaking the commandments in order to receive forgiveness of our sins, transgressions, and iniquities.**

A Guideline for Repenting

As an example, I have included the Ten Commandments with space between each commandment. Take each commandment and search your soul for a sin against that commandment. Acknowledge the sin, tell

God that you're sorry and that you will not do that again. Do this exercise for each of the commandments every day. I recommend that you do this at least seventy times seven times or 490 times. This is the number of times that Yeshua said for Peter to forgive his brother for sins against him. (Matthew 18:22).

The Ten Commandments
(From ONMB)

I. YOU WILL HAVE NO OTHER GODS BEFORE ME.

_____
_____
_____
_____
_____
_____

II. YOU WILL NOT MAKE ANY GRAVEN IMAGE FOR YOURSELF, OR ANY LIKENESS OF ANYTHING THAT IS IN HEAVEN ABOVE, OR THAT IS IN THE EARTH BENEATH, OR THAT IS IN THE WATER UNDER THE EARTH. YOU WILL NOT BOW DOWN YOURSELF TO THEM, OR SERVE THEM, FOR **I AM** THE LORD YOUR GOD, A JEALOUS GOD, VISITING THE INIQUITY OF THE FATHERS UPON THE CHILDREN UNTO THE THIRD AND FOURTH GENERATION OF THEM THAT HATE ME AND SHOWING MERCY UNTO THOUSANDS OF THEM THAT LOVE ME AND KEEP MY COMMANDMENTS.

_____
_____
_____

III. THOU SHALL NOT TAKE THE NAME OF THE LORD IN VAIN: FOR THE LORD WILL NOT HOLD THEM GUILTLESS THAT TAKETH HIS NAME IN VAIN.

IV. REMEMBER THE SABBATH, TO KEEP IT HOLY. YOU WILL LABOR SIX DAYS AND DO ALL YOUR WORK, BUT THE SEVENTH DAY IS THE SABBATH OF THE LORD YOUR GOD, YOU WILL NOT DO ANY WORK, YOU OR YOUR SON OR YOUR DAUGHTER, YOUR MANSERVANT, OR YOUR MAIDSERVANT OR YOUR CATTLE OR YOUR STRANGER WHO IS WITHIN YOUR GATES. FOR IN SIX DAYS THE LORD MADE HEAVEN AND EARTH, THE SEA, AND ALL THAT IS IN THEM AND HE RESTED THE SEVENTH DAY, THEREFORE THE LORD BLESSED THE SABBATH, AND SANCTIFIED IT.

V. HONOR YOUR FATHER AND YOUR MOTHER: THAT YOUR DAYS WILL BE LONG UPON THE LAND WHICH THE LORD YOUR GOD GIVES YOU.

VI.　YOU WILL NOT MURDER.

VII.　YOU WILL NOT COMMIT ADULTERY.

VIII.　YOU WILL NOT STEAL

IX.　YOU WILL NOT BEAR FALSE WITNESS.

X. YOU WILL NOT COVET YOUR NEIGHBOR'S HOUSE, YOU WILL NOT COVET YOUR NEIGHBOR'S WIFE, OR HIS MANSERVANT, OR HIS MAIDSERVANT, OR HIS OX, OR HIS DONKEY, OR ANYTHING THAT IS YOUR NEIGHBOR'S.

CHAPTER 35

The One New Man

MOST CHRISTIANS KNOW THE STORY of Paul. Paul was a very gifted Jewish man from the city of Tarsus in Cilicia. As a child, and according to Jewish tradition, he was required to memorize the Torah, which is the first five books of the Scriptures. He was taught the Torah by Gamaliel, and the Scriptures tell us he was zealous for God.

Although he did not believe that Yeshua was the Messiah and he persecuted His followers, Yeshua selected him to carry His message to the Gentiles. The Jews originally agreed to be priests for God on Mount Sinai. When Yeshua came, He took His ministry to the Jews. Now Yeshua picks the man who will take His message to the Gentiles.

THE OLIVE TREE

Now we know that the olive tree has been used in several scriptures in order to convey a picture of mankind. King David said that he was like a green olive tree in the house of the LORD (Psalm 52:8). Paul also used the analogy of the olive tree in his teachings.

In Romans 11, Paul is explaining to the Gentiles that the Jews have become apostate and many had rejected Yeshua as the Messiah. Paul went on to remind them of the prophet Elijah who lived in a time when a majority in Israel worshipped a false god called Baal. He also reminded them that God still preserved a remnant of true worshippers. So many branches of the olive tree are broken off with only a remnant left.

Paul then explains that Gentiles who accept Yeshua as the Messiah are to provoke the Jews to jealousy.

> *Therefore I say, did they stumble so they would fall forever? God forbid! But by their [Jews] transgressions the salvation for the Gentiles is to provoke those [Jews] to jealousy. And if their [Jew]) transgression is riches for the world and their loss riches for the Gentiles, how much more will their fulfillment be riches.* (Romans 11:11–12 ONMB)

Then Paul explains how the Jewish branches are broken off the olive tree so that Gentile believers can be grafted in.

> *And if the First Fruits is holy the whole batch is also: and if the root is holy, the branches are also.* (Romans 11:16 ONMB)

Note: First Fruits refers to the first portion of dough that was used for the bread of the Presence in the sanctuary.

Paul is saying that when the Gentile believers are grafted in the olive tree of the LORD, then they are holy because the root that bears the tree is holy.

> *But if some of the branches are broken off, and you since you are a wild olive tree, were yourself grafted into them, then you would be a participant for yourself of the richness of the root of the olive tree.* (Romans 11:17 ONMB)

Then Paul gives a message to the Gentile believers who are grafted into the olive tree.

> *Stop boasting of the branches: but, if you do boast, you do not support the root, but the root supports you.* (Romans 11:18 ONMB)

Paul exhorts a strong warning to the Gentile believers who are grafted in by faith that they are not to be proud or boastful, but rather they should be fearful. The Jewish branches were broken off by their unbelief that Yeshua was the Messiah.

> *For if God did not spare the natural branches,* **neither will He in any way spare you**. (Romans 11:21 ONMB, emphasis added)

Paul is telling the Gentiles that they are grafted into the tree of God that was given to the Jews. They are to be faithful to the promises of the Messiah.

Yeshua said the following to the Samaritan woman about salvation:

> *You worship whom you have not known; we are worshipping whom we do know, because salvation is by the Jewish people.* (John 4:22 ONMB)

The Call for a One New Man

Paul also carried the message of the Jewish roots that the Gentile believers are to walk in. The Gentiles were told to worship the Living God of Abraham, Isaac, and Jacob. Paul explains that that formerly they were heathens in the flesh, uncircumcised in the flesh by human hands, and were separated from citizenship of Israel, making them alien to the promises of the covenants between God and Israel.

Paul tells them they have been saved by grace through faith in Yeshua because of the blood of Yeshua.

In Ephesians 2, Paul calls for the Jewish and non-Jewish people to form one body called the "One New Man" congregation.

> *By his nullifying the tradition of the commandments by decrees, so that he could create the two; Jewish and non-Jewish, into One New Man, establishing peace so He could reconcile both in one body to God through the cross as God killed the enmity by means of Him, Yeshua.* (Ephesians 2:15 ONMB)

The Messiah, Yeshua, picked Paul to carry His message to the Gentiles and the Jews. So the instruction to form a One New Man congregation comes direct from Yeshua. This is His instruction to all the Christians to join with the Jews.

Across the world we see Gentile Christians and Jews joining together to form One New Man congregations. We see the Jewish roots and names being restored to the Scriptures, giving us a clearer picture of the truth of the Scriptures.

Of course, you are given a choice to either be grafted into the olive tree of the Lord or not. If you remove everything Jewish from your testimony, the Scriptures say you are not grafted in. Remember, the root bears the branches, not the branches bearing the root.

Obedience is required to the Jewish roots to keep your branch from being cut off of the olive tree of the Lord.

The Remnant
YHVH speaks to us in our dreams.
Both in the Hebrew Bible and in the Gospels it says that God speaks to us in our dreams.

> *And it shall come to pass afterward, that I will pour out my spirit upon all flesh; and your sons and your daughters shall prophesy, your old men shall dream dreams, your young men shall see visions.* (Joel 2:28, Acts 2:16 kjv)
>
> *For God speaketh once, yea twice, yet man perceiveth it not. In a dream, in a vision of the night, when deep sleep falleth upon men, in slumberings upon the bed; then he openeth the ears of men, and sealeth their instruction.* (Job 33:14–16 kjv)

Most of the time, we discount our dreams. We believe that it was due to indigestion and we ignore or forget them. The Scriptures, however, tell us that our dreams contain messages and we should pray for understanding.

Through dreams and visions many are called to do the will of the Father. We know this because hundreds of evangelists have told their story of a dream or vision they experienced that caused them to become a teacher to others.

The Scriptures say we are called

There are many examples of people in the Scriptures and today's world being called into a ministry of teaching the Scriptures and the Gospels. Probably the most significant one called was Paul. Paul, a persecutor of the apostles of Jesus, was struck blind on his way to Damascus. Yeshua spoke to Paul to tell him what his new mission would be.

In the Epistle to the Romans, Paul tells us that not all Israelites are committed servants of God. Paul goes on to explain this by the example of Jacob and Esau.

> *For although they were not yet born and had not done anything good or evil, so that the plan would remain according to the chosen purposes of God, not because of works, but the* **calling**, *it was said to her that "the older will serve the younger," just as it has been written, "I loved Jacob, but I hated Esau."* (Romans 9:11–13 ONMB, emphasis added)

This verse says that God decided the future of both men before they were born.

Paul said many will claim this to be injustice by God. Paul explains that God had previously told Moses that he would be merciful to whomever he pleases and have no compassion for whomever He pleases (Romans 9:14–15).

Paul goes on to say that salvation depends on the mercy of God. He gives the example of Pharaoh whom He raised so that He could show His power and cause His name to be proclaimed all over the earth.

Many will say this is injustice because our desires and efforts are not considered. Paul replies that we are the clay molded by God and we have no right to judge God. God's purpose is making known His glory by His mercy.

God calls a Remnant of Jews and Gentiles

> *And whom He **called**, not only us [remnant] from the Jewish people but also from those (remnant) from the heathens (Gentiles).* (Romans 9:24–26 ONMB, emphasis added)

And also He says in Hosea, "I shall call those not my people, my people and she who has not been loved, my beloved" (Hosea 2:21). "And it will be in the place of which he spoke to them, you who are not my people, there they will be called children of the loving God."

God very clear that He is calling a remnant of Gentiles and Jews.

In the book of Isaiah, God says only a **remnant of Israel** will be saved (Isaiah 10:22–23).

The Gentile believers live by faith in Yeshua. Paul says that if you confess with your mouth the Lord Yeshua and you would **believe** in your heart that God raised Him from the dead, you will be saved. The Jewish understanding of the belief requires a change in behavior or that you must turn away from your sins. Since sin is the transgression of the commandments of God, then start living them or doing the commandments.

> *For he believes for himself in his heart into righteousness, and confesses for himself with his mouth into salvation. For the scriptures says, "No one will who believes in Him will be put to shame." For there is no distinction between Jewish or Greek, for the same one is Lord of all, and He is rich, abundantly blessing all those who call upon Him. For everyone who will call upon the name of the Lord will be saved.* (Romans 10:10–13 ONMB)

Many are called but few are chosen

Yeshua said the following:

> *These will make war against the lamb but the lamb will conquer them, because he is Lord of Lords and King of Kings and those with Him are **called** and **chosen** and **faithful**.* (Revelation 17:14 ONMB, emphasis added)

So many are called and their names are written in the Book of Life. However, a warning is given also about having your name removed from the Book of Life.

> *The one who conquers will be clothed in this way, in white garments, and I shall not wipe out his name from the Book of Life and I shall confess his name before My Father and before His angels.* (Revelation 3:5 ONMB)

To me this means that many are called. Maybe they are faithful in following Yeshua's commandments. Maybe they accept Yeshua as their Lord, but they really don't follow His commandments, then at Judgment Day their names are blotted out of the Book of Life and they are not accepted in heaven.

CHAPTER 36

Salvation

IN THE PROCEEDING CHAPTERS WE learned what the Scriptures said about the importance of doing the commandments of God. **By doing the commandments, we are expressing our love for Yeshua and He in return will save us. This is called grace.**

When Yeshua (Jesus) was crucified, He rose from the dead after three days and three nights. After a few days, he ascended to heaven. Yeshua conquered death and defeated Satan. He accomplished what the angel Gabriel had prophesied to Daniel while he was captive in Babylon.

In the book of Daniel, the angel Gabriel told Daniel that the Messiah would come and deliver the believers by doing the following:

> *Seventy weeks are determined upon thy people and upon thy holy city, To finish the **transgression**, and to make an end of **sins**, and to make reconciliation for **iniquity [without Torah]**.* (Daniel 9:24 KJV, emphasis added)

(Remember these are the different levels of sins we talked about in chapter 34).

With His death and resurrection, Yeshua defeated Satan by taking on the curse of the Torah and the commandments of God.

> *Therefore because the children had partaken of blood and flesh, then likewise He shared with them, so that through death He would make ineffective the one who had the power of death, this is the devil...for*

*this reason He was obligated to become like His brothers in every way, so that he could become a merciful and faithful High Priest in the things relating to God for the **propitiation** for the sins of the people.* (Hebrews 2:14, 17 ONMB, emphasis added)

Note: The word *propitiation* means "to be the agent through whom forgiveness, atonement, can be achieved."[367]

He did his part for you. Now you must do your part if you want salvation.

So what instructions did Yeshua give us so that we could do our part?

Let's start with forgiveness. The orderly progression in the act of forgiveness is as follows: [368]

1. **Forgive others.**
   A sinner must forgive others first before you can be forgiven by God.
2. **Forgive yourself.**
   Always forgive yourself after you forgive others.
3. **Seek forgiveness from others.**
   This is the hardest one to accomplish, but you must reconcile yourself with others before you can be forgiven by God.
4. **Bridle the tongue.**
   Yeshua said we are to give an account of every word that comes out of our mouths. He also said we are condemned or justified by our words. If something blurts out, repent immediately. Some say that idle words come from the strong man demon that lets other really bad demons in.
5. **Then repent.**
   This is where you repent for the iniquities (without Torah) of your actions. As we said in an earlier chapter, we should too repent according to the Ten Commandments for our iniquities.

Remember that Yeshua's death covered sins committed in error. Yeshua said in Hebrews 10:17 (ONMB):

And I shall never, ever remember their sins and their iniquities.

This is a quote from Jeremiah 31:33. In this verse *iniquities* is the Hebrew word for sin (*hata-ah*), which means sins committed in error. Repentance is required for all sins (willful sins) not committed in error.

6. **Confess Yeshua (Jesus) as your Savior publicly to other people.**

   Therefore everyone who will confess me in front of people, then I shall confess him before my father, the One in heavens: But whoever would deny Me before people, then I will shall deny him before My Father, the One in the heavens. (Matthew 10:32–33 ONMB)

7. **Forgiveness comes from God.**

   This is a result from the acts of forgiving, repenting, turning away from your sins, and doing the commandments.

Yeshua gave us two major standards to judge us by.
The first is righteousness.

> *For I say unto you, that except your **righteousness shall exceed** the righteousness of the scribes and Pharisees, ye shall in no case enter into the kingdom of heaven.* (Matthew 5:20 KJV, emphasis added)

This is saying that your righteousness must exceed the righteousness of the Pharisees of His time. The Pharisees were extremely righteous in following the written and the oral Torah (Teaching) from God. Unfortunately, the Pharisees were guilty of adding many instructions to the worship of YHVH through the *"Torah Sheba'al Peh"* (Oral Law). Yeshua accused them of being hypocrites (see chapter 4). However, the Pharisees were extremely righteous in following the written Torah but were called hypocrites for adding traditions to the oral Torah.

The lesson here is just follow what YHVH (God) teaches in the Torah, but we must stop twisting the Scriptures in order to justify a different way of worship. If you add or take away, you are in opposition to God.

So what does righteousness mean?

We are made righteous by faith and grace, but **righteousness is also action.** The word *righteousness* is taken from the Hebrew word *Ts-d-k* and the Greek verb *Dikaio*. They both mean "to do right" and "to be just." They are verbs that require action by the subject of the verb. So when we are made righteous by our faith, our behavior has to change.[369]

This is how we perfect our righteousness, which means "as it should be."[370] Remember, we discussed earlier that we are spirit, mind, and body. We must strive to make all three parts of us holy. We must not judge others, but we are commanded to forgive their offenses and bless them to come to the full knowledge of Yeshua's teachings. Yeshua must live in you. A great example was given by Yeshua when He was crucified and He prayed for YHVH's forgiveness for His crucifiers.

Persuade your heart to be holy and your body will be made holy. Then, with belief, your prayers will be heard.

To be righteous means every day you should be focused on obedience to God and faith in Yeshua.

THE SECOND STANDARD IS EXPRESSING LOVE FOR YESHUA.
What did Yeshua say about this in the Scriptures?

As I have previously mentioned, **doing the commandments is the way we show Yeshua that we love Him.** If you don't show Him your love by doing the commandments, then you cannot go to heaven. This is according to Yeshua Himself:

> *Not everyone who says to Me Lord, Lord will enter the Kingdom of the Heavens, but one who does the will of my Father, the One in the Heavens.* (Matthew 7:21 ONMB)

The will of the Father is the Torah and the Ten Commandments.

The next verse clearly says that Yeshua is speaking to Christians on Judgment Day and they are pleading their case that they were good Christians that loved the Lord.

> *Many will say to me in that day, "Lord, Lord, Did we not prophesy in your name? And we cast out demons in your name; we did many miracles in your name?"* (Matthew 7:22 ONMB)

Yeshua answers with His judgment:

> *And then will **I declare to them, I never knew you: you working without Torah [Teaching] must continually depart from me.*** (Matthew 7:23 ONMB, emphasis added)

The King James Version refers to "ye that work iniquity." *Iniquity* comes from the Greek word that means without Torah.

This verse is telling us that there are Christians that do not follow the Torah. They obviously are not grafted into God's olive tree, and they are rejecting the Jewish roots of the faith.

The Torah contains the Ten Commandments. The fourth commandment is the seal of God. Maybe this means the rejection of Sabbath worship and the acceptance of Sunday worship. The answer will be clear on Judgment Day, and there is no appeal if you get it wrong. Choose wisely.

Yeshua is plainly telling everyone on earth that your choices of either following the **commandments of men or the commandments of God** will determine your salvation or judgment on the great Day of Judgment.

> *This people honors me with their lips but their hearts are far distant away from me, and they worship me in Vain teaching teachings that are the commandments of men.* (Matthew 15:8–9 ONMB)

The Parables
Yeshua also spoke often about salvation in His parables. When questioned by the disciples regarding the parable, He answered:

> *"The sower of the good seed is the Son of Man, and the field is the world, and these good seeds are the sons of the kingdom: and the darnel are the sons of the evil one, and the devil is the enemy who sows them, and the harvest is the end of the age, and the harvesters are the angels. Therefore as the darnel is gathered and consumed in fire, so will it be in the end of the age: the Son of Man will send His angels and they will gather them from His kingdom all **those drawn into error** and those who were doing **wickedness**, and they will cast them into the oven of the fire: in that place there will be **weeping and gnashing of teeth**."* (Matthew 13:37–42 ONMB, emphasis added)

Darnel was a weed that resembled wheat, but was not an edible grain.

Also **"those who are drawn into error"** could also be stated as **"doing without Torah'"** or not doing what is taught in the first five books of the Scriptures. If you are following the commandments of men instead of the commandments of Yeshua (Jesus), then the Scriptures say this is a serious problem for you if your are seeking salvation. The seriousness of this verse requires that we look at other translations for other witnesses of what Yeshua is preaching regarding salvation.

> *As the darnel, then, is gathered and burned in the fire, so shall be it at the end of this age. The Son of Adam [Man] shall send out His messengers [angels], and they shall gather out of **His reign** all the stumbling-blocks, and those doing lawlessness.* (Matthew 13:40–41 ISR, emphasis added)

His reign refers to all nations.

In the ISR's translation of Matthew 13:41, it refers to "stumbling blocks" as the darnel, which the devil sowed and sprouts and takes shape in the form of lawless "believers."

In the HRV's translation of Matthew 13:41, it refers to the darnel as the ones who offend and the wickedness as "Torahlessness."

In the Word of Yahweh Bible's translation of Matthew 13:41, it refers to the darnel as all things that offend.

In the King James Bible's translation of Matthew 13:41, it refers to the darnel as all things that offend.

Offend comes from the Greek word *skandalon*, which means "scandals, offends, a stumbling block, a snare."

The different English translations of the Scriptures all seem to agree that wickedness or lawlessness is referring to the ones without the Torah.

All these translations from the Greek seem to be saying that there are Christians who lead others to follow the Torah, and Christians who do not follow the Torah.

Now, in my own experience in attending several different Protestant denominations following the Torah was never taught. Some even say that the Old Testament is not relevant and the New Testament teaching of grace is the answer.

Yeshua gave us this parable to show us the heart of YHVH: "To love your neighbor as yourself" (Leviticus 19:18).

There are many other parables taught by Yeshua that show what is expected of a Christian.

The Scriptures tell us that Yeshua went to the cross and died for us; He took the punishment for your sins and iniquities (without Torah). After this He expects you to express your love for Him by trying to keep the Torah and doing His commandments.

According to the Scriptures, doing the commandments is the only proof to Him that you love Him.

So the standard is to be obedient in following Yeshua's commandments (you must do them), keeping your heart, mind, and spirit focused on **Him**.

When you confess your sins to Yeshua (Jesus) and ask for forgiveness, this is referred to as being saved. It covers all your sins from birth to that moment. We must be born again and follow Yeshua's teachings by doing His commandments. However, since we will also continue to sin, then we are to do the following daily:

Repent daily!
The very first commandment from Yeshua after returning from the wilderness was:

> *From then on Yeshua began to preach sand to say "You must **continually repent:** for the Kingdom of the heavens has come near."* (Matthew 4:17 ONMB, emphasis added)

At the Sermon on the Mount, Yeshua said "Blessed are those who forgive, because they will be forgiven." He also said to be humble, to thirst for righteousness, to be pure in heart, and to be peacemakers.

He also taught that when we are persecuted for His name's sake to be joyful. You must love your enemies and pray for them. Do not stand against an evil person, but give him whatever he wants. Treat every person a though they were Yeshua (Matthew 25:42–45).

You are to let your heart shine by doing good deeds. Give charitable gifts in secret so that YHVH will reward you publicly. Everything that you would want that people to do to you, in that way you must do to them.

Guard your thoughts, and remove all anger against anyone from your thoughts and heart.

Do not think lustful thoughts, for it is the same as adultery. Divorce should be avoided at all costs because it will lead to adultery.

Do not judge others, or you will be judged by the same measure in which you measure. Instead, pray a blessing over them to come to the full knowledge of the Yeshua's ministry.

Yeshua said that everyone who asks takes, everyone who seeks finds, and everyone who knocks, it is opened to them. Therefore, pray for the promises of YHVH (God) to be part of your life.

Yeshua is telling you to keep His commandments in your actions and in your heart. He wants you to invite Him to live in you. If you do this, you will be born again as a new creature in Yeshua (Jesus).

Ponder and meditate on the words of Yeshua in the Scriptures (preferably one with the best Greek translation).

May YHVH bless you in your overcoming the world and hearing the words from Yeshua

His lord said unto him, well done, thou good and faithful servant: thou hast been faithful over a few things, I will make thee ruler over many things: enter thou into the joy of thy lord. (Matthew 25:21 KJV)

Finally, we must have faith in Yeshua.

The ones that are with Yeshua at the end are described as "called and chosen and faithful" (Revelation 17:14 ONMB).

Yeshua appeared to Paul and gave him a mission to preach to the Gentiles.

To open their eyes, and to turn them from darkness to light, and from the power of Satan unto God, that they may receive forgiveness of sins, and inheritance among them which are sanctified by faith that is in me. (Acts 26:18 KJV)

Do His commandments to show you love Him and keep faith that He will save you. Always love others and proclaim the gospel to them. Finally, openly confess to others that Yeshua (Jesus) is your Lord and you are obedient to Him.

THE POTTER'S WHEEL AND THE CLAY

The story in the Scriptures of the potter, the potter's wheel, and the clay gives us a picture of the sovereignty of God over men and shows us that He is in control of our destiny. For example, man was created from clay of the earth:

> *Then God said,* ***"We will make mankind in our image, after our likeness and have dominion over the fish of the sea, and over the fowl of the air, and over the cattle, over all the earth, and over every creeping thing that creeps upon the earth." So God created mankind in His own image****; He created him in the image of God. He created them male and female.* (Genesis 1:26–27 onmb, emphasis added)
>
> *And no plant of the field was yet on the earth and no herb of the field had yet grown, for the* Lord *God had not caused it to rain upon the earth, and there was not a man to till the ground. But there went up a mist from the earth, and* ***it watered the whole face of the ground****. And the* Lord ***God formed man from the dust of the ground****, and blew into his nostrils the breath of life; and man became a living being.* (Genesis 2:5–7 onmb, emphasis added)

God watered the dust to form clay, and then He formed the clay into a man. *Formed* comes from the Hebrew word *yatsa*, which means to mold as a potter molds in clay.

Most of you are familiar with stories in the Scriptures regarding the potter and the clay. The Potter is God, and the vessel of clay is mankind. The message in Isaiah is this:

> *Woe unto him that strives with his Maker! Let the potsherd strive with the potsherds of the earth. Will the clay say to him that fashions it, what are you making? Has your work no hands?* (Isaiah 45:9 onmb)

God is the Potter of the clay vessels. We are the clay vessels. Again in Isaiah 29:15–16, God warns Isaiah that Judah has become apostate and uses the potter and the clay analogy to get His message across to Isaiah. God asks the question, "Shall the potter be regarded as the clay?"

The clay vessel is man, and God says to Isaiah, "Woe to him that strives with His maker, an earthen vessel with the potter." Paul brings the message from Yeshua that the potter has the absolute right over the clay vessel. If the clay vessel is not perfect for the purposes of God, He discards the vessel to the trash heap. God has compassion for those He chooses. The Scriptures say that God brought up Pharaoh for the purpose of God showing His power.

Paul goes on to explain man is not to answer back to God. God makes the earthen vessel of a man, and man has no right to answer back to God. God calls whom He wishes to call—both Gentile and Jew. We don't have any say in that decision, just as we don't have any right to make up our own rules of worship.

God created the universe, and He specifically made man for His own pleasure. God is sovereign in control of man and entire nations. The potter has absolute control and right over the clay. He shapes both nonbelievers and believers for His purposes. In grace God allows the clay of our humanity to cooperate with the Potter. Our cooperation in following the commandments of God allows Him to make us beautiful clay vessels in His sight.

The clay vessel houses our spirit and soul, and we are given a new resurrection body to house our spirits in heaven. God and Yeshua have given us the instructions in the Scriptures of how we are to live and worship so that the Potter in heaven will remake us for His purposes.

CHAPTER 37

The Final Choice

THE FINAL CHOICE IS NEAR

No one would argue that we are not very close to the end of the age. The war in the Middle East could start any day. America is on the verge of becoming a socialist country. The Scriptures tell us there will be a war between Israel and her Muslim neighbors. So when the war comes, then we will know we are at the seven-year benchmark before Yeshua returns. This is when Satan's plan for controlling the earth outlined in Revelation 13 will take place. This is when everyone on planet Earth will have to make a choice to worship the Antichrist or God.

The Scriptures tell us that most will choose the mark of the Antichrist because they are deceived. They will think they are doing the correct thing. Now we know that the mark of the beast is going to be a number that will be used by the one-world government to control the economic situation of every person on earth. And we know that the only ones who will refuse the mark and will do so because they know it means they will be worshipping the Antichrist.

> *And the great dragon, the old serpent, the one called Devil, and Satan, the one who **deceived the entire inhabited world**, was cast to the earth, and his angels were cast out with him.* (Revelation 12:9 ONMB, emphasis added)

SO HOW DO YOU DECEIVE BILLIONS OF PEOPLE?
It is quite simple. A national Sunday law will be passed. The ones who refuse will be breaking the law. The economic mark of the beast or their national ID number will be invalidated. This is done to compel them to go to church on Sunday. You will not be able to work or buy or sell.

This new law will not be rigidly enforced until the Antichrist is revealed in Jerusalem.

It will be through a counterfeit religion. When the false prophet mimics Elijah and brings fire down from heaven in the rebuilt temple in Jerusalem, the whole world is going to think the Messiah has returned. The counterfeit religion will be endorsed by the false prophet, and you will believe it.

This event ushers in the one-world religion to worship the Antichrist. And remember it is estimated that Satan will have at least one-third of the angels who were in heaven to help in deceiving us into worshipping the Antichrist.

WILL THERE BE ANY MUSLIM INFLUENCE IN THE ONE-WORLD RELIGION?
Because of these verses, many believe Sharia Law will be imposed on Christians.

> *And they paid homage to the dragon, because he gave his great authority to the beast and they paid* **homage to the beast** *saying, "Who is like the beast and who is able to war against him?"* (Revelation 13:4 ONMB, emphasis added)

Homage is the way Muslims pray where they fall down on their knees and touch their forehead to the ground.

> *Then I saw thrones and those that sat upon them and judgment was given to them, and I saw the lives of those* **who had been beheaded** *because of the testimony of Yeshua [Jesus] and because of Word of God*

and who did not worship the beast or his image and did not take the mark upon their foreheads or upon their hands. Then they became alive again and lived and reigned with the Messiah one thousand years. (Revelation 20:4 ONMB, emphasis added)

Beheading is the normal way Muslims execute people.

What about the remnant mentioned in the Scriptures?

The Scriptures also tell us YHVH will preserve a remnant of true believers. This is a remnant of Jews and Christians.

And the dragon was angered on account of the woman and left to make war with the rest of her seed, of those [remnant] who keep the commandments of God and have the testimony of Yeshua. (Revelation 12:17 ONMB)

The choice seems to be either to keep the commandments of God or the commandments of men.

Investigative Judgment

The Scriptures also tell us that an investigative judgment takes place in heaven and ends before Yeshua comes. After the seventh angel blows his trumpet and the mystery of YHVH is completed, then the temple in heaven fills with smoke. Since prayers cannot be brought before God at this point that means prayers for forgiveness for sins are not heard by God. Then the seven last plagues come, and everyone who made the wrong choice and is worshipping the Antichrist will suffer from the plagues. This will include many Christians, and they will wonder why they are suffering through these plagues. They will not understand what they did wrong in their worship. They had trusted their pastors to teach them correctly in their worship. Finally, they will realize that they had been worshipping according to the commandments of men. During this period, the call from YHVH is to come out of the Babylonian church as the mystery of Babylon is exposed. Your choice of worshipping the Antichrist will result in suffering due to the plagues. Will you heed the warning before it is too late?

The Scriptures tell the story of what happens when the Gentiles cry out to YHVH about their suffering during the plagues.

> *O LORD, my strength, and my fortress, and my refuge in the **day of affliction, the Gentiles** shall come unto thee from the ends of the earth, and shall say, **surely our fathers have inherited lies, vanity, and things wherein there is no profit**.* (Jeremiah 16:19 KJV, emphasis added)

Remember the day of affliction is also called the period of the Great Tribulation during the last three and a half years just before Yeshua returns.

> *O YHVH, my strength, and my stronghold, and my refuge, in the **day of distress the gentiles** shall come to you from the ends of the earth and say, **"Our fathers have only inherited falsehood, futility, and there is no value in them."*** (Jeremiah 16:19 ISR, emphasis added)
>
> *Therefore, behold, I will this once cause them to know, I will cause them to know mine hand and my might; and they shall know that my name is The LORD.* (Jeremiah 16:21 KJV, emphasis added)
>
> *Therefore see, I am causing them to know, this time I cause them to know my hand and my might. And they will know that my name is Yehovah.* (Jeremiah 16:19 ISR, emphasis added)

From these verses in the book of Jeremiah, it appears we may be given one last chance to recognize that most of the churches have not taught the true worship. For those who recognize the true worship, they will call on YHVH for the truth. They will be seeking out Jews to learn the truth. Also, these verses can only be describing events at the end of the age because they are describing the Gentiles who have been misled in true worship.

DON'T BE FOOLED BY THE RAPTURE
Many believe that the rapture will occur before the great affliction in the second half of the seven year period before Yeshua returns. The Scriptures say that the saints are killed during the tribulation. So how can the saints be raptured before the great affliction and then be killed by the antichrist during the great affliction? It is impossible and the Scriptures say that the rapture happens when Yeshua returns to destroy the antichrist and the false prophet after the great affliction.

Yeshua said the rapture would occur after the great affliction.

ONMB Mat 24:29 But **immediately after the affliction** of those days the sun shall be darkened, and the moon will not give its light, and the stars will fall from the sky, and the powers of the heavens will be shaken.

ONMB Mat 24:30 And then the sign of the Son of Man will be revealed in the sky, and then all the tribes of the earth will be cut off and they will see the Son of Man upon the clouds of the sky with power and great glory.

ONMB Mat 24:31 Then He will send his angels with a great shofar call, and they will gather His chosen ones from out of the four winds as far as the uttermost parts of the heavens.

When you see the above things start to happen, then you will know that everyone is going to be deceived if you are wise to the scriptures.

SO WHAT WILL BE YOUR CHOICE?
Each of us has choice in worship. Soon the Antichrist and false prophet will be in charge. Will you be grounded enough in the Scriptures to make the wise choice?

You will have to make a choice to either receive the mark or starve to death. If you make it to when the antichrist starts the Great affliction, you will be thrown in jail. Ten days later they will kill you.

If you accept the mark, the Scriptures say you will be damned to hell with no forgiveness.

ONMB Rev 14:9 Then another, a third angel, followed them saying in a loud voice, "If someone pays homage to the beast and his image and takes his mark on his forehead, or upon his hand,

ONMB Rev 14:10 Then he will drink from the wine of the wrath of God which has been poured undiluted in the cup of His wrath and he will be tortured in fire and sulfur before holy angels and before the Lamb

ONMB Rev 14:11 And the smoke of their tormenting fire ascends forever, and those who pay homage to the beast and his image do not have rest day or night, even if someone just takes the mark of his name.

The choice is to reject the mark and be killed or accept the mark and spend eternity in hell.

You see it is not a question of what is right or wrong, but it is a question on whether you understand the Scriptures so that you know what you must do to be saved. Yeshua made this clear in the Scriptures.

Yeshua has given you a promise of salvation by faith in Him if you can love Him by keeping His commandments. He died in agonizing pain for you, and all He asks of you is to show your love by doing His commandments. All anyone has to do is repent of their sins and do His commandments. Then you can receive the grace of salvation.

It is not too late to recognize the truth of the Scriptures, to repent and be obedient to YHVH's commandments so you can be saved. Soon the Antichrist will also give you a choice to worship him, and you will have to make a final choice then.

If you want a personal relationship with Yeshua and you want to be saved, pray the prayer located in Appendix A and be obedient to YHVH's commandments.

APPENDIX A

The Sinner's Prayer

Yehovah (God), please save me.
I have sinned against you.

I ask YOU to forgive me for all my sins.

I ask YOU to come into my heart and change me.

I believe that Yeshua (Jesus) died for me
And HE rose again.
I receive Yeshua as my master and savior.
Please send me the Holy Spirit to lead me.
In the name of my master Yeshua, I pray.

Amen.

APPENDIX B

The Lord's Prayer

(Hebrew Matthew Version)

Our Father in heaven,

May your name be sanctified

May your kingdom be blessed.

Your will shall be done in heaven and on earth.
Give us our bread continually. Forgive us the debt of our sins
As we forgive the debt of those who sin against us.

Do not bring us into the hands of a test, and protect us from all evil.
Amen.

APPENDIX C

The Power of Blessings

Purpose

Blessings declare the intentions of YHVH for each of us. Most Christians are familiar with Aaron's blessing of the Hebrews. YHVH spoke to Moses and said to bless the people as follows:

> *"Yehovah bless you and keep you; Yehovah make His face shine on you; Yehovah lift up His face upon you, and give you peace." "In this way they are to put my name on the people of Israel, so that I will bless them."* (Numbers 6:24–27)

The power of the tongue pronouncing blessings was an important part of the Hebrews life in the Old Testament. There are many verses in the Scriptures where the sons received the blessings of their father. These blessings were spoken over the ones to be blessed and YHVH blessed them. Blessings are for everyone, not just the Hebrews.

The power of the tongue is like a two-edged sword. You can bless someone, or you can curse someone. The problem of the curse is that you receive the curse.

Now if you say something negative against someone, then YHVH is against you. The Scriptures tell us that YHVH loves us and wants everyone to be saved. So if you say something negative against anyone, then YHVH is against you because you are against Him.

The Scriptures say to bridle your tongue and manage every word that comes out of your mouth. Be slow to speak and never say anything negative against anyone. Criticizers and complainers are hated by YHVH.

So how should we bless others?

To bless someone, you should declare the intentions of YHVH for them. The Scriptures tell us that the will of YHVH for us is that we should not perish but that all should come into the knowledge of YHVH. Blessings are a prophetic declaration of the intentions of YHVH for you for the way He intended you to be.

Sample blessing for others:
May YHVH release you to fulfill all the purposes of YHVH that He has called and ordained for you; may you fulfill all the desires that YHVH has for you and that your life come into full destiny.

Sample blessing for those who offend you:
May YHVH release you to fulfill all the purposes of YHVH; I declare over him that he will come into the full knowledge of the son of YHVH, that he would be a blessing to his family and he would fulfill the calling and essence of his new life.

APPENDIX D

A Morning Prayer

This prayer is rephrased by Cindy Trimm from Deuteronomy 28:1–14

(Blessed)

I am blessed in the city; I am blessed in the field

I am blessed in my down setting; I am blessed in my up rising

I am blessed socially

I am blessed physically

I am blessed mentally

I am blessed psychologically

I am blessed relationally

I am blessed interpersonally

I am blessed, I am blessed

I am blessed physiologically

I am blessed

Every part of my life is blessed

(I speak)

I speak into my day
I download prosperity into my day
I download success into my day

I speak over those that I love
I speak prosperity and success

I speak to my government that they will come into Divine alignment so that they will lead morally and ethnically
I speak into my business
I speak that my business is successful
That we are increasing and there is no decrease

I speak into my home
That my home is a haven of peace

I speak into my loved ones
I speak that their lives as coming back into alignment

I decree and declare that wealth and riches are in our house

I speak into my mind peace

I speak into my heart courage

I speak into my feet
That there are paths I can walk on so that I can overcome every obstacle

(I am special to God)

I am the head and not the tail

I am the first and not the last

I am above and not beneath

I am loved by God

I am chosen by God

I am protected by God

Today shall come into direct alignment with the plans and purposes of God

Every good and perfect gift comes from God

Today is my gift; therefore it will end perfect and it will end good.

In Jesus's name,

Amen.

APPENDIX E

The Prayer of Transformation
(By Dr. James Richards)

Heavenly Father, search my heart and discover the origin of this (thought or feeling) of _____

Go to the very root of my being and resolve this origin in order to bring every aspect of my spirit, soul, and body into harmony with your truth and my true identity in Christ.

Search through every generation, every cellular memory, every action, and every expression of this (thought/feeling) of _____
_____

Heal me completely according to the finished work of Jesus until Your life, light, love, righteousness, peace, and joy empower me to completely forgive myself for every inappropriate expression, distorted perception, and destructive behavior, and forgive every person or circumstance that has contributed to this (thought or feeling) of _____
_____

I choose to express my love for myself and my right as a child of God by allowing every mental, emotional, spiritual, and physical disease and inappropriate behavior based on this root problem recorded in my DNA to be transformed.

I choose being _____
_____

I choose feeling _____

I am _____

It is done! It is finished; it is mine by the resurrection of Jesus!

Thank you, Holy Spirit, for the grace to live in the fullness of my identity as a child of God and a new creation in Christ.

I give thanks, Yehovah my Healer, who is good and only good. You are my God, my strength, my hope, and my salvation!

REFERENCES

1. The Revised King James Version of the Scriptures.

2. The Scriptures translated by the Institute of Scripture Research.

3. The Hebrew Roots Version Scriptures

4. The Word of Yahweh Scriptures

5. The Complete Jewish Bible

6. The Hebrew Book of Matthew by George Howard (2nd edition)

7. The 1611 King James Bible

8. The Apocrypha

9. One New Man Bible

10. "Byblos" Article by Embassy of Lebanon

11. "Origin of the term "Holy Bible" from the www.vbvbc.org website

12. "What is the Torah" from the www.restoringtheway.org website This reference is under copyright.

13. The Aleppo Codex Article from the www.aleppocodex.org website

14. "Secrets in the Torah" by Restoring the Way Ministries from www.restoringtheway.org website.

15. "Brit-Am Bible Codes" from the www.britam.org website

16. Messianic Prophecies Full filled by Jesus Christ article by George Konig and Ray Konig

17. "Old Testament Prophecies Fulfilled in Jesus' Life" from the www.askapastor.org website.

18. "Messianic Prophecies" from the www.clarifyingchrisitianity.com website.

19. Index of Old Testament Prophecies from the www.pw2.netcom.com website

20. "Journey Toward Creation" by Hugh Ross

21. "The Evolution of the Creationist" by Dr. Jobe Martin

22. The Dead Sea Scrolls by Wikipedia

23. Noah's Ark article by Wyatt Archaeological research Inc. from www.wyattmuseum.com website

24. Red Sea Crossing article by Wyatt Archaeological Research Inc. from www.wyattmuseum.com website

25. Mount Sinai article by Wyatt Archaeological Research Inc. from www.wyattmuseum.com website

26. Ark of the Covenant article by Wyatt Archaeological Research Inc. from www.wyattmuseum.com website

27. Hebrew Bible by Wikipedia

28. The Septuagint by Wikipedia

29. The Vulgate by Wikipedia

30. History of the Authorized King James Bible by Wikipedia

31. "A Brief history of the King James Bible" by Dr. Laurence M. Vance

32. "A Timeline of different Greek Translations of the Scriptures" from www.Google.com website

33. "The Leningrad Codex" by Curt Leviant from the www.jewishvirtuallibrary.org website

34. "The Leningrad Codex" article from the www.usc.edu website

35. Names of God in Judaism by Wikipedia

36. The New American Bible, Revised edition by the United Conference of Catholic Bishops.

37. Pharisees by Wikipedia

38. Judah by Wikipedia

39. "Ancient Hebrew Lexicon of the Bible" by Jeff A. Brenner

40. "His Hallowed Named Revealed Again" by Keith Johnson

41. The Book of Enoch by Heaven Net

42. The Hebrew Names for God from www.hebrew4chrisitians.com website

43. The Messiah's Name from the www.nazarite.net website.

44. "A Prayer to Our Father" by Keith Johnson.

45. "The Hebrew Yeshua versus the Greek Jesus by Nehemiah Gordon.

46. Aramaic Language from Wikipedia

47. Papias of Hierapolis from Wikipedia

48. "Raiders of the Lost Book" by Michael Rood.

49. Hebrew Gospels of Matthew from Wikipedia

50. A Collection of evidence for and against the traditional wording of the baptismal phrase in Matthew 28:19 by A. Ploughman from the www.jesus-messiah.com website.

51. Matthew 28:19 a rebuttal to Robert Turkel by Pastor G. Reckart from the www.jesus-messiah.com website

52. Matthew 28:19 evidence against the Trinity by Dr. G. Reckart from the www.jesus-messiah.com website.

53. "The Creator's Calendar" by Michael Rood.

54. Calendar Origins from the www.calendar-origins.com website.

55. Egyptian Calendar from Wikipedia.

56. Greek (Attic) Calendar from Wikipedia.

57. Babylonian Calendar from Wikipedia.

58. Roman calendar form Wikipedia.

59. Gregorian Calendar and Pagan Assumptions from the www.hebrew-4chrisitians.com website.

60. Julian calendar from Wikipedia

61. Prophecies in the Spring Feasts of the Lord by Michael Rood from the www.aroodawaking.tv website

62. Prophecies in the Fall Feats of the Lord by Michael Rood from the www.aroodawaking.tv website.

63. "Satan's Dirty Little Secrets" by Bill Foss.

64. Satan by Wikipedia

65. "(Almost) The Beast" by Charles Wheeling

66. "To long in the Sun" by Richard Rives.

67. "From Sabbath to Sunday" PHD Thesis by Samuel Bacchiocchi, PhD

68. "The Birth of the Messiah" from the www.nazarite.com website

69. 'The Jonah Code" by Michael Rood

70. The Great Secret of Solomon's Temple and the Hiding of the Ark of the Covenant" by Michael Rood

71. The star of Bethlehem and Birth date of Jesus from the www.ed5015.tripod.com website.

72. "The 70 Week Ministry of Messiah" by Michael Rood

73. Harmony of the Gospels from the Nelson King James Study Bible.

74. Commentary of "The Jonah Code" by the www.wyjd.org website

75. Commentary on "The Jonah Code" by the www.kayceskorner.com website.

76. Assyriology, Scientific Dating the Reign of Artaxerxes from the www.harvardhouse.com website.

77. Artaxerxes I of Persia from Wikipedia

78. The Babylonian Talmud

79. Which day did the Messiah rise on, Saturday or Sunday? From the www.nazarite.net website.

80. Fox's Book of Martyrs

81. Siege of Jerusalem from Wikipedia

82. Mithra, Light of the World

83. Planetary week of the Romans, pages 241–244 from the book "From Sabbath to Sunday" PHD Thesis by Samuele Bacchiocchi, PhD:

84. Reflexes of sun worship, pages 252–261 from the book "From Sabbath to Sunday" PHD Thesis by Samuele Bacchiocchi, PhD:

85. Antoninus Pius from the www.roman-emperors.org website.

86. Constantine the Great from Wikipedia

87. First Council of Nicaea from Wikipedia

88. Arianism from Wikipedia

89. 538A.D. the degree of Justinian and its Significance from www.bigchurch.com website

90. 538 A.D. to 1798 A.D. from the www.wwco.com website

91. Middle Ages Torture from the www.middle-ages.org.uk website

92. The History of Romanism, book 8, Cha. 1, pp 542,543 by John Dowling.

93. First Council of Ephesus from Wikipedia.

94. John Wycliffe from Wikipedia

95. The Ninety-Five theses from Wikipedia.

96. On the Babylonian Captivity of the Church from Wikipedia.

97. Martin Luther from Wikipedia

98. Protestant Reformation from Wikipedia

99. "Don't Be Fooled Study Guide" by Doug Batchelor of Amazing Facts Ministry.

100. Why Churches Keep Sunday from the www.the trumpet.com website.

101. The Westminster Confession of Religious worship and the Sabbath-day from the www.creeds.net website

102. "Catholic Catechism of Catholic Doctrine" by Peter Geiermann

103. The Seventh Day Sabbath Sought Out (1657) by Thomas Tillam. This book is available from the www.sealingtime.com website

104. Sentinel, Pastor's page (Fr. Leo Broderick), Saint Catherine Catholic Church, Algonac, Michigan, may 21, 1995. from the www.biblelight.net website.

105. Sabbath vs. 1st day Debate; Samuele Bacchiocchi and Tom Lewis from www.bible.ca website

106. Scientology from Wikipedia

107. Church of Scientology from the www.bonafidescientology.org website

108. New Age from Wikipedia

109. The New Age Movement: What Christians Should Know from www.victorious.org

110. Oprah Winfrey Opens Church, Founds Religion from www.westerngh.com website

111. What is New age Religion from www.victorious.org website

112. New Age Spirituality from www.religioustolerance.org website.

113. Statics on religion in America Report from www.religions.pewforum.org website

114. The Seven Churches by Perry Stone of Perry stone Ministries at the website www.voe.org.

115. God's War on Terror by Walter Shoebat

116. Islam from Wikipedia

117. Muhammad from Wikipedia

118. Tawhid from Wikipedia

119. Hadith from Wikipedia

120. Black Stone from Wikipedia

121. Caliphate from Wikipedia

122. Mahdi from Wikipedia

123. Crescent from Wikipedia

124. The Crescent Moon from the www.islam.about.com website

125. Islamic calendar from Wikipedia

126. Islamic view of Jacob from Wikipedia

127. Sharia Law from Wikipedia

128. Hira from Wikipedia

129. Banu Quravza from Wikipedia

130. Monotheism from Wikipedia

131. Islamic View of Abraham from Wikipedia

132. Islamic View of Isaac from Wikipedia

133. Islamic View of Jacob from Wikipedia

134. Jesus in Islam from Wikipedia

135. First inauguration of George Washington from Wikipedia.

136. The Harbinger Part 1: The Warning by Jonathan Cahn

137. Daytonian in Manhattan: The 1766 St. Paul's chapel from the www.daytoninmanhattan.blogspot.com website

138. Buttonwood Agreement from Wikipedia

139. President Obama's Address to Congress from the www.nytimes.com website

140. The Harbinger part 2; the Shaking by Jonathan Cahn

141. Shemittah; The Jewish sabbatical Year by Lisa Hershman

142. Abraham Lincoln's Proclamation Appointing a National Day of Prayer from the www.showcase.netins.net website

143. National Day of Prayer from the www.snopes.com website.

144. Obama and the National day of Prayer from the www.urbanledgends.about website

145. President Obama Proclaims National Day of Prayer from the www.chrisitianpost.com website

146. The Watchman, 911 and the Harbingers from the www.archivesmb.wordpress.com website.

147. World council of Churches from the www.oikoumene.org website

148. American Churches to embrace Islam on June 26,2011 from the www.thedayofnoah.wordpress.com website

149. Muslims, Christians, Jews Share Pulpits, Debunk Myths from the www.faithinpublic.org website

150. Faith Shared—Uniting in Prayer and Understanding from the www.faithshared.org website

151. Tony Blair Faith Foundation includes Muslim Brotherhood from the www.globalmbreport.org website.

152. ISNA Officials attend tony Blair Interfaith Foundation Event from the www.globalmbreport.org website.

153. Chrislam—Rick Warren Controversy from the www.agapemovement.com website

154. Pope Presides over Interfaith call for Peace from the www.voanews.com website.

155. A Common Word Accomplishments from the www.acommonword.com website.

156. A response to A Common Word in Love, freedom and peace from the WEA.

157. Chrislam 3—The coming One-World Religion from the www.professorjt2012.wordpress.com website

158. Vance Havner from the www.friendsofvancehavner.org website

159. The Counterfeit Millennium from the www.cornorstonebooks.org website.

160. Ambassador for Christ: Counterfeit from the www.ambassador4christ-david.blogspot.com website

161. Vance Havner—Defending, Contending from the www.defendingcontending.com website.

162. The case of The Counterfeit Christian from the www.sermons.logos.com website.

163. The Masonic Dollar Bill from www.atlanteanconspiracy.com website

164. Satan on Our Dollar from the www.jesus-is-savior.com website

165. League of Nations from the www.historylearningsite.co.uk website

166. Yalta conference from Wikipedia.

167. The New World Order by Irving Baxter

168. "Caritas in Veritate"–Encyclical letter of His Holiness Benedict XVI…from the www.vatican.va website.

169. Vatican-Israel Agreement on Jerusalem from the www.bibleplus.org website

170. Secrets of Oslo by Joel Bainerman from the www.joelbainerman.com website.

171. Replacement Theology—Origins, teachings and Errors from the www.shema.com website

172. Vatican Agenda from the www.angelfire.com website

173. Israel rejects 1967 Border Proposal from the www.msnbc.msn.com website.

174. Quartet response to the Palestinian request from the www.usforeignpolicy.about.com website.

175. "Perestroika" Summary from the www.enotes.com website

176. Popes of the New World order from the www.howlongolord.com website

177. Chaplin who prayed in Jesus name convicted from the www.wnd.com website

178. Blog; Houston cemetery bans the Word "god" from military funerals from the www.americanthinker.com website

179. The prophecy Code by Doug Batchelor of Amazing Facts

180. Oslo accords from Wikipedia

181. Second Intifada from Wikipedia

182. The Four Horses in Revelation by Irvin Baxter

183. The Worst genocides of the 20th Century from the www.scaruffi.com website

184. Weber: The Protestant ethic and the spirit of capitalism from the www.wikisum.com website

185. Religions of the world: numbers of Adherents from the www.religioustolerance.org website.

186. Revelation Studies from the www.666man.net website

187. The Justinian Code and the Catholic faith from the www.biblelight.net website

188. Great Dreadful beast of Daniel 7 from the www.666man.net website

189. Ottoman wars in Europe form Wikipedia.

190. The Holy Roman Empire Reborn by Irvin Baxter from the www.endtime.com website.

191. Holy Roman Empire from Wikipedia.

192. Charlemagne Births the Holy Roman Empire from the www.kimmillerconcernedchrisitians.com website

193. The Treaty of Rome (1957) from the www.historiasiglo.org website

194. The Treaty of the European Union from the www.historiasiglo.org website.

195. Czech president Vaclav Klaus signs EU Lisbon Treaty from the www.telegraph.co.uk/news website

196. The Antichrist by Irvin Baxter from the www.endtime.com website

197. The Great Apostasy from the www.endtimepilgrim.org website

198. The False Prophet by Irvin Baxter from the www.endtime.com website

199. The USA in Bible Prophecy by Dough Batchelor of Amazing Facts

200. World War III by Irvin Baxter from the www.endtime.com website

201. "Zechariah's Thermonuclear War" by Michael Rood from the www.aroodawaking.tv website.

202. Scud from Wikipedia.

203. Range of a Scud missile from the www.hypertexbook.com website

204. How big is a biblical Cubit of measurement form the www.answers.yahoo.com website

205. Do scud missiles really matter from the www.xinhauanet.com website

206. "Order of Battle" article from the Lion and lamb Ministries magazine, July 2010, Vol. 16, No. 7

207. "On the Brink of War" article from the lion and Lamb Ministries magazine, January 2012, Vol. 18, No 1

208. Libya war a precursor to Ezekiel 38-39 from the www.oilinisrael.net website.

209. The Latter rain Revival form the www.endtimepilgrim.org website.

210. location of Solomon's Temple from the www.endtimepilgrim.org website

211. The Final Seven years—the road to Armageddon from the www.prophecyandtruth.com website

212. Tribulation by Dough Batchelor of Amazing Facts ministry

213. Final Events by Doug Batchelor of Amazing Facts ministry

214. "Its Supernatural" by Sid Roth

215. "Prayers of the Heart" by Dr. Mark Virkler

216. "The Power of the Blessing" by Kerry Kirkwood

217. Healing by Dr. Joan Hunter

218. "Opening the Gates of Heaven" by Perry Stone

219. "The Mystery of Iniquity" by Michael Rood

220. "Activating the promises of God" by Dr. James Richards from the website www.impactministries.com.

221. "The Perfect Storm is Coming" by IBE, Inc.

222. One New Man Bible by edited by William J. Morford

223. "How Perfect Should a Christian Be? By Dough Batchelor from the website www.amazingfacts.org

224. "3 Days That Changed Your Life" by Dr. James Richards from the website www.impactministries.com.

225. "I have seen the future of America" by Shane warren from the website www.firstassemblywm.org.

226. "When God Judges the Iniquities of the Fathers by Perry Stone of Perry Stone Ministries at the website www.voe.org.

227. "Last Days Signs and Wonders" by Mel Bond from the website www.agapechurch.addr.com.

228. "Expected End Ministries" by Katie Souza from the website www.expectedendminisitries.com.

IN MEMORY

In loving memory of my wonderful husband, mentor, and soul mate.

This is a mission you put your heart and soul into against all odds, and I am honored and proud to be able to simply bear witness to your experience.

You truly believed in Hosea 4:6 My people are destroyed for lack of knowledge, because thou has rejected knowledge, I will also reject thee.

To All those who search their soul and look for the truth, it is HERE in the Scriptures **REVEALED!**

As Jerry would say, "Hope to see you on the other side."

JERRY'S BIO

I have a BS-Electrical Engineering from Clemson University, Postgraduate Curriculum toward MSEE, (Master of Science in Electrical Engineering) Clemson University. 1963

During my career I designed electrical systems for all areas of paper mills, petrochemical plants, refineries, chemical plants and infrastructure projects in the USA. I also designed a water project in Syria and a 33KV transmission line in Abu Dhabi. I have traveled to almost all of the states in the US and have traveled to the Middle East and Europe. I started my own engineering company MEP which peaked at 65 people.

Out of all of my ventures, my study and revelations of the Holy Scriptures has been my greatest accomplishment. Now to reveal to all those that have an Ear to Listen! May you be Blessed as I have been!

Made in the USA
San Bernardino, CA
19 May 2017